SOUTHERN LITERARY STUDIES
Fred Hobson, Editor

SOUTH TO A NEW PLACE

Region, Literature, Culture

Edited by **Suzanne W. Jones and Sharon Monteith**

Foreword by **Richard Gray**

Louisiana State University Press)|(Baton Rouge

First printing

12 11 10 09 08 07 06 05 04 03
5 4 3 2 1

Designer: Amanda McDonald Scallan
Typeface: Sabon
Typesetter: Coghill Composition Co. Inc.
Printer and binder: Thomson-Shore, Inc.

The editors are grateful to the following journals and publishers for permission to reprint: Graham Holderness, General Editor of *Critical Survey* (New York and London: Berghahn Press), for versions of the essays by Amy J. Elias, Carolyn M. Jones, Michael Kreyling, Barbara Ladd, and Scott Romine, all of which appeared in Volume 12, no. 1 (2000), of that journal, a special issue titled "South to a New Place" edited by Suzanne W. Jones and Sharon Monteith; New York University Press for passages from Robert McRuer, *The Queer Renaissance: Contemporary American Literature and the Reinvention of Lesbian and Gay Identities* (1997); Vanderbilt University Press for passages from Deborah Cohn, *History and Memory in the Two Souths: Recent Southern and Spanish American Fiction* (1999), and Peter Lang for a version of Cohn's essay in *Do the Americas Have a Common Literary History?* ed. Buchenau and Paatz (2002); Rutgers University Press for sections from Helen Taylor, *Circling Dixie: Contemporary Southern Culture Through a Transatlantic Lens*, © 2001 by Helen Taylor, reprinted by permission of Rutgers University Press; and Louisiana State University Press for sections from Richard Gray, *Southern Aberrations: Writers of the American South and the Problems of Regionalism* (2000); and *Studies in American Fiction* for a version of Paul Lyons, "Larry Brown's *Joe* and the Uses and Abuses of the 'Region' Concept," Volume 25, no. 1.

ISBN 0-8071-2823-6 (cloth); ISBN 0-8071-2840-6 (paperback)

For our mothers

CONTENTS

Acknowledgments   xi

Richard Gray
FOREWORD: Inventing Communities, Imagining Places:
Some Thoughts on Southern Self-Fashioning   xiii

Sharon Monteith and Suzanne W. Jones
INTRODUCTION: South to New Places   1

PART I   **SURVEYING THE TERRITORY**

Scott Romine
WHERE IS SOUTHERN LITERATURE? The Practice of Place
in a Postsouthern Age   23

Barbara Ladd
DISMANTLING THE MONOLITH: Southern Places—Past,
Present, and Future   44

Carolyn M. Jones
RACE AND INTIMACY: Albert Murray's *South to a Very
Old Place*   58

Jon Smith
SOUTHERN CULTURE ON THE SKIDS: Punk, Retro,
Narcissism, and the Burden of Southern History   76

Paul Lyons
LARRY BROWN'S *JOE* AND THE USES AND ABUSES OF
THE "REGION" CONCEPT 96

PART II **MAPPING THE REGION**

Suzanne W. Jones
I'LL TAKE MY LAND: Contemporary Southern
Agrarians 121

Wes Berry
TONI MORRISON'S REVISIONARY "NATURE
WRITING": *Song of Solomon* and the Blasted Pastoral 147

Eric Gary Anderson
NATIVE AMERICAN LITERATURE, ECOCRITICISM, AND
THE SOUTH: The Inaccessible Worlds of Linda Hogan's
Power 165

Robert McRuer
QUEER LOCATIONS, QUEER TRANSFORMATIONS: Randall
Kenan's *A Visitation of Spirits* 184

Matthew Guinn
INTO THE SUBURBS: Richard Ford's Sportswriter Novels and
the Place of Southern Fiction 196

Martyn Bone
PLACING THE POSTSOUTHERN "INTERNATIONAL
CITY": Atlanta in Tom Wolfe's *A Man in Full* 208

Maureen Ryan
OUTSIDERS WITH INSIDE INFORMATION: The Vietnamese
in the Fiction of the Contemporary American South 235

Amy J. Elias
POSTMODERN SOUTHERN VACATION: Vacation
Advertising, Globalization, and Southern Regionalism 253

PART III **MAKING GLOBAL CONNECTIONS**

Michael Kreyling
ITALY AND THE UNITED STATES: The Politics and Poetics
of the "Southern Problem" 285

Christine Gerhardt
NORTH, SOUTH, EAST, WEST: Constructing Region in
Southern and East German Literature 303

Deborah Cohn
"OF THE SAME BLOOD AS THIS AMERICA AND ITS
HISTORY": William Faulkner and Spanish American
Literature 320

Helen Taylor
THE SOUTH AND BRITAIN: Celtic Cultural
Connections 340

Diane Roberts
AFTERWORD: The South of the Mind 363

Contributors 375
Index 381

ACKNOWLEDGMENTS

The editors would like to thank the University of Richmond and the University of Nottingham, and colleagues at each institution for their support and interest in *South to a New Place*. We especially appreciate the comments and suggestions of those colleagues and friends who read many of the essays submitted for the collection, most especially Barbara Ewell, Richard H. King, Pete Messent, Dave Murray, Robert Nelson, Frank Papovich, and Nahem Yousaf. We would also like to acknowledge the final contributors themselves for being so willing to read each other's work following acceptance. In addition, at the University of Richmond Toni Blanton and Kathy Zacher helped to prepare the manuscript, and graduate student Melanie Clore created the index.

We are indebted to Fred Hobson for his thorough reading of the manuscript and to the anonymous reader for Louisiana State University Press. At the press, we would like particularly to single out John Easterly for his unflagging support of this project, and for securing such a careful copy editor in Margaret Dalrymple.

We owe a special thanks to Art Werger for the use of his image "Homeward."

Finally, we would like to thank each other. This project came together over a number of years of close and happy collaboration between the South—Virginia—and another place—Nottingham in the U.K. Despite the distance, rarely a day went by without our corresponding, re-reading, developing, and modifying, or commenting in some way on the project as it developed. We saw each other when we could and mailed and talked on the phone when we couldn't: throughout, we have been each other's best support.

FOREWORD

Inventing Communities, Imagining Places:
Some Thoughts on Southern Self-Fashioning

Richard Gray

"The life and people of certain favoured regions are seen as essentially general, even perhaps normal, while the life and people of certain other regions are, well, regional."[1] The words are those of Raymond Williams, and they make a point that, within the context of American history— literary and otherwise—has a peculiarly southern edge to it. The word *region* is usually applied to an area judged to be on the fringes; *regional* and *regionalist,* in turn, tend to be applied by "us," the members of a culturally dominant group, to "them," a group or area whose interest very largely stems from its not being at the center of things. So, Thomas Hardy is a "regional" novelist and Charles Dickens is not; Willa Cather and Ellen Glasgow are "regional" writers, while Edith Wharton is some-thing else. This is not all there is to regionalism, of course, but it is worth saying, as Williams does, that somewhere along the line regionalism can be seen, and often is, as a symptom of centralized cultural dominance. To

---

1. Raymond Williams, *The Country and the City* (1973; London: Chatto and Windus, 1976), 199. The two books where Williams explores regionalism and its literary dimen-sions most fully are *The English Novel: From Dickens to Lawrence* (London: Hogarth, 1970) and *The Country and the City.*

call a text or body of writing "regional," in turn, is, however innocently, to assign it a marginal status, the measure of its "regionalism" being the extent of its deviation from the national norm—a norm that, by a strange but common irony, its deviations have probably helped to determine. The "center" is what the "mainstream" culture establishes and then ensures through a series of contrasts with its "regional" other; it is whatever the "regional" culture is not, just as it is not whatever the "regional" culture is. The circular character of this is perhaps obvious: the cultural "norm" serves to define the "regional" and the "regional" serves to define the "norm" in a process that could be described as reciprocal—or, less kindly, tautological. Clearly circular and arguably redundant as this process is, though, it occurs as a matter of cultural practice whenever one group seeks to map its boundaries by deciding what lies outside them. In other words, it happens and has happened throughout history. Even within the relatively small world of the literary history of the United States, there are many instances of this particular cultural practice. But perhaps the most telling instance is offered by the acceptance of the writing of the American South as distinctively regional—an acceptance that distinguishes many writers from the southern states themselves as they struggle with the sense of being different, writing somewhere of and from the periphery.

That sense of difference, of distance, is there, for instance, in the story of Margaret Mitchell. In 1932, Mitchell wrote to a friend about what she called her "family curse." "I remember so well, saying when I was twenty that God being willing, the curse . . . would never fall on me," she recalled. She then tried to explain the nature of that curse and relate it to the book she had written: "The curse I refer to is loving land enough to give everything you've got to get it. Never would I own a foot of it, city or country land. If I had spare money it would stay in the bank or the stock market but never in red clay. Then about two years ago when I set out to write the great American novel I was confronted by the fact that whether I liked it or not, it was a story of the land and a woman who was determined not to part with it."[2] As far as dates are concerned, Mitchell was telling something other than the truth. As her biographer

2. Darden Asbury Pyron, *Southern Daughter: The Life of Margaret Mitchell* (New York: Oxford University Press, 1991), 290. The letter is to Harvey Smith, 14 July 1932. See also p. 291. William Faulkner expands on the theme of loving and hating the South in "Mississippi," in *Essays, Speeches and Public Letters,* ed. James B. Meriwether (London: Random House, 1967), 11–43.

points out, "she had not begun to write in 1930; on the contrary, she had by then effectively completed" *Gone With the Wind.* The emotional truth of what she said, however, is utterly convincing. It also seems utterly southern in the sense that attachment to the southern land—or, as William Faulkner would have it, loving and hating that land—has always been taken as a determining feature of what it means to be southern.

Nonetheless, it has never really been possible to talk about the South in the singular; that would only be feasible for a culture frozen in time— and that the South decidedly never was. It has grown ever more impossible, as the pace of change has accelerated and cultural pluralism (and, not least, our perception of that pluralism) has steadily grown. So the slippage of meaning at work in regional self-identification has become inescapable. To be southern could always mean many things, despite the attempts of those like the Nashville Agrarians who tried to align it with relatively specific notions of human culture and the body politic ("relatively" because, of course, the Agrarians differed among themselves). And those many things have now become more.

Writing about the South some fifty years after Margaret Mitchell completed *Gone With the Wind,* another, very different southern writer, Alice Walker, said this: "No one could wish for a more advantageous heritage than that bequeathed to the black writer in the South: A compassion for the earth, a trust in humanity beyond our knowledge of evil, and an abiding sense of justice. We inherit great responsibility as well, for we must give voice to centuries not only of silent bitterness and hate but also neighborly kindness and sustaining love."[3] A very different writer and a very different experience and idea of the South. In their confessional moments and in their work, Mitchell and Walker may both give voice to the sense of being rooted in a dear, particular place and, with that, to a feeling for the past that is part of their earth and therefore a part of them. Where exactly that place may be, however, how that past is constituted and what place and past may signify are hardly identical; whatever the correspondences or points of congruence between these two ideas of a region, they are in no sense one and the same. Walker's description of the inheritance of the black writer in the South echoes the suggestion sounded in the work of Ernest Gaines that if any writer now has a seminal role to play in the rewriting of the South, it is the African American. And, set beside Mitchell's disclosure of her "family curse," it brings us

---

3. Alice Walker, "The Black Writer and the Southern Experience," in *In Search of Our Mothers' Gardens* (New York: Harcourt Brace, 1983), 21.

right back to the vital point that those who call themselves southern have this in common, whatever else they may have, much or little: that their southernness is defined against a national "other." There is a familiar series of oppositions at work here: "southern" versus "American"/"northern" (the slippage between these two terms is, in itself, a measure of the southern sense of aberrance) = place versus placelessness = past versus pastlessness = realism versus idealism = community versus isolation. As an act of self-definition, the oppositions are usually and defiantly weighted in the way I have just suggested. Admittedly, not everyone has been willing to go quite so far, or to argue in quite so morally loaded a way as William Lowndes Yancey, the antebellum politician and orator from South Carolina, did, when he declared:

> The Creator has beautified the face of this Union with sectional features. Absorbing all minor sub-divisions, He has made the North and the South; the one the region of frost, ribbed in with ice and granite; the other baring its generous bosom to the sun and ever smiling under its influence. The climate, soil, and productions of these two grand divisions of the land, have made the character of their inhabitants. Those who occupy the one are cool, calculating, enterprising, selfish, and grasping; the inhabitants of the other are ardent, brave and magnanimous, more disposed to give than to accumulate, to enjoy ease rather than to labor.

Nevertheless, this primary act of setting "the one" against "the other" was and still is a commonplace in southern self-fashioning. So is the sense of arguing against an "other" that is too commonly taken as the norm. "The world will not hear our story," a young Georgia girl wrote in her diary just after Lee surrendered to Grant at Appomattox, "and we must figure just as our enemies choose to paint us." Stripped of the bitterness provoked by war and its aftermath, and the anger ("I hate the Yankees more and more," the Georgia girl added, "every time I . . . read the lies they tell about us"), that feeling of being sidelined is commonly there. The other is not named as the enemy, certainly—but it is, more often than not, seen as more successful in getting its story told. The South, in short, *any* South, tends to be named and identified *against* the historical tide.[4]

This is the first of four points or thoughts that I would like to pose here. The South has customarily defined itself against a kind of photo-

4. John W. Du Bose, *The Life and Times of William Lowndes Yancey,* 2 vols. (New York: P. Smith, 1942), I: 301; Eliza Frances Andrews, *The War-Time Journal of a Georgia Girl, 1864–1865* (New York: D. Appleton, 1938), 371 (entry for 18 August 1865).

graphic negative, a reverse image of itself with which it has existed in a mutually determining, reciprocally defining relationship. The South *is* what the North *is not*, just as the *North* is what the *South* is not. It may be that all cultures do this. The difference with the southern strategy is that it usually begins from a consciousness of its own marginality, its position on the edge of the narrative. The constitutive otherness of the North or the American nation is considered central; the South, in whatever terms it is understood, is placed on the boundary, posed as an (albeit probably preferable) aberration. This is a piquant reversal of customary cultural self-positioning. It would never have occurred to those who constructed the idea of the Orient, for example, to see their object of study as anything other than inferior to the enlightened West and on the dangerous borders of Western culture. The lesser breed was, famously, without the law. The idea of southernness may—or may not—carry a moral burden; it may project on to the typology of itself, and its opposite, a sense of its own superiority and a claim to historical centrality (of the kind Allen Tate was thinking of when he said "The South was the last stronghold of European civilization in the western hemisphere"[5]). Nevertheless, the claim cannot be made effortlessly, without a powerful sense of past exclusion, present discontent, and future peril. Southerners start seeing others with a more than usually astringent sense of how others see them; their arguments begin, as it were, *within* an argument already made that has shifted them on to the edge.

A word of caution is necessary here, which brings me to the second point I would like to pose. These acts of regional self-definition are not, of course, simply fake. It is not that the South and the North or the American nation—even in the crudely simplistic terms imagined by a William Lowndes Yancey—are merely falsehoods, fables, no more in touch with historical contingencies than, say, stories of the lost city of Atlantis. They are, however, *fictive*—and in a double sense. They are fictive, first, because they involve a reading of existence as essence. What Anwar Abdul Malek has to say about Orientalism is relevant here. Orientalists, he points out, "adopt an essentialist conception of the countries, nations and peoples of the Orient under study, a conception which expresses itself through a characterized ethnist typology."[6] In short, they form a notion of a cultural "type" based on a real specificity but divorced from

5. Allen Tate, *Jefferson Davis: His Rise and Fall* (New York: Minton, Balch and Co., 1929), 301.

6. Anwar Abdel Manwak, "Orientalism in Crisis," *Diogenes* 44 (1963), 107–8.

history. Similarly, the cultural work that has evolved ideas of the South and southerners, and their opposites, occurs in history and is a result of the forces working in the field of historical evolution. But its end result is to transfix the beings, the objects of study, and leave them stamped with an inalienable, nonevolutive character—to sever them from the living tissue of their moment in time. These constructions of regional types are fictive also in the sense that perhaps Yancey had at the back of his mind when he conveniently skipped over what he called "all minor subdivisions." The South—and this is the third point or thought I would like to propose—has never *not* been made up of a number of castes, classes, and smaller communities that at best live in uneasy coexistence with each other and at worst are in active conflict—and some of which, at least, choose to claim that *their* South is *the* South, their story the master narrative. Readings of the South are just that, readings—of its past, present, and possible futures, the plurality of its cultures; for better or worse, they involve selection and abstraction; they involve a figuring and, in the purest sense of that word, a *simplifying* of history.

In trying to get at what goes on in this reading and figuring of southern history, one of the more common critical practices of recent years has been to see a link between southern self-fashioning and nationalism. So Michael O'Brien, writing in 1979, discerns a connection between southern sectionalism and the tendency of Romanticism to locate "the wellspring of man's being in national groups"; and John Shelton Reed, writing three years later, finds in some arguments for the South, at least, what he calls "more than glimmerings of the typical nationalist responses: cultural defense, economic autarchy, even political self-determination."[7] The nationalist analogy is an interesting, potentially productive one. As both O'Brien and Reed indicate, though, it begs the question, what is a nation? What compels a series of discrete individuals and interest groups, despite all their differences, to admit not necessarily a communality of purpose but a certain common cultural ground?

The answer seems to come back to figuring. "Nationalism is not the awakening of nations to self-consciousness," argues Ernest Gellner, "it invents nations where they do not exist." " 'Nationalism,' " declares Tom Nairn in his book on British nationalism, "is the pathology of modern

7. Michael O'Brien, *The Idea of the American South, 1920–1941* (Baltimore: Johns Hopkins University Press, 1979), 7; John Shelton Reed, "For Dixieland: The Sectionalism of *I'll Take My Stand*," in *A Band of Prophets: The Vanderbilt Agrarians After Fifty Years,* ed. Louis D. Rubin Jr. (Baton Rouge: Louisiana State University Press, 1982), 51.

developmental history, as inescapable as 'neurosis' in the individual, with much the same essential ambiguity"; while Hugh Seton-Watson in his *Nations and States* sadly admits, "I am driven to the conclusion that no 'scientific definition' of the nation can be devised"—and yet he adds, "the phenomenon has existed and still exists." The shared perception here—whatever the differences of judgment—is that the nation is a cultural arti-fact. "All I can find to say," says Seton-Watson, "is that a nation exists when a significant number of people in a community consider themselves to form a nation, or behave as if they formed one." A nation is, in this sense, what Benedict Anderson has christened an "imagined commu-nity." No community larger than what Anderson terms a "primordial vil-lage" is "real" in the sense that everyone in it knows everyone else. No community is one based on the denial of difference and conflict. To call myself English, for instance, is not to say that I am either the same or have precisely the same origins, aims, or interests as anyone else who de-scribes himself as English; the term allows for multiple signification—even more so, if I substitute "British" for "English." Similarly, Margaret Mitchell and Alice Walker may both call themselves southern, but that permits difference; their common term is also a fluid one, a distillation of a complex crossing of discrete historical forces. "Communities are to be distinguished," Anderson has argued, "not by their falsity/genuineness, but by the style in which they are imagined."[8] And it is "style" that distin-guishes that strange resistance to the American "norm"—itself made up of a whole series of internal resistances—known as the South.

This "style," the terms in which the South has been imagined, depends on many things. The book is only one of them. Communities are con-structed, changed, defended, and resisted by language (spoken as much as, or perhaps, as I have already intimated, even more than written), by monu-ments (to the Confederate soldier, to Martin Luther King Jr.), by maps and museums—and, more recently, by a mass technology that enables differ-ence up to a point to both consumer and producer. Difference to the con-sumer comes from the media-making of the South; southerners can see themselves in terms of the many Souths imagined on film, television, and

8. Ernest Gellner, *Thought and Change* (Chicago: University of Chicago Press, 1964), 169; Tom Nairn, *The Break-Up of Britain* (London: NLB, 1977), 359; Hugh Seton-Watson, *Nations and States: An Enquiry into the Origins of Nations and the Politics of Nationalism* (Boulder, Colo.: Westview Press, 1977), 5; Benedict Anderson, *Imagined Communities: Reflections on the Origin and Spread of Nationalism* (1983; rev. ed., London: Verso, 1991), 6.

other electronic/mass media. Difference to the producer comes from the chance that the newer information technology gives for cultural diversity; it is, quite simply, easier, thanks to the multiple opportunities now for publication—which is to say, communication beyond the immediate face-to-face community—for any group to make its voice heard. The mistake made by some commentators is to see these newer forms as invention in the sense of *fabrication* and *falsity* (just as the mistake made by some observers of nationalist movements and ideology is to assume that, if nations are invented, then nationalism is fake and irrelevant). They are not *necessarily* that; as I intimated earlier, they are simply some of the terms in which southerners now come to think of themselves, and the South. They are no more false, inevitably, than were, say, the old tales and telling that generations of earlier southerners employed to make up and transmit *their* identity. They simply offer new ways of working at the interface between consciousness and history; their potential is as new tools for old habits.

This is the fourth point or thought I would want to work with: the potential for southern self-definition offered by recent social and economic change. The potential and also the peril. To say that there are new tools for old tendencies made available by the developing technologies is not to ignore the other possibility—that the net effect of mass culture may be to homogenize and commodify. Either the flattening out of cultural diversity that the logic of the global marketplace dictates, or the devotion to surface image demanded by the logic of late capitalism could wipe out all the benefits to cultural diversity promised by the exponential increase in forms of communication. To put it simply, southerners may be too busy being "Confederate consumers"[9] to continue imagining *any* kind of community, and/or they may buy, rather than invent, themselves. The evidence here is certainly mixed. But if any generalization is to be ventured at all, it is surely that change has brought an even more acute self-consciousness and an even greater pluralism than ever before. The South is still a concept active in the everyday lives and exchanges of communities; it is still there as a determining part of their mental maps and speech acts. The difference now is that inventing or imagining—or simply *assuming the existence of*—the South occurs within an environment where the sheer diversity of information available and the multiplicity of systems supplying that information make cultural insularity close to impossible. More than ever before (and with more deliberation than ever before), acts of regional self-identification have to be made against the

9. John Peet, "A Survey of the South," *Economist*, 10 December 1994, 6.

grain. Rapid change, increasing social mobility, and the accelerating exchange between cultures all mean that any reading of the South now requires a peculiarly intense and focused gaze.

So why does it still happen? Why does southern self-fashioning continue? The answer, or the closest thing to an answer, has surely not altered since the invention of the South. It is a matter of *language* and
communal ritual, the human habit of positioning the self with the help of
the word and others, giving a local habitation and a name to things to
secure their and our identity, and establishing a connection or kinship
with other people that is also an anchorage, a validation of oneself. There
are many possible ways of illustrating this; as usual, the poets and storytellers have put it better than probably anyone, and certainly I, can. As
for language and its compulsions, few southern writers have expressed
the matter more memorably than Eudora Welty. A remark of hers is well
worth repeating: "The mystery," Welty has said, "lies in the use of language to express human life." To this extent, we can infer, inventing the
South is a product of an aboriginal impulse we all share—to render life
comprehensible through the use of the spoken and written word. Welty
describes her own discovery of that impulse in her account of what she
terms her "sensory education"; in the process, she cannily measures both
its strength and the drastic limitations of its reach. "At around six, perhaps," she recalls:

> I was standing by myself in our front yard waiting for supper, just at that
> hour on a late summer day when the sun is already below the horizon and
> the risen full moon in the visible sky stops being chalky and begins to take
> on light. There comes a moment, and I saw it then, when the moon goes
> from flat to round. For the first time it met my eyes as a globe. The word
> "moon" came into my mouth as though fed to me out of a silver spoon.
> Held in my mouth the moon became a word. It had the roundness of a
> Concord grape Grandpa took off his vine and gave me to suck out of its
> skin and swallow whole, in Ohio.[10]

The beauty of a passage like this is that Welty manages to convince us
simultaneously that words are everything *and* nothing. They are everything because they constitute all the world we make for ourselves. Issuing
out of a fundamental, definitively human rage for order—not only to see,

---

10. Eudora Welty, *One Writer's Beginnings* (Cambridge: Harvard University Press,
1984), 10. See also Linda Kuehl, "The Art of Fiction: Eudora Welty," *Paris Review* 55
(1972), 77.

but to know—they are as vital to us as breath. They register for us the irresistible otherness of things in terms that are, at their best, vivid and sensory. Another writer, William Carlos Williams, suggested that a thing known passes from the outer world to the inner, from the air around us into the muscles within us. And the word *moon* seems to achieve the same vital transit. As Welty remembers it, "moon" is not just an abstract, arbitrary sign, it has the "roundness" of a sensory object; it generates the sense that contact between the namer and named has taken place. This is the gift, given with "a silver spoon," that we are all offered. And it can fill us with a sense of presence, as it does the six-year-old girl recollected here: we, like her, can feel that we know and can participate in the world through the word. It is everything, then. It is, however, quite literally nothing. The word *moon,* despite the way it assumes shape and fullness in the mouth, is "no thing." It is, at best, a powerful, sense-laden sign for the mysterious, distant object that shimmers in the evening sky. There is probably no need to labor the point that, in the talk and writing of generations of southerners, the word *South* and its variants have assumed the same power and pathos as the word that came into Welty's mouth at a seminal moment in her sensory education. It has become a vital instrument of knowledge, linked to the broader human project of trying to spin a sense of reality out of language. It is also a palpable sign of ignorance to the extent that the histories it maps must remain irreducibly other, constantly altering and apart. One of the determining concepts of American history, it is a measure of how much and how little that history can be known—or, for that matter, of the scope that any of us have for making sense of our own individual and collective lives.

As for communal ritual, that is linked to language even though it is not confined to it. We know who we are and where we belong, after all, because we engage in social exchanges that substantiate and complicate our sense of belonging. And those exchanges are, many of them, vocal; talk, speech is our link between external and internal worlds. Verbal exchanges embody and then re-embody the changing relations between classes, sexes, and races, help to shape beliefs and behavior—and, in general, exist in a genuinely dialectical relationship with the developing rituals of a group. "As a social animal, man is a ritual animal," the anthropologist Mary Douglas has observed, "ritual focuses attention, by framing; it enlivens the memory and links the present with the past. In all this," she adds, "it adds perception because it changes the selective principles. . . . It does not merely externalize experience . . . it modifies experience in so expressing it." "Ritual and beliefs change," Douglas insists, "they are extremely plastic," and their plasticity, as she sees it, derives above all from their being used, spoken, and energetically debated. They can be engaged in and argued over in what Fredric Jameson has termed "the privileged meeting places of collective life," which in the South include the bar and restaurant, the dinner table and shopping mall and the courthouse square. They can be engaged in and argued over inside the head. Either way—or, rather, both ways, since the two are inseparable—rituals become a site of struggle as different groups, classes, and individuals seek to appropriate and use them. And inventing the South—in turn, an idea of being and belonging *somewhere*—becomes a field of ideological contention in which those same groups, classes, and individuals seek to control the sign "South" and imbue it with their own meanings.[11]

The South is an imagined community made up of a multiplicity of communities, similarly imagined. Some of those communities are more imagined than others (where, say, there is little or no immediate contact). Some individual southerners, perhaps most, belong to several communities (think, for instance, of all the writers who write in one southern place about another). Some are more active and aware in their imagining. Still, what all these communities have in common *is* the act of imagination. And what all members of all those communities share, in turn, is what links them to the young girl whom Eudora Welty remembers and to the young woman whom Zora Neale Hurston describes in *Their Eyes Were Watching God,* for instance—the need to make a place in the world with the aid of talk and ceremony, language and communal ritual. This, both Welty and Hurston intimate, is a determinately human need since we are, by definition, verbal and social creatures. It is also a need that issues out of the aboriginal process of self-awareness and self-recognition ("Who am I?")—a process that involves the discovery of both resemblance ("I am like this") and difference ("I am not like that"). Less abstractly, it is something that drives southerners to position themselves *with* others in their locality, communality of interest or area, and *against* or *apart from* others elsewhere. It is also something, a need, a compulsion that, in satisfying, enables them to make some sense of their lives and histories. This is why southern self-fashioning has played such a decisive part in the making of America, and it is why, surely, southerners will go on doing what they do—insisting on their vital connection with some, many, or all other southerners in their difference.

11. Mary Douglas, *Purity and Danger: An Analysis of the Concepts of Pollution and Taboo* (1966; rprt., London: Routledge, 1984), 64, 62; Mary Douglas, "Couvade and Menstruation," in *Implicit Meanings* (London: Routledge and Paul, 1975), 61; Fredric Jameson, "Metacommentary," *PMLA* 86 (1971), 15.

SOUTH TO A NEW PLACE

Introduction: South to New Places

Sharon Monteith and Suzanne W. Jones

Place? It isn't that we don't *have* roots anymore. There is still a unique continuity to the southern experience. . . . We have roots, yes, but we have become like those plants that send . . . rootlets out into the air: a sense of *places,* not a sense of place.
> —Jack Butler, "Still Southern After All These Years"

To write, form rhizomes, expand your own territory by deterritorialization.
> —Gilles Deleuze and Felix Guattari, *On the Line*

At the end of Alan Gurganus's *Oldest Living Confederate Widow Tells All* (1989), his elderly protagonist gazes out of an airplane window as she flies over Georgia. Her view is a bird's-eye view, tracing the route Sherman's army took through the South. Tom Dent and Gary Younge track similar paths in *Southern Journey* (1997) and *No Place Like Home: A Black Briton's Journey Through the American South* (1999), following the route the Freedom Riders took in 1961.[1] In each case, it is the historical framework through which an individual views the South that determines what is seen. One is reminded of Eudora Welty's child protagonist in "A Memory", who watches the world through the frame she makes with her fingers. It is possible both to delimit what one sees and to create a paradigmatic framework through which to see further and more clearly—or simply differently from those who studied the South before you. Walker Percy's urban, apocalyptic vision frames the South very differently from William Alexander Percy, whose *Lanterns on the Levee*

---

1. See also Townsend Davis, *Weary Feet, Rested Souls* (New York: W. W. Norton, 1998), which concentrates on a sense of southern place by mapping the locales in which civil rights demonstrations and events took place.

(1941) is one of the most nostalgic (and reactionary) of place-defining southern memoirs. The Mississippi Delta that Larry Brown describes, with its rabid consumerism and depressing poverty, extends our apprehension of the places expatiated upon by predecessors like Percy, Welty, Faulkner, and Wright. For Richard Ford, who lived in the Delta, the Delta is "the South's South," supporting James C. Cobb's thesis that the region from Memphis to Vicksburg is "the Most Southern Place on Earth."[2]

The South's custodians, conservators, and gatekeepers have been many and various. They figure in diverse ideological contexts, as the tensions between what has become known as the "Rubin generation" and "post-Rubin" scholars demonstrate so well. Fred Hobson claims in *The Southern Writer in the Postmodern World* (1991) that there are few contemporary fictions that explore what he calls the "old" southern themes. Hobson asserts that since the "old albatross of segregation" has been thrown off, novelists inevitably also cast off "the old southern subject" of race and racial conflict, "the old setting" of the rural South, and "the old theme" of community. For Hobson, contemporary southern fiction is hardy but depleted in specific ways. He has been followed closely by others, like Jan Nordby Gretlund, who, despite examining the South from a very different nonsouthern perspective, sees the region's fiction in the same way. There is a notable and disturbing tendency to limit one's critical perspective by judging new writers according to old precepts. Gretlund, while finding new southern writing "impressive" and arguing for its appreciation, continues to compare Larry Brown to Faulkner, or Clyde Egerton's humor to Faulkner's in "Spotted Horses," and feels the need to test how writers of the 1980s compare "in determination and achievement" to Faulkner's "stoic resolve." As long ago as 1983 in "No More Monoliths, Please," C. Hugh Holman warned critics not to "shut too many doors to the fresh, the vital, and the new" in what he called the "Multi-Souths." In *South to a New Place*, the American South remains the datum, a given whose mythic properties have traditionally exceeded its realities and that consequently impels continued investigation, but the novum, the new places that extend our understanding of the South beyond traditional conceptions of regionalism, demand our special attention.[3]

2. Richard Ford, quoted in James C. Cobb's *The Most Southern Place on Earth: The Mississippi Delta and the Roots of Regional Identity* (New York: Oxford University Press, 1992), 325.

3. Fred Hobson, *The Southern Writer in the Postmodern World* (Athens: University of Georgia Press, 1991); Jan Nordby Gretlund, *Frames of Southern Mind: Reflections on the*

Most theories of national literature function metonymically, as in Jay B. Hubbell's discussion of the South's literary dependence on the North or Sacvan Bercovitch's *The American Jeremiad* (1978), where the South exists only as a footnote to a thesis in which the Puritan North is the seat of American identity, deriving its cultural credibility from its elevation over the Old South. But disavowing the South is simply one way of registering its presence, and elsewhere in American literary history "Souths"—Old and New, antebellum and postbellum, Upper and Lower, and Deep, together with Souths of the mind and imagination, and Nu-Souths and postmodern Souths—have proliferated.[4] Telling about the South in order to ratify its regional distinctiveness has a long and successful history through texts with titles like *The Everlasting South* (1963), *The Enduring South* (1974), and *The Prevailing South* (1988). Carl Degler argues, by predicating place over time, that the idea of the "South" overrides modernity, and in his essay in *The Prevailing South,* Louis D. Rubin Jr. ensures that place is capitalized (as is the Past and southern Problems) when he adjudges that a "firm identification with a Place" is a defining trope of southern literature. Rubin is hardly unusual in this claim, but many more critics like Leonard Lutwack have written of the "pain of placelessness" in modernist and postmodernist writing. Southern place is becoming a much more fluid concept than such parochial axioms would imply. For Jack Temple Kirby, for example, the "solid

---

Stoic, Bi-Racial and Existential South (Odense: Odense University Press, 1998), 248 and passim; C. Hugh Holman, "No More Monoliths, Please: Continuities in the Multi-Souths," in *Southern Literature in Transition,* ed. Philip Castille and William Osbourne (Memphis: Memphis State University Press, 1983), xiii–xxiv. The editors first had the idea for this project when they planned a special issue of the British journal *Critical Survey* called "South to a New Place." An MLA panel followed, and the interest generated in the U.S. and Europe is evidence of the continuing importance of place in southern studies.

4. Jay B. Hubbell, *The South in American Literature 1607–1900* (Durham: Duke University Press, 1954); Sacvan Bercovitch, *The American Jeremiad* (Madison: University of Wisconsin Press, 1978), xiii. "Defining" southern texts, from the apologist to the deconstructionist, include, for example: W. J. Cash, *The Mind of the South* (New York: Alfred A. Knopf, 1941); Clement Eaton, *The Mind of the Old South* (Baton Rouge: Louisiana State University Press, 1964); C. Hugh Holman, *The Roots of Southern Writing* (Athens: University of Georgia Press, 1972); Fred Hobson, *Tell About the South: The Southern Rage to Explain* (Baton Rouge: Louisiana State University Press, 1983); Richard Gray, *Writing the South: Ideas of an American Region* (Cambridge: Cambridge University Press, 1986); Michael O'Brien, *Rethinking the South: Essays in Intellectual History* (Baltimore: Johns Hopkins University Press, 1988), Lewis P. Simpson, *The Fable of the Southern Writer* (Baton Rouge: Louisiana State University Press, 1994); and, of course, the work of Louis D. Rubin over half a century.

South" dissolved in 1976 with the election of Jimmy Carter, and Richard Gray has consistently problematized backward-looking sectionalism by detecting forward-thinking regionalism. Jon Smith in his essay here reminds us of the six thousand South Carolinians who in January 2000 came out in force to keep the Confederate flag flying over their statehouse.[5]

Many of the contributors to this volume revisit Eudora Welty's discussion in "Place in Fiction," wherein location is the "ground conductor of all the currents of emotion and belief and moral conviction that charge out from the story in its course." Welty, Faulkner, Percy, and the Vanderbilt Agrarians have each spelled out in differing ideological contexts the significance of southern place. But in a postmodern world, premodern and modern conceptions of place are inevitably insufficiently fluid. For Welty's insider-writer, the region signifies home, but ideas of nationhood, and the global as well as the local, complicate any discussion of regional veracity. Most tellingly, turning assertions about the "Americanization" of the South around, critical debate about the "Southernization of America" has established a model whereby the South is both a cultural filter and the barometer for the health (or sickness) of the nation. In a recent issue of *Virginia Quarterly Review*, Leslie W. Dunbar argues that the South has polluted America with its racism and violence. But writers, critics, politicians, and historians as different as James Dickey, Peter Applebome, Carl Degler, James C. Cobb, John Lewis, V. S. Naipaul, and John Hope Franklin have claimed that the South is a place of reconciliation, and this feeling strengthened over the last decades of the twentieth century. John Lewis asserted in 1966 that "here in the South where racial divisions were once the deepest, I can see the day breaking when this will be considered a region of hope." More recently in his autobiography *Walking with the Wind* (1998), Lewis believes his prediction has come true: "Despite the setbacks of recent years, there remains in the South, an inherent sense of purpose, of belief, of people pulling together and actually effecting change. Despite all the failures and frustrations of the past

---

5. Carl Degler, *Place Over Time: The Continuity of Southern Distinctiveness* (Baton Rouge: Louisiana State University Press, 1977); Louis D. Rubin Jr., "Changing, Enduring, Forever Still the South," in *The Prevailing South*, ed. Dudley Clendinen (Atlanta: Longstreet Press, 1988), 26; Leonard Lutwack, *The Role of Place in Literature* (New York: Syracuse University Press, 1984); Jack Temple Kirby, *Media-Made Dixie: The South in the American Imagination* (Rev. ed.; Athens: University of Georgia Press, 1986), 172. For Richard Gray's most recent work, see *Southern Aberrations: Writers of the American South and the Problems of Regionalism* (Baton Rouge: Louisiana State University Press, 2000).

three decades, there is still a *spirit* in the South, a spirit that was not and *is* not felt in the same way in the North." In 1972, John Hope Franklin was careful and coded in "The Great Confrontation: The South and the Problem of Change." But later he advances the belief that the South, the nation's most visible crucible of national racial guilt, is nevertheless the nation's hope for racial peace.[6]

Much has been invested in the contemporary South's abilities to redeem the nation at the end of the twentieth century and the beginning of the twenty-first, despite the kinds of inherent regional contradictions that Peter Applebome has summarized: "Looked at one way, it's a place of grace and faith that has purged most of its old sins while maintaining most of its old virtues, a place that for all its bloody past and the ambiguities and unresolved issues of the present, offers the nation's best blueprint for racial peace. Looked at another way, it's a Potemkin Village of mirrors and trap doors, where old inequities are cloaked in new forms, a chameleon South changed only on the surface, now pumping old poisons into new veins, a place where even in the most neutered suburbs, what was still lives, beating insistently away like Poe's telltale heart." A number of southern writers keenly demonstrate a sense of the South as appalling as well as enthralling. For Carson McCullers, a visit to Columbus, Georgia—a key setting for her fiction—was "a stirring up of love and antagonism," and James Baldwin, visiting Martin Luther King Jr., encountered a "great, vast, brooding, welcoming and bloodstained land, beautiful enough to astonish and break the heart." When Eudora Welty writes "Where Is This Voice Coming From?" immediately following the news of Medgar Evers's assassination in her hometown of Jackson, Mississippi, on June 12, 1963, she succeeds in apprehending the smoldering hatred that gives rise to a racist killing.[7]

---

6. Eudora Welty, "Place in Fiction," in *The Eye of the Story: Selected Essays and Reviews* (New York: Vintage, 1979), 128; Leslie W. Dunbar, "The Final New South?" *Virginia Quarterly Review* 74, no. 1 (Winter 1998): 49–58; John Lewis, "Statement" to the Voter Education Project, Atlanta, 13 January 1966, as quoted by Stephen A. Smith in *Myth, Media, and the Southern Mind* (Fayetteville: University of Arkansas Press, 1985), 92–93; John Hope Franklin, *The Color Line: Legacy for the Twenty-First Century* (Columbia: University of Missouri Press, 1994).

7. Applebome, *Dixie Rising, How the South Is Shaping American Values, Politics, and Culture* (New York: Harcourt Brace and Company, 1997), 20; Carson McCullers, "The Flowering Dream: Notes on Writing," in *The Mortgaged Heart* (Boston: Houghton Mifflin, 1971), 279; James Baldwin, *No Name in the Street* (New York: Doubleday, 1972), 68; Eudora Welty, "Where Is This Voice Coming From?" in *The Collected Stories* (London: Penguin, 1983), 603–7.

The southern landscape has always meant more than the sum of its parts. For nonsoutherners traveling through the South, it is often the bloody past that remains the most pervasive. They often begin their journeys trapped within confining and predetermined expectations; travelers to and through the southern states, from whites like Frances Trollope and Harriet Martineau in the nineteenth century to blacks like Eddy Harris and Gary Younge at the end of the twentieth, tend to revise their preconceptions.[8] New York journalist Harris, who rides South to "confront the source of [his] anger" on behalf of those "tempered in the kiln of Jim Crow," is surprised to find that by the end of his journey the South feels like home. Like Baldwin before him, he finds that it is the contradictions that fuel his conclusions. Gary Younge finds himself turned away from a motel in Senatobia, Mississippi, with a racist assumption that spurs him to remember the "bad old" 1960s rather than bask in the "new" 1990s. But he continues to long for the "heartfelt affinity that both blacks and whites in the South seemed to have with their environment," and his disaster-filled predictions are slowly transformed into clear-sightedness. Southern *place-ness* has obsessed those outside the South, like Jean Renoir, whose films *Swamp Water* (1941) and *The Southerner* (1945) celebrated the land and the struggle of those who work it.[9] The South has captured the imaginations of those not born in the region but who seek to tell "southern" stories, like Octavia Butler in *Kindred* (1979), Sherley Anne Williams in *Dessa Rose* (1986), Toni Morrison in *Beloved* (1987), and Pete Dexter in *Paris Trout* (1988). As Suzanne W. Jones and Wes Berry point out in their essays, African American writers often turn to the South in order to explore personal and family history forged in the crucible of slavery and segregation.

An ever-evolving critical axis of investigation widens the parameters

8. See Frances Trollope (mother of Anthony), *Domestic Manners of the Americans* (1832) and *The Life and Adventures of Jonathan Jefferson Whitelaw* (1836), and Harriet Martineau, *Society in America* (1837), as discussed in detail by Diane Roberts in *The Myth of Aunt Jemima: Representations of Race and Region* (New York: Routledge, 1994); Eddy Harris, *South of Haunted Dreams: A Ride Through Slavery's Old Back Yard* (New York: Simon and Schuster, 1993), 22–23, 238; Gary Younge, *No Place Like Home: A Black Briton's Journey Through the American South* (London: Picador, 1999), 24.

9. Joel Williamson, in his biography of William Faulkner, selects the word *place-ness* as the single word that conveys his sense of Faulkner's South. In his context, it resonates with the designation of specific places and social spaces to blacks and whites in ways that worked to uphold segregation. Williamson, *William Faulkner and Southern History* (New York: Oxford University Press, 1993), 403.

within which the South may be examined, critiqued, and understood. Brian Morton, in an essay on the South published in the British press, argued recently that "the American South has never had to rely on the theories of strangers." Morton reworks the idea that "the" South has been elaborated over generations by southerners for southerners. In *Inventing Southern Literature* (1998), Michael Kreyling opens out such ideas to scrutiny, allowing that "cultural waves originating outside the South" may "wash through its literature and change it." And when George Brown Tindall in *Natives and Newcomers* (1995) allows for a keen sense of ethnic diversity in southern places, he forces us to acknowledge that we are almost as likely to encounter new southern fictions by Vietnamese Americans on the Gulf Coast or by Cuban Americans in Florida as we are to find the myth of southern place still tied to the biracial small town. For Tom Dent, small towns are "more interesting, more resistant to change, more reflective of the South as a region," but in contemporary novels like Roberto G. Fernández's *Holy Radishes!* (1995), Lan Cao's *Monkey Bridge* (1997), and Susan Choi's *The Foreign Student* (1998) those same small southern towns are changed forever by new immigrants. In a strangled effort to convey his homeland in terms that may mean something to his United States audience, Korean Chang Ahn (otherwise known as Chuck) asserts in Choi's novel, "Korea is a shape just like Florida. Yes? The top half is a communist state, and the bottom half are fighting for democracy!" He tries to compare the thirty-eighth parallel with the Mason-Dixon Line, casting around for "southern" tropes through which southerners might begin to imagine his homeland. It is to a sense of place that he turns: "You maybe don't believe it but Korea, the land, looks very much like Tennessee." He feels the comparison looking out over the Tennessee hills as he studies at Sewanee in the late-1950s: "sometimes he woke in the morning and just for an instant was sure he was home." Edward Said attests that home is always provisional, and exiles crossing borders "break barriers of thought and experience." Negotiating a sense of place involves reassessment of one's past in a new present, and writers like Choi provoke a cultural remapping of the region that allows us to inquire into new coordinates of southern identity.[10]

10. Brian Morton, "Not So Much a Region, More a State of Mind," *London Sunday Times*, 24 July 1994, 10–11; Michael Kreyling, "The Extra: Southern Literature: Consensus and Dissensus," *American Literature* 60, no. 1 (March 1988): 83–95 (for a fuller discussion, see Kreyling, *Inventing Southern Literature* [Jackson: University Press of Mississippi, 1998]); George Brown Tindall, *Natives and Newcomers: Ethnic Southerners and Southern Ethnics* (Athens: University of Georgia Press, 1995); Tom Dent, *Southern Journey: A Return to the Civil Rights Movement* (New York: William Morrow, 1997) (this

In Cao's *Monkey Bridge,* Falls Church, Virginia, just a few miles from Washington, D.C., becomes Little Saigon, and her protagonist Mai builds horizontal communities with others to find her way through moral panics in the press over immigration, and the "eerie topography" of her memories of Vietnam. Such novels can be read as syncretic models in which the fusion of cultures overrides what Freud once described as "the narcissism of minor difference," wherein communities living on the boundaries of one another make manifest their inclination toward aggression by undermining each other. New immigrant writers turn a mirror on the South, and the images refracted tell the South in new ways. They complicate the South's predominantly biracial literary history and reveal the South's demographics as complex and changing. A key text in this regard remains Robert Olen Butler's Pulitzer Prize-winning *A Good Scent from a Strange Mountain* (1992), explored in detail by Maureen Ryan in this collection.[11]

Comparative studies are sometimes viewed with suspicion by those who maintain that hegemonic centers of power leave the comparative context auxiliary and inferior. In a special issue of *South Atlantic Review* dedicated to "The Worldwide Face of Southern Literature," the editors point to Poe's artistic reception in France and Twain and Faulkner's in Japan, but it is difficult to reconcile just why the successful exportation of southern writers should come as such a surprise to them: "conferences on southern authors have taken place, often more than once, in the United Kingdom, France, Spain, Germany, Austria, Italy, Norway, Denmark, Poland, Soviet Georgia, and Japan." A tinge of provincialism remains in the assumption that southerners rather than South-watchers will inevitably discover new ways of eliciting meaning from southern places. A socio-cultural approach to literature, which examines the South

---

quotation appears on the dustjacket); Susan Choi, *The Foreign Student* (New York: Harper Perennial, 1999), 51–53; Edward W. Said, "Mind of Winter: Reflections on Life in Exile," *Harper's,* September 1984, 54.

11. Lan Cao, *Monkey Bridge* (New York: Penguin, 1999), 16; Sigmund Freud, *Civilization and Its Discontents* (1930) in *Standard Edition of the Complete Psychological Works of Sigmund Freud,* ed. James Strachey (London: Collins, 1927–31), Vol. 21, 123. For exemplification of the biracial literary tradition, see Suzanne W. Jones's anthology of short stories, *Crossing the Color Line: Readings in Black and White* (Columbia: University of South Carolina Press, 2000), and for critiques of interracial connections, see, for example, Minrose C. Gwin, *Black and White Women in the Old South: A Peculiar Sisterhood* (Knoxville: University of Tennessee Press, 1985) and Sharon Monteith, *Advancing Sisterhood? Interracial Friendships in Contemporary Southern Fiction* (Athens: University of Georgia Press, 2000).

from a distance or sets the South at the periphery, can draw out distinctions, break open frontiers, and question those boundaries that hermetically seal the South, as in, for example, Robert H. Brinkmeyer Jr.'s *Remapping Southern Literature* (2000). Essays on transcultural crossovers—Deborah Cohn's study of Faulkner and Latin American writers and Helen Taylor's circum-Atlantic reorientations of traditionally southern tropes in European contexts, for example—focus on particularized "new places." But across the volume, "traveling theory," especially when related to contemporary interrogations of regionalism and to postmodern geographies, helps to change the contours of southern studies. Writers revisit specific southern terrain (from cities to small towns and rural places), and what they find in the representations they read allows us to inquire into new coordinates of southern identity.[12]

In 1971, Albert Murray published *South to a Very Old Place*. Commissioned by the editor of *Harper's* magazine, Willie Morris, to write about "home" in a series of articles, the African American writer produced much more: *South to a Very Old Place* is memoir, travelogue, and social commentary. Orchestrated as a jazz-and-blues composition, it is a meditation on the American South. Taking his title as our starting point, we have gathered contributors who are critically and creatively remapping the American South, a region that exasperates as it inspires definition(s). Just as Murray's blues-informed jazz forms are open-ended, improvised, and hybrid, the blues metaphor and jazz form are key to our collection, which surveys representations of the South within a postmodern, diverse, inclusive, and international context. In fact, when V. S. Naipaul began his "turn" in the South, he visited Albert Murray in Harlem, and Murray helped the writer to "see" differently: "with Al's help, my eye changed. Where at first I had seen only Harlem gloom, I began . . . to see . . . the splendor of the original Harlem design." Heading south with *A Turn in*

12. Pearl Amelia McHaney and Thomas L. McHaney, eds., *South Atlantic Review* 65, no. 4 (2000): 2; Robert H. Brinkmeyer Jr., *Remapping Southern Literature: Contemporary Southern Writers and the West* (Athens: University of Georgia Press, 2000). This study examines those writers like Cormac McCarthy, Barry Hannah, and Doris Betts who head west in their plotlines but whose fiction, Brinkmeyer argues, remains thematically and stylistically rooted in the South. For a fuller discussion of transcultural crossovers, see Deborah N. Cohn, *History and Memory in Two Souths: Recent Southern and Spanish American Fiction* (Nashville: Vanderbilt University Press, 1999) and Helen Taylor, *Circling Dixie: Contemporary Southern Culture Through a Transatlantic Lens* (Piscataway, N.J.: Rutgers University Press, 2001).

the South (1989), Naipaul is initially surprised to discover that what he feels are "some of the most important 'American' things" are actually southern—"Coca-Cola, and country music, and even the idea of supermarkets." Whereas Naipaul fails to examine many of the southern clichés that prompt his search for southern distinctiveness, once his eyes are accustomed to the South he does succeed in elucidating points of comparison with the Caribbean, ones that draw on past associations via slavery and other pointed parallels between the historical area of Charleston, with its horse-drawn carriages and souvenir stalls, and "the tourist Caribbean of today."[13]

As recently as 1999, Randall Kenan, following Murray, entitled the final section of his epic *Walking on Water: Black American Lives at the Turn of the Twenty-First Century* "Home to a Very Strange Place." Raised by his grandfather in Wallace, North Carolina, and in nearby Chinquapin by his great-aunt, he casts back to a place that was "unincorporated and rural, largely tobacco fields and cornfields and hog farms," but that now "coexists" with a world that includes cyberspace. Freighted with memories, some of which are harbingers of fear and the desire to leave, Kenan realizes that "the many feelings engendered by life in a small town are much more complex and tangled than most people who've never lived in one, belonged to one, could ever imagine," and he ensures that his own small-town experience—"strange" now to the grown man who has lived in New York—is incorporated into the epic sweep across the changing social geography of African American lives.[14]

South to a New Place begins to chart connections with "other" Souths in ways that open up spaces and places from which we might read the region as a site of exchange. Taking as our starting point Wendell Berry's incredulity that contemporary scholars of the American South could attempt to "redefine Southernness without resort to geography," we have collected essays that tie the mythic southern balloon down to earth. Our contributors examine both new southern places and old southern landscapes—from fiction set in postsouthern suburbs to a Thoreauvian impulse in contemporary southern writing about nature. The essays pay attention to the ways that regional typologies are fictive, as Richard Gray points out in his foreword to this collection. Gray demonstrates one of the key conceptions that underpin *South to a New Place*—that it opens

13. V. S. Naipaul, *A Turn in the South* (New York: Vintage, 1990), 22, 105, 77–78.

14. Randall Kenan, *Walking on Water: Black American Lives at the Turn of the Twenty-First Century* (New York: Alfred Knopf, 1999), 607–8, 624.

up to scrutiny the literary and cultural practice that has come to be known as "regionalism." Larry McClain in "The Rhetoric of Regional Representation" has argued that regional writing is afforded canonical status only when region is disguised in a "vague 'American' universalism" and that, in this way, "the boundaries of 'mainstream' literature are patrolled." Whereas McClain believes that one only explores regional counter-traditions by examining noncanonized regional fiction, Gray in his foreword and other contributors to this collection succeed in opening up debates about regionalism precisely through their examination of canon and context.[15]

Part I, "Surveying the Territory," theorizes definitions of place and region. In "Where Is Southern Literature? The Practice of Place in a Postsouthern Age," Scott Romine wraps his mind around southern literary regionalism from the 1930s to the present, skillfully analyzing the evolution of southern literary scholarship and its fascination with place. Finding that throughout its history the South has been variously defined as a region—geographically, economically, ideologically, culturally, historically, and orientationally—Romine argues that "all these 'Souths' have been subject to or implicated in distinctive forms of representation." He wonders which criteria will be necessary for southern literature to survive and concludes by speculating on the effect that the loss of southern distinctiveness will have on the writing of southern fiction. In "Dismantling the Monolith: Southern Places—Past, Present, and Future," Barbara Ladd takes a look around Atlanta and its outlying suburbs as she speculates about how contemporary scholars might theorize place. Ladd's wide-ranging study shows that, although the symbolic landscape of "the South" continues to shape many of our perceptions, the South is continually undergoing demographic changes. She demonstrates that the South is neither insular nor homogenous, and she argues that while "the *experience* of place remains dynamic and vital," it is the theorizing of place that is problematic. Sharing a concern with Michael Kowalewski that we "lack a vocabulary with which to ask engaging philosophical, psychological or aesthetic questions about what it means to dwell in a place, whether actually or imaginatively,"[16] Ladd proposes a number of new

15. Wendell Berry, "Writer and Region," *Hudson Review* 40, no. 1 (Spring 1987): 25; Larry McClain, "The Rhetoric of Regional Representation: American Fiction and the Politics of Cultural Dissent," *Genre* 27, no. 3 (1994): 227–53.

16. Michael Kowalewski, "Writing in Place: The New American Regionalism," *American Literary History* 6, no. 1 (Spring 1994): 174.

areas for exploration, many of which other contributors begin to map in detail. Together she and Romine expand the conceptual framework in which the South has traditionally been mapped and monitored.

In "Race and Intimacy: Albert Murray's *South to a Very Old Place*," Carolyn M. Jones returns to Murray in order to rethink what it means to dwell in a place. Murray recognized the hybridity of southern culture long before the concept became trendy in contemporary theoretical circles. He showed how the South has, within its indigenous African American musical forms, some of the tools it needs to reconstruct its society and to think differently about its region. Via Toni Morrison's ideas of "intimate things in place," Jones argues that in the structure of *South to a Very Old Place*, Albert Murray illustrates how the blues-inspired jazz form can become a model both to locate the self and to improvise new communities. Through his conversations with white southerners— Robert Penn Warren, C. Vann Woodward, Edwin Yoder, Walker Percy, and others—Murray, playing the role of the trickster, tests to see if they will acknowledge the hybridity of southern culture, all the while hoping to spot the "downhome angle of vision" beneath their cosmopolitan intellectualism and their southern politeness. Much less "polite" are Jon Smith's subjects in "Southern Culture on the Skids." Southern rock music with its lyrics about Civil War rebels and nostalgia for the "Lost Cause" is a resistant romanticization of "history" and "home," as Paul Wells and Ted Ownby have discussed.[17] But for Jon Smith, it is punk-influenced subcultures that function to reveal white southern self-presentation as especially fetishistic and narcissistic. Deploying psychoanalytic paradigms, he shows how subcultures can operate to maintain a specific identity and the extent to which "love of place" can be a self-displacement. In a wide-ranging piece that reads southern signifiers from flags to ads, trucks to perfume and Elvis Jell-O molds, Smith studies the punk dynamic alongside southern surf bands to survey an intrinsically southern popular-cultural terrain.

The final essay in this section develops out of a keenly theorized sense of place. Paul Lyons argues that Larry Brown's *Joe* (1991) is "an exem-

---

17. Paul Wells, "The Last Rebel: Southern Rock and Nostalgic Continuities," in *Dixie Debates: Perspectives on Southern Culture*, ed. Richard H. King and Helen Taylor (London: Pluto Press, 1996), 115–29; Ted Ownby, "Freedom, Manhood, and White Male Tradition in 1970s Southern Rock Music," in *Haunted Bodies: Gender and Southern Texts*, ed. Anne Goodwyn Jones and Susan V. Donaldson (Charlottesville: University Press of Virginia, 1997), 369–88.

plary test-case for critiquing the usefulness of theories of global/local conjunctions and American cultural remapping for the residual regionalism" that he detects in contemporary southern literature. In this sense, *Joe* is a liminal text; Larry Brown's characters lack a sense of "place-history" which, though it signifies a lack of future direction, may also inspire a certain "freedom to pursue their order of things." The only job that Joe manages to secure in rural Mississippi is poisoning trees; his job is to "kill" a forest. But through Joe's introspection, the novel opens up "glimmers" of eco-consciousness, and Lyons calls for a "critical regionalism" in his discussion of the "uses and abuses of the region concept" based in and on the land itself.

Part II, "Mapping the Region," examines different representations of contemporary southern places. The essays in this section serve as a reminder that the South is rhizomic in the sense of Deleuze and Guattari, whereby diverse literary speculations on southern places connect and intertwine like crabgrass—or, more appropriately in the southern landscape, like kudzu—with multiple crossings and taproot systems flourishing everywhere. The contributors to this section consider rural landscapes and small towns, cities and suburbs, as well as the liminal zones in which new immigrants make their homes. Anxiety over place—Stephen Flinn Young's idea that some southerners have become "prisoners of our fascination with the 'sense' of place" rather than "aware of the living thing that place really is"—provides a starting point from which to begin to read the essays.[18]

Revising Agrarian definitions of the South and southern literature, Suzanne W. Jones's "new agrarians," Ellen Douglas and Madison Smartt Bell, refute the pastoral, conservative South of the Vanderbilt credo. Instead, the South to which their protagonists return in *The Rock Cried Out* (1979) and *Soldier's Joy* (1989) is the post-Vietnam and post–civil rights South. Bell writes lyrical landscapes but underpins them with a keen appreciation of the tangled racialized economics of land ownership for blacks and for whites even toward the end of the twentieth century, as Jones's reading of the end of *Soldier's Joy* makes clear. Jones shows how Douglas pushes interracial agrarianism a step further than Bell, by rewriting Ike McCaslin's story in "The Bear." Jones locates her contemporary agrarians from their writerly beginnings. Bell grew up with the

18. Gilles Deleuze and Felix Guattari, "Rhizome," in *On the Line* (New York: Semiotext[e], 1983), 1–65; Stephen Flinn Young, "Post-Southernism: The Southern Sensibility in Postmodern Sculpture," *Southern Quarterly* 28, no. 1 (Fall 1989): 41.

Vanderbilt Agrarians from whom he draws but whose tenacious romanticism he revises. Douglas, from an older generation of writers, recalls Faulkner, but in her fictional Homochitto (Natchez) she reasserts the southern landscape by "unburdening" it of Faulkner's "mythic configuration." Wes Berry turns to ecocritics and environmental philosophers (Lawrence Buell, William Cronon, Barry Lopez) in "Toni Morrison's Revisionary 'Nature Writing': *Song of Solomon* and the Blasted Pastoral" to explore "the healing potential of southern woodlands" when those very landscapes are fraught with historic violence. In Morrison's novel, Milkman Dead returns to his ancestral "homeland." Berry tracks the "regenerative moments," the disquieting experiences that pull him up short in his merging with a "more-than human nature." He concludes that the strain of African American pastoralism that Buell detects together with the "language of ego-dissolution" in Euro-American writing combine in Morrison's progressive and historically inflected "nature writing."

Other contributors to *South to a New Place* shift our attention from the rural to the urban and suburban South. One of the most succinct descriptions of the origins of suburbia in the 1950s occurs in a novel set in the South. In Julius Lester's *And All Our Wounds Forgiven* (1994), John Calvin Marshall, a fictional Martin Luther King Jr., declares: "for centuries we had been rooted to place. home and work and leisure occurred in one place and created a whole—community. the interstate highway system made it possible to live thirty, forty, fifty, sixty miles away from where you worked. work and home and place ceased to be interrelated. . . . you could live without belonging to a community. . . . the interstate highway system brought into being a geo-political entity called sub-burbs."[19] Matthew Guinn in "Into the Suburbs" reminds us that Richard Ford has visited many different locales in his fiction. It is the rootlessness of protagonist Frank Bascombe that prompts Guinn's exploration of postmodern writing in which "the local and the regional have been subsumed by an anarchic mix of architectual references." For Ford, the past recedes in favor of a continuous present. Guinn reads the shifts in postmodern place and placelessness from Ford's *The Sportswriter*

---

19. Julius Lester, *And All Our Wounds Forgiven* (New York: Harcourt and Brace, 1994), 5. For a detailed reading of the novel, see Sharon Monteith, "Revisiting the 1960s in Contemporary Fiction: 'Where Do We Go from Here?'" in *Gender and the Civil Rights Movement*, ed. Peter J. Ling and Sharon Monteith (New York: Garland, 1999), 215–38. See also Alex Harris, ed., *A New Life: Stories and Photographs from the Suburban South* (New York: W. W. Norton, 1997), especially Alan Gurganus's afterword, "Toward a Creation Myth of Suburbia."

(1986) to *Independence Day* (1995), and Martyn Bone pursues the term *postsouthern* in the specific literary context of Tom Wolfe's *A Man in Full* (1998). Engaging with Lewis Simpson and Michael Kreyling's discussions of the term as well as with postmodern geographies, Bone embarks upon an examination of both the capitalist production of suburban spaces and the fetishization of place, focusing on Atlanta. In "Placing the Postsouthern 'International City,'" Bone explores a postconsensus South in an examination of Wolfe's much-hyped depiction of capitalist land-speculation. In Bone's reading, Wolfe exposes how the spectacle of the "panorama-city" is a real-estate projection, and he raises issues of race and place, capital and real estate against the "concrete geography" of Atlanta. Whereas Tom Wolfe and Richard Ford left the South and Larry Brown stayed, reading their novels as closely as Bone, Guinn, and Lyons do in this collection serves to open up a wider discussion of how significant region has been in the development of individual consciousness in local and national context.

Robert McRuer in "Queer Locations, Queer Transformations," a study of Randall Kenan's 1989 novel, *A Visitation of Spirits,* examines how stories of "difference" are told as stories of location, via Kenan's fictional Tims Creek in rural North Carolina. McRuer contends with Henry Louis Gates Jr., who in his praise for the novel expresses the hope that Kenan will take his protagonist Horace "to the big city" in his next book. Gates suggests a path that has been well trodden by lesbian and gay characters migrating from country to city, whereas what is much more interesting to McRuer is the fact that "queer transformations can begin in the queerest of locations." Tims Creek is a fundamentalist Christian and African American locality, and Horace's suicide is firmly set against any mythical, pastoral sense of community. Eric Gary Anderson contends with another kind of fragile presence in the South—Florida Indians in a novel by Linda Hogan, a Chickasaw novelist at several times remove from the South. Anderson provides a nuanced ecocritical reading of a landscape we know best through the writing of Zora Neale Hurston and Marjorie Stoneman Douglas but are also coming to know through the novels of Connie May Fowler. Anderson asks how we should locate Hogan's *Power* (1998) on the southern literary map when it is impossible to retrieve so many lost stories of American Indian culture. He probes this question of inaccessibility and concludes that we are beginning to "stretch and complicate our understanding" of both American Indian literature and the South.

For novelists and for critics, the "region concept" is transmogrified by the changing dictates of transnational postmodernism, not least of which is the recent influx of immigrants to the South. Maureen Ryan's intervention into debates about southern place is distinguished by its focus on some of the South's newest citizens, those Vietnamese refugees for whom the land itself is a sacred constant (one is reminded that the word *country* translates as earth and water in Vietnamese). Most tellingly, traditional Vietnamese emphases on family, home, the land, and the past echo agrarian concerns from earlier decades, as Ryan points out. But Ryan counters the "changeless" South with the changing South in which the Vietnamese make their new homes following the fall of Saigon. She examines a large cast of Amerasian and Vietnamese characters across fictions by Robert Olen Butler, Wayne Karlin, Lan Cao, and Mary Gardner, set in Louisiana, Maryland, Virginia, and Texas. Across the South, these novels not only address the melee of feelings that persist around the Vietnam War, the "watershed event" of late-twentieth-century America, they open up what Ryan calls a "new frontier of cultural hybridism."

Amy J. Elias unpacks the irony that just when southern writers and critics are questioning the notion of a unique southern literature, "popular culture and the travel industry seem intent upon constructing and marketing southern regional identity." In "Postmodern Southern Vacation: Vacation Advertising, Globalization, and Southern Regionalism," Elias emphasizes how the construction of the American South has become a global issue, and she examines the ways in which some advertisements recuperate the Old South's construction of race and others illuminate the New South's anxieties about ethnicity. Her focus on the lifestyle magazine *Southern Living,* with a readership of twelve million, reveals a complex fantasy South, which has become a playground for consumers from all over the United States and around the world. *Southern Living* has long been a lifestyle primer for middle-class southerners in which emblems of the former Confederacy and of the New South sit intriguingly, if uncomfortably, side by side. In reading representative advertisements for southern vacationing, Elias uncovers a wealth of contradictions, and her cultural-studies approach elicits our understanding of mass cultural theory and reception studies in a very specific southern context.

The essays in Part III, "Making Global Connections," challenge notions of southern distinctiveness like those mass-mediated in *Southern Living* by reading the region through comparative frameworks: Southern Italy, East Germany, Latin America, and the U.K. Such frameworks facilitate other telling comparisons, too. A glance across to South Africa, for example, leads us to recall Steve Biko's correlation between Black Consciousness in South Africa in 1976 with the African American freedom struggles that developed out of southern civil rights initiatives of the 1950s and 1960s. The "South" in Africa and the United States acts as a focalizer through which the American South and the struggles of the black population can be set in a transnational context.[20] Rob Nixon, for example, faces the other way in *Homelands, Harlem, and Hollywood: South African Culture and the World Beyond* (1994), and Ann Seidman's comparative approach has recently exposed specific links between South African and Appalachian mineworkers. In this section of *South to a New Place,* Michael Kreyling goes to Italy in "Italy and the United States: The Politics and Poetics of the 'Southern Problem' " to illuminate how both southern regions were "made" in the 1860s and have been remade since. Via a range of texts and contexts—from early reconciliation romances through the works of Antonio Gramsci, the Southern Agrarians, Norman Douglas, and William Faulkner to the rural expeditions of urban intellectuals James Agee and Carlo Levi—Kreyling argues that in both countries the idea of the "South" functions similarly in national discourse. In 1945 at the end of the Second World War, Ralph McGill found himself discussing Caldwell's *Tobacco Road* with a Roman bookseller: "The American South was a regional abstraction with a capital S. It possessed, like his Naples and Sicily, a stubborn, often unjustified, pride; it was easygoing and yet violent when it chose to be; it shared as did Southern Italy, a common mystique in which there is grandeur, and pathos, and a note of falseness too. . . . Now fluid as quicksilver, now rigid and cruel in its adamant injustice and wrongs, now soft and merry, it was difficult to put into words." McGill searches for an Italian story with a southern angle as exemplification. He doesn't immediately find one. In his essay for this collection, Kreyling detects a series of "coincidences" linking Italian and American literature and history, and goes on to demonstrate that the place of the South in both countries shifts from "historical urgency" to "cultural politics," and thus from historical to ideological discourse.[21]

20. See, for example, John W. Cell, *The Highest State of White Supremacy: The Origins of Segregation in South Africa and the American South* (Cambridge: Cambridge University Press, 1982)

21. Rob Nixon, *Homelands, Harlem and Hollywood: South African Culture and the World Beyond* (New York: Routledge, 1994); Ann Seidman, "Apartheid and the U.S. South," in *Imagining Home: Class, Culture and Nationalism in the African Diaspora,* ed. Sidney Lemelle and Robin D. G. Kelley (London: Verso, 1994), 209–221; Ralph McGill,

Gunter Lenz has written at length about the ways in which an intercultural approach to the United States and Germany provides insights into how cultures "reproduce, represent, and reshape within themselves axes or fault-lines of difference."[22] Here, by examining the particular transnational context of the former German Democratic Republic and the American South, Christine Gerhardt enters the debate by engaging with contemporary definitions of regionalism in order to argue that region remains "a productive category of cross-cultural comparison." Gerhardt compares six representative fictions that help her to gauge the ideological strictures that sustain regional identities by protecting their boundaries. Most tellingly, in her pairing of Welty's "No Place for You, My Love" and Gabriele Eckart's "Feldberg und Zurück," protagonists who visit the South and East Germany help to show how regions—as heterotopic spaces—can resist attempts to penetrate them, or can resist those who crave an authenticity of place they can never find. In a very different comparative context, by examining Faulkner's influence on a range of Spanish American writers from Borges to Márquez, Rulfo to Bombal, Deborah Cohn tests Faulkner's legacy most specifically with younger Latin American authors, such as Rosario Ferré for whom "Faulknerian method" continues to resonate with cross-cultural meanings. Puerto Rican Ferré reorients traditionally Faulknerian themes of incest, miscegenation, and the plantation household. Building on her work in *History and Memory in Two Souths* (1999), Cohn demonstrates the continuity of Faulkner's appeal at the same time that she reveals a new "South" American literary sensibility that seeks to revise shared histories regarding issues of race and gender.

When places are set in manichean opposition (North America over the American South; West Germany over the former German Democratic Republic), the strategies deployed to compare fictions of place and placelessness necessarily involve an understanding of sectarianism and nationalism as well as regionalism. Helen Taylor's context here is rather different since it is the globalizing of the American South—its popular-cultural currency—that motivates her investigation of the British fascina-

---

"There Are Many Souths," in *The South and the Southerner* (Boston: Little, Brown and Company, 1963), 6.

22. Gunter Lenz, "Historians, Histories, and Public Cultures: Multicultural Discourses in the U. S. and Germany," in *TransAtlantic Encounters: Multiculturalism, National Identity and the Uses of the Past*, ed. Gunter Lenz and Peter Ling (Amsterdam: Vrije Universiteit Press, 2000), 63–103.

tion with the American South. Specific place-defining fictions—the chivalric novels of Sir Walter Scott in the mid-nineteenth century; Erskine Caldwell's *Tobacco Road* and *God's Little Acre* and Margaret Mitchell's *Gone With the Wind* in the early twentieth—help us to see how peculiarly resonant images of places have been when produced at particular historical moments. Taylor extrapolates from Scott's influence over a tradition of cavalier romances and Carlyle's espousal of the Confederate cause to examine the way "the Celtic card" is played now by groups like the League of the South, Christian Identity, and Neo-Nazis. She traces the way that the white "cracker," originally a Scottish term for "a noisy, boastful fellow," has come to designate a specific southern type in an essay that exposes the intercultural penetration and pervasiveness of Celtic myths. It is most especially to *Gone With the Wind* (1936), Alexandra Ripley's sequel, *Scarlett* (1991), and finally Alice Randall's *The Wind Done Gone* (2001) that Taylor turns in her analysis of how contemporary updates of a classic southern novel draw on new markets to consume a specifically southern mass entertainment. They also create controversy. Taylor's reading of Randall's novel is especially interesting, not only because of the furor surrounding its publication but also when one remembers that Randall stated that her influences were diverse: a Caribbean novel, Jean Rhys's *Wide Sargasso Sea* (1966); and eighteenth-century English novels like Defoe's *Moll Flanders* (1722) and Richardson's *Clarissa* (1747); as well as southern classics like Hurston's *Their Eyes Were Watching God* and, of course, the mythical *Gone With the Wind* in its Georgia setting.

Together, the essays in *South to a New Place* examine the roles that economic, racial, and ideological tensions in the South have played in the formation of "southern" identity through many different representations of southern places. Our contributors recognize how problematic narratives of regional consciousness and portraits of southern places continue to be, and they challenge southern boundaries and southern regional myths as they move "South" toward a "new place" in literary studies.

PART I   SURVEYING THE TERRITORY

Where Is Southern Literature? The Practice of Place in a Postsouthern Age

Scott Romine

Of the several stock answers to the perennial question "What is southern literature?," the importance of "place" (or the presence of "sense of place") surely ranks near the top of the list. Immediately we are faced with a paradox—how can any regional literature be distinguished on so ambiguous a basis? Places are, after all, found everywhere and in all literatures, and it is doubtful that even a rigorous poetics could reliably identify a "sense of place" that is distinctively southern. To complicate matters, "sense of place" often seems to imply being located not merely in a distinctive region, but in a distinctive way; the term connotes something that is not just *geographically* different (a southern variation of a thing that exists elsewhere) but *qualitatively* different (a thing distinctive to the South). "Sense of place," then, serves as both a description (southern literature has it) and a distinction (southern literature has more of it than other literatures). For my purposes here, it is precisely the nebulous content of "place" that makes it so useful as a point of entry into examining how critics have defined and practiced southern literature; because of place's conceptual instability, what stability it does possess can be ascribed almost exclusively to how it has been used. Arguably, the location of "place" is not so much in the South or in southern literature as in the critical discourse about those things. I do not take this as an indication that "sense of place" is imaginary, only that its validity is pragmatic in nature: "place" is dependent upon practice. And where practice is concerned, a consensus has emerged. Traditionally, "place" has signified a nexus of *is* and *ought,* a describable outside metonymically associated with a network of imperatives, codes, norms, limitations, duties, obligations, and relationships. "Place," therefore, is both subject to representation and suggestive of things that resist representation—hence the "texture" often associated with it. "Sense of place" has usually signified a positive orientation toward that determinative texture: place located you, told you who you were, and did so in a way that provided comfort and security (if occasional restlessness). At worst, "place" is what you were alienated from, or what you loved and hated simultaneously, with the love running just a little bit deeper.

But things have changed, both in the South and in southern literature, and the practice of place has begun to show clear signs of wear. One reason, clearly enough, is that southern places have become less identifiably southern. Another is that the basic assumptions we make about literary texts have changed—sometimes dramatically. Consequently, many practices whose validity appeared self-evident as southern literature was emerging as an academic discipline have either begun to lose their pragmatic coherence or have survived vestigially in the absence of the assumptions that originally informed and motivated them. By tracing, in a very schematic manner, the evolution of place as it has been implicated in theories of regionalism and of representation, I hope to show how "place" has been variously used to link the geographical and qualitative components of "southern literature"—or, to state the matter negatively, how it has been used to prevent "southern literature" from becoming an arbitrary geographical designation. In the end, it may be that the question "What is southern literature?" necessarily turns on the question "Where is southern literature?" Is it, for example, in the South (conceived as a location, a "place," a set of determining conditions) or in the literature (conceived as a style, a "sense," a set of representations)? If we answer the former, which conditions are determinative, and which are peripheral? Can southern literary regionalism be defined in positivist terms, or is it contingent upon a structural relationship with other literatures, other regions? My purpose is not so much to answer these questions systematically as to pose them as a way of clarifying the crisis of place—and of southern literature—in a time of transition.

*   *   *

Because of its conceptual flexibility, "sense of place" allows for a durable practice. A recent collection entitled *Southern Writers at Century's End* (1997), edited by Jeffrey J. Folks and James A. Perkins, offers a case in point. If the title of the volume suggests some vague tension between a continuous tradition and the end times, place constitutes an important site where those tensions are negotiated. Of the half-dozen or so essays that deal substantively with the topic, Hugh Ruppersburg's is the only one to mark a clear break between southern places past and present. In an analysis of James Wilcox's fiction, Ruppersburg asserts that the increasing heterogeneity of southern places has "largely deprived [southern writing] of the myths that formerly gave it a regional identity separate from mainstream American literature." At the other end of the spectrum lies James A. Grimshaw on Clyde Edgerton: "Place transcends the geographical location in which Edgerton sets the action of his novels. Thomas Hardy has his Wessex, William Faulkner has his Yoknapatawpha County, and Clyde Edgerton has his Hansen County." Between these models of relatively pure discontinuity and continuity lies a group of essays for which I will claim a certain representative status; these attempt to refashion place as a distinctively southern trope. Discussing the "limbo between place and placelessness" in Anne Tyler's work, James Grove observes a "persistent tenuousness" in the "use of place [that] gives her fiction a solid base of reference and a Southern flavor." Like Welty, Tyler "connects place to many of the recurrent concerns within her fiction," but according to Grove the inheritance is only partial. In another essay, John Cawelti describes Cormac McCarthy's quest motif as a reaction against the South's stable "symbology of 'down home,'" but one symptomatic of "that restless drive toward the West that has been a key motive in Southern culture since the first long hunters crossed the Appalachians in search of more game and the plantations began their long push from the Tidewater through the deep South to the plains of Texas." The "anti-southern" content of McCarthy's work is thus redeemed as ur-southern. Using a slightly different logic, Jeffrey Folks argues that Richard Ford "approaches the mythology and literary conventions of Western fiction from the perspective of a native Southerner"—one whose regionalist "sense of place" is, as it were, transportable.[1]

1. Hugh Ruppersburg, "James Wilcox: The Normality of Madness," in *Southern Writers at Century's End*, ed. Jeffrey J. Folks and James A. Perkins (Lexington: University Press of Kentucky, 1997), 33; James A. Grimshaw, "Clyde Edgerton: Death and Dying," in *ibid.*, 239; James Grove, "Anne Tyler: Wrestling with the 'Lowlier Angel,' " in *ibid.*, 135; John Cawelti, "Cormac McCarthy: Restless Seekers," in *ibid.*, 165; Jeffrey J. Folks, "Richard Ford: Postmodern Cowboys," in *ibid.*, 212, 216.

The general pattern of these essays can be adumbrated, without too much distortion, as one in which traditional concepts of place are still salient enough that deviations from them can be recuperated as markers of southern literary identity; a kind of discontinuous continuity exists even if place isn't what (or even where) it used to be. If this continuity appears strained in some cases, it is worth remarking that the pattern itself is nothing new. In fact, it appears in two of the founding texts of modern southern literary criticism, Allen Tate's "The Profession of Letters in the South" (1935) and "The New Provincialism" (1945). It was in these two essays that Tate famously attributed the regionalist explosion of the postwar period to the South's "re-enter[ing] the world" while retaining its "conscious[ness] of the past in the present," a set of circumstances, Tate claims, "not unlike, on an infinitesimal scale, the outburst of poetic genius at the end of the sixteenth century when commercial England had already begun to crush feudal England." Tate defines regionalism as "that consciousness or that habit of men in a given locality which influences them to certain patterns of thought and conduct handed to them by their ancestors." Against regionalism, he opposes "provincialism" defined in a special way. Retaining its pejorative connotation, Tate despatializes the term; "provincialism" is isolated from "civilization" in time, not space, and thus signifies an antitraditionalist, utilitarian society "locked in the present."[2] Although regions could presumably exist in isolation, literary regionalism (at least in the case of southern literature) results only from contact with the provincial world—the very contact, ironically enough, that would eventually spell its doom. As Michael O'Brien observes, "Three ideas were crucial to Tate's interpretation of the Southern Renaissance: the mutation of economic and social order, the decline of religious coherence, the briefly energizing value of witnessing these changes." Restating Tate's Renascence thesis in 1956, Robert Penn Warren identified "some strange mixture of continuity and discontinuity" at the heart of southern writing. It may prove that an overdeveloped eschatological sense is one of the more enduring characteristics of the southern literary tradition: the southernness of place, it seems, is always in danger of expiring.[3]

2. Allen Tate, "The New Provincialism: With an Epilogue on the Southern Novel," in *The Man of Letters in the Modern World: Selected Essays, 1928–1955* (New York: Meridian Books, 1955), 330, 331, 325; Tate, "The Profession of Letters in the South," ibid., 319. In the quotation from "The New Provincialism," Tate glosses his earlier interpretation, from which he quotes directly at the end of the essay.

3. Michael O'Brien, *Rethinking the South: Essays in Intellectual History* (Baltimore: Johns Hopkins University Press, 1988), 177; Robert Penn Warren, "On the Art of Fiction,"

Although I will want to return to the Agrarians momentarily, let me observe for the time being that Tate's thesis highlights a central feature of regionalism and the "sense of place" attendant upon it: both are embedded in oppositional relationships with locations that are not regions or even places.[4] If place is normally, as Eudora Welty says, one of fiction's "lesser," "lowlier" angels, it usually receives a discernible promotion in regionalist literatures. Regionalism, traditionally conceived, implies a kind of geographical determinism; a regional text is assumed to display certain characteristics deriving from place. In *A Certain Slant of Light: Regionalism and the Form of Southern and Midwestern Fiction* (1995), David Marion Holman states the formula succinctly: "It is locality and surroundings . . . that constitute the impulses behind the artist's creation of the work itself, and often behind the form it takes." As Barbara Ladd observes in her essay later in this book, regions emerged historically as peripheral places defined in relation to some center; one of the working premises of regionalism is that the geographical determinants of the periphery are more powerful than those of the center. This is why "southern novel" is a more descriptive label than "American novel," why we know more about the one without reading either. As a qualitative adjective, "southern" signifies the presence of place as a limitation and not merely a location. A "southern novel," then, is not merely a novel set in the South, or a novel written by a southern person; "southern" is, finally, irreducible to geographical criteria. But at the same time, geographical criteria can never be removed from the equation. The law of regional determinism dictates that it must remain a purely hypothetical question to ask whether, if we started without a map and proceeded to classify all literature on a purely inductive basis, we would end up with a category similar to "southern literature" as we now conceive it. *Where* southern literature is—in the South, obviously—can never be dissociated fully from *what* it is.[5]

---

in *Talking with Robert Penn Warren,* ed. Floyd C. Watkins, John T. Hiers, and Mary Louise Weaks (Athens: University of Georgia Press, 1990), 29.

4. In theories of regionalism, this opposition is usually spatial (e.g., southern place/region versus American non-place/non-region). Tate subordinates this spatial opposition to a temporal one (past place/region versus present non-place/non-region), although he subtly insinuates a spatial, North/South opposition as well.

5. Eudora Welty, "Place in Fiction," in *The Eye of the Story: Selected Essays and Reviews* (New York: Vintage, 1979), 116; David Marion Holman, *A Certain Slant of Light: Regionalism and the Form of Southern and Midwestern Fiction* (Baton Rouge: Louisiana State University Press, 1995), 110.

This is not to assert that southern literature has no internal integrity, only that the integrity it does possess is at least partially indebted to its peripheral relationship to a center. In fact, it is a fully defensible proposition that southern places have in themselves asserted an identifiable determinative pressure, and that this pressure is reflected in literary texts. To say that "sense of place" is a distinctive—that is, structurally situated—characteristic of southern literature is by no means to say that it is not descriptive as well. Nevertheless, this does nothing to clarify that descriptive dimension, nor the relationship between the South's literary regionalism and its status as a sociopolitical region of the United States.[6]

In turning to these questions, some clarifications are in order regarding a central question, "To what does 'southern' refer?" Below are a few of the criteria by which the South has been defined or differentiated as a region: (1) geographically, as a region defined by political or other boundaries; (2) economically, as a region having a distinctive system of labor; as a material "base" in the classic Marxist sense; (3) ideologically, as a region differentiated by collective (or at least public) norms, laws, practices, and codes that determine or influence both behavior and subjectivity; as a hegemony; (4) culturally, as a region with distinctive patterns of speech, leisure, folkways, ritual, food preferences, and the like; (5) historically, as a region defined by its past or by the presence of "the past in the present"; as a character in a historical plot; (6) orientationally, as an identification with or positive orientation toward one or more of the preceding "Souths." (As I shall suggest, this usage explains the historical exclusion of African Americans from the category "southern.") Although this list is neither exhaustive nor precise, it does indicate some important ways in which the South has been figured as a qualitative geography—as a place. Historically, all of these "Souths" have been subject to or implicated in distinctive forms of representation, but which one(s), in addition to the geographical "southern," are necessary for southern literature to survive?

6. Instead of the traditional North/South opposition, recent scholarship has remapped the South in relation to other places, notably the American West (Robert H. Brinkmeyer Jr., *Remapping Southern Literature: Contemporary Southern Writers and the West* [Athens: University of Georgia Press, 2000]), Spanish America (Deborah N. Cohn, *History and Memory in the Two Souths: Recent Southern and Spanish American Fiction* [Nashville: Vanderbilt University Press, 1999]), and the Caribbean (George Handley, *Family Portraits in Black and White: Postslavery Literature in the Americas* [Charlottesville: University of Virginia Press, 2000]). This trend promises to further destabilize the South's status as "Uncle Sam's other province."

Can it survive, for example, without mimetic reference at the economic or ideological levels? Can "southern" come to describe a set of representations that no longer have a referent, or an increasingly indistinct one? Can place be revised indefinitely as a marker of southern literary identity?

These questions would have been quite inconceivable when "sense of place" became part of critical practice, and for reasons that are instructive. The story will begin, as many do, with the Agrarians. In *Inventing Southern Literature* (1998), Michael Kreyling offers a perspicacious critique of how the Agrarians attempted to control representation of the South at a specific historical moment. According to Kreyling, the Agrarian project was one of performing a (provincial) style as a way of obfuscating local practices that might have proven unpalatable to their contemporary audience. The Agrarians, Kreyling argues, "manipulated the image of the problem of their time so that their solution seemed unavoidable," an act triggered not so much by "the South itself" as by "competing 'orders' of cultural power [Humanists, Chapel Hill Sociologists] that threatened to imagine the South in other ways." According to Kreyling, then, the Agrarian icon derives not from imitation per se, but from the strategic manipulation of images conceptually prior to their "southern" referent. As Kreyling shows, the preferred mode of representation for the Agrarians was myth (although, as we shall see, they did not conceive of it as a preference). Myth served as an antidote or prophylactic to scientific modes of representation perceived as committing the heresy of the statistic. For the Agrarians, scientific representation had a curious ability to disrupt the world by reacting back on it: "$e = mc^2$" looks descriptive, they might say, but in the end it can blow things up. So might, insofar as it enabled "social planning," a statistical chart in Howard Odum's *Southern Regions of the United States* or (worse) Arthur Raper's *Preface to Peasantry,* a book in which, according to Donald Davidson in a 1937 review, Macon County, Georgia, "has become a type and stopped being a beloved place to which men cling with more than rational attachment." Presenting his own impressions of Macon Country as "what any normal person could not help seeing and hearing informally," Davidson registers the negation of his normative "sense of place" by Raper's quantitative geography.[7]

For Davidson and the Agrarians generally, scientific representation of

---

7. Michael Kreyling, *Inventing Southern Literature* (Jackson: University Press of Mississippi, 1998), 5, 6; Donald Davidson, "A Sociologist in Eden," *American Review* 8 (1936): 184, 178.

the South amounted to, in effect, an apostasy against their theory of mythic emergence. Southern places, they held, exerted a distinctive valence such that perceptions, attitudes, and representations emerge in a predictable, normative, and "natural" way. They were therefore not "describing" the South in a mythic manner but merely registering the spontaneous emergence of myth from a specific way of life—returning "place," as it were, to the farms and the small towns of the South. And where myths emerged naturally, statistics were imposed as a false mode of representation. For Donald Davidson especially, emergence tropes carried over into the domain of art, which mirrored the mythic reality of place in the form of folk music, architecture, and other noncommodified, "everyday" artistic forms. Moreover, the situation was ripe, he asserted in "A Mirror for Artists," for the emergence of higher art forms that "are not luxuries to be purchased but belong as a matter of course in the routine of [the artist's] living."[8] According to Davidson, this autochthonous relationship would naturally produce a vital and distinctive regionalist literature. As we have seen, Tate's perspective was slightly different, since his theory of literary regionalism presumes a process of dispossession— his mirror for artists was necessarily cracked—and thus is predicated on a dialectical relationship that Davidson's model eliminates. But even if we recognize the rather obvious prescriptive component in both models—that is, the orientational imperative implicit in "southern"—or, less obviously, the priority of "sense" to "place" that Kreyling observes, we are left to consider whether "place" has to be there at all. Would other locations, that is, have served just as well for the "emergence" of the Agrarian mythology of place? In short, were farms necessary?

The Agrarians were adamant that they were. In denouncing the "abstract" Humanism of Irving Babbitt in *I'll Take My Stand*'s "statement of Principles," John Crowe Ransom affirmed that the South's "genuine humanism, was rooted in the agrarian life of the older South and of other parts of the country that shared in such a tradition. . . . It was deeply founded in the way of life itself—in its tables, chairs, portraits, festivals, laws, marriage customs." The South's "native humanism" could not be recovered by adopting an abstract Humanist program "that is critical enough to question the contemporary arts but not critical enough to question the social and economic life that is their ground." "[S]oft mate-

8. Donald Davidson, "A Mirror for Artists," in Twelve Southerners, *I'll Take My Stand: The South and the Agrarian Tradition* (1930; rprt., Baton Rouge: Louisiana State University Press, 1977), 51–52.

rial poured in from the top" would not suffice. For a symposium nearly entitled *Tracts Against Communism* authored by a core group of incipient New Critics, the interdependence of art and economics here might seem perplexing, and the similarity between Agrarian and Marxist critiques of capitalism has been duly noted. But there are important differences in addition to the Agrarians' desire to retreat from capitalism rather than progressing past it toward some communist utopia. More significantly from the Agrarian perspective, a scientific, causal relationship between base and superstructure was quite inconceivable. This can be observed in their use of *religion* (in an almost totally nonspecific way) where a Marxist would use *ideology*; the former can be "rooted" or "founded" in a "way of life" in a way that the latter, conceived as the causal product of material modes of production, cannot. (We might also note the obvious: *religion* is a term of approval, *ideology* of disapproval.) Tropes of organic emergence again predominate over tropes of mechanical causality.[9]

To see how this opposition relates to the representation of place, we might turn to Davidson's 1937 review of John Dollard's *Caste and Class in a Southern Town*. Dollard's book, Davidson reports, produces a need for "something to clutch": "Familiar things have suddenly taken on a pasty, unreal complexion. The world has assumed a dizzy effervescence, like the nauseous boiling stir of termites under a wooden plank. Still worse, the perspective has altered sickeningly. All that was big has become little. All that was little has swelled up fantastically." Davidson could tolerate a relatively pure empiricist like Odum, but he invariably saw red when liberals such as Raper and Dollard brought to bear their "prejudice"—in the latter's case, a "Yankee" prejudice—upon southern places. Consider, however, the form that Dollard's prejudice takes. "It is a little hard," Davidson reports, "for a Southerntowner to get Dr. Dollard's notion straight in his head, but I shall do my best to state what I gather he means." Here is part of Dollard's notion as Davidson gathers it: "The whole thing is, he says, an enormous conspiracy of the dominant whites to keep themselves in the relative position they enjoyed when the whites were masters and the Negroes were slaves. White society, we must understand, is organized around a fiction which establishes whites as the superior caste and Negroes as the inferior caste." Where Davidson sees a

---

9. Twelve Southerners, *I'll Take My Stand,* xliv. For an insightful discussion on the ambiguous use of *religion* by critics of southern literature, see O'Brien, *Rethinking the South,* 159–61.

"well accepted . . . *modus vivendi*," Dollard sees ideology and oppression.[10] But what seemed preposterous to Davidson is axiomatic today, and therein lies an institutional paradox. The assumptions that enabled the Agrarian "sense of place" are with us today only in highly refracted ways: appeals to "religion," for example, appear less often in the post-Rubin era, and Walter Sullivan's *Requiem for the Renascence* (1976) was probably the last major scholarly work to extend the Agrarian discourse of religion. If "sense of place" has survived as a marker of southern literary identity, it has done so by surviving a radical shift in the assumptions that originally enabled it.

We have already noted that these assumptions had shifted slightly by the time Allen Tate formulated his founding narrative of the Southern Renascence. Nevertheless, Tate's use of "southern literature" continues to designate a geographically, materially, ideologically, culturally, and historically coherent region; it indicates, moreover, an identification with that region. To be sure, Tate's identification is leavened with alienation; "sense" has begun to escape "place" rather than existing in autochthonous harmony with it. But Tate's South is continuous and unstratified, and his use of *southern* remains radically prescriptive. As O'Brien observes, Tate was responsible for "delimiting a canon, of those who exemplified his definition" of southern writing.[11] With only minor revisions, this canon and the assumptions that enabled it formed the basis of southern literature as it began to emerge as an academic discipline, a point of origin often marked by the 1953 publication of Louis D. Rubin and Robert D. Jacobs's *Southern Renascence*. For various reasons—mainly orientational ones—T. S. Stribling, Lillian Smith, and Richard Wright did not make the grade. If, in *Black Boy,* Richard Wright represented a place that was geographically, materially, ideologically, and culturally southern, he most certainly did not have a "sense" of that place according to the Agrarian usage. For Wright, place was the antagonist, the cause of alienation and not its antidote. In the past two decades, it has proven attractive to dismiss the orientational dimension of "southern" in the case of Wright, who is now indisputably a part of southern writing. But in order thus to incorporate *Black Boy,* it is necessary to revise the Agrarian definition of place and its relationship to southern writing; further revisions are necessary if *Native Son* is to be included. The past two decades have

10. Donald Davidson, "Gulliver with Hay Fever," *American Review* 9 (1937): 152, 154, 153.

11. O'Brien, *Rethinking the South,* 166.

seen a long-overdue expansion of the southern canon, but with the result
of a conspicuously imprecise use of *southern* to designate a specific set of
texts or the qualities they share. But insofar as a canon continues to exist
and to evolve, it is simply naïve to assume that our canon is empirically
superior to Tate's. The tautology O'Brien observes is inescapable; canons
always depend on definitions, and "southern writing" will always turn
on how *southern* is conceived. In turning now to some of these revised
conceptions, I mean to indicate some ways in which place continues to
help define southern literature.

One obvious and widespread revision is simply to adopt Arthur Raper's
conception of place as a set of material conditions coextensive with a pernicious ideology. In fact, that is precisely what we find another Raper,
Julius Rowan, doing in a 1990 essay entitled "Inventing Modern Southern Fiction: A Postmodern View." "In modern Southern literature,"
Raper claims, "the sense of place takes on a role better played by a sense
of self." Arguing that mimetic representations of place are complicit in
the "control of reality" exerted by "ideologues of the age," Raper calls
for an antimimetic style that will not emerge from place but be deployed
against it in the form of postmodern subversions of verisimilitude. As a
Jungian, Raper looks to a collective unconscious to provide the mythic
structure of self that the mythology of place (as a pathological surrogate
for selfhood) has undermined. Like other critics who appeal to universals
(justice, for example) to leverage southern oppression, Raper figures
southern places as obstacles to be overcome. His endgame thus extends
southern literature by calling for its deconstruction. Nevertheless, as long
as southern places erode individual autonomy in distinctive ways, there
will remain an antimimetic space in which to "dispense with the grandi-
ose loyalties grounded in the piety of place."[12]
   Where Raper looks at the old places in new ways, Fred Hobson, in
The Southern Writer in the Postmodern World (1991), looks to new
places to find old ways of representing them. In attempting to rehabilitate
Davidson's autochthonous ideal for the postmodern era, Hobson casts
his argument as an aesthetic critique. The "contemporary writer," he
writes, "is indeed in danger of writing a sort of twentieth-century local
color," of "giv[ing] in to southern stereotypes," of "becoming too much
the self-conscious regionalist, one who begins with the recognition that

---

12. Julius Rowan Raper, "Inventing Modern Southern Fiction: A Postmodern View,"
Southern Literary Journal 22, no. 2 (1990): 10, 3, 13.

he or she is primarily a 'southern writer' with an opportunity and obligation to present or interpret Southerners to the rest of the nation." While
"the South" still exists prior to representation, the contemporary writer
must not reify or hypostatize it as such lest the writing devolve into *mere*
local color unable to "transcend the moment or region." Hobson's rhetoric of transcendence—his insistence that great writing focus not "on what
is distinctive in the region, [but] what is universal in man"—is not, however, an ethereal one: the concrete, the particular, and the local remain
positive words in his lexicon. His program is thus to reinject referentiality
into southern literature, but in a such a way that access to the universal
follows without impediment. Place exists as an opportunity for transcendence, rather than, as with Raper, as an obstacle to it. And yet certain
places do not appear to offer this opportunity—Bobbie Ann Mason's settings, for example, which are saturated with generic forms of mass culture and thus produce characters mired in "emotional and spiritual
poverty" and an author who is "not a New South so much as a No South
writer."[13] Although Hobson is not uniformly critical of Mason's fiction,
his preference is to stabilize place as a reliable marker of southern literary
identity at the level of traditional culture and folkways—places, that is,
where "sense of place" can continue to emerge in organic, autochthonous ways.

It is instructive, however, that Hobson leaves the Agrarian South in
order to find exemplars, Fred Chappell and Ernest Gaines, who fulfill this
criterion. I do not mean to allegorize Hobson's choices except to indicate
that the places he recuperates as quintessentially southern tend elsewhere
to be perceived as less than representative at the homogeneous level of
region. The places of which Chappell and Gaines write, that is, appear
often in critical discourse not as local synechdoches of "the South" so
much as local attachments to places defined along subregional or social
lines. Chappell considers himself more an Appalachian than a southern
writer, and although Gaines has not rejected the label, his "place" would
not, for obvious reasons, have been marked "southern" under the old
dispensation. And yet the criteria by which "southern" was marked under
that dispensation allow Hobson not only to recuperate Gaines as southern but to recuperate southern literature through Gaines, who, like
"other contemporary black writers . . . taken as a whole, tend to be more
concerned with community, place, and the past and its legacy—and to

13. Fred Hobson, *The Southern Writer in the Postmodern World* (Athens: University
of Georgia Press, 1991), 81, 79, 81, 80, 13, 81.

ground their fiction more fully in a rich traditional folk culture—than do most of their white counterparts." "As much as any writer since Faulkner," Hobson continues, "Gaines has appropriated a particular limited territory in the southern provinces, has set most of his fiction there and made it his own."[14] But if Gaines is bound to Faulkner by "the southern provinces" and his "sense" of place, community, past, and culture, it is worth remarking that these things have different referents in Gaines than they do in Faulkner. (In Gaines's past, for example, the Civil War counts as a victory.) The old skins may hold, but the wine is new.

Despite their differences, Raper and Hobson continue to conceive of southern literature as dependent upon distinctive southern places; for Raper, the distinction is primarily ideological, for Hobson, cultural. One senses, however, especially in the latter's case, that the dissemination of mass culture, the end of the Civil Rights Movement, and the material prosperity of the Sunbelt era have eroded the South's distinctiveness, with marked effects on its literature. The boundary of the southern provinces begins to feel a bit arbitrary; what James McBride Dabbs called the "massive, concrete South" begins to feel thin and abstract. Although Hobson's inclusion of black writers within southern literature is part of a pervasive liberal-pluralist trend theorized elegantly by Thadious M. Davis, his inclusion of Chappell countervails a general critical tendency to locate smaller, more meaningful loci as the salient contexts in which texts are placed. Nowhere is this trend more prominent than in the field of Appalachian literature, well on its way to becoming a separate place, institutionally speaking. Davidson's "southerntown" seems increasingly anachronistic, and W. J. Cash's influential formulation—"if it can be said there are many Souths, the fact remains that there is also one South"—is emphasized differently than it was in 1941. Hugh Holman started a poly-southern trend when he identified three distinctive subregions in *Three Modes of Southern Fiction* (1966); Joseph M. Flora and Robert Bain identified eight in their introduction to *Contemporary Fiction Writers of the South* (1993). Of the criticisms made of the landmark *History of Southern Literature* (1985), many were directed toward the volume's mono-southern tendencies. Whereas Hobson typifies a liberal tendency to preserve "the South" as a metadiscursive space, an opportunity for negotiation and consensus, the economic and ideological substrata that provided cohesion for earlier "one Souths" have been eroding for some time. In addition, the postmodern geographies of Doreen Massey, Ed-

14. Ibid., 92, 95.

ward Sojo, and David Harvey have shown not only the fracturing of social space engenderd by urbanization and globalization but the varying
experiences of space among different socioeconomic groups. Moreover,
postmodern skepticism toward grand narratives and other forms of totalizing discourse, and a corresponding preference for micropolitics and
highly localized "language games" have found their way into our practice of place. As Jean-François Lyotard (whose views I have just been
summarizing) puts it, "consensus has become an outmoded and suspect
value." The institutional place of southern women's writing, for example, bears witness to this suspicion. Under the influence of the separate-
spheres model of American feminism and important scholarly works by
Anne Firor Scott, Anne Goodwyn Jones, Lucinda MacKethan, Louise
Westling, and others, women's writing has undergone at least a partial
institutional separation that emphasizes the distinctive experience of
women in the South. Microcommunities based on race, class, gender, and
ethnicity have largely supplanted the holistic concept of community pervasive in the scholarship of an earlier generation.[15]

Will, then, "the South" become, as the journalist Henry Waterson predicted a century ago, "simply a geographical expression"? Responding to
this question in *One South: An Ethnic Approach to Regional Culture*
(1982), John Shelton Reed answers with an unambiguous no, and with
substantial empirical evidence to back up his assertion. Reed sees no
future for continued economic distinctiveness, nor for such historically
distinctive ideological traits such as "parochialism, fatalism, authori-
tarianism, ethnocentrism, and categorical resistance to innovation."[16]
Culturally, Reed predicts, the South will survive. But most provoca-

---

15. James McBride Dabbs, *The Southern Heritage* (New York: Alfred A. Knopf,
1958), 168; Thadious M. Davis, "Expanding the Limits: The Intersection of Race and Re-
gion," *Southern Literary Journal* 20, no. 2 (1988): 3–11 (for an opposing view, see Krey-
ling, *Inventing Southern Literature,* 76–99); W. J. Cash, *The Mind of the South* (New York:
Alfred A. Knopf, 1941), viii; C. Hugh Holman, *Three Modes of Southern Fiction: Ellen
Glasgow, William Faulkner, Thomas Wolfe* (Athens: University of Georgia Press, 1966);
Joseph M. Flora and Robert Bain, eds., *Contemporary Fiction Writers of the South: A Bio-
Bibliographical Sourcebook* (Westport, Conn.: Greenwood Press, 1993), 3–5; Jean-
François Lyotard, *The Postmodern Condition: A Report on Knowledge,* trans. Geoff Ben-
nington and Brian Massumi (Minneapolis: University of Minnesota Press, 1984), 66.

16. Reed notes that this "bundle of traits"—labeled the "traditional values orientation" by Harold Grasmick—is closely correlated with agrarian societies worldwide. This
bundle, he observes further, includes "some of the things [the Agrarians] cherished most
about the south." See *One South: An Ethnic Approach to Regional Culture* (Baton Rouge:
Louisiana State University Press, 1982), 170.

tively, Reed argues that southern "ethnicity" or "group identification"—what I am calling the identitarian South—may, paradoxically,
become stronger as the South becomes less distinctive in other areas.
Citing a common history as one reason "why group identification, once
established, can exhibit a surprising degree of autonomy, surviving the
circumstances that brought it into being," Reed goes on to assert that the
"same experiences that heighten this sort of identification—exposure to
outsiders, actual or (through education or the media) vicarious—
undermine the cultural characteristics on which it is based; the process
that brings about awareness of [group] similarity can destroy the similarity itself."[17]

Significantly, the components of Reed's "enduring South" are precisely the ones put forward by Louis D. Rubin Jr. in his introduction to
The History of Southern Literature (1985):

> The facts are that there existed in the past, and there continues to exist
> today, an entity within American society known as the South, and that for
> better or for worse the habit of viewing one's experiences in terms of one's
> relationship to that entity is still a meaningful characteristic of both writers
> and readers who are or have been part of it. Yet in the year 1984, as this
> history is being prepared for the printers, to consider writers and their
> writings as Southern still involves considerably more than a geographical
> grouping. History, as a mode for viewing one's experiences and one's iden-
> tity, remains a striking characteristic of the Southern literary imagination,
> black and white.[18]

Like Reed, Rubin overcomes the problem of empty geography by recuperating "southern" at the level of history and of identification, both of
which require only minimal material grounding and thus resist being represented as "place." The identitarian South especially might conceivably
gravitate toward a condition of pure textuality impervious to material,
ideological, or even cultural content, or, alternatively, might produce
those things as effects—that is, by producing southern "content" in order
to verify identification. This, I take it, is the way certain persons eat grits.
It is also the way a certain kind of critical discourse, both academic and
journalistic, finds that any remotely "southern" setting demonstrates

17. Ibid., 20, 18. Using data from a 1971 North Carolina survey, Reed notes that
whites from Appalachian regions and blacks are less likely than non-Appalachian whites to
identify themselves as southerners, although majorities of both groups do so (21).

18. Louis D. Rubin Jr., "Introduction," *The History of Southern Literature,* ed. Rubin
et al. (Baton Rouge: Louisiana State University Press, 1985), 5.

"sense of place," any representation of dialect evinces the South's "oral tradition," any vaguely eccentric character is a "southern grotesque," and any historical reference displays "the past in the present." Lastly and most unfortunately, I fear, it is the way certain writers litter their work with conspicuous southernness.

In a 1936 essay entitled "Don'ts for Regionalists," Robert Penn Warren admonished that "even literary regionalism is more than a literary matter, and is not even primarily a literary matter. If it is treated as a purely literary matter it will promptly lose any meaning, for only in so far as literature springs from some reality in experience is it valuable to us." Two years earlier, Donald Davidson had made a similar point in "The Trend of Literature," an essay he contributed to *Culture in the South,* a volume dominated by his Chapel Hill antagonists. "If the South did not occupy," Davidson writes, "a somewhat peculiar and separate relation to the United States, there would be no need of an essay on southern literature and this book itself would be nonsense. . . . I must look for the native distinction that one would seek to encounter in the South alone, or else have nothing to say about southern literature as a separate manifestation." For both Warren and Davidson, a regionalist literature intuitively presupposes a region, even if "southern" becomes applicable to literary representation deriving from that region. But what if "place" and "region" are effects, not causes, of representation? What if southern literature is determined by southern literature, not by "the South itself"? Can southern literature perpetuate itself in a referential vacuum?[19]

In a 1996 essay entitled "The Discourse of Southernness," Jefferson Humphries answers in the affirmative to most of these questions. According to Humphries, "the South" derived from a "discursive exigency" imposed by antagonistic, quasi-colonialist narratives originating in the antebellum North. In a South "only related to geographical place by pure arbitrary contingency," a South that is "nothing in the world but an idea in narrative form, a discourse or rhetoric of narrative tropes, a story made out of sub-stories, a lie, a fiction to which we have lent reality by believing in it," there is nothing "southern" there to represent, only a "South" produced by representation and made real through identitarian practices—that is, by "believing in it." Insofar as the content of "south-

19. Robert Penn Warren, "Don'ts for Regionalists," *American Review* 8 (1936): 150; Donald Davidson, "The Trend of Literature," in *Culture in the South,* ed. William Terry Couch (Chapel Hill: University of North Carolina Press, 1934), 183, 184.

ern" is concerned, Humphries defines seven paradigmatic "characterizations"—Thomas Jefferson, Edgar Poe/Roderick Usher, Sut Lovingood,
Robert E. Lee, Uncle Remus and Aunt Jemima/Nat Turner, the belle, and
the southern middle class—before asking (rhetorically), "if any reasonable person who knows any part of the South today . . . can deny that
the types, the narrative characterizations I just listed, continue to determine and therefore describe accurately (or to describe accurately and
therefore determine) much of the appearance, comportment, and ideology of persons living today from Virginia to Texas?"[20] Leaving aside the
potentially objectionable nature of these characterizations, it becomes
clear that, despite his parenthetical non sequitur, Humphries conceives of
economic and cultural "Souths" as mere effects of oppositional narratives: ideology derives from stories, not the other way around. However
counterintuitive this may seem, it is not difficult to envision how the organizing trope of place might fit within Humphries's pattern of narrative
exigency. Place is, after all, what the deracinated Yankees don't have, no
matter how prosperous their locations. Within Humphries's model, then,
"sense of place" would be just that—a sense, an idea—but one with real
effects, since we believe in the stories told about it. And for Humphries,
these stories are imitated with little loss of energy as the discourse of
southernness perpetuates. If the South is a narrative, then one assumes
that this bodes well for southern (literary) narrative, but Humphries is
not explicit on this point; although he subtitles his essay "How We Can
Know There Will Still Be Such a Thing as the South and Southern Literary Culture in the Twenty-First Century," he refers to hardly any contemporary writing, and we are left to assume that he sees this continuity as
consisting of combinations, permutations, and slight variations of the
southern metanarrative already in place.

In contrast, Michael Kreyling offers a distinctly literary model of the
postsouthern era, and one that encompasses the discontinuity of post-
Renascence writing. By postsouthern, Kreyling indicates a condition in
which the "real South" no longer offers itself as an object available to
mimesis, since it has been massively mediated by "coded representations
of the South" that are "always already there." Coming after the master
code and coder "Faulkner," post-Renascence writers respond to their

---

20. Jefferson Humphries, "The Discourse of Southernness: Or How We Can Know
There Will Still Be Such a Thing as the South and Southern Literary Culture in the Twenty-
First Century," in *The Future of Southern Letters,* ed. Jefferson Humphries and John Lowe
(New York: Oxford University Press, 1996), 120, 131.

own lateness through the literary mode of parody. Because parody takes as its primary object not a thing but a style or system of representations, the postsouthern writer has "no recourse to the totalizing and totally authoritative referent."[21] There is no place, no South, there to imitate, only previous imitations of place there to parody. Kreyling's is therefore a strictly literary model, and as such offers the southern writer a degree of awareness and autonomy absent in more deterministic versions of regionalism, where the valence of place tends to reduce the writer to a relatively passive position. But at the same time, the southern writer is not a free agent either. Even without a mimetic South to imitate, the South remains as an absent cause, an imperative (implicit on Kreyling's part) for Barry Hannah to parody Faulkner and not Ernest Hemingway; postsouthern literature can be delineated, as it were, only by its relationship to earlier writing that could imagine itself as Southern (capital S, no quotation marks). Whence this imperative, it is difficult to determine precisely, since Kreyling's examination of the "collision of the southern 'immovable object' and the postmodern 'irresistible force'" tends to remain at the level of representation—that is, in opposing a "natural" southernness to one "utterly mediated through representation"—rather than analyzing the origin of the new dispensation or interrogating the constitution of the "real South" (a concept he does not reject entirely). And although it is clear that Kreyling sees no future for any elite, neo-Agrarian control of southern representation where literary texts are concerned, his vision is more concerned with diagnosis than prognosis.

Can southern literature survive indefinitely in a parasitic, parodic relation to the ur-host, "Faulkner," or in some other purely textual form? If there's no there there, can a regionalist literature—can "place"—endure?[22] It is surely too soon to tell, and those who perceive that the end times have finally arrived must acknowledge that, for over a century, reports of the South's demise have been greatly exaggerated, and for half a century

21. Kreyling, *Inventing Southern Literature*, 159, 155.

22. In an essay on southern poetry, Dave Smith answers in the affirmative. Smith argues that the changing "visible habits of the new South—the ubiquitous strip malls with their chain stores and the equally commonplace imitations of southern-ness glossily spread in the pages of *Southern Living*" do not necessitate discontinuity in southern poetry, which, "if it exists, cannot be a function of matter, for that would be only sociological, not aesthetic definition. The poetry exists in the tone, the attitude, the structuring vision of the language, precisely where traditional definition of 'the South' has focused its attention." See Smith, "Speculations on a Southern Snipe," in *The Future of Southern Letters*, ed. Humphries and Lowe, 147.

now, similar reports have issued forth on the subject of southern literature. Nevertheless, it seems inevitable that the erosion of economic and
ideological distinctiveness will radically alter the meaning of place. One
need not be a radical materialist to accept the premise that a distinctive
set of material and ideological conditions affected southern writing of the
Renascence era—Richard Wright as well as William Alexander Percy—in
a way that no longer obtains. Even myths, as Roland Barthes observed,
require literal reference as "nourishment," and the mythology of place
is probably no exception. Perhaps Tate's eschatology was correct, only
premature; it may be premature yet. But it is striking to compare his prediction of the new provincials—forever alienated from local traditions
and thus condemned to live nowhere, to "see *with*, not *through* the
eye"—with the observation of a more recent commentator, Jean-François
Lyotard: "But capitalism inherently possesses the power to derealize
familiar objects, social roles, and institutions to such a degree that the
so-called realistic representations can no longer evoke reality except as
nostalgia or mockery, as an occasion for suffering rather than for satisfaction." Even if we allow that the disappearance of many distinctive
southern institutions is a cause for celebration and not suffering—and
that capitalism played no small role in their elimination—it is nevertheless revealing to note how Tate foreshadows Lyotard's diagnosis of the
postmodern condition.[23]

Almost certainly, place as a marker of southern literary identity cannot continue under the aegis of verisimilitude and mimesis, although this
is not necessarily to pronounce a postmortem. Raper and Kreyling both
indicate ways that an antimythology of place might survive, at least for a
while, and as Kreyling observes, the South continues to figure prominently
in the Culture Wars.[24] In all likelihood, however, the prognosis is more
dubious where narrative is concerned, since regionalism, traditionally
conceived, presupposes "place" not as mere geography but as a deterministic geography—that is, as a distinctive limitation of the possibilities of
plot, character, and narrative subjectivity. The determinants of even the
most isolated southern hamlet are increasingly dispersed to other locations: an Indonesian labor force willing to work at low wages, a board
of directors' meeting in New York, a Hollywood film set. It is difficult to
imagine how southern places will continue to exert a distinctive pressure,

23. Roland Barthes, *Mythologies*, trans. Annette Lavers (New York: Hill and Wang,
1972), 118; Tate, "New Provincialism," 331; Lyotard, *Postmodern Condition*, 74.
24. See Kreyling, *Inventing Southern Literature*, 167–82.

or how regionalism can be squared with the historicist and materialist models of literary production that have dominated the academy in the recent past. But at the same time, it is difficult to disagree with Kreyling's contention that " 'the South' is the richest site yet discovered in the U.S. cultural terrain for the study of and participation in the reinvention of culture," and it is quite possible that the South will survive a postmodern reinvention. It would be a fool's bet that the South will simply cease. If Jean Baudrillard's theory of postmodern simulation is predictive, the identitarian South may inflect representation long after the material South has retired into memory. The following list is adapted from Baudrillard's "successive phases of the image" as he defines them in *Simulations* (1983):

1. It is the reflection of a basic reality
2. It marks the absence of a basic reality
3. It distorts and subverts a basic reality
4. It masks the *absence* of a basic reality
5. It bears no relation to any reality whatever: it is its own simulacrum.[25]

If we substitute "South" for "basic reality," we have a useful heuristic tool for organizing southern modes of representation: (1) the autochthonous tradition; (2) the tradition of alienation and dispossession; (3) the protest tradition, the school of guilt and shame, the parodic tradition; (4) the school of conspicuous southernness. Where Renascence writers worked mainly in the second and third modes, it is the fourth, with its bad-faith effort to maintain the pretense of reality, that seems to plague so much contemporary writing. "When Is Southern Literature Going to Get Real?" asked Marc K. Stengel in a 1990 edition of *Nashville Scene.* Confronted with an unreal, idealized, and sentimental picture of a vanished society, an earlier Nashville-based magazine had pronounced its intention to flee "from nothing faster than from the high-caste Brahmins of the Old South."[26]

25. Baudrillard's list is as follows: "• it is the reflection of a basic reality / • it masks and perverts a basic reality / • it masks the *absence* of a basic reality / • it bears no relation to any reality whatever: it is its own simulacrum." See *Simulations* (New York: Semiotext[e], 1983), 12.
26. Marc K. Stengel, "When Is Southern Literature Going to Get Real?" *Nashville Scene,* 12 April 1990 (as Stengel notes, southern cities are conspicuously underrepresented in contemporary fiction); Foreword, *Fugitive* 1 (1922): 2.

Now it is the Agrarian South that has the fuzzy edges and threatens to produce a decadent nostalgia. A neo-Fugitive movement may already be among us. The genericized places of Bobbie Ann Mason and Frederick Barthelme might represent the shape of things to come. But if "getting real" is to become less southern, it may also be that southern literature will become less real. It might, in fact, dispense with reality altogether, which would eliminate the sleight-of-hand and trickery that taint conspicuous southernness. The hyperrealism of Barry Hannah and Lewis Nordan, whose distinctively southern texts seem to generate their own worlds without especially borrowing from ours, can be viewed as a step in this direction. For a culture that even recently resisted the Disnification of its history, it would surely be ironic should the South come to exist as a weightless simulacrum, a displaced identification, a condition of pure performativity. But as C. Vann Woodward pointed out many years ago, irony and the South have never been strangers.

Dismantling the Monolith: Southern Places—Past, Present, and Future

Barbara Ladd

Most of us in southern literary studies have taken for granted the idea that southern literature is grounded in a "sense of place," but questions about the meaning and significance of that sense of place have been troubling, particularly when linked in U.S. literature (as seems always to be the case) with the idea of "regionalism." Is a literature "grounded in place" necessarily a "regional" literature? Many—including Eudora Welty—would say that it is not: " 'Regional' is an outsider's term," she writes, that "has no meaning for the insider who is doing the writing, because as far as he knows he is simply writing about life." Nevertheless, for Welty, "*Location* [italics mine] is the ground conductor of all the currents of emotion and belief and moral conviction that charge out from the story in its course."[1] "Place," in other words, is a matter of "location," of "situation," a "conductor" of the currents that move through a literary text; and unlike "region" as it has usually been understood, "place" and "location" are subjective, experiential insiders' terms. If this

1. Eudora Welty, "Place in Fiction," in *The Eye of the Story: Selected Essays and Reviews* (New York: Vintage, 1979), 132, 128.

is so, why has the sense of place been so closely linked with regionalism in U.S. literary history? It is especially odd when one considers that the sense of place suggests something that "centers," whereas regionalism evokes ideas of the periphery, so that the literatures of the periphery are often said to be "centered" in that famous "sense of place," whereas those literatures of the "center" are presumably unplaced. The answer probably has something to do with the fact that Americans imagine change and possibility in terms of a flight from, or liberation from, place. This has been one very powerful version of the American Dream. But change and possibility, those forces that move narrative, might be more accurately imagined as a transfiguration of—rather than as a flight or liberation from—place.

What is place now, for scholars and critics and literary theorists, in the age of late modernism?[2] What was it in the premodern context, and what will it be in the postmodern context? The question "What is place?" might best be answered by rephrasing a bit: "What is *a* place? What are *places*?" For geographers and cartographers and urban planners, a place is a specific organization or representation of space. For historians and chroniclers and other storytellers, a place is as much a specific representation of a time. Of course, mapmakers are also interested in the capacity of place to organize time, as storytellers are interested in the capacity of place to mobilize space. New Historians find themselves interested in "social spaces," in borders and boundaries and margins and frontiers. New Geographers draw "deep maps" to record evidence of change over time. According to one of these, "literary mappings of American places have increasingly involved an interest in metaphors of depth, resonance, root systems, habitats, and interconnectedness."[3] As this assessment im-

---

2. I situate the present as the era of "late modernity" rather than "postmodern," following Anthony Giddens, who argues that whereas "postmodernism" can accurately refer to a movement (or set of movements) in aesthetics that characterize our own period, it is a mistake to term this period itself as "postmodern." "Postmodernity," according to Giddens, "usually means that we have discovered that nothing can be known with any certainty, since all pre-existing 'foundations' of epistemology have been shown to be unreliable; that 'history' is devoid of teleology and consequently no version of 'progress' can plausibly be defended; and that a new social and political agenda has come into being with the increasing prominence of ecological concerns and perhaps of new social movements generally" (Anthony Giddens, *The Consequences of Modernity* [Stanford: Stanford University Press, 1990], 46). The "postmodern" perspective is not yet widespread enough to characterize our own era.

3. Michael Kowalewski, "Writing in Place: The New American Regionalism," *American Literary History* 6, no. 1 (Spring 1994): 182. For other valuable discussions of place, see the following: Jim Cheney, "Postmodern Environmental Ethics: Ethics as Bioregional

plies, the South's places have never been simply geographical—especially where literature and literary criticism are concerned. Although they are that as well, the places of literature and literary criticism are more viable and interesting when they are conceptualized in ways that are also fundamentally aesthetic, rhetorical, historical, ideological, cultural. But for all of us (whether geographically or historically enabled), a sense of place provides a sense of relative permanence. So a sense of place might be defined as the sense of stability amid flux. Although place has often been imagined as something solacing or protective, it doesn't have to be.[4] A place is as often a site of horror or brutality—I think, for instance, of Toni Morrison's "Sweet Home" in *Beloved*.

This leads toward two issues: the issue of memory and the issue of change. For many students of memory, no remembering is possible without "a sense of a place" where something happened to you or where you witnessed something happening. Pierre Nora titled a groundbreaking essay "Les Lieux de Mémoire" or the "Sites of Memory."[5] Topoi (sites, entrances) have traditionally been the means of accessing memory. A memory calls something up from past time, but it calls that something up through the passage of (and often in the form of) an imagined sight or sound—in the form of a place (geographically or historically speaking).[6] But topoi are also the means of conceptualizing the imagination or invention. Heuristics is based on the idea of topoi. In a way, then, both the past (memory) and the future (invention) are evoked in terms of places— and it is hard to imagine that memory could withstand the destruction of place, or that the future could be imagined except as a place (in both time and space).

Narrative," *Environmental Ethics: An Interdisciplinary Journal Dedicated to the Philosophical Aspects of Environmental Problems* 11, no. 2 (Summer 1989): 117–34; Roberto Maria Dainotto, " 'All the Regions Do Smilingly Revolt':The Literature of Place and Region," *Critical Inquiry* 22 (Spring 1996): 486–505; David Harvey, *Justice, Nature, and the Geography of Difference* (Malden, Mass.: Blackwell Publishers,1996), 19–45; and Allan Pred, "Place as Historically Contingent Process: Structuration and the Time-Geography of Becoming Places," *Annals of the Association of American Geographers* 74, no. 2 (June 1984): 279–97.

4. For a sense of "place" as "solacing," see, for example, W. J. Keith, *Regions of the Imagination: The Development of British Rural Fiction* (Toronto: University of Toronto Press, 1988), 10 and passim.

5. Gerald Kennedy, "Place, Self, and Writing," *Southern Review* 26 (1990): 500; Pierre Nora, "Between Memory and History: Les Lieux de Mémoire," *Representations* 26 (Spring 1989): 7–25.

6. The senses evoke memories, but are not themselves memories.

What are some of the "places" or "topoi" that animate southern literature, that construct memory and shape the future? Speaking geographically and historically, those places were "the states of the former Confederacy, along with Missouri and Oklahoma"—or something like that; they were slave markets, cotton fields, working plantations (first with slaves, later with sharecroppers), small farms (with black day-laborers hired for practically nothing), tobacco fields and tobacco barns, small towns, "niggertowns," the sheriff's office and town hall where Snopeses and Sartorises divided the spoils according to their own very different sense of fairness and honor.

More recently, the slave markets have become arts and crafts bazaars, former plantations have become museums and theme parks[7]; tobacco barns have been turned into homes for white-collar workers with a preservationist bent (mostly from out of town); tobacco fields have become mobile-home parks where sons and daughters of former farmers now own half-acres or, worse, rent; and suburban neighborhoods of seemingly prosperous African Americans in split-level homes back up into public-housing projects. Recently, southern places are to be found in Atlanta, full of bankers and Baptists; in Savannah, with its good old boys (white and with money and most from out of town) who get along pretty well with everyone as long as there is murder and scandal to bring them together in defense of the community. Southern places are streets and schools formerly named for Civil War heroes and renamed for civil rights leaders; integrated (and racially polarized) city governments; white-only county governments; integrated (and nervous) city neighborhoods; segregated suburbs. Even more recently, southern places are crossroads where legal or illegal aliens from Mexico are seen trudging in small groups home to rundown apartment complexes from minimum-wage work as landscapers or better-paid work on construction crews; southern places are Asian American business districts where gangs are said to exact tribute from owners of small businesses.

But despite the current anxiety surrounding place—and particularly surrounding southern places—which I hope the above list of southern places reveals, Michael Kowalewski is right when he suggests that many of us "lack a vocabulary with which to ask engaging philosophical, psychological, or aesthetic questions about what it means to dwell in a place,

---

7. Either completely without references to slaves or with slavery sanitized into a melodrama fit for television featuring only victims, villains, heroes, and few adequately "placed" or "situated" characters.

whether actually or imaginatively."[8] He and others have gone on to suggest that our inability to ask these engaging questions about place stems from the way place has been conceptualized—which is either as an inert category (a background, a setting, evoked chiefly by the descriptive) or sometimes as a "character" in a work of literature (i.e., the "Mississippi River" as a "character" in Mark Twain's work). Whereas those who want to speak of place as a character may well be responding to a sense that place is not merely a matter of "background" or "setting"—that it is in some sense an active presence in a literary work, an agent in the sense of "a force or substance that causes some change" or "a means or a mode by which something is done or caused"—to talk about place as a *character* generates a number of problems; they are, however, problems that clarify.

"Place" is not "person," especially in the U.S. or, more broadly, Western cultural context where to be a "person" implies, first, to be a "human being" or an "organization" (i.e., incorporated as a human being in some respects) possessed of "certain legal rights or duties" (*American Heritage Dictionary*). Here we can probably discern a suggestion as to why postcolonial scholars, environmentalists, and feminists have been among those most interested in reconceptualizing "place"—ironically, they are all dealing with disfranchised *populations*—i.e., with populations not possessed of the "legal rights and duties" capable of ensuring them the status of persons, with populations whose relationship to the "natural" or "cultural" background, or place, would seem to be more or less "predial" in a culture in which the relationship of real "persons" to "place" is "proprietary." To the extent that postcolonialists, environmentalists, and feminists seek to understand naturalized or marginalized populations, they are engaged with questions about what constitutes subjectivity and agency, with questions about ways such naturalized or marginalized (i.e., placed) populations can be empowered as subjects, as agents. And thus, for complex reasons, they are engaged with questions about ways that place or what has been in some sense "owned" as cultural property can be emancipated, about ways that place can make movement and change possible rather than simply serving as a way of talking about resistance to change.

We might then reconceptualize place as a site of cultural dynamism. What are some of the implications of such a reconceptualization for southern studies? In the first place, it enables us to shift our focus from

8. Kowalewski, "Writing in Place," 174.

moments or sites of narrative (or historiographical) stability to moments/ sites of narrative and historiographical process. So, rather than pointing to the plantation system or cotton production as defining the South, for example, we would point to the moment and to those places where plantations are relatively new means of economic and social organization or relatively archaic ones. Rather than defining the South in terms of its relationship to a specific kind of chattel slavery, we might look for those temporal and geographical sites where chattel slavery did not define a locale as "southern," or at "southern" sites where chattel slavery did not exist. A different reading of *Gone With the Wind*, for instance, would not focus so exclusively on the pre–Civil War plantation life of Scarlett O'Hara as a former paradise "gone with the wind," but (reading against the grain) would look instead for signs of the economic, social, and historical narratives that the plantation tale displaces. I am thinking, in particular, of the significance of Scarlett's Irish genealogy and the plantation's setting in Georgia, an area settled later than Virginia and South Carolina, and by a population that was significantly different (politically, socially, economically, historically, culturally) from the population that established Virginia's and South Carolina's plantations. But one might also look at the way the publication of the novel in 1936 displaced or functioned intertextually with other narratives of the thirties for readers of popular fiction. We might also read *Gone With the Wind* as part of a group of novels that includes tales of plantation slavery in the Caribbean. (Thus far, novels like Mitchell's and like Stark Young's *So Red the Rose* have not been read with novels of the Caribbean like Claude McKay's *Banana Bottom*.) And, by implication, we might begin to focus on ways that the narrative rewrites (or unwrites) the history of African Americans in the South, in the United States, and in America more broadly conceived. The recontextualizing of *Gone With the Wind* as part of a larger literature that spans the U.S. South and other sites of plantation slavery makes it possible to do just that.

Concerns about the place and placing of persons are intensified, too, by the conditions of late modernity, in particular by the alienations experienced by human populations in an age in which territorial boundaries are clearly delineated with respect to a sovereign state (i.e., legally) but in which cultural and economic boundaries are much less clearly marked with respect to that sovereign state.[9] In other words, one has a sufficiently

9. See Anthony Giddens's discussion of this issue in *The Consequences of Modernity*, particularly pp. 17–54.

wide range of movement to make it possible (indeed inevitable) to make money or even a family in any number of locations, but one is enfranchised in only one location (i.e., in one "nation-state"). With rare exceptions, one cannot be a citizen of two states (i.e., the United States and Mexico), whereas—and this is key—in premodern cultures, communities and societies "were not terrritorial in the same sense as [our present] state-based societies."[10] So, again ironically, in the late modern age we are possessed of a capacity to move (our bodies, our voices, our texts) or to transgress boundaries between one culture and another while we are bound politically and legally to a sovereign government that controls a particular territory. In the premodern age, human beings were not possessed of such a wide range of movement (whether of bodies, voices, or texts) but were less strictly bound with respect to a governmental entity. In the premodern period (all other things being equal, which of course they never were), one was a citizen of the place where one really spent one's time. Space and time were, in a sense, *grounded* if not bounded; and under such conditions, place is relatively unproblematic; under such conditions, to speak of a social location is to speak of a geographical location. Under such conditions, place is dynamic and vital; if not (strictly speaking) a character in any cultural narrative, neither is it (strictly speaking) a background or object (i.e., distanced or removed from the character, from the human being or social organization).[11]

Now and then I teach a student with a name like Juan Chen; his complexion might be light or dark; his features Asian, Hispanic, Caucasian, or African; he speaks like any other urban southerner, which means he sounds a little like Al Gore. He is a U.S. citizen; he is from the South—but he is also Asian or Hispanic or African—and often more significant for him than his Asian or Hispanic or African roots is his hybridity, which seems in some instances to define and in others to threaten his identity as an American, or as a southerner.

10. Ibid., 14.

11. One might argue that until World War II, the American South could be said to have been, in some ways, premodern, where to speak of a geographical location was indeed to speak of a social location. I have some reservations about this, however, when dealing with southern literature. Certainly there were (and are) still some "folk" populations within the South. What kind of difference they make to southern literature is unclear to me—although I believe they do make a difference. Often southern literature "deals with" them—in much the same way that the state has always "dealt with them." Much clearer is the fact that southern writers and publishers and most readers of this literature are not themselves "folk," although they sometimes pretend to be, sometimes for admirable reasons and sometimes for reprehensible ones.

The *experience* of place remains dynamic and vital. It is the *theorizing* of place that is problematic. Kowalewski is right; we *have* failed to theorize place in ways that enable us to ask significant questions about its influence in and impact upon literature and literary study. Place signifies much more for literature and literary studies than "a conceptual index of social attitudes and representational practice," which is more or less what it has signified for social scientists. The reality, as Kowalewski suggests, is that neither literature nor literary study is simply a matter of indexing the conceptual or anything else. To be useful in literary studies, he writes, place "must be reimagined as a texture, a metabolism, a temperament, an etiquette"—i.e., it must be imagined more like the way that Eudora Welty imagines it; and literary critics need to develop a vocabulary for the discussion of the way place animates a text, governs movement, and makes change possible. The new geography has not yet grappled adequately with this problem, although "literary mappings of American places have increasingly involved an interest in metaphors of depth, resonance, root systems, habitats, and interconnectedness—factors that together put places into motion, making them move within their own history, both human and nonhuman."[12] At the beginning of this essay, I mentioned the irony of peripheral/regional literatures being "placed" while the literatures of the "center" are "unplaced." It may well be that place and regionalism are more or less incompatible concepts, linked only by an ideology that understands persons, but not places, as agents of change.

Why has the sense of place been so closely linked with the idea of regionalism in U.S. literature? The word *regionalism* appeared in the vocabulary in the late nineteenth century in response to the centralizing discourse of state-sponsored nationalism. The first recorded use refers to the national unification effort in Italy, and more precisely to resistance to that unification effort on the part of the populations of different regions of the country.[13] By 1881, then, regions were becoming geographical or historical provinces within the nation-state, those provinces surrounding the metropolis that drew from each region the best of its talent and re-

12. Kowalewski, "Writing in Place," 174, 182, 181.
13. The first use, according to the *OED*, was in February 1881, when the *Manchester Guardian* referred to "that unfortunate 'regionalism' of Italy, which has been described by recent writers of the country," and in 1887 in the *Edinburgh Review*: "The spirit of local individualism—in politics somewhat inharmoniously dubbed 'regionalism.' "

turned to the region gifts in the form of information from the "outside" world, government, progress, and economic and cultural improvements. Resistance to these forces was termed resistance to "change" or to "progress" and was dealt with largely in those terms. In the U.S., the literary and artistic production of the region was often written into literary history as "local color," and (as much recent work has demonstrated) much of the potential subversiveness of these cultural processes was packaged and directed as various forms of resistance to *progress*.

The accuracy of this version of regionalism might be tested by comparing regionalism in U.S. literary history to regionalism as it functioned and continues to function elsewhere in the Americas where state control was either much more distant (i.e., in Europe or Great Britain) or much more contested. The political and cultural vitality of regional literatures in Central and South America and in the Caribbean has been much greater than in the U.S., where the South has been one of the few regions to sustain a truly vital (and visible) literature—no doubt chiefly because of the political history of the South.[14]

In the words of one scholar, Horst Frenz—although many others, including Edgar Allan Poe, writing a century earlier, have shared the sentiment—it is politics "that helped to create a national literature." But, as Philip Rahv observes, if the nature of American literary life was formerly determined by national forces, "now it is international forces that have begun to exert a dominant influence." Rahv's assessment appeared more than half a century ago, not long before the the U.S. entered World War II, so the international forces he had in mind were probably coming chiefly from Europe, Asia, and the Soviet Union. World War II and the Cold War that followed are now over, but the internationalization of American literary life continues. Today, however, we would include Africa, the Caribbean, and Central and South America among the regions

---

14. The reasons for the vitality and visibility of literature in the American South no doubt have a great deal to do with the Civil War, the memory of which has provided a locus of political and ideological resistance well into the late twentieth century; but it also has to do with the discourses of slavery, race, and racism (which continue to provide a locus for political and ideological resistance on several fronts) within southern literature and literary study. But the memory of the Civil War has vanished into history. In other words, the experience of the Civil War has become for most of us vicarious, displaced (rather than evoked) by representations (i.e., biographies, histories, national parks, museums, documents, relics, theme parks). The Civil Rights Movement is a more vital "site of memory" for contemporary southerners, although these memories too are becoming vicarious—increasingly experienced through biographies, histories, national parks, museums, theme parks, etc.

exerting economic, political, cultural—and more specifically literary—influences on American literary life.[15]

But as I stated earlier, the discourse of any region, including the American South, has never been solely geographical; it is also historiographical, aesthetic, rhetorical, and ideological. For example, the cultural impact of the Caribbean and Mexico on the American South is not new; rather, its long history has been obscured by the nationalism that has structured American historiography. American history in the Deep South, many people assume, begins with the Louisiana Purchase and the coming of U.S. citizens into the region. What precedes that migration is held to be marginal to the inevitable nationalistic narrative in one way or another, but however marginal in the nationalistic stories themselves, the impact of colonial experience in the Deep South has been and continues to be experienced, precisely because it leaves traces, and the new migrations of Caribbean peoples into the Deep South in the early twentieth century, in the mid-twentieth century, and in the future will no doubt expose those old traces as returning populations once again make their lives—and thereby construct both memories and histories—in places from which they have been, for a time, cut off.

Insofar as the United States South is concerned, these movements of people between the Deep South and the Caribbean and Africa are nothing new—despite the claims of (mostly white) literary nationalists that, in comparison with the rest of the United States, the South has been relatively insular and relatively homogeneous. The problem, of course, is that the people who have constructed the South in these terms have been exclusively focused on the white South's troubled relationship to the nation-state. Most would argue that the Civil War was (and still is) the defining moment for the South as a discrete entity; that the South prior to the Civil War is the South only to the extent that it is developing the economy, the politics, and the ideology that would lead to secession and the Civil War; that the South following the Civil War is the South to the extent that the Civil War determines its economies, its politics, and its ideology; that the South today is and the South in the future will continue to be the South to the extent that the Civil War remains a defining event

15. Horst Frenz, "Nationalism and Cosmopolitanism in American Letters: A Backward Glance," *Proceedings of the IVth Congress of the International Comparative Literature Association,* Vol. 1 (The Hague: Mouton, 1966), 453; Philip Rahv, "The Cult of Experience in American Writing" (1940), reprinted in *Literature in America,* ed. Philip Rahv (New York: Meridian Press, 1957), 372.

in its history and continues (however obliquely) to shape its economy, its politics, and its ideology.

Certainly the activities of any chamber of commerce in any southern city or town would substantiate the continuing importance of the Civil War as a shaping event in the American symbolic landscape. And, as Barry Lopez has observed, most educated Americans (and particularly historians and literary critics, I would add) do reside in a largely imaginary and highly symbolic landscape, often unable to see the actual landscape for the symbolic one.[16] Despite the multinationalization of American literary and cultural life in the past fifty years, a symbolic landscape shaped largely by nationalist ideology continues to determine—and, I would argue, to distort—our sense of the past, our sense of place, our sense of what the present is all about, and the way we imagine the future.

What will happen to southern literary studies if we decenter the Civil War and decenter the discourse of nationality that surrounded it and delineated the parameters and the meaning of southern literary study? What if we take a look at southern literary life (past, present, and future) within a multinational context and within a longer and more complex history than the one afforded by the historiography of the Civil War? Reasons for doing so are compelling. Human history in the region began centuries before 1861. Although the traditional narrative of the South tells the story of the displacement of Native Americans, the introduction of slave labor from Africa, the growth and decline of an agricultural (and plantation) economy, the Civil War, Emancipation, Reconstruction, segregation, fundamentalism, the Civil Rights Movement, integration, and the resurgence of a southern conservatism (anti-feminist, anti–Affirmative Action, anti–government assistance; or pro-family; pro-individual, pro–self reliance—depending on your perspective), there are many other stories to be told. Some of these stories meander toward the mainstream; some do not. Perhaps some of them would make more sense to Juan Chen than the ones he has heard from nationalist historiographers who write textbooks.

Such a rethinking of region will necessarily have an impact on the way we think about place. Wendell Berry has written that most of us in the United States occupy "a regionalism of the mind"; in other words, the

---

16. Barry Lopez, "The American Geographies," in *Openings: Original Essays by Contemporary Soviet and American Writers,* ed. Robert Atwan and Valeri Vinokurov (Seattle: University of Washington Press, 1990), 55.

"maps" that we use to get around—ideologically and culturally speaking—have no "territory." Certainly for many literary and cultural critics, the maps we use to think about American literary life and history were drawn up by the first generations of U.S. literary and intellectual historians (Bancroft, Frederick Jackson Turner, and others) for whom the United States was made up of an intellectual New England, a cosmopolitan Mid-Atlantic, an agricultural Midwest, a defeated but resurgent South, and a West of opportunity and promise. These topoi, or places, may have been useful to previous generations' efforts to experience the present and define the future, but they have become less useful in our own day. Barry Lopez has described these ideological maps as "false geographies" or "memorized landscapes," no longer always directly relevant to the way place is experienced in America. Lately, the literature of New England is more and more gothic (leading one to wonder what has happened to the New England mind). The West no longer represents possibility, and those characters in literature who go west expecting to discover new possibilities are often violently disabused of their dreams. The cosmopolitan is found as easily (or with as much difficulty) in Los Angeles or Atlanta or Miami as in New York or San Francisco. In fact, there are deep regions in New York and San Francisco where modern civilization seems never to have dared to go; and globalization (for all the rosy pictures painted by those who stand to profit from it, called "globaloney") is as likely to extend the territory of the Third World as to extend the territory of the First—the two being (and promising to remain) mutually constitutive.[17]

How well we theorize place for the future depends on our being able to rethink the region. The literary mapping of regions needs to be vastly different in the decentralized, multinationalized, hybridized era of late modernism. First, regions are no longer comprehensible as provinces surrounding a centralized national authority; in other words, the traditional distinction between the center and the margin, the metropole and the provinces—a distinction upon which the idea of regionalism in art and literature was based—does not hold. Specifically, with the movement of people back and forth across increasingly permeable boundaries (borders permeable not only by bodies but by economic and political and cultural transactions), the mapping of regions will change as will the writing of history and culture within specific regions. Regions are more and more

17. Wendell Berry, "Writer and Region," *Hudson Review* 40, no. 1 (1987): 24, 25; Lopez, "The American Geographies," 65.

provinces that surround not a national but a transnational center, or multinational crossroads; in other words, the traditional distinction between
the center and the margin, the metropole and the provinces, cannot hold
precisely in the same way in the twenty-first century when the places constructed by metropolitan centers of business and cultural transactions
will vie more and more with the places constructed by sovereign nation-
states to define a region. Atlanta, like most major cities, is more and more
a transnational crossroads. In other words, Atlanta is as viable a metropolitan center involved in organizing regions or being incorporated into
regions (i.e., economic and cultural geographies) in Asia, Africa, and
South America as it is a metropolitan center for Georgia and/or the
United States. What impact will this have on southern places?

Is place or the "sense" of it to become something phantasmagoric?
Must the sense of place refer only to something lost and longed for, like
the longing for presence in language? Must it refer only to a locus of desire, or can a phantasm, can desire, *do* anything? Is there any sense in
which place can *function,* can become *viable* or even *dynamic* and *vital,*
a *vehicle* or *engine* for *desiring,* in contemporary literary studies?

I think place can be a dynamic and vital force in literary study. More
and more, place needs to be constructed not as a stable site of tradition
and history within a progressive nation but as something more provisional, more fleeting, more subversive, and likewise more creative—a
locus for economic, political, discursive, and more broadly cultural transactions, a site of memory and meaning both for the past and the future.
Places, like memories, are always in transition, always redefined, resitu-
ated, by experience over time. If nationalism sought to stabilize place as
background for a drama of national progress, thus far transnationalism
seems inclined to construct place itself as dramatic and fleeting, produced
by encounter, contingent.

I don't really believe that southern places are in danger of disappearing anytime soon. Raymond Williams writes that "the explosion of the
international economy and the destructive effects of deindustrialization
upon old communities" have revealed "*place*" to be "a crucial element
in the bonding process—more so perhaps for the working class than the
capital-owning classes." He adds that "when capital has moved on, the
importance of place is more clearly revealed."[18] Whether capital is going
to move on or move in to the rural South is unclear to me. I do think

---

18. Raymond Williams, "Decentralism and the Politics of Place," in *Resources of
Hope: Culture, Democracy, Socialism,* ed. Robin Gale (London: Verso, 1989), 242.

southern places will continue to be (as they have always been) in the process of being constructed and reconstructed as solacing or terrifying sites of only relative permanence within time and change. In southern literature as in southern literary study of the twenty-first century, there will continue to exist both southern utopias and southern dystopias because the South continues to mean something. Increasingly, however, it means something different, and in new places.[19]

19. See, for example, the meaning that Clinton's "southernness" has on the national and international arena. People like Toni Morrison can call him our "first black president," and he turns out to be the first U.S. president to do an extensive visit to Africa. Irony of ironies: this is a southern white man.

Race and Intimacy: Albert Murray's *South to a Very Old Place*

Carolyn M. Jones

In her essay "Place in Fiction," Eudora Welty describes place as identity. We put a poetic claim on, give a name to, a part of landscape that has put a claim on us. Place, therefore, is space to which meaning has been ascribed—as Scott Romine expresses it, "a network of imperatives, codes, norms, limitations, duties, obligations and relationships." As we name, therefore, we create, as Welty describes it, a crossroads, "a proving ground." That place is the South, and the South is the ground of the novel. Yet, so often, as Barbara Ladd so rightly reminds us, place can become "something phantasmagoric . . . something lost and longed for . . . a locus of desire"—a dream rather than a reality. Can place, she asks, function, become viable, dynamic, and vital?[1]

Such a rethinking of the notion of place calls for a rethinking of the

1. Eudora Welty, "Place in Fiction," in *A Modern Southern Reader,* ed. Ben Fortner and Patrick Samway, S.J. (Atlanta: Peachtree Publishers, 1986), 537–46; Erica Carter, James Donald, and Judith Squires, *Space and Place: Theories of Identity and Location* (London: Lawrence and Wishart, 1993), xii. See also, herein, Scott Romine, "What Is Southern Literature? The Practice of Place in a Postsouthern Age," and Barbara Ladd, "Dismantling the Monolith: Southern Places—Past, Present, and Future."

function of the novel—particularly the southern novel, which has been so closely tied to place. In an essay called "Home," Toni Morrison ties home and place to race and discusses the project of the novel as a way of shifting the focus of the "racial project." To domesticate the project of thinking about race, for Morrison, shifts the questions to an altered space that offers new possibilities for thought and discourse. The task that Morrison suggests is to write not as mistress or opponent of the master's voice but in one's own deconstructive voice; the task is to avoid creating a redesigned racial house through what we call diversity or multiculturalism and to create a space that is "psychically and physically safe." Imaginary landscape cannot be substituted for inscape; utopia can never be substituted for home.[2]

Albert Murray's *South to a Very Old Place* searches for this altered space in which to examine the South as place and home and southernness as identity. The work is categorized generally as a travelogue, finding its center and meaning in Murray's actual homecoming, described in the chapter called "Mobile." This chapter, coming after the fourth bar in the blues-structured work, seems to constitute Murray's break—the point at which, for Murray, as he puts it in "Regional Particulars," the blues hero is faced with "the Moment of Truth . . . that disjuncture which should bring out [his or her] personal best." The chapter is indeed a break with the form of discourse that has gone before in the work. It is the place where the "comb and scissors historians"—the folk of Murray's childhood community—get their say about the intellectual matters that have been discussed in the rest of the memoir.[3] It would be a mistake, however,

---

2. Toni Morrison, "Home," in *The House That Race Built*, ed. Wahneema Lubiano (New York: Vintage Books, 1998), 3, 10, 11. "So much," she writes,

of what seems to lie about in discourses on race concerns legitimacy, authenticity, community, belonging. In no small way, these discourses are about home: an intellectual home; a spiritual home; family and community as home; forced and displaced labor in the destruction of home; dislocation of and alienation within the ancestral home; creative responses to exile, the devastations, pleasures and imperatives of homelessness as it is manifested in discussions on feminism, globalism, the diaspora, migrations, identity, hybridity, contingency, interventions, assimilations, exclusions. The estranged body, the legislated body, the violated, rejected, deprived body—the body as consummate home. In virtually all these formations, whatever the terrain, race magnifies the matter that matters. (5)

3. Albert Murray, "Regional Particulars," *Callaloo* 12, no. 1 (Winter 1989): 6; Albert Murray, *South to a Very Old Place* (New York: Vintage Books, 1971), 116. Henceforth, this volume will be cited parenthetically in the text.

to equate these voices uncritically with Murray's voice. To do so, I think, is to miss the point of the memoir.

Although Murray's journey is, as Warren Carson puts it, an Odyssean journey to get home, it is, beyond that, an interrogation of American culture as "home" for black Americans. As Toni Morrison so eloquently puts it in her review of the work: "Murray's going home, like the return of any black born in the South, takes on a special dimension. Along with an intimacy with its people and ties to its land, there is a separateness from both the people and the land—since some of the people are white and the land is not really his. This feeling of tender familiarity and brutish alienation provides tension and makes the trip down home delicate in its bitterness and tough in its joy." Murray's interrogation of the blue-steel edge of our "kinship and aginship" (14), the "familiar difference and similar otherness" (15)—the tension-filled intimacy between black and white southerners—is what I want to explore here.[4]

The color line—the boundary in the South—is not a solid line but a porous one: the site of numerous relationships. Murray's speculation on W. E. B. Du Bois's assertion that the color line is the problem of the twentieth century recognizes, as Satya P. Mohanty puts it, that "the color line does not merely divide and separate; it also involves a dynamic process through which social groups can be bound, defined, and shaped." Through this dynamic process, the colonized is characterized as "inferior," while the colonizer forms a superior identity that has been characterized as "white" and that narrates and enforces "ideas, ideologies, and interests."[5]

Murray, playing on the idea of such a charged relational boundary, begins his memoir with quotations from James Joyce, W. H. Auden, and Thomas Mann. The key themes of those quotations are mixture and intimacy: from Joyce, "Miscegenations upon miscegenations"; from Auden, "The true ancestral line is not necessarily a straight or continuous one"; and from Mann, a hero of Murray's, touching universes, "in our interwovenness [we] arrive at [our] goal." Home, intimacy, and interwovenness are explored in the areas of education and upbringing and are

4. Warren Carson, "Albert Murray: Literary Reconstruction of the Vernacular Community," *African American Review* 27, no. 2 (1993): 287; Toni Morrison, "Going Home with Bitterness and Joy: *South to a Very Old Place*," *New York Times Book Review*, 2 January 1972, 5.

5. Satya P. Mohanty, "Drawing the Color Line: Kipling and the Culture of Colonial Rule," in *The Bounds of Race: Perspectives on Hegemony and Resistance*, ed. Dominick LaCapra (Ithaca: Cornell University Press, 1991), 314.

interrogated in Murray's conversations with white intellectuals like Robert Penn Warren, C. Vann Woodward, Hodding Carter, and Walker Percy—conversations that make up most of the memoir. In these conversations, Murray looks most critically and honestly at the "trouble spots" that intimacy and home are and, like the trickster that he is, asks these white intellectuals to do it with him. Home, as Murray expresses it, may be the site of belonging, but it is also the place of monsters, the origin of "boo-boo badness" (6). That is, home is both a stable space and a contended space; a place of conflict and negotiation as well as a place of self-expression and safety. Ashis Nandy's concept of the "intimate enemy" illuminates Murray's sense of intimacy and home as it involves the color line. The idea of the "intimate enemy" involves both the colonizer and the colonized's unconscious participation in and, finally, conscious acknowledgment of the relationships in culture that are the sources of understanding and self-definition as well as of cultural tensions. In other words, as Nandy puts it, colonialism includes "codes" that both the rulers and the ruled share: "As a state of mind, colonialism is an indigenous process released by external forces. Its sources lie deep in the minds of the rulers and the ruled."[6]

This concept is particularly apt for describing race relations in the South. James Baldwin recalls in an essay on Martin Luther King the silence that he encountered on an integrated bus not long after the Montgomery boycott was settled. This silence, Baldwin realizes, comes from the white riders' sense of order violated, and the silence and anger betray the intimacy of the relationship between black and white southerners:

> This silence made me think of nothing so much as the silence which follows a really serious lovers' quarrel: the whites, beneath their cold hostility, were mystified and deeply hurt. They had been betrayed by the Negroes, not merely because the Negroes had declined to remain in their "place," but because the Negroes had refused to be controlled by the town's image of them. And without this image, it seemed to me, the whites were abruptly and totally lost. The very foundations of their private and public worlds were being destroyed.[7]

As the social arrangement authorized by the whites breaks apart, the whites feel betrayed in an intimate space, not realizing that consent to these arrangements was forced. Confronting these issues of intimacy and

6. Ashis Nandy, *The Intimate Enemy: Loss and Recovery of Self Under Colonialism* (Delhi: Oxford University Press, 1988), 3.

7. James Baldwin, "The High Road to Destiny," in *Martin Luther King, Jr.: A Profile*, ed. C. Eric Lincoln (New York: Hill and Wang, 1970), 95.

social configuration ideologically has failed again and again in America. Our political discourse does not have the flexibility or insight to handle them. How, then, may we begin to confront them? Albert Murray seeks an answer by deconstructing the discourse of politics with the discourse/ performance of blues.

For Murray, we begin with the "blisses of the commonplace." Toni Morrison's phrase, "intimate things in place," illuminates Murray's "blisses of the commonplace." Morrison, in an interview with Robert Stepto, talks about the meaning of place in her novel *Sula*. She says that place for her is detail: "a woman's strong sense of being in a room, a place, or in a house." Morrison suggests that, as a woman, she does "intimate things 'in place' "—in a rooted, definite location.[8]

Morrison's phrase has a double implication: that women do intimate things in a located space and that, in that located space, they put intimate things "in place," where they belong. She uses the example of black women who, moving across the boundaries of intimate spaces— homemaking and housekeeping—have dealt most directly in the exchanges between cultures. In this responsibility, Morrison suggests, is freedom and a model of what to do: locate meaning in particular people, places, and things. Similarly, home is a concrete and located site for Murray. He argues that "the condition of [the hu]man is always a matter of the specific texture of existence in a given place time and circumstance." Both writers take this down-home knowledge, which has been called local, particular, folk, and which has been disparaged, appropriated, and, most of all, misunderstood, and give it a universality and a particularity that make it extraordinary (229). And art, Murray and Morrison suggest, is the model of a place in which we might locate ourselves.[9]

This location does not defeat the West: instead, it acknowledges the Western culture within us and, as Ashis Nandy says, "domesticates" the West. This location does not deny history; instead, it affirms myth over history and thereby orders history in a new way. This location does not deny suffering; it embraces and heals suffering. This location does not rule; it hides—that is, it may choose silence and survival over confronta-

---

8. Albert Murray, *The Blue Devils of Nada: A Contemporary American Approach to Aesthetic Statement* (New York: Pantheon Books, 1996), 174; Toni Morrison, " 'Intimate Things in Place': A Conversation with Toni Morrison," in *Chant of Saints: A Gathering of Afro-American Literature, Art, and Scholarship,* ed. Michael Harper and Robert B. Stepto (Chicago: University of Illinois Press, 1979), 213.

9. Morrison, " 'Intimate Things in Place,' " 219; Murray, "Regional Particulars," 3.

tion and violence. It is home—or as bell hooks calls it, "homeplace," stressing location as well as function; this place is a revitalized community of equal persons in mutual interactions. Home is not homogeneous; at home, as Charles Hartmann puts it in *Jazz Text*, voice is born "from a matrix of voices." Home is a polychronic, polychromic, multilocated, and fluid "structure," which may be both actual and in the consciousness, in which we accept difference, negotiate conflict and, most important, can love one another. From that located homeplace, which Murray shows us has become, in the modern world, more a mode of consciousness—down-home southern consciousness—than, finally, a place, Murray can look at American culture in general and offer a theory of identity and culture that he sees as most conducive to freedom.[10]

America, Murray argues in *The Omni-Americans*, is a mulatto culture. Shaped by the conjunctions of influences from the Yankee to the Native to the Black, America is a "composite" nation of "multicolored people . . . [who] are all interrelated one way or another." This fact is, he continues, the essence of national creativity but also the source of our greatest tensions. How can we creatively and meaningfully negotiate this intimacy? Murray asks, as does Edward Said in *Culture and Imperialism*, how, in looking at our overlapping histories, we can find an alternative "secular interpretation" to a politics of denunciation, regret, blame, and "the even more destructive politics of confrontation." Historian of religions Charles H. Long, in "Freedom, Otherness, and Religion: Theologies Opaque," says that this new form of freedom must not be a flip-flop of power: "If this freedom is not to be simply the sentimental initiation of the lordship-bondage structure with a new set of actors, it would have to be a new form of freedom." Murray, in his conversations in *South to a Very Old Place*, embraces both notions: the need for a secular interpretation and for one that moves beyond a redistribution of the same destructive power. He rethinks intimacy in community with other intellectuals to articulate a secular notion of culture that can acknowledge the existence and interdependence of a multiplicity of selves. That reconstruction can help us to create a form of expression through which free and mutual selves can interact. He argues that this form already exists, that it is a southern indigenous form, and he calls it the blues idiom.[11]

10. Nandy, *The Intimate Enemy*, 108; Charles Hartmann, *Jazz Text: Voice and Improvisation in Poetry, Jazz, and Song* (Princeton: Princeton University Press, 1991), 47.

11. Albert Murray, *The Omni-Americans: Black Experience and American Culture* (New York: Vintage Books, 1970), 22, 3; Edward W. Said, *Culture and Imperialism* (New York: Vintage Books, 1993), 19; Charles H. Long, "Freedom, Otherness, and Religion:

The blues idiom, enacted by the blues hero, respects the concreteness of life and what Warren calls the southern fear of abstraction. Murray presents the South as a context that offers a locus of motivations and a context for heroic action. Southern roots "dispose and also condition [one] to function in terms of the rootlessness that is the basic predicament of all humankind in the contemporary world at large." Like Murray, Jon Michael Spencer suggests in *Blues and Evil* that the blues life is a "moral sojourn" that includes a ritual recollection of the religious upbringing and a reworking of the codes and creeds of that upbringing. The "story within the story" that the blues musician lives, works out, and finally narrates includes facing a historical reality of pain and suffering and connecting the personal knowledge gained to black history; for Spenser, the connection extends to the sacred history of the biblical narrative, and for Murray, to the canon of the West. The "I" in the blues is communal as well as individual, connected to black history, especially slavery, and to economic hardship. The blues musician, through the play that is interplay—between the individual and the tradition as well as between persons and groups—is able to move beyond the good/evil, master/slave binaries to integrate what is problematic into the self and thereby to move toward wholeness. The blues idiom is, to use Homi K. Bhabha's terms, a structure of cultural liminality—which I am calling home—within the nation, a performative space that moves between the authorized discourse and the space of the people.[12]

The people are both object of authority and subjects of a process of signification that redeems, iterates, and reproduces meaning.[13] Murray contrasts the subjective-authorial poetic form of the blues to the objective-authorizing social-scientific idiom that he believes dominates our discourse about race and that makes us see black people as social problems. Murray prefers the metaphorical to the scientific. He says of Duke Ellington and James Weldon Johnson that they regarded themselves as "flesh and blood human being[s], as person[s] of capability with many possibilities . . . not as if they were mostly social problems in urgent need of white liberal compassion." Murray's argument with the social-scientific idiom

---

Theologies Opaque," in *Significations: Signs, Symbols, and Images in the Interpretation of Religion* (Philadelphia: Fortress Press, 1986), 197.

12. Murray, *The Blue Devils of Nada*, 17, 30; Jon Michael Spencer, *Blues and Evil* (Knoxville: University of Tennessee Press, 1993), 66, 74; Homi K. Bhabha, *The Location of Culture* (New York: Routledge, 1994), 147.

13. Bhabha, *The Location of Culture*, 145.

is that it pretends to capture all of experience and to explain it. Murray argues that this cannot be done without reduction and oversimplification. Scientific categories and formulations presume that the human response in a given situation is already known. Science "dehumanizes experience in the very process of coming to terms with it. Whereas literature . . . always humanizes or dramatizes experience."[14] The social sciences disregard play, imagination, and creativity.

Murray, always on the side of play, imagination, and creativity, argues instead for the importance of metaphor. The capacity of metaphor both to render experience and to leave experience open to further interpretation is its strength. The poetic metaphor, because its "net" has a looser weave, can trap and, most important for Murray, stylize[15] larger areas of experience. Style is essential for Murray. Individual experience and regional particularities can be stylized into significance for the whole: "Art is the ultimate extension, elaboration, and refinement of the rituals (and hence reinforce the basic orientation towards experience) of a given people in a given time, place, and circumstance." Art is indispensable to human existence because it is a process of play that "gives rise to the options out of which come the elegance that is the essence of the artistic statement." The artist is one who, in creating forms and images, "creates the very basis of human values, defines accurately or not what is good and what is not, and . . . exercises immeasurable influence on the direction of human aspiration and effort." The blues is such a form—Murray sees the blues tradition as one of "pragmatic American existentialism" that offers "affirmation in the face of adversity" and "improvisation in situations of disruption and discontinuity."[16]

Significant areas of disruption, because they are the significant intimate issues for southerners and for Americans in general, are those ties of, as he says in *South to a Very Old Place*, "blood and household" (61). Blood and household take us back to Murray's definition of American culture and its forms as mulatto. In the intimacy of the home space and in the miscegenation of races, America became and remains a mixture. The blues idiom, which Murray demonstrates and calls others into in the memoir, is for him the poetic response that can represent this miscegenated culture because it is a miscegenated form: *"It is the product of the most complicated culture, and therefore the most complicated sensibility*

14. Murray, *Nada*, 25, 171.
15. Murray, *The Omni-Americans*, 54.
16. Murray, *Nada*, 13, 96, 220–21, 180, 94.

in the modern world" (166, italics Murray's). The blues idiom, he argues, in *The Omni-Americans,* "represents the most comprehensive and the most profound assimilation. It is the product of a sensibility that is completely compatible with the *human* imperatives of modern times and American life." I would also argue, using Robert Detweiler's definition of poetic metaphor as erotic, that the blues idiom's greatest virtue is its capacity to forge relationships—dare we say, create communities— between selves who may see themselves as nonrelated.[17]

The blues hero knows, Murray says, that there are no clear-cut solutions for the human situation (167). What the blues idiom offers is a way to make a response to the human condition that is meaningful, significant, and individually stylized (58). As a performative construction of identity and community, the blues offers a form of communication between "self" and "other" that breaks stagnant binary and hierarchical structures. The gap between "self" and "other" becomes the break in which the artist plays the self in the context of the community, but also in potentially transgressive ways. In this mode, voice, as Charles Hartmann puts it in *Jazz Text,* is born from a matrix of voices, and voice is "authorial but not exactly authoritative . . . [Its] function depends on others." Jazz and the blues presuppose mixture.[18] Whereas the blues is often a "guy and a guitar," the blues or jazz band embodies the extension and multiplicity of voice, allows the individual to be a self while being in community with others, and involves both continuity and difference.

The "affirmative, heroic response" can be made only in and from this situation of paradox and limitation. The blues hero plays with the possibilities that exist, and this performative self can live with cultural ambiguity and with ambiguity in the self. Such a self does not claim a single, static, finished identity. Instead, it is, as Edward Said has expressed it in "Criticism, Culture, and Performance," "multiple identity, the polyphony of many voices playing off against each other, without . . . the need to reconcile them, just to hold them together. . . . More than one culture, more than one awareness, both its negative and its positive modes." Improvisation depends on challenge, on contrapuntal themes. Murray, in *The Blue Devils of Nada,* quotes Hemingway saying that he "had used the word 'and' consciously over and over in the first paragraph of *A Fare-*

17. Murray, *The Omni-Americans,* 60 (italics Murray's); Sharon E. Greene, "A Conversation with Robert Detweiler," in *In Good Company: Essays in Honor of Robert Detweiler,* ed. David Jasper and Mark Ledbetter (Atlanta: Scholars Press, 1994), 434.
18. Hartmann, 147, 94.

well to Arms the way Mr. Johann Sebastian Bach used a note in music when he was emitting counterpoint." This capacity to function in times of confrontation with discipline and courage, but also realistically and with flexibility, suggests to Murray that music and art become models for life, "fundamental equipment for living." The blues offer a creative, disruptive counterstatement and a model that, for Murray, can deal with tragedy, comedy, melodrama, and farce simultaneously: "In a fully orchestrated blues statement, it is not at all unusual for the two so-called elements [of comedy and tragedy] to be so casually (and naturally) combined as to express tragic and comic dimensions of experience simultaneously." The blues statement "expresses a sense of life that is affirmative."[19]

Murray is the returning exile from the South who seeks the affirmative counterpoint to his memory and his experience in his conversations with white intellectuals in *South to a Very Old Place*. When Murray converses with the white southerners he seeks out, he is asking them to acknowledge that the reality of racial contact in the South long ago moved beyond a simple master/slave dichotomy—a binary in which the self not only *confronts* an "other," but in the attempt to establish the "self" as "self" *creates* an "other." This static binary cannot account for exchange—or conversion, as Jerry Bentley, in *Old World Encounters* calls it, suggesting to me both the chemical process and the religious conversion as a micromodel of an internal process of personal change and as a broader process that results in the transformation of culture. In what is created from exchange, from a process of relationality between two self-defining consciousnesses, the authorized changes in culture emerge. In the creolized forms, as Edouard Glissant calls them, is revealed a culture that is, as Murray puts it, "dynamic, ever accommodating, ever accumulating, [and] ever assimilating."[20]

19. Una Chaudhuri, Bonnie Marranca, and Marc Robinson, "Criticism, Culture, and Performance: An Interview with Edward Said," *Performing Arts Journal* 37 (January 1991): 26; Murray, *Nada*, 182, 201, 105, 14–15, 203–4, 208.

20. Jerry H. Bentley, *Old World Encounters: Cross-Cultural Contacts and Exchanges in Pre-Modern Times* (New York: Oxford University Press, 1993), 6, 8 (Bentley describes conversation through voluntary means, through pressure, and through assimilation); Murray, *The Omni-Americans*, 180. Hegel, who articulates the master-slave dichotomy in a way that has dominated Western thought, may have seen this more nuanced reality. He suggested in *Phenomenology* that "this movement of self-consciousness in relation to another self-consciousness has . . . been represented as the action of *one* self-consciousness, but this action of the one has itself the double significance of being both its own action and the action of the other as well. . . . the action has a double significance not only because it is directed against itself as well as against the other, but also because it is indivisibly the

Murray wants to see if Edwin Yoder, Robert Penn Warren, Walker Percy, and others will acknowledge this exchange and interdependence or if they have lost their "downhome angle of vision" (203), their "seed-store-feed-store courthouse-square dimension of Southern sensibility" (214) as they moved through the intellectual world. These conversations become a site of exchange and conversion. Murray, ever the trickster, conducts the conversations on two levels. The surface is the exchange between two intellectuals; Murray approaches these scholars, writers, and journalists as a "book-oriented Southerner" (204) like themselves. He introduces the conversational melody, usually about studies of slavery or social-scientific studies of African Americans. The surface also involves southern politeness: the code of hospitality that dictates the ways a guest is received, and Murray's own mask. *"Why,"* he asks, *"is nothing ever made* [in contemporary discourse] *of the fact that to be Afro-American is to be derived at least in part from a mask-wearing tradition?"* (65, italics Murray's).

The depth of the conversation is reached and revealed in the counter-statement of the white intellectual, the improvisation from the "other" on the melodic line. The degree to which the "other" can play his response, to Murray's statement, honestly, skillfully, and with style, and the amount of genuine hospitality and not routine politeness that Murray receives dictate the degree of intimacy that Murray allows and offers. The point, Murray says, is "not to have to ask. . . . Because at bottom the point is . . . how much Remus-type insight he brings to bear upon things as a matter of course" (56). It is Robert Penn Warren, reminding Murray most fully of down home, of Red Scarborough in the old Texaco filling station out on old Telegraph Road (16), who meets the test on the level of hospitality and puts it best in intellectual exchange:

> The wrongs of slavery are beyond words, simply beyond words. No question about that, and there is no way that any of it can be excused. . . . But another thing to remember, and now this you always have to remember. Always. And of course this is the horror of it, too: that it was also a human thing, institution—not to say humane—a system made up of human beings, and in such a system—any system—where what is involved is human beings, every possible, every imaginable, every *imaginable* combination of human social relationship is likely to exist. *And did exist.* Now that's what it was. (31–32)

---

action of one as well as of the other." G. W. F. Hegel, *Phenomenology of Spirit*, trans. A. V. Miller (Oxford, Eng.: Clarendon Press, 1977), 111–12.

Working from this confirmation of relationality, Murray moves to what he sees as the central exchange in black/white relationships: the modes of education that shape identity and community. Murray asks Warren and the others what they got from blacks and how they shaped that knowledge, then he shows us in the chapter on Tuskegee what he received from white culture and how he and his classmates reshaped it.

What white southern culture got from black slave culture, Murray argues, is Uncle Remus and Aunt Hagar, who represent an often-discredited knowledge, authority, parental bond, and love. While being very critical of white sentimentality about and misunderstanding of the relationships between white children and black adults, Murray nevertheless makes the acknowledgment of that shared upbringing a litmus test in his encounters. Do these intellectuals know that "the whiteness of white skin is only skin deep and that the rest is mostly human nature and tradition or conditioned conduct?" (67).[21] Does Edwin Yoder exhibit "an Uncle Remus (or Uncle Remus–derived) dimension of downhome or blues-idiom orientation to the ambiguities of human actuality, an Uncle Remus–derived respect for human complexity, a Brer Rabbit–derived appreciation for human ingenuity?" (55). Would Jonathan Daniels admit to Murray that his "Mammy" Harriet was someone else's mother, that he and Murray share an upbringing?—"But how much connection between that profoundly intimate part of his childhood and your own would he have been prepared to acknowledge? and once that acknowledgement was made, how ready would he have been to see the contrast that you insist on pointing out?" (48–49). Murray attempts to make, with these white intellectuals, a blues statement. The white intellectuals are able to take the break when Murray challenges. The disjunction is bridged in the blues encounter that contains the familiar and the similar in creative tension with difference and otherness through the acknowledgment of common roots. This allows Murray to "vouch" (25) for these white folks, "saying yes, one of mine, so to speak, me" (25). Murray asserts that you cannot play unless you have already acknowledged who *all* your ancestors are.

The play between Murray and the white men he talks to reveals that these white intellectuals have recognized the essential inhumanity of antebellum white slaveholding and of contemporary oppressive society. In

21. Murray always puts "black" and "white" in quotation marks. I think the reason is his insistence on this common heritage. For Murray, while there are black and white people, there is no "black" and "white" in American cultural terms.

The Blue Devils of Nada Murray says that: "The oppressor who is already so dehumanized at the very outset that he can regard fellow human beings as chattels becomes even more dehumanized in the all-consuming process of maintaining an inhuman system. The violation of the humanity of others becomes for him a full-time occupation, a preoccupation, a way of life." The oppression of others is an inauthentic and limiting way of life. Hence, Murray is eternally suspicious of codes: code heroes or codes of honor. For Murray, living, thinking, reading, and writing lead to the flexibility in being through which one can know what one feels—and, I would add, thinks—rather than what one is supposed to feel and think according to societal codes.[22]

It is in Robert Penn Warren—who, like Murray, is a fugitive, who knows home, and who is a relentless interrogator of codes—that Murray most sees himself, sees home: "Because that was not only old book-reading, book-writing Telegraph Red himself on his way from, say, Tuscaloosa or Auburn not to murder and flight but to the *Southern Review,* the *Sewanee Review,* and the *Kenyon Review.* It was also Gerald Hamilton at Tuskegee. It was also Ralph Ellison at Tuskegee and it was also you" (37). Book-oriented Warren, who is book-oriented Murray, provides the transition, the bridge, between New Haven and Tuskegee.

Books—being "book-oriented"—and being southern bridge the break between New Haven, Atlanta, and Tuskegee. At Tuskegee particularly, the "blue steel implications" (151) of being a black intellectual are physically symbolized. They are symbolized, first, by the physical presence of the Alexander House, the plantation house near the campus that represents the "living past that so deeply concerned, haunted . . . tormented, and ensnarled" (116) southerners. A second symbol is the spiritual presence of Booker T. Washington himself, who, having been dead only twenty years when Murray was a student at Tuskegee, links Murray's generation to slavery (120). Even as they are conscious of the proximity of pedestals to pillories and of apotheosis to ostracism (149), Murray, Ellison, and their classmates soak up Western culture, in its African American, European, and Euro-American expressions. Murray's landscape is shaped by the canonical works of Mann, Hemingway, and Steinbeck, even as he reshapes them with his own heritage: "[My] enthusiasm for Thomas Mann's dialectic orchestration went hand in hand with [my] all-consuming passion for the music of Duke Ellington and Count Basie. [It] proved that [I] was one on whom Chaucer and Shakespeare were not lost" (110).

22. Murray, *Nada,* 207, 169.

This creolizing of the tradition is an essential foundation of what he calls the epical commitment of those "beknighted [*sic*] pathfinders and trailblazers" (147) who were called to seek their people's fortunes in the world. The epic, for Murray, is an account of a hero involved with elemental problems of survival and a genre that gives attention to the implications of ambiguities (166). For Murray, Ellison, and the rest, therefore, there is no separation between literature and politics, between music and the demand for freedom. Their commitment means using every means at hand to penetrate "frontiers and thereby [expand] your people's horizons of aspirations" (132). This is the blues consciousness, and this is liberation (91). Thus, Murray works in the Western tradition with a signifying blues attitude that "establishes perspective. Adds proper (and anticipated) dimension of down-home ambivalence." And, I would add, keeps the tradition vital. Murray, in "Regional Particulars and Universal Statement in Southern Writing," argues that Faulkner's *The Sound and the Fury* is a novel about the absence of heroic action: "Neither poor Benjy, sad Quentin, nor mean Jason can riff or solo on the break, or set a personal pace for a truly swinging ensemble. They are all stuck with stock tunes that only add up to sound and fury, signifying a mess." So too are our lives without the power of improvisation. Only through the capacity for improvisation can the cycle of violation and counterviolation be broken, and only through improvisation "does man the player become man the stylizer and by the same token the humanizer of chaos; and thus does play become ritual, ceremony, and art."[23]

Improvisation, the blues idiom, is to riff from the tradition the method that can make the solution fit the indigenous style. The blues "knows all the other music and is looking for something better" (168). That is what the conversations in Mobile illustrate primarily. Murray's particular home, in Mobile, has been destroyed by the Scott Paper Towel Company. In Mobile, Murray faces the questions of how to be at home when home is, in one sense, no longer there, and how to maintain southern down-home knowledge in a changing world. Home is a place of "very old horizon-blue dreams" (138), of achievement and disappointment. With place gone, Murray visits people, from old folks who talk about Lyndon John-

---

23. Ibid., 11; Murray, *The Omni-Americans*, 191–92, 58; Murray, "Regional Particulars," 6. Murray continues his discussion of Faulkner in *The Blue Devils of Nada* (178–80). He sees Faulkner caught up in the Greco-Roman tragic cycle of "destiny, the fateful curse, doom, of honor, hubris, and outrage" (180) to the point that he cannot utilize the blues idiom, which is part of his work, to break out of the cycle of violation and counterviolation.

son as a white southerner who can face other white racist southerners, to former teachers who recognized Murray's potential and formed it, to men who want to talk with "New York" about the important matters of the day. Warren Carson argues that the word *nigger* is Murray's entrance into the community. Indeed, he transforms the meaning of the word to say that when black people use it about other black people, they mean "the best part" (141). The word comes to mean, in the course of the chapter, a kind of clarity in thought that is the capacity for analysis, signification, and improvisation that, as each member of the community speaks, comes together in an ensemble—Murray refers to the voices as instruments—piece-voicing a community's—and America's—concerns. As Carson points out, the jam-session metaphor emphasizes the improvisational quality of the discourse but also the "escalating intensity of the discussion" as its core issues are approached.[24]

Murray and his people fear that this capacity for improvisation is disappearing among young people. They criticize the turn in the Civil Rights Movement of the 1970s as "loud and wrong," and they see white silence—when, they argue, in the past white people would have laughed at such antics—as an encouragement to get young blacks to follow the wrong people (159). They criticize Afrocentrism, arguing that the common experience of America is more important than Africa (164) as a unifying force for black Americans. Most important, a way of being in the world and a black intellectual heritage are being disrupted. The way of being in the world is for each generation to push the next forward. This was done for Murray, and his conversational partners fear that it is disappearing. One of them says: "[We're] doing nothing but trying to make it *possible* for them. That's what the old folks did for us and mine always told me the way to thank them is to do the same for the next generation and any child of mine get up there saying I ain't done my part is just a bigmouth lie and I bet he won't tell me to my face" (172). Revolutionary rhetoric is taking the place of local, community, and individual action. This is changing black intellectual life. A whole generation's education has been disrupted by distance from home: "Then for the outchorus: . . . 'Some of our kids now seem to think that heritage is something in a textbook, something that has to be at least a thousand years old and nine thousand miles across the sea' " (175). Home, place, is being lost. For Murray, this means that the fundamentals are lost and that shucking is taking the place of riffing, of improvisation that can make change (174).

24. Carson, "Albert Murray," 289.

Murray's identity, to be sure, is important in this chapter. As Carson tells us, Murray begins to make connections between "what was and what is, between the then and the now, between what he himself was and what he has become."[25] As Murray leaves, heading to New Orleans to meet Walker Percy, we realize that the memoir's themes built to the "Mobile" visit and continue from it. The African American voice is one intellectual riff in this work, commenting on what has come before it, signifying on it, and opening Murray to his final thoughts as he walks in Memphis, the home of the blues, as the blues hero.

What is at stake in Murray's conversations with Warren and the other white intellectuals, in the improvisations on the tradition that he and his classmates do at Tuskegee, and in the jam-sessions in Mobile is the same—survival. Survival means, as what comes before Murray's unspoken but written ruminations shows us, an embeddedness in the particular that makes changes in the political and social possible. For Murray, "the question of endurance comes before that of surpassing" (217). As Ashis Nandy suggests, violence may crown an immediate victor, but perhaps freedom is in survival: adapting, staying on the stage, appearing "dead in somebody else's eyes, so as to be alive for one's own self." This is, Charles Long says, "the power to be, to understand, to know even in the worst historical circumstances, and it may often reveal a clearer insight into significant meaning of the human venture than the power possessed by the oppressor." This may involve, even necessitate, silence. If, for Murray, language is the "dancing of an attitude," so, under certain conditions is silence. In the context of a discourse, "ellipses, omissions, and silence are also verbal actions and as such also represent the dancing of an attitude." In the blues, silence is a technique, especially in terms of the individual jazz musician playing an instrument; it is the positive and negative ground through which blues contours are defined. Silence, as Charles Long says, is also a mode of defining the contours of existence: it "is radically ironic. . . . [It] forces us to realize that our words, the unities of our naming and recognition in the world, presuppose a reality which is prior to our naming and doing." Silence is a "fundamentally ontological position . . . which though involved in language and speech exposes us to a new kind of reality and experience." The question of whether we can play, therefore, is the question of our capacity, first, to stay on the stage, in the conversation, perhaps through critical silence, and second, to stylize images that can represent and imagine solutions

25. Ibid., 290.

that can address creatively and effectively the complexity and interrelatedness of the American South—and by extension. America itself.[26]

The blues style allows—indeed, demands—complexity and a creative confrontation with the facts of life. It is that quality of identity that, as Murray says in *The Hero and the Blues*, "enables [oppressed peoples] to extemporize under pressure and in the most complicated circumstances." This mode of constructing the self, if successfully accomplished, becomes a way of creatively engaging the historical and political realities of oppression through creativity and relationality. This mode of individual identity is, as Toni Morrison puts it, located yet fluid—capable of negotiating multiple tasks, of managing and creating a world. Blues is, for Murray, the "music for good times earned in adversity. A sound track for an affirmative life-style riffed in resilient blue steel from the least congenial of all American circumstances" (218).[27]

Uncle Remus and Aunt Hagar, who link black southerners to white southerners and who are the foundation of the way that both deal with their intellectual and cultural inheritances, are the "source of all the stone foxiness" (220) that it takes to survive and to create. They become a down-home metaphor for a mode of consciousness and a set of resources that allow one a sense of home wherever one is. They are, as Murray expresses it, part of the pantheon: "[A] pantheon is not a natural temple of any sort but rather a metaphorical place. In this sense, it refers to all the gods, heroes, and outstanding champions and achievers of a particular people or nation (or even an organization or line of endeavor) taken collectively as if existing somewhere in an imaginary place . . . [which is] a metaphor."[28] This "place" is accessible through people and through the imagination whether the Scott Paper Company has power or not, and it not only forms who we are but also exists as a critical presence. Having found that down-home quality in a few white folks and affirmed its importance in his hometown. Murray wonders how to get more intellectuals, white and black, from everywhere, to see that they need what Uncle Remus and Aunt Hagar teach and represent—that is, intimacy with place and concern and precision about particularities—and, as important, that

26. Nandy, *The Intimate Enemy*, 111; Long, *Significations*, 195, 60, 61; Murray, *Nada*, 31.

27. Albert Murray, *The Hero and the Blues* (Columbia: University of Missouri Press, 1973), 25; Toni Morrison, Interview with Bill Moyers, "The World of Ideas," PBS Television broadcast, 14 September 1990.

28. Albert Murray, "The Vernacular Imperative: Duke Ellington's Place in the National Pantheon," *Boundary 2* 22, no. 2 (Summer 1995): 20.

Uncle Remus and Aunt Hagar and their descendants have been and are watching them, evaluating them, and judging them from down home.

The novelist, Eudora Welty argues, should write of home. Only one situated in the intimacy and otherness of place can explain and reframe the importance of place. The blues idiom, for Murray, finally, is an intellectual locus that is a recognition, reframing, and reinforcement of roots. Murray says that "when you talking about somebody come from where us folks come from you talking about somebody come from somewhere. You talking about people been through something, you talking about somebody come out of something. And is therefore ready for something" (229). In the multivoiced explorations in *South to a Very Old Place*, Murray, I think, is calling southerners and, since all roads lead home, Americans, to attention and to action. The issues that, in the past, were characterized as southern—race, exploitation, violence—are really, Murray proves, American issues. The urgency of our situation in America, Murray suggests, does not leave the luxury of time for "stock tunes." Our commitment to ourselves and to America must be one of "conditioned unforgetfulness" (230) that sounds loudly, like "rhapsodized thunder and syncopated lightening" (230). "Going to the Territory," to borrow Ellison's phrase, is what Murray does. That journey is a journey into the past, yes, but it is also the journey into the future of a very cool blues man who links, converts, exchanges, preserves, and creates—who takes the old and makes the new out of it. Ellison says that the slaves knew that geography—as a symbol of the known and of the unknown—was fate. The metaphor of travel over an actual and a symbolic landscape that Murray plays out in his memoir reminds us, as Bakhtin does, that we communicate by crossing boundaries and that we assimilate and alter as we speak and move. Murray, crossing north to south and back, covers and maps the territory, the territory of his own existence and ours: that intimate place where we belong and from which we are exiled—the land and the American soul. We carry our common and complex roots within us in memory, in our bodies, and in our culture, and because of migration—diaspora—we can find them "[any]where people do certain things a certain way." Examining and accepting these roots disposes and conditions us to function in the rootlessness that is the condition of humanity in the modern world. And, as Murray reminds us in the outchorus, this ain't new: "all of this is nothing if not down home stuff."[29]

29. Murray, "Regional Particulars," 6.

Southern Culture on the Skids: Punk, Retro, Narcissism, and the Burden of Southern History

Jon Smith

I was talking with a friend of mine about this the other day: that country life as I knew it might really be a thing of the past and when music people today, performers and fans alike, talk about being "country," they don't mean they know or even care about the land and the life it sustains and regulates. They're talking more about choices—a way to look, a group to belong to, a kind of music to call their own. Which begs a question: Is there anything behind the symbols of modern "country," or are the symbols themselves the whole story?
—Johnny Cash, *Cash: The Autobiography*

If "the search for meaning in difficult pasts" is what most closely binds the U.S. South to other New World cultures, as Deborah N. Cohn has argued,[1] critics would do well to ask exactly why these cultures so frequently seem to remain permanently mired in such pasts (or, worse, in permanent denial of their impact). By far the most exciting work in the past decade on understanding how cultures relate to their difficult pasts has to be that done by Holocaust historians and theorists, particularly those who apply at the cultural level psychoanalytic ideas about healthy and unhealthy ways in which the individual psyche deals with past trauma. Like postwar Germany, the postbellum, post-Reconstruction white South has had to deal with trauma and guilt, and the psychic processes involved have at points been very similar.[2] These correspondences

1. Deborah N. Cohn, *History and Memory in the Two Souths: Recent Southern and Spanish American Fiction* (Nashville: Vanderbilt University Press, 1999), 1. The author wishes to thank Deborah Cohn, George Evans Light, Robert L. Phillips, Jr., and Scott Romine for their helpful and patient readings of early drafts of this essay.

2. For one discussion of Latin American responses to trauma, see Idelber Avelar, *The Untimely Present: Postdictatorial Latin American Fiction and the Task of Mourning* (Durham: Duke University Press, 1999).

suggest two particular reasons why the white South has been unable to work through its trauma. First, far from liberating white southerners from, say, the alienation and homogeneity of northern U.S. culture, several clichés of white southern identity—the senses of community, place, and history—have more often tended to reinforce particularly crippling forms of narcissism. Second, particular modes of white southern self-representation (i.e., as "southern") have operated as kinds of fetishism (in psychoanalytic terms, a related kind of overinvestment in object-cathexes). Supplementing the psychoanalytic method with a subcultural/semiotic one, however, suggests a third, more hopeful conclusion: that various punk-influenced white southern subcultures have served healthily to negate the fetishism implicit in traditional iconic representations of white southernness, even as they offer new problems in white southern culture's ongoing negotiation with the past.

Perhaps *all* varieties of identity politics are to some degree forms of narcissism. Walter Benn Michaels, not usually considered a psychoanalytic critic, seems to suggest as much when he claims that "nativist modernism helped to make identity itself into an object of cathexis, into something that might be lost or found, defended or surrendered." The connection between identity, narcissism, and the object-cathexis requires some elaboration. For Robert Stolorow, "narcissism refers not to the love of oneself but to the love of one's mirror image" and "[n]arcissistic object relationships are understood as regressive efforts at identity maintenance through mirroring in the object." Or, as Hanna Segal and David Bell put it, "Narcissus is trapped, gazing at something that he subjectively believes is a lost loved object but that objectively is the idealized aspect of his own self. He believes himself to be in love. He dies of starvation, however, because he cannot turn away toward a real object from whom he might have been able to get what he really needed." Obviously, the shared diction between the "lost loved object" and the so-called "Lost Cause" of the Confederacy, which represents the white South's "idealized aspect of [its] own self," points up an immediate connection between white southernness and narcissism as defined here. The connection between Michaels's observation about identity as "heritage" and narcissism should be clear: in both cases, identity is projected onto idealized objects outside the self, onto what Freud called *object-cathexes*. In the white South, I would suggest, the "Lost Cause" is only one such object-cathexis; narcissistic mirroring, clinically defined, also describes several of the more general properties traditionally associated with white southern literature and, by extension, with white southern culture: the senses of community, place, and history (insofar as "the presence of the past" is conceived to be a determinant of white southern identity).[3]

Reading Cleanth Brooks's famous dictum that "a true community . . . is held together by manners and morals deriving from a commonly held view of reality," Scott Romine in *The Narrative Forms of Southern Community* reminds us that "insofar as it is cohesive, a community will tend to be coercive" and that "community is enabled by practices of deferral." He identifies the dominant cultural work of selected white southern fiction and memoir broadly as "an attempt to defer reflexivity, to recuperate the autochthonous ideal, and to reclaim the tacit ground that enables the production of an objective social world."[4] This deferral, I would argue, may also be characterized as a species of what Holocaust historian Eric Santner calls "narrative fetishism,"

the construction and deployment of a narrative consciously or unconsciously designed to expunge the traces of the trauma or loss that called the narrative into being in the first place. The use of narrative as fetish may be contrasted with that rather different mode of symbolic behavior that Freud called *Trauerarbeit* or the "work of mourning." Both narrative fetishism and mourning are responses to loss, to a past that refuses to go away due to its traumatic impact. The work of mourning is a process of elaborating and integrating the reality of loss or traumatic shock by remembering and repeating it in symbolically and dialogically mediated doses; it is a process of translating, troping, and figuring loss. . . . Narrative

3. Walter Benn Michaels, *Our America: Nativism, Modernism, and Pluralism* (Durham: Duke University Press, 1995), 141; Robert D. Stolorow, "Towards a Functional Definition of Narcissism," in *Essential Papers on Narcissism*, ed. Andrew P. Morrison (New York: New York University Press, 1986), 199; Hanna Segal and David S. Bell, "The Theory of Narcissism in the Work of Freud and Klein," in *Freud's "On Narcissism: An Introduction,"* ed. Joseph Sandler, Ethel Spector Person, and Peter Fonagy (New Haven: Yale University Press, 1991), 198.

Julius Rowan Raper, arguing that "in modern Southern literature the sense of place takes on a role better played by a sense of self," in some ways prefigures my argument about place. Raper proceeds from a Kohutian framework and is more concerned with a distinction between modern and postmodern southern literatures. See his "Inventing Modern Southern Fiction: A Postmodern View," *Southern Literary Journal* 22, no. 2 (1990): 3–18. Scott Romine helpfully pointed me to Raper's essay at a point when work on the present piece was substantially completed.

4. Cleanth Brooks, "William Faulkner," in *The History of Southern Literature*, ed. Louis D. Rubin Jr. et al. (Baton Rouge: Louisiana State University Press, 1985), 339; Scott Romine, *The Narrative Forms of Southern Community* (Baton Rouge: Louisiana State University Press, 1999), 2, 4, 21.

fetishism, by contrast, is the way an inability or refusal to mourn emplots traumatic events; it is a strategy of undoing, in fantasy, the need for mourning by simulating a condition of intactness, typically by situating the site and origin of loss elsewhere. Narrative fetishism releases one from the burden of having to reconstitute one's self-identity under "posttraumatic" conditions; in narrative fetishism, the "post" is indefinitely postponed.[5]

In other words, the post-traumatic deferral involved in the fantastic construction of "community" in white southern literature and culture is less about maintaining white male privilege or power than about what Stolorow calls "regressive attempts at identity maintenance through mirroring in the object." The idealized community becomes a fetish, an object-cathexis.[6] The emphasis on manners in particular, of course, is intimately tied to narcissism as well. Segal and Bell note that "patients who make excessive use of projective identification are trapped in a world made up of projected aspects of themselves. The profound denial and projection lead to a weakening of the ego, which becomes less able to cope with anxiety, leading to further splitting and projection: a truly malignant vicious circle." In *Gone With the Wind*, for example, when the northerner Mrs. Calvert makes the horrible social gaffe of actually praising her employee, Mr. Hilton, "a flush went over Cade's white face and Cathleen's long lashes veiled her eyes as her mouth hardened. Scarlett knew their souls were writhing in helpless rage at being under obligations to their Yankee overseer." Insofar as Mitchell allows *any* sympathy for ineffectual people, the reader's sympathy here largely goes out to Mrs. Calvert, who "never knew what not to say to her stepchildren, and, no matter what she said or did, they were always so exquisitely polite to her." In its depiction of white southern hypersensitivity and passive-aggressive courtesy, the scene suggests what Melanie Klein has identified as the "close connection between envy and projective identification." As Segal and Bell paraphrase Klein, "the envious person cannot accept things from the object [here, the overseer], for to do so means to ac-

5. Eric Santner, "History Beyond the Pleasure Principle: Some Thoughts on the Representation of Trauma," in *Probing the Limits of Representation: Nazism and the "Final Solution,"* ed. Saul Friedlander (Cambridge: Harvard University Press, 1992), 144.

6. According to Charles W. Socarides, "the relationship to the object in all forms of perversion may be described as 'narcissistic.' . . . The fetish, for example, represents the self free from disintegration and fragmentation." See Charles W. Socarides, *The Preoedipal Origin and Psychoanalytic Therapy of Sexual Perversions* (Madison, Conn.: International Universities Press, 1988), 84.

knowledge its worth and separateness," its goodness, its existence as something other than the narcissist's projection. There is, however, a more basic point here: manners are most important in a narcissistic society because the narcissist's weakened ego cannot cope with the anxiety that comes from even the smallest perceived slight.[7]

The traditional notion of community, of course, depends on a notion of place. For the Agrarians, any community not rooted in place (united, instead, by class or ethnic affiliation, say) is not really a community. But place, as the Agrarians conceive it, is not really place at all. As Edward Relph points out, "the meanings of places may be rooted in the physical setting and object and activities, but they are not a property of them—rather they are a property of human intentions and experiences." Thus, concludes Lawrence Buell in *The Environmental Imagination*, "if we idealize the sense of place as a panacea for the disaffections of modern up-rootedness, we run almost as great a risk of cultural narcissism as when we accept the myth of place-free, objective inquiry." The white southerner's love of place is, in short, largely just cultural self-love dis-placed onto natural objects. Although not going as far as Buell, even Eudora Welty in writing of the mystery of place acknowledges this projection: "Might the magic lie partly, too, in the *name* of the place, since that is what *we* gave it? Surely, once we have it named, we have put a kind of poetic claim on its existence; the claim works even out of sight—may work forever sight unseen."[8] Indeed, what makes Welty's sense of place, and by extension that of so many twentieth-century white southern writers, so different from those of environmentalist writers (southern and otherwise) is that in Welty nature is always a mirror. In *Delta Wedding*, for example, the whirlpool and the Yazoo River are just more figures for the womb, and glancing into them is really yet another example of Fairchild narcissism, a kind of (not to mix metaphors) gazing into their own beautiful navels. Peering into pools, they are quite literally a family of Narcissi.[9] Any at-

7. Segal and Bell, "The Theory of Narcissism," 203, 205; Margaret Mitchell, *Gone With the Wind* (New York: Avon, 1973), 485.

8. Edward Relph, *Place and Placelessness* (London: Plon, 1976), 47; Lawrence Buell, *The Environmental Imagination: Thoreau, Nature Writing, and the Formation of American Culture* (Cambridge: Harvard University Press, 1996), 253; Eudora Welty, "Place in Fiction," in *The Eye of the Story: Selected Essays and Reviews* (New York: Vintage, 1979), 119.

9. Eudora Welty, *Delta Wedding* (New York: Vintage, 1946). When William Bartram looks into a sinkhole, or Rick Bass contemplates the Yaak River—to cite two southern writers rarely discussed as such—something less anthropocentric, less *culturally* narcissistic, is going on, even when the same word, *magic*, and even a similar metaphor linking the river

tempt to make them figures for the white South as a whole—James C. Cobb, after all, has called the Delta "the most southern place on earth"—is complicated by little white Laura McRaven's outsider point of view, but even Laura, ever the Fairchild herself, does quite a bit of navel-gazing too, peering not only into the Yazoo but up into the tower of Marmion; the gaze causes her to have "a moment of dizziness and [feel] as if she looked into a well."[10] And the loss of the mother—the definitive trauma that in psychoanalytic theory generates doomed psychic attempts to re-posit wholeness (attempts that include narcissism and fetishism)—is, of course, the underlying trauma of the entire novel.

In *Absalom, Absalom!*, of course, history and memory are the pools into which various narrators narcissistically gaze. Each of the narrators whom Quentin hears in one way or another fetishizes his or her narrative of the past, and as a result each seems fundamentally unable to mourn. Quentin's task, with the help of his analyst, Shreve, is to sort through these various narrative fetishes to arrive at the "real" trauma. Since the coming of poststructuralist criticism, especially reader-response criticism, *Absalom, Absalom!* has often been discussed in terms of the reader's role in constructing narrative. Yet it may be closer to Faulkner's vision to describe the process, as psychoanalytic critics once did, as one of transference (and countertransference), projection, and introjection. Everyone partakes of this process in the making of meaning (as Nancy Chodorow forcefully reminds us in *The Power of Feelings*), but in the white South, the "difficult past," or what Santner calls "a past that refuses to go away

---

and the inside of the body, are being deployed: "It's not about fishing. It's about being in the Yaak. It's about feeling the magic of all the little feeder creeks, cedar streams, not so rich in nutrients, but rich in magic, emptying into the Yaak's little belly." In Bass, some of the magic lies, of course, in the name of the place—Bass highlights that magic in titling his book *The Book of Yaak*—but here the name is an emblem of wildness, not culture: a bleat, a noise, "the Kootenai word for arrow." The appeal of the name, that is, lies in its invention by *another* culture, one apparently romanticized as "natural," as so much European American writing on Indian cultures has tended to do. Rick Bass, *The Book of Yaak* (Boston: Houghton Mifflin, 1996), 131, 1. See also William Bartram, *Travels in Georgia and Florida, 1773–74: A Report to Dr. John Fothergill*, in *William Bartram: Travels and Other Writings* (New York: Library of America, 1996), 484–87.

10. James C. Cobb, *The Most Southern Place on Earth: The Mississippi Delta and the Roots of Regional Identity* (New York: Oxford University Press, 1992). Marmion is also, of course, the name of Laura's doll, made and named by her mother "as if everything, everything in that whole day's fund of life had gone into the making of the doll and it was too much to be asked for a name too." To contemplate the miracle or mystery of Marmion is to contemplate the miracle or mystery of the self. Welty, *Delta Wedding*, 264, 321.

due to its traumatic impact," makes the question of present-day identity formation and maintenance a good deal more difficult, and often a matter of bad faith. We all know that Shreve's question "Why do you hate the South?" and Quentin's famous reply recapitulate the analyst's question "Why do you hate your [mother/father]?" and the analysand's characteristic denial in response. Yet perhaps the white South's problem might better be thought of not in oedipal terms but in preoedipal ones, in issues involving unresolved anxiety about *separation* from the cultural and historical mother. Despite his suicide in *The Sound and the Fury*, in *Absalom, Absalom!* Quentin has always struck me as the sanest of the southerners because, from the perspective of the development of a self, it is slightly better to be a barracks full of backward-looking ghosts than to be such a ghost oneself. A barracks, for all its deficiencies, is a structure, a stable, solid entity. A ghost is not a self; its narcissism comes from its desire to return to its own body, not the mother's, but in psychic terms that difference is relatively trivial. (In Toni Morrison's *Beloved*, in fact, it is nonexistent.) Here, I think, Faulkner's own transferential gifts may have enabled him to tell about the South a truth that his more conscious attempt to deploy (or satirize) the psychoanalytic situation belied.[11]

Curiously, when one moves from white southern high literary modernism to contemporary popular representations of southernness, not much seems to have changed. Fetishism abounds. In January 2000, for example, six thousand white South Carolinians turned out to keep the Confederate flag—perhaps the ultimate narrative fetish, for if flags stand for anything they stand for historical narratives—flying over the Statehouse dome.[12] Yet in our "postmodern" visual culture, conservatives are hardly the only ones to indulge in such fetishism. Many southern liberals, white and black, have been taken with the NuSouth emblem, a Confeder-

---

11. William Faulkner, *Absalom, Absalom!* (New York: Vintage, 1986); Nancy Chodorow, *The Power of Feelings* (New Haven: Yale University Press, 1999).

12. See Jim Davenport, "Thousands in S.C. Stand Behind Confederate Flag," *The Memphis Commercial Appeal*, 9 January 2000, A4. Lest the demonstrators be written off as unrepresentative extremists, it is worth noting that the major Republican presidential candidates refused to take a moral stand on the issue: "Texas Gov. George W. Bush said South Carolinians should decide for themselves whether the flag should fly atop their Statehouse. Publisher Steve Forbes also called it a local issue." In April 2000, John McCain, having bowed out of the race, apologized for his own failure to call for the flag's removal. "I feared that if I answered honestly, I could not win the South Carolina primary," the *New York Times* quoted him as saying. "So I chose to compromise my principles. I broke my promise to always tell the truth." Steven A. Holmes, "McCain Admits He Wasn't Candid on Confederate Flag Issue," *New York Times* 20 April 2000, A1.

ate flag done over in the African American colors of red, green, and black. The commercially copyrighted emblem, which first appeared on the cover of a rap album, is now used as a clothing logo, perfectly combining narrative and commodity fetishism. "Threads [get it?] that connect us/Words that free us/NuSouth," flashes the company's Web page (www.nusouth.com) in the familiar American idiom of freedom through commodity consumption, promising in the simple act of purchase "freedom" from the past and "connection" between blacks and whites in the present. Indeed, as the South becomes more "Americanized"—as identity becomes more and more structured as a lack to be filled by consumption—the paradoxical result may be the increasing commodity-fetishization of southernness itself. In the course of reporting on a new perfume called "Southernness," which bizarrely incorporates floral scents from twelve different southern states, a recent article in the *Memphis Commercial Appeal* happens to note that the perfume's inventor, who "worked 20 years as a free-lance market researcher focusing on the tastes of affluent Southern women," has been involved with "a $2.3 million study by a large private company exploring what it would mean to be Southern in the 21st Century."[13] (The contributors to this volume may have missed our calling.) And one cannot listen to the evening news south of the Mason-Dixon Line without having it drummed into one's head—via the typical Madison Avenue ploy of generating desire by describing that desire as though it already exists—just how much "the South loves trucks/ That's all there is to it."

In the investigation of identity construction, such relatively private, fungible icons can actually tell us more than public ones. The Confederate battle flag, that is, is in many ways more interesting as icon when displayed as a license plate, as an emblem of *personal* identity. More interesting still are those icons that have changed over time (for white southern personal identity has always been, to a degree, fetishized and iconic): the columned "big house" to which such middle-class white male southerners as Allen Tate and William Faulkner aspired, and into which they eventually moved, has yielded since the sixties, among such men, to more working-class emblems: the pickup truck, blue jeans, boots. As Amy Spindler has recently noted, "fashion trends are about one thing: a collective yearning."[14] Southern or otherwise, when a bourgeois man

13. Barbara Bradley, "Bottled Up and Ready to Wear, Sweet Smell of the South for Sale," *Memphis Commercial Appeal,* 26 September 1999, G1, G3.

14. Amy Spindler, "What Your Clothes Make of You: Dressing and Identity," *New York Times Magazine* 14 November 1999: 85–87.

who doesn't work with his hands affects a pickup truck or work boots, he generally expresses not an identity but a yearning for one.

Such yearnings have not gone unexamined by academics, nor have academics been immune to them. Indeed, although "southernness" has often been perceived as an advantage in studying the South, white male academics who do so but who also self-identify as southern—regardless of how critical their stance toward the region may be—have tended, and quite possibly *must* tend, to construct (their) southernness as a collection of object-cathexes, of mirror-objects and fetishes. Using only white men as his examples (and I can think of no major southern intellectual women who fit this mold, though a similar phenomenon is observable in some male black public intellectuals), Michael O'Brien has argued that "the southern intellectual has masked his intellectuality in order to survive" in an anti-intellectual culture: "he has become folksy."[15] Yet given the institutional protections that southern intellectuals now enjoy, even the likes of Jesse Helms pose no real threat to their survival (at least, no greater than to intellectuals who do not specialize in southern cultures).

To explain the exaggerated "southernness" of some middle-class southern white male intellectuals, we must look elsewhere. In *Redefining Southern Culture: Mind and Identity in the Modern South*, James C. Cobb takes issue with what he sees as a pernicious trend in white southern music of the 1990s: the rise of what he calls "southern smart-ass groups," particularly Southern Culture on the Skids, which he calls "a phenomenally popular college band whose name suggests both its repertoire and, quite likely, its social significance as well." For Cobb, such bands "threaten to turn the South of popular perception into nothing more than a homegrown caricature of itself."[16] Cobb's uncharacteristic, paradoxical intemperance—his perception of Southern Culture on the Skids as a "threat" to southern culture and his simultaneous attempt to dismiss its "social significance"—is in its essential lineaments comparable to the conflict between teddy-boy revivalists and punks over the symbolism of dress that Dick Hebdige wrote about in the now-classic *Subculture: The Meaning of Style*.

The dispute, that is, is more closely about the validity of iconic or fet-

---

15. Michael O'Brien, *Rethinking the South: Essays in Intellectual History* (Baltimore: Johns Hopkins University Press, 1988), 213.

16. James C. Cobb, *Redefining Southern Culture: Mind and Identity in the Modern South* (Athens: University of Georgia Press, 1999), 142–43; Dick Hebdige, *Subculture: The Meaning of Style* (New York: Methuen, 1979).

ishistic strategies for representing identity. Cobb has presented his "southern" credentials on the previous page, proclaiming himself "the owner of one of the most ostentatious pickup trucks in Hart County, Georgia, and the not-the-least-bit-sheepish author of the *Encyclopedia* [*of Southern Culture*]'s entry on Herschel Walker." What lies behind Cobb's self-representation (both in Hart County, Georgia, and, perhaps more interestingly, in the *Georgia Review*, where this chapter first appeared) is a concept of identity as structured through a relatively naïve notion of signification: for Cobb, pickup trucks and Herschel Walker in varying ways *signify*—serve as icons, badges, or artifacts of— southernness. I do not mean to single Cobb out here, nor to miss the humor with which he presents these credentials. In a recent *Oxford American* interview, Charles Reagan Wilson, director of the University of Mississippi's Center for the Study of Southern Culture, discusses what the magazine calls his "Southern tacky collection," and expatiates on one item in that collection, his "plastic Jell-O mold shaped like a bust of Elvis":

> *Uncle Art:* Tell us of the object's provenance.
> *Dr. Wilson:* My friend Lisa Howorth gave it to me. I don't know where she found it. She suggested it could be used for a centerpiece at some Center event, but I couldn't bear to desecrate his image. . . .
> *UA:* So what does it mean to have a Jell-O mold shaped like a bust of Elvis?
> *DW:* It suggests Elvis as an icon of everyday life. You could—if you wished—eat a piece of the great man's head.

Despite the surprisingly complex layers of irony in Wilson's remarks— Elvis is simultaneously tacky and (as I interpret Wilson's remark) genuinely "great," for example, though the fact that the bust is of the later "fat Elvis" complicates things—Wilson asserts that such a mold has an iconic meaning. Indeed, he seems to deflect, quite modestly, what in context appears to be for our purposes an interesting if intrusive question— "what does it mean [*for you?*] to have" such a mold—into a more general scholarly one: "It suggests. . . . You could. . . ." The assumption underlying both question and answer, however, is that both the mold and *having* the mold express something about being southern or about southern being. However ironically, they *mean*. They have *significance*.[17]

---

17. Cobb, *Redefining Southern Culture*, 142; "Dr. Wilson's Cabinet of Wonders," *Oxford American* 31 (January/February 2000): 11. For Wilson's more scholarly work on southern icons, see, for example, Charles Reagan Wilson, *Judgment and Grace in Dixie: Southern Faiths from Faulkner to Elvis* (Athens: University of Georgia Press, 1995).

To explain punk, however, which Hebdige considers unique even within the surreal semiotic practices of subcultures in general, Hebdige must draw not on *significance* but on Julia Kristeva's notion of *signifiance*. Contrasting the teddy-boy culture with punk, Hebdige notes:

> Teddy boys interviewed in the press regularly objected to the punks' symbolic "plundering" of the precious 50s wardrobe (the drains, winklepickers, quiffs, etc.) and to the ironic and impious uses to which these "sacred" artefacts were put when "cut up" and reworked into punk style. . . . Behind punk's favorite "cut ups" lay hints of disorder, of breakdown and category confusion. . . . We can express the difference between the two practices in the following formula: one (i.e. the punks') is kinetic, transitive, and concentrates attention on *the act of transformation* performed upon the object; the other (i.e. the teds') is static, expressive, and concentrates attention on the *objects-in-themselves*.

Southern Culture on the Skids does to such (neo)traditional symbols of the South as pickups, Elvis Jell-O and Herschel Walker what punks, mods, and teddy boys did to "the conventional insignia of the business world—the suit, collar and tie, short hair, etc. [The insignia] were stripped of their original connotations . . . and transformed into 'empty' fetishes, objects to be desired, fondled and valued in their own right." To *signifiance* we might also add *signifyin(g)*. Hebdige traces, among other sources, the Afro-Caribbean and African American roots of the punk movement. Certainly his opening claim that "we are interested . . . in those subordinated groups . . . who are alternately dismissed, denounced, and canonized; treated at different times as threats to public order and as harmless buffoons" almost perfectly describes not only African American culture's relationship to the white U.S. (and U.S. southern) mainstream but also white U.S. southern culture's relationship to the U.S. mainstream.[18] But in their ironical and impious emphasis on the *act* of transformation, Southern Culture on the Skids is specifically punk (as opposed to both bourgeois and more traditional subcultural signifying practices such as the teddy boys' or, despite their own irony and impiety, Cobb's and Wilson's). On the band's bright-orange "Hillbilly Racing Team" T-shirt, for example, two traditional symbols of white southern identity—

18. Hebdige, *Subculture*, 123–24, 104–5, 2. Obviously influenced by Hebdige in its emphasis on subversive exaggeration and *bricolage*, Shane White and Graham White's more recent *Stylin': African American Expressive Culture from Its Beginnings to the Zoot Suit* (Ithaca: Cornell University Press, 1998) usefully contextualizes Hebdige's argument and my own.

the hillbilly and NASCAR—become emptied of (apparently transparent or "natural") meaning through a kind of over-the-top juxtaposition or "category confusion." Like punks, the band members self-consciously "*display* their own codes . . . or at least demonstrate that codes are there to be used and abused." Because of this symbolic emptying, Southern Culture on the Skids adopts the punk position as the southern southernist's subcultural Other: "a scandal," Hebdige writes, citing Roland Barthes on the petit-bourgeois, "which threatens his existence."[19]

When middle-class white male southerners adopt the pickup truck to signify identity, however, more is at issue than southernness. Historically, the pickup is, like Elvis, an emblem of particularly *working-class male* white southern identity, as teddy boys' accoutrements were of one working-class white male British identity. But the adoption of the pickup—to focus on that icon in more detail—in middle-class southern white male culture reflects something different from what the codings of working-class Englishmen do: an attempt to alleviate a bourgeois sense of having *no (masculine) identity at all*. There has never really been a viable middle-class southern white masculine identity—the middle class is the great unmarked signifier in the South even more than in the rest of the United States—so that class has been forced to ape the signifiers of those above and below it. Exactly when the paradigm of white southern masculinity leapt from the planter directly over the merchant to the laborer is unclear; I posit the sixties above, but recent work also suggests that the decline of the gentlemanly ideal may have been a longer process, though still one resulting from a sense of its insufficient masculinity. Indeed, the automotive affectations of some southern bourgeois men, intellectual and otherwise, may derive from a concern that, unlike "real" men, bourgeois men do not work with their hands.[20]

19. Hebdige, *Subculture*, 101, 97. This punk aesthetic and its mainstream response are not surprising, given that the band "started out as basically a Cramps cover band in 1984." See Rick Miller, "Interview with Carl Wilson," *Hour Magazine*, 22 September 1997, 7 October 1999 <http://www.scots.com>.

20. For useful discussions of gender anxieties surrounding the notion of the southern gentleman, see Part Two of *Haunted Bodies: Gender and Southern Texts,* especially Caroline Gebhard's essay "Reconstructing Southern Manhood: Race, Sentimentality, and Camp in the Plantation Myth." It is not clear to me, however, that the present fetishization of working-class white male southernness is any less shaped by contradictions, insecurities, and anxious yearnings than the fetishization of aristocratic white male southernness that preceded it. Anne Goodwyn Jones and Susan Donaldson (eds.), *Haunted Bodies: Gender and Southern Texts* (Charlottesville: University Press of Virginia, 1997).

Susan Faludi's argument in *Stiffed* does not always map well onto the subjects I'm discussing, but the following passage from her conclusion is worth noting here: "The men who

On its breakthrough third album, *Ditch Diggin'*, Southern Culture on the Skids specifically parodies the working-class affectations of such college-educated white southerners. Though the title song of the album draws a standard, if unsubtle and rather adolescent, blues analogy between its overt topic and sex (proclaiming the song to be about a "new dance" called the "ditch digger," the singer eventually claims he is "gonna dig your ditch/till my back gets sore"), it also makes a somewhat subtler ironical analogy between digging ditches and the sort of work that non-working-class southerners do. Purporting to teach the listener how to dig ditches (an activity that is, of course, the paradigmatic form of unskilled labor), Rick Miller sings, "Let's dig some ditch," before highlighting his own *skilled* labor with a guitar solo. The back cover of the CD shows Miller in overalls (another self-consciously displayed "southern" code) wielding his guitar through a series of four obvious shoveling motions. Musicians, the album suggests, don't really work with their hands either—and all this fetishization of working-class southern traits is just another code. In the context of the punk aesthetic, such songs as "Put Your Teeth Up on the Windowsill," "My House Has Wheels," and "Chicken Shit Farmer" need to be read less as satirizing (working-class) southern culture—balancing the ironical lyrics is the band's obvious and affectionate mastery of a very broad range of traditional working-class southern musical idioms, from bluegrass gospel harmony to country guitar—than as displaying and ironizing the cultural codes that some white southern bourgeois men use to mystify class distinctions and enforce a "unified" definition of southern identity: to give themselves perhaps less a "usable past" than a "usable present."

As the preceding argument implies, it might therefore make more sense to talk about the "southernness" of middle-class white people, especially white men, less as a kind of ethnicity, as John Shelton Reed's pioneering early work suggested, or as the kind of nationalism that Michael Kreyling and Richard Gray, following Benedict Anderson (and, for that matter, Michael O'Brien), deconstruct as an "imagined community," than as a kind of subculture in the Hebdigean sense: a set of fetishized

---

worked at the Long Beach Naval Shipyard didn't come there and learn their crafts as riggers, welders, and boilermakers to *be* masculine; they were seeking something worthwhile to *do*. Their sense of their own manhood flowed out of their utility in a society, not the other way around. Conceiving of masculinity as something to *be* turns manliness into a detachable entity [fetish? object-cathexis?], at which point it instantly becomes ornamental, and about as innately 'masculine' as fake eyelashes are inherently 'feminine.' " Susan Faludi, *Stiffed: The Betrayal of the American Man* (New York: William Morrow, 1999), 607.

cultural codes bestowing the solace of an identity. Of course, because more than twenty years have passed since Hebdige's analysis, things are no longer quite so simple. More recently, anthropologist Ted Polhemus, perhaps the most important successor to Hebdige, has argued that we now, in fact, live in a "post-subcultural" age: "unlike those who feel and express a consistent commitment to a particular subculture, 'Clubbers' delight in promiscuously 'cruising' through all manner of clothing and musical styleworlds. . . . It is this 'surfing' (as in 'Channel Surfing' or 'Surfing the Internet') that most tellingly identifies 'clubbing' as a post-subcultural phenomenon. And which, in so doing, defines this world and those within it as Post-Modern."[21]

Though I will argue below with Polhemus's assertion that post-subculturalism is postmodern, the post-subcultural model provides something that neither Reed's nor Kreyling's can give us: the possibility of being only part or half southern. In an era when ethnic studies has thoroughly deconstructed such racial binarisms as black/white, and queer theory has dealt the death blow to such simple gender binarisms as masculine/feminine, both southernists and—till very recently—southerners in general have found it impossible to conceive of anyone as half, or simply partly, southern. Reed's studies always assume that binarism, even though, as he admits (with a characteristic lack of dogmatism), the binarism runs counter to his own ethnic model: "I think this is a place where the ethnic analogy breaks down: you've got folks who tell us they're Southern although neither parent was, or that they're not when both were. . . . In that respect, Southern-ness is more like nationality than ethnicity. (Winston Churchill's mother was American, but that didn't make him 'half-English.')"[22] But nationality doesn't work either. Because Kreyling draws on Anderson for his model rather than on later postcolonial theorists such as Gayatri Spivak and Homi Bhabha (my one criticism of what is otherwise an outstanding and overdue book), a nationalist model simply cannot account for, or consider, the possibility of southern hybridities.

21. Ted Polhemus, *Style Surfing: What to Wear in the 3rd Millennium* (London: Thames and Hudson, 1996), 91. See also Michael Kreyling, *Inventing Southern Literature* (Jackson: University Press of Mississippi, 1998), x–xviii; Richard Gray, *Southern Aberrations: Writers of the American South and the Problems of Regionalism* (Baton Rouge: Louisiana State University Press, 2000), 497–511; Benedict Anderson, *Imagined Communities: Reflections on the Origin and Spread of Nationalism* (1983; rev. ed., London: Verso, 1991); Michael O'Brien, *The Idea of the American South, 1920–1941* (Baltimore: Johns Hopkins University Press, 1979).

22. John Shelton Reed, personal communication, 16 March 1999.

Yet at the beginning of the twenty-first century, it is just about impossible (except in very bad faith) for any individual anywhere on the planet to be anything *but* hybrid, globalized, postcolonial. It is this concern with hybridity and globalization that brings me back to Southern Culture on the Skids. In focusing only on Southern Culture on the Skids's modes of (not) signifying southernness, as Cobb and I have done, we have neglected even to consider their musicianship, which happens to be very good, particularly in an odd area: the group is arguably one of the best bands in the current global revival of the surf-guitar movement originally associated with early-sixties Southern California. Of the fifteen tracks on *Ditch Diggin'*, five are straight-ahead surf instrumentals (four originals and a cover of Link Wray's "Jack the Ripper"), and several others use surf music in more hybrid ways: "New Cooter Boogie," for example, fuses strong surf guitar and drums, Jerry Lee Lewis–style vocals, and a lyrical paean to an *Andy Griffith Show* character's reptilian namesake. The band is, in fact, about equally anthologized in two very different sorts of subcultural collections: alternative country and surf guitar. Just as "Too Much Pork for Just One Fork," the first track on *Ditch Diggin'*, appears on the K-Tel anthology *Exposed Roots: The Best of alt. country*—between such classics as Steve Earle's "Guitartown" and Johnny Cash's "Folsom Prison Blues," no less—the album's last track, "Rumors of Surf," appears on the Relativity Records anthology *Bikini World* between the Untamed Youth's version of "Tube City" and the Boardwalkers' "It's a Bikini World."[23]

23. In *Utopia and Cosmopolis: Globalization in the Era of American Literary Realism* (Durham: Duke University Press, 1998), Thomas Peyser argues that the 1890s represent the beginnings of American globalization. Yet Barbara Ladd has persuasively argued for "the power of the South and the southern author to challenge the ideology of nationalism" and of the "legacies" in the South "of French and Spanish colonialist cultures . . . throughout the nineteenth century." Barbara Ladd, *Nationalism and the Color Line in George W. Cable, Mark Twain, and William Faulkner* (Baton Rouge: Louisiana State University Press, 1996), xiii. The South has been global for a long time.

For a good account of the characteristics of surf guitar—an instrumental rock genre popularized in Southern California in the very early 1960s as an attempt to recreate aurally the rush of riding wave through such technologies and techniques as lots of reverb, staccato picking, glissando runs, big drums, etc.—see the Cowabunga FAQ page <http://pages. prodigy.com/cyclops/cowabunga.html>, an unusually reliable Web source, which can also direct you to a variety of more traditional print sources. If you have heard the *Pulp Fiction* soundtrack, you know the sound—Dick Dale's "Miserlou" dominates and even, according to director Quentin Tarantino, inspired the film. Several other surf guitar pieces are heard as well.

In other words, Southern Culture on the Skids is very much a post-subcultural band, "promiscuously 'cruising,'" in Polhemus' phrase, "through all manner of . . . musical styleworlds." Rick Miller articulates the relationship between surf and southernness as follows:

> If you've ever gone to a bluegrass festival, you'll realize that a lot of blue-grass banjo and mandolin picking, man, is basically surf music. It's the double-picking, staccato stuff.[24] And I kinda see us as Appalachian surf music. But I didn't grow up in a cabin, isolated in the middle of Appala-chia, right? I've got some belly-dancing records in my collection, and I've also got some surf music. I lived in Southern California for a while when I was in high school, and I came back to North Carolina to go to college— but my dad has always lived out here—but, you know, it goes back to the whole thing I was talking about earlier, you're from the South, you've grown up here, but you've got influence from a million different places and you can see where they overlap, and the grey area.[25]

Despite betraying a slight anxiety about inherited identity—"my dad has always lived out [?] here"—Miller's overall discussion of his influences runs directly counter to any attempt to cordon off southernness as a sepa-rate identity, as a distinct burden or legacy, as half of anyone's binarism. It is also worth noting that, in good postmodern fashion, Miller's account of his influences is spatial, rather than historical. Though he knows full well that some of the roots of the original surf-guitar movement lie in the South—Link Wray hails from Dunn, North Carolina, three of the origi-nal Tornadoes moved as teenagers to California from Alabama, where they grew up playing country music, and so on—his account is indifferent to chronology, calling bluegrass "basically surf music" instead of the other way around, though bluegrass antedates surf by (at most) two dec-ades. In place of a single, determining "past" (or isolated "place"), the guitarist sees a full set of influences arranged around him like a record collection. No Quentin Compson, Rick Miller is a record warehouse, not a barracks full of ghosts.

Yet the past is not absent, either, for most of the punk-rooted subcul-tures presently at full swing in the South—the retro-country of BR-549,

24. Even the note-bending characteristic of surf guitar—the use of the whammy bar to bend sustained notes and chords, balancing the staccato double-picking—can be approxi-mated on the (quintessentially staccato) five-string banjo by depressing the drum head, among other techniques. Dick Dale's "The Wedge," for example, does not sound too bad on the five-string banjo.

25. Miller, "Interview with Carl Wilson."

the rockabilly and punkabilly that have lingered around Memphis as well as Los Angeles since at least the early eighties, the swing revival that came out of rockabilly (think Brian Setzer), the surf-music revival—are self-consciously retro phenomena. Though Southern Culture on the Skids does not affect uniform early-sixties garb—suits and skinny ties like Tuscaloosa's Penetrators or matching bowling shirts like SoCal's Bomboras—their "look" on *Ditch Diggin'* is clearly vintage: bassist in a bouffant, drummer in a fedora, and *where* did Miller get that *shirt*? In less eclectic (or less post-subcultural) forms, the visual image of a certain postwar, preboomer hipness (along with a surfin' and spyin' or atomic-age lounge atmosphere) is very much a part of the image and appeal of many of the other groups in the retro subcultures spawned by punk. In *The Conquest of Cool*, Thomas Frank argues that "retro's vision of the past as a floating style catalog from which we can choose quaint ward-robes but from which we are otherwise disconnected is, in many respects, hip consumerism's proudest achievement: it simultaneously reinforces contemporary capitalism's curious ahistorical vision and its feverish cy-cling of obsolescence."[26]

It is not quite correct, however, either to identify retro with capital-ism's "feverish cycling of obsolescence"—the implication of retro, in fact, is that nothing is ever "out"—or to say that it implies a past from which we are otherwise disconnected. What Richard Goldstein recently wrote in the *Village Voice* about World War II and the swing revival can also be applied to much of the Cold War and the surf revival, about which, despite the popularity of the *Pulp Fiction* soundtrack, much less has been written: "In an age when culture and politics reek of either decadence or fanaticism, something in the mall-weary American soul yearns for the consolation of a seemingly pure time, when we shared a common enemy and a set of beliefs that united us, for better or worse. . . . For the emer-gent young, it's an erotic masquerade, the first time as tragedy, the second time as fetish." Krin Gabbard, writing on the upcoming boom in movies about jazz, which Hollywood is gambling will be the next wave, notes that "we can sway to the echoes of both innocence and innocence lost in a deconstructive age when we aren't sure which we cherish more, or if either was real." Gabbard's basic argument about jazz applies neatly to the punk-derived retro movements in general, perfectly to surf in particu-

26. Thomas Frank, *The Conquest of Cool: Business Culture, Counterculture, and the Rise of Hip Consumerism* (Chicago: University of Chicago Press, 1997), 227.

lar, and remarkably well to Southern Culture on the Skids: it is "music that accommodates nostalgia and nihilism alike."[27]

Surf *is* like that. On one hand, the covers of the old albums portray happy, clean-cut young men with surfboards and their bouffant-coiffed girlfriends. Dick Dale plays for Frankie and Annette. Yet the glamour and terror of the space race and Cold War are there, too, with the Ventures titling their first hit album *Telstar* and bands appearing with names like The Astronauts. Laika and the Cosmonauts, a Finnish band who started playing surf music in the late eighties before the end of the Cold War (and who are named, of course, for the Soviet dog launched to its death in a Sputnik in November 1957), understand the dualism perfectly. While Dick Dale gushes on the back cover of their 1994 album *Instruments of Terror* that "listening to Laika and the Cosmonauts' new CD makes me feel that I'm standing toes over on that endless wave in the midst of a tropical sunset," the songs (which often do have that feel) include covers of the themes from *Mission: Impossible, Psycho* (1960), and *Vertigo* (1958), along with original numbers with such titles as "Space Base" and "Six Seconds in Dallas."

Southern surf bands pick up on these themes as well, sometimes pushing them to the edge of high concept. The Penetrators have constructed an elaborate Website in which they portray themselves as "agents" of the "Southern Surf Syndicate," answering "to a man known only as Simon." They wear suits, skinny ties, and sunglasses, and adopt such stage names as "Rip Thrillby" and "Ilya 'Stix' Stichkin." Auburn's Man or Astroman?, who purport to be aliens who meant to land in 1962 but missed by thirty years, joke in their own Website, "luckily for us, landing in Alabama was a benefit. As the kind folks from this fine state are well known for their reports of flying saucers, no-one really paid attention to their claims that we had, in fact, crashed." Southernness as place is not repressed or banished, nor is it prevalent and overdetermining; it's just a small part of what structures these performers' identities—one of their influences, retro and otherwise, "from a million different places." One of these influences, however, *is* especially noteworthy. What no one has quite said is that what is present in most of these retro movements—surf in particular—is what might rather deliciously be called a nostalgia for

27. Richard Goldstein, "World War II Chic," *Village Voice,* 13–19 January 1999 (<http://www.villagevoice.com/features/9902/goldstein.shtml>); Krin Gabbard, "Innocence Lost: American Movies Revisit Jazz," *Chronicle of Higher Education,* 3 September 1999, B11.

postmodernism. If, as increasing numbers of critics are asserting, post-modernism ended with the fall of the Berlin Wall, then such movements enact a campy nostalgia for a kind of Pynchonesque paranoia now experienced as stylistic sublimity.

What is utterly absent from the southern surf revival—as, indeed, from retro-country and, as Jesse Berrett notes, from most of the swing revival as well—is any mention of the Civil Rights Movement taking place at the same time. America in this vision is not racially divided but united, as Goldstein points out, against a common foe. Yet what is going on is not exactly historical denial. In a post-subcultural world, what Goldstein observes of the traditional gender roles in swing dancing is true of most of the peculiarities of surf and other retro subcultures: swing "provides a playing field on which to try out roles that may not extend beyond the dance. It is tempting to mistake this experiment—laced with irony and a generational gift for synthesis—as blind devotion to the way we were." The fetishes—the costumes, the martinis, the album-cover art-work—are not *narrative* fetishes. And whereas some subcultures do seem to provide an otherwise absent identity, the general effect of the post-subcultural "style surfer" is one of comfort with his or her self.[28]

At least when it comes to signifying southernness, I think, it has been difficult for cultural critics accustomed to traditional accounts of signification to come to terms with the unique irony and synthesis of recent retro movements. To many, four pudgy young white men in skinny ties do not look "cool"; they look like the same young white men in skinny ties chanting to keep James Meredith, say, out of Ole Miss—or others out of any other of dozens of public southern colleges in the early 1960s. But to see them that way is, ultimately, to miss the point: the young men are practicing *signifiance* and, most of all, stylin'. What is now happening in the middle-class white South is not the disappearance of the past but the appearance, through a multiplicity of media, of multiple pasts embedded in multiple places. There are so many of these pasts and places, in fact, that it is becoming possible to assemble an "identity" self-consciously out of an assortment of so many ironized object-cathexes that, unlike the mirror-objects and narrative fetishes of white southern modernism, designed to prevent a fragile, narcissistic ego from disintegrating, and unlike the commodity-fetishes of a kind of middle-class baby-

---

28. Jesse Berrett, "Swing Kids! A Revival Tries to Make History of Its Own," *Village Voice*, 2–8 September 1998 (<http://www.villagevoice.com/arts/9836/berrett.shtml>); Goldstein, "World War II Chic."

boomer white-male subcultural southernness, designed to provide an identity where none exists, we can expect to see from this new generation of middle-class southern whites a new attitude toward cultural coding. Some will embrace the "southern" subculture exclusively, but most will see that subculture's iconography, codes, and fetishes not as determinant legacies or burdens, but—along with the icons of whatever other subcultures they come to select—as ingredients in the recipe they use ironically to construct themselves. By foregrounding the arbitrariness of cultural codes, punk may—for those young white southerners alert to the implications—have freed white southern identity from its long, narcissistic gaze at its own ancestral navel.

Larry Brown's *Joe* and the Uses and Abuses of the "Region" Concept

Paul Lyons

What we seek in history is difference—and, through difference, a sudden revelation of our elusive identity. We seek not our origins but a way of figuring out what we are from what we are no longer.

—Pierre Nora, "Between Memory and History"

The problem of "regionalism" goes to the heart of U.S. cultural politics today and has become a key "site" for theorizing the effects of global culture and postmodernity on contemporary subjectivities. Until recently a derogatory term in the mainstream academy, where it was reserved for "country cousins," "regionalism" has come to be considered by many as "a more appropriate frame within which to read literature than . . . nationalism."[1] At the same time, the tendency among cultural theorists to describe every ex-centric challenge to a posited centric mainstream as "regional" has transfigured the once-stable place-term into an un-

1. W. H. New, quoted by Roberto Maria Dainotto, " 'All the Regions Do Smilingly Revolt': The Literature of Place and Region," *Critical Inquiry* 22 (Spring 1996): 487. For a more historicized version of the formation of American regionalism, see Robert L. Dorman, *Revolt of the Provinces: The Regionalist Movement in America, 1920–1945* (Chapel Hill: University of North Carolina Press, 1993), and Robert Brinkmeyer Jr.'s essay-review of the book, which notes that the region concept largely failed during the war years because its "emphasis on particularism and indigenous culture appeared . . . chauvinist, regressive, and racist—for many observers regionalism was the seedbed of fascism," in "Modern American Regionalism," *Mississippi Quarterly* 46 (1994): 650.

bounded space "within" which to imagine or contest communities. *Mu-tatis mutandis,* what were "regional" texts seem to have lost their purchase in contemporary discussions of "regionalism," in part because of their perceived hostility to multiculturalism. To what (if not to where), one might ask today, might "regionalism" refer?

In this sense, Philip Fisher's account of American Studies tracks devel-opment of the term *region* as much as it does a shift within American Studies from (nationalist) myth to contending (regionalist) rhetoric. Applying the logic of a long line of regional sociologists—who have con-sidered region as an ethnicity—Fisher argues that the first part of the twentieth century saw the rise of "regionalism that was not geographic but ethnic." The latter part of the century, Fisher continues, saw "a fur-ther episode of regionalism" centered around gender, race, queerness, and any other group that "sets out its claims against" the "central tech-nological culture" and "the older forces of education and mass represen-tation." In an elegant critique of this "metaphoric translation" of identity-politics into "regionalism," Roberto Mario Dainotto questions whether "regionalism's goal is different from . . . a centralized notion of nationalism" and finds that regionalism and nationalism "speak the same language" and "foster the same desires, menacing and childish, of purity and authenticity."[2] However, Dainotto's deconstruction of the region/na-tion binary seems to accept, as Fisher's account of the trajectory of Amer-ican Studies does, the collapse point between metaphoric uses of region and uses of the term connected to specific narratives about land, many of

2. Philip Fisher, "American Literary and Cultural Studies Since the Civil War," in *Re-drawing the Boundaries: The Transformation of English and American Literary Studies,* ed. Stephen Greenblatt and Giles Gunn (New York: Modern Language Association, 1992), 241, 242; Dainotto, " 'All the Regions,' " 505.

On interplays among region and ethnicity, see George Brown Tindall, *Natives and Newcomers: Ethnic Southerners and Southern Ethnics* (Athens: University of Georgia Press, 1995), and, in a different key, the works of John Shelton Reed, especially *One South: An Ethnic Approach to Regional Culture* (Baton Rouge: Louisiana State University Press, 1982) and *Southerners: The Social Psychology of Sectionalism* (Chapel Hill: University of North Carolina Press, 1983). For Reed, with occasional qualifications, the southerner is white, and the South, as a distinct ethnic culture, has long been "multicultural" *avant la lettre.* For a symmetrically opposed viewpoint, see Thadious M. Davis, who argues con-vincingly in "Race and Region," in *The Columbia History of the American Novel,* ed. Emory Elliot (New York: Columbia University Press, 1991), that whereas "race and re-gion" were "once considered inseparable, in the case of the South [they] are now two dis-tinct and discrete areas of inquiry," in that black literature cannot now be treated responsibly through southernist frames such as Reed's (436).

which have always emphatically considered themselves sub-nationalisms: "not quite a nation within a nation, but the next thing to it," as W. J. Cash said of the South. Neither Fisher nor Dainotto suggests that there are meaningful distinctions to be made among understandings of regionalism, whether in terms of U.S. cultural politics or in terms of attempts to view historic regions as critical sites of social resistance, reactionary or progressive. Fisher can write of "the full spectrum of regionalized culture" as including "Native American, Chicano, gay, black, lesbian, female" regionalisms, as if "Native Americans" did not have over five hundred distinct and federally recognized "nations." Dainotto's cautionary *overview* of the region concept likewise loses sight of the histories of struggle of peoples committed to place in specific locations, and considers the identification of Americans with region as a recent phenomenon. In a similarly unhistorical manner, "postmodern geographers" often imply that the "turn" to "localism" is largely to be understood as a reflexive resistance to economic encroachment. Such readings charge (or credit) transnational corporatism (TNCs) with forcing the local to the surface of consciousness, as if place-bound identities had somehow previously been repressed.[3]

Scholars of what might be provisionally (re)considered as American "sectionalism" know, of course, that regional "dividing lines" have a history in America going back to the colonial period, and that these have repeatedly been discussed in terms of nationalism. For instance, in "The

---

3. Fisher, "American Literary and Cultural Studies," 242; Dainotto, "'All the Regions,'" 500. TNCs seemingly respond to post-Fordist critiques by presenting themselves as proactive brokers for global cultural preservation. IBM's "Solutions for a Small Planet" campaign, for instance, suggests that laptop computers protect "culture," linking disparate groups in ways that enable them to maintain traditional ways. The literature on global/local conjunctions is extensive and by no means homogenous in arguing that transnational and local formations have superseded statism. For exemplary post-Fordist accounts, see Edward W. Soja, *Postmodern Geographies: The Reassertion of Space in Critical Social Theory* (London: Verso, 1989); Robert Reich, *The Work of Nations: Preparing Ourselves for 21st-Century Capitalism* (New York: Knopf, 1991); Masao Miyoshi, "A Borderless World? From Colonialism to Transnationalism and the Decline of the Nation State," *Critical Inquiry* 19 (Summer 1993): 128–51; Arif Dirlik, *After the Revolution: Waking to Global Capitalism* (Hanover, N.H.: Wesleyan University Press, 1994); Rob Wilson and Wimal Dissanayake, eds., *Global/Local: Cultural Production and the Transnational Imaginary* (Durham: Duke University Press, 1996); and Rob Wilson, *Reimagining the American Pacific: From "South Pacific" to "Bamboo Ridge" and Beyond* (Durham: Duke University Press, 2000). All are concerned with the cultural problem, as Miyoshi puts it, of how "to balance the transnationalization of economy and politics with the survival of local culture and history—without mummifying them with tourism and in museums" (147).

Significance of the Section in American History" (1925), Frederick Jackson Turner argued (conventionally, even then) the persistence of distinct "sections" in America and expressed guarded optimism about sections "becoming more and more the American version of the European nation." At the same time, Turner saw "section" as working in a stabilizing dialectic with the national political party system, in which each party of necessity works to "conciliate sectional differences within itself." In their monumental *American Regionalism*, Harold Odum and Harry Moore likewise expressed fears about sectionalisms as inherently separatist and nationalistic, and counterposed the integrative powers of the "region" concept. Given the sedimented history of the "problem," then, members of venerable institutions like southern literature are understandably reluctant to redefine their projects in relation to a post-statist theory that posits the "local" as a discovery, or to proliferating "regional" claims upon a reopened American cultural frontier. For them, the post-statist tendency to act as if U.S. historic regions were suddenly obsolescent (a matter for antiquarians and tourist boards), while privileging abstract notions of the "local," might seem to work in the service of the globalization it critiques. At the same time, the widespread sense of "regionalism" as a now-legitimate frame for resisting what Frank Chin calls "death by assimilation" makes the concerns of regional institutions resonate against those of an increasingly pluralistic mainstream American Studies. This coincidence of interests affords opportunities on all sides and suggests the uses of bringing geopolitically regional outlooks into dialogue with culturally regional ones.[4]

4. Frederick Jackson Turner, *History, Frontier, and Section*, introduction by Martin Ridge (Albuquerque: University of New Mexico Press, 1993), 112, 93. On American sectionalism, see Wallace Stegner, "Variations on a Theme by Crèvecoeur," in *The American West as Living Space* (Ann Arbor: University of Michigan Press, 1987), 63–86; and the essays in *All Over the Map: Rethinking American Regions*, ed. Edward L. Ayers et al. (Baltimore: Johns Hopkins University Press, 1996), especially Peter S. Onuf, "Federalism, Republicanism, and the Origins of American Sectionalism," 63–82, and Stephen Nissenbaum, "New England as Region and Nation," 38–61.

See "From Sectionalism to Regionalism," in Harold W. Odum and Harry Estill Moore, *American Regionalism: A Cultural-Historical Approach to National Integration* (New York: Henry Holt and Company, 1938), 35–51. For the purposes of this chapter, and in the face of a critical scene in which *region* means many things, I posit *sectionalism* as involving a sublimation of both "local" and "global" into a concept of *region* that acts as a sub-nationalism and ultimately resists a more critical regionalism.

For an exemplary overview and critique of the complexities of a "politics of location," in which, following Adrienne Rich, the gendered body functions as "location" and subjectivity may have transnational "locations," see Cindy Franklin, *Writing Women's Identities:*

This conjunction might be empowered by an ongoing redefinition of the value of regionalism that differs in emphasis from Fisher's agonist notion of regionalism as "Civil War within representation." In "Place in Fiction," Eudora Welty wrote that the term "regional . . . has no meaning for the insider doing the writing, because as far as he knows he is simply writing about life." The danger in "as far as he knows," of course, was that this sort of regional writer did not know very far—was essentially provincial. James D. Houston distinguishes between such provincialism and a "new and upgraded regional feeling": "Provincialism implies a narrowness of perspective, a stubborn attachment to the only place one really knows. It springs, as often as not, from a fear of other places and possibilities. This new regionalism is characterized by conscious choice, together with a growing awareness of our options." Houston's "upgraded regionalism," in its emphasis on "conscious choice," suggests a regionalism that recognizes broad connections to diverse cultures, and acknowledges the need not just to assert one's own experience as central but to put it in relation to other cultures from which it might learn without being swallowed in the process. In making no distinction between economic refugees and back-to-nature yuppies, Houston's "choice" suggests that regionalism offers nomad and indigene alike a set of sedimented but nonexclusive alternative values that the long-time resident of a place will not necessarily choose.[5]

The architectural critic Kenneth Frampton builds the political dimension of form-place into a conception of "critical regionalism." For Frampton, critical regionalism is a consciously selected *arrière-garde* position capable of cultivating "a resistant, identity-giving culture while at the same time having discreet recourse to universal technique." In critical practice, this means "distancing oneself equally from the Enlightenment myth of progress and from a reactionary, unrealistic impulse to return to

Contemporary Multigenre Anthologizing Practices (Madison: University of Wisconsin Press, 1997). This is an appropriate place to express my indebtedness to Franklin for incisive critiques of this paper.

5. Eudora Welty, "Place in Fiction," in *The Eye of the Story: Selected Essays and Reviews* (New York: Vintage Books, 1979), 132; James D. Houston, "One Can Think About Life After the Fish Is in the Canoe: Some Rambling Notes on the Regional Feeling," in *One Can Think About Life After the Fish Is in the Canoe and Other Coastal Sketches* (Santa Barbara: Capra Press, 1985), 60. For another vision of "New American Regionalism" that has the virtue of advocating a de-ruralizing of the concept of place, see Michael Kowalewski, "Writing in Place: The New American Regionalism," *American Literary History* 6, no. 1 (Spring 1994): 171–83.

. . . forms of the preindustrial past." Such a regionalism cannot gel as a "national" movement or as a theory proper, since it depends on decentralization and local/regional histories, but it can imagine mutually enriching dialogues and must recognize the need to work against the xenophobic aspects of place-bound "tradition." For Turner and Odum, the question of region is primarily part of an internal, nationalistic dialectic. For Frampton, on the other hand, critical regionalism responds to a pervasive crisis in (post)modernity. It registers momentous changes in the global system and seeks strategies to "mediate the impact of universal civilization," while avoiding romantic history, opportunistic invocations of place, or regressive conceptions of region.[6]

Among the most regressive of these conceptions is that which sees regions as dying "on and on," and regards this as symptomatic of historical decline, fall from grace, fracturing of value. This tenacious structure persists in ironic elegiac sayings like "even nostalgia's not what it used to be," which read as nostalgia for nostalgia. Like trick birthday candles, sectionalisms only seem to "go out." The South, for instance, has always been "postsouthern" but never "post," and has persistently sung gorgeous, doom-filled requiems for itself. As Jefferson Humphries acknowledges, "it is part of our pleasure . . . to assert that, as a literary culture, we are near the end in the South." Such discussions, fraught with the semiotics of a paralyzingly self-serving nostalgia, are less expressions of *fin-de-region* than demonstrations of reluctance to mobilize critically. Post-South discourse only discloses an anxiety-ridden awareness that, while the category southern is *not* imperiled by "post"-nesses, the rigor, politics, and popular significations of the term are increasingly visible. As much as ever, a mesh of southern "sublime objects"—signature clothes, music, architecture, eats, pulpit styles, and behaviors—"believe" southernness for the viewer within expanded American and global audiences. These "objects" may appear outdated, but if so they refuse to heed their expiration dates in uncanny ways, and even circulate back into regional consciousness from "without."[7]

6. Kenneth Frampton, "Towards a Critical Regionalism: Six Points for an Architecture of Resistance," in *The Anti-Aesthetic: Essays on Postmodern Culture,* ed. Hal Foster (Port Townsend, Wash.: Bay Press, 1983), 20, 21.

7. Jefferson Humphries, "Introduction: On the Inevitability of Theory," in *Southern Literature and Literary Theory,* ed. Jefferson Humphries (Athens: University of Georgia Press, 1992), xvii. Wallace Stegner makes the point succinctly: "We have been forever bidding farewell to the last of the Mohicans . . . or the vanishing wilderness. . . . We have made a tradition out of mourning the passing of things." *Where the Bluebird Sings to the Lemon-*

Faced by their images in the global media—or in a host of foreign discussions of "southernness" (as in the German academy)—"insiders" may appropriate or internalize behaviors attributed to them. It becomes hard to say which came first, the stereotype or the behavior—demand or product. In this, one might, following Raymond Williams, distinguish between emergent and residual place-bound literatures. With emergent literatures, communal self-imagining involves countermemory, or conscious renunciation of "prior" representations. But with sectionalism part of the project is precisely retaining contact with prior cultural production. The heritage that stereotypes attach to may not be attractive, but to do away with them might involve destroying vital grounds of identity. In Flannery O'Connor's words, "The anguish that most of us have observed for some time now has been caused not by the fact that the South is alienated from the rest of the country, but by the fact that it is not alienated enough, that every day we are getting more and more like the rest of the country, that we are being forced out not only of our many sins, but of our few virtues."[8]

In a world marked by the increasing intermingling of peoples, not disengaging the virtues from the sins threatens disastrous balkanization, and a perpetuation of ugly stereotypes into the foreseeable cyberspace future imagined by the likes of Neal Stephanson, whose southerner appears with confederate flag and "a baseball cap perched on the top of his head, tilted way back to expose the following words, tattooed in block letters across his forehead: MOOD SWINGS/RACIALLY INSENSITIVE."[9] Under-

---

ade Springs: Living and Writing in the West (New York: Penguin, 1992), 203–4. However, following Raymond Williams in The Country and the City (New York: Oxford University Press, 1973), one might consider such "mourning" a repetitive "structure of feeling" at the base of European modernity (12). Likewise, John Shelton Reed argued that "interaction with nonSoutherners can raise the regional consciousness of Southerners . . . by exposing them to regional differences and leading them to generalize about those differences: in other words, by generating regional stereotypes in Southerners." Southerners, 38. On the devastating effects of regional stereotypes on Appalachian communities, see Stephen William Foster, The Past Is Another Country: Representation, Historical Consciousness, and Resistance in the Blue Ridge (Berkeley: University of California Press, 1988).

8. Flannery O'Connor, Mystery and Manners: Occasional Prose, ed. Sally and Robert Fitzgerald (New York: Farrar, Straus and Giroux, 1962), 28–29.

9. Neal Stephanson, Snow Crash (New York: Bantam, 1992), 300–1. On the threat of balkanization today, see Tony Horwitz, who writes of "a cultural war flaring across the South . . . fuelled by a burgeoning and sophisticated cadre of Southern 'nationalists' who feed on modern fears of dwindling status and on nostalgic images of a South that is cohesive, distinct, and independent from the rest of America." "A Death for Dixie," New Yorker, 18 March 1996, 65. The article cites John Shelton Reed as saying that the "deepest

standing the historical contingency of regional identity on attitudes about race (and "race" as an effect that has meaning within time-place) would seem crucial for reenvisioning the future. As Arif Dirlik, who moves toward a syncretic mode of working through the trauma of postmodernity argues, "the local is valuable as a site for resistance to the global, but only to the extent that it also serves as the site of negotiation for abolishing inequality and oppression inherited from the past, which is a condition of any promise it may have for the future." Dirlik does not say how consensus will be reached about the nature of justice and can seem to be reinstalling a center-periphery model of Reason. At the same time, Dirlik argues, like Frampton, that "it is neither possible nor desirable to dismiss the new awareness that is the product of modernity as just another trick of Eurocentrism." Rather, it is now necessary to speak of "critical localisms" that subject "the present to critical evaluation from past perspectives" but retain "in the evaluation of the past the critical perspectives afforded by modernity."[10] What still needs to be heard, in the reading of regional texts, are the affirmative resonances of historic sections in this moment when present answers to past, and local resists global.

*   *   *

If there be no constructive impulse behind the historical one, if the clearance of rubbish be not merely to leave the ground free for the hopeful living future to build its house, if justice alone be supreme, the creative instinct is sapped and discouraged.

    —Friedrich Nietzsche, "On the Uses and Disadvantages of History for Life"

Larry Brown's *Joe* (1991) immediately suggests ways in which, however much the South has changed (or at however different paces the Souths

---

grievances are cultural," in that "they feel that they don't get any respect, and that their ancestors are being dissed" (72). However, a myriad of contemporary Hollywood films, such as *A Time to Kill* and *Dead Man Walking*, present the redneck as suffering less from cultural grievance than from a blind xenophobia emerging from faulty baptism.

    10. Dirlik, *After the Revolution*, 108. See also Dirlik's fine essay, "The Global in the Local," in *Global/Local*, ed. Wilson and Dissanayake, 21–45. There is a sense, however, in which the term *local* as it is used in such analyses refers to what Benedict Anderson calls "imagined community." For Anderson in *Imagined Communities: Reflections on the Origin and Spread of Nationalism* (1983; rev. ed., London: Verso, 1991), "all communities larger than the primordial village . . . are imagined. Communities are to be distinguished not by their falseness/genuineness, but by the style in which they are imagined" (6). For this paper, it might be good as well to retrieve the quite different nineteenth-century American understanding of *local* as related to "local-color" movements. See, for instance, Josephine Donovan, "Breaking the Sentence: Local-Color Literature and Subjugated Knowledges," in

are changing), it elicits books that *are experienced* as southern by readers, publishers, reviewers, critics, and that cannot simply be considered "retro," forms of nostalgia, aesthetic recycling, or literary tourism. If southernness is a market term, this need not contradict the pride that authors feel in asserting their affiliation, however fraught such affiliation might be in American culture.

Beneath its taut, gritty narrative of rural life in a contemporary Mississippi more strewn with ramshackle structures than malls, *Joe* reads as, among other things, an enactment of tensions between a sectional preoccupation with a fantasmal "pre-" and an anxiety before an atavistic "post-." Nostalgia need not be for a simpler, purer, more integrated society. In *Joe,* it involves a hard-nosed, blue-collar attachment to individual freedom, without illusions about some less-violent, homier past, or fear of losing the "sense of home." The "post," in contrast, foresees loss through integration, destructive corporatism, over-regulation, a legal system stacked against the poor and psychically repressive. Because of its intonation of caught-in-betweenness, *Joe* functions as an exemplary text case for critiquing the usefulness of theories of global/local conjunctions and American cultural remapping for the residual regionalist. The book might be read as constituting one literary mode of "approaching" critical regionalism in that, in its very recalcitrance, it implicitly evokes tension between tenacious sectionalist modes and tropes (with their troublesome organicism) and a critical regionalism that might involve re-signifying these tropes of affiliation from within, and resituating southernness on its own shifting grounds. A book that leaves legible its own "betweenness" suggests the possibility of affirmative choices.

Whatever else reviewers comment on about *Joe,* they celebrate its southern "authenticity," though the review form precludes engaging the problem of what secures authenticity. One might, for brevity's sake, argue that if nothing guarantees it (and that, historically, "authenticity" is an outsider's term that self-servingly elides internal differences), this does not mean it cannot be useful to make tentative definitions, or distinctions between grounded and tourist invocations of place. Historians have never considered "region" or "section" as deterministically real concepts; although Turner spoke, in the Crèvecoeurian mode, of waves

---

The (Other) American Traditions: Nineteenth-Century Women Writers, ed. Joyce W. Warren (New Brunswick, N.J.: Rutgers University Press, 1993), 232, on how local-colorist black and women writers resisted an internal colonization with which regionalism was at times complicit. For Donovan, *local-colorist* (female/black) is thus a more "insurrectionary" term than "the tamer, more acceptable, *regionalist*" (male/white).

of migration "pouring their plastic pioneer life into geographic moulds," he also invoked an eclectic amalgam of other factors: "a geography of political habit—a geography of opinion, of material interests, of racial stocks, of physical fitness, of social traits, of literature, of the distribution of men of ability, even of religious denominations." For reading regional texts, Paula Gunn Allen's definition, which foregrounds region as process while retaining the aboriginal context muted in Turner's analysis, is particularly useful: "A truly Southwestern work almost inevitably combines the ancient, the medieval, and the contemporary in ways that yield maximal meaning comprehensible within several contexts." For Gunn Allen, "cultural geography is more important than the geopolitical place" (seen as borders that have crossed people, as well as landscapes that various groups have placed borders around). To this might be added a concern with cultural maintenance, along with a rendering of regional "complicities of language, local references, and the unformulated rules of living know-how."[11]

By all of the above criteria, *Joe* is certainly authentic. One *could*, perhaps, read *Joe* out of southernist frames, but much would be lost by doing so. The book "convinces" the reader through the specificity of its landscapes, ethnoscapes, languages, and its participation in a strand (white masculinist)[12] of southern tradition. It has the aura of having grasped some substance of culture that percolates up into a convincing

11. Turner, *History, Frontier, and Section*, 106, 111; Paula Gunn Allen, "Preface," in *Writing the Southwest*, ed. David King Dunaway and Sara L. Spurgeon (New York: Plume, 1995), xxiii. For more detailed developments of this concept, see Leslie Marmon Silko's essays "Language and Literature from a Pueblo Indian Perspective," in *English Literature: Opening Up the Canon*, ed. Leslie A. Fiedler and Houston A. Baker Jr. (Baltimore: Johns Hopkins University Press, 1981) and "Landscape, History, and the Pueblo Imagination: From a High and Arid Plateau in New Mexico," *Antaeus* 57 (1986); and Richard Hamasaki, "Mountains in the Sea: Emerging Literatures of Hawai'i," in *Readings in Pacific Literature*, ed. Paul Sharrad (Wollongong, Australia: University of Wollongong Press, 1993). Marc Augé, *Non-Places: Introduction to an Anthropology of Supermodernity*, trans. John Howe (London: Verso, 1995), 101. Augé also invokes Vincent Descombes's notion of a character's "rhetorical country" that "ends where his interlocutors no longer understand the reasons he gives for his deeds and actions, the criticisms he makes or the enthusiasms he displays" (quoted, 108).

12. Since the Civil Rights movement and the rise of feminism in the sixties, "new" strands of southern fiction have contributed to the reconceptualizing of southern studies. Within some anthologies that claimed to speak for "the South" as a whole, white women fared much better than persons of color, in part perhaps because of a troublesome relation between regionalism (with its exclusionary, conservative tendencies) and a multiculturalism that is, in a disturbing sense, what provincial regionalisms defend against.

present, where cultural mores change slowly. This suggests that if the local is fully subject to the global, as postmodern geographers assume, *Joe* might be heard asking, "So what?" Postmodern geographers may see the local as fully global, while subjects whose affiliations are primarily regional may in complex, imperfectly conscious ways appropriate what suits them from the global without priorities in their lives being reordered by the encounter. For instance, in *Joe* TVs, VCRs, and radios are often on, but only highlight Joe's psychic distance from the consumer culture around him: "He twisted the dial around, and the radio snarled and whined while quick-speaking Spaniards exhorted their wares and somebody screamed CASH MONEY and the twangy garbled country music flared and diminished amidst the roading and fuzz and static until finally he snapped it off. The road twisted through strands of pine, hills of hardwood timber green as Eden."[13] Joe Ransom's search through the no longer exclusively white/black voices of an increasingly consumer-oriented South ends in static.

If materialistic Spaniards (Hispanics?) are within his band-width, he need not listen to them. If the "outside" is "inside," it *can* be "snapped off," tuned out. The repetition of "twisted" in relation to the radio "dial" and then country "road" sets the two up as cognitive alternatives for Joe: the seductions of a "twisted" garish multicultural consumer society that "garble[s] country music," *or* the road back into the lyric and Edenic "hills of hardwood." Likewise, when Joe watches TV he sees "things happening on the television screen without seeing them and [hears] the words the actors [are] saying without hearing them . . . like dreams, real but not real" (30).[14] It isn't clear what the book thinks of these TVs, which seem always half-ignored—"they had a movie going on the TV and VCR but the sound was low" (267). The TV seems neither something to resist nor something that makes individuals feel romantically or futilely anachronistic, demanding change.

Part of the book's "southern" mode is its refusal to establish "theoriz-

---

13. Larry Brown, *Joe* (Chapel Hill: Algonquin Books, 1991), 75 (hereafter cited parenthetically in the text).

14. This quality of minimizing the importance of references to popular culture seems a deliberate characteristic of a certain kind of regional literature. In *Bastard Out of Carolina* (New York: Penguin, 1993), which might be seen as a woman-centered perspective on a community whose male characters share many predilections with those in *Joe*, Dorothy Allison typically refers to characters watching TV without mentioning what they are watching: "Daddy Glen was sitting in the living room in front of the television set with the sound turned down low" (77).

ing" vantage points outside the literary matrix. The book's "literariness" is thoroughly traditional, an implicit argument for regional reproduction: its stakes are, as allegorically as ever, a concern for the eradication of the ancestral landscape, and the theme still feels like an epochal metaphor, redolent of Faulkner. In *The Bear*, for instance, Faulkner emblematizes the "final" moment of a mode through the interlocked figures of Boon, Lion, and that metaphor on hind legs, Old Ben: "It fell all of a piece, as a tree falls, so that all three of them, man dog and bear, seemed to bounce once." The connection between bear and forest is literalized when the reader learns that hunting has stopped because "the lumber company moved in and began to cut the timber."[15]

The "hero" in *Joe* no longer hunts in the forest for sport; rather, he hunts the forest itself in the least sportsmanlike manner, for profit, without any sustaining connection to the land or traditional coming-of-age rituals. Brown suggests an inversion of old hunter myths in an episode where Joe carves up a deer found snagged in barbed wire. In part through his complicity in such inversions, Joe becomes representative of a generation that participates uneasily in cutting itself off from crucial aspects of an identity that imagines itself nonetheless connected to a "first settler," rebel mentality. Joe, with his "scarred knuckles, outsized, knotty with gristle" (256), and Gary, the young illiterate worker he befriends (a "kindred soul" whose imitation of Joe suggests a perpetuation of ways), are pulled toward an unregulated "settler" past where the region's guiding philosophy was established. As Joe puts it, "Ain't nobody gonna run my life for me" (123). In the present, this involves a largely class-based distrust of the legal process, so that vigilante justice will ultimately be heroicized. The linkage of past-present emerges in connection with the collapsing cabin that Gary restores.

Gary seems designed to represent a consciousness cut off from contemporary consumer culture: "The boy was fascinated by the logs. He touched their axed surfaces, felt the dried mud chinked in the cracks. He thought he would have liked living in times when men built houses like this one" (32). Likewise, Joe mentally associates the house with a pioneer

---

15. Elsewhere, in the hilarious and uncharacteristically metafictional story "Discipline," Brown satirizes the literary establishment's obsession with Faulkner (and a hyperventilating southernness) through the figure of a writer on trial for "secretly copying Faulkner . . . using heavy, frightening imagery. . . . Ignoring punctuation . . . making your characters talk like Beeder Mackey on LSD." See Larry Brown, *Big Bad Love* (Chapel Hill: Algonquin Books, 1990), 131–32. William Faulkner, *Go Down, Moses* (New York: Vintage Books, 1990), 237, 301.

ethos: "From where he lay Joe could see under the house and see the sandstone foundation, the logs resting on strategic rocks maybe chipped flat by some pioneer with high boots and a muslin shirt. The logs had long cracks and they were huge and they bore on their sides many axe marks" (313). Joe's connection to this frontier mentality is underscored throughout the narrative: "He backed out into the road and headed west, toward where there were dirt roads and big deer green-eyed in the light and no lawmen patrolling the old blacktopped roads. He got a beer from the cooler and opened it and rolled down the window and stuck his arm out. There was good music on the radio. The dark trees enveloped the road in a canopy of lush growth" (293). The passage shows the persistence of the impulse to "head west" along dusty roads into a wilderness without "lawmen"; "old" impulse and new "products" don't seem in contradiction. With a writer like Brown, who has the rowdy, heavily inflected southern stuff, the ability to turn sorry squalor comic-side out while remaining tuned in to and honest about social realities (including the pleasures and costs of alcoholism), the southern tradition cooperates powerfully to absorb product references.

Joe's opening places the reader familiar with southern literature in a domain of familiar images:

> They trudged on beneath the burning sun, but anyone watching could have seen that they were almost beaten. They passed over a bridge spanning a creek that held no water as their feet sounded weak drumbeats, erratic and small in the silence that surrounded them. No cars passed these potential hitchhikers. The few rotting houses perched on the hillsides of snarled vegetation were broken-backed and listing, discarded dwellings where dwelled only field mice and owls. It was as if no one lived in this land or ever would again, but they could see a red tractor toiling in a field far off, silently, a small dust cloud following. (1)

The seemingly beaten, anthropomorphized setting, the oppressive sun that makes the language seem dusty and monotonous like a documentary spool, the abandoned, collapsing houses and rapacious vegetation are tropes long associated with southern fiction. This is the vanquished, evacuated setting of aftermath, emptied of all sound but that feebly brought into it, the site of a disastrous heat that dehydrates the spirit and the soil and makes characters, tractors, and prose toil to move. No one watches the unnamed "they"; the creek holds no water; disembodied feet drum out a defeated marching beat; no cars pass so the hitchhikers are not hitchers; no one dwells in the "discarded" houses; the dust of the landscape shrouds the tractors and the perspective minimalizes their importance, returning the reader to a structure of the long run—of the old interplay between laborer and land.

*   *   *

The starting point of critical elaboration is the consciousness of what one really is, and is "knowing thyself" as a product of the historical process to date which has deposited in you an infinity of traces, without leaving an inventory. . . . Therefore it is imperative at the outset to compile such an inventory.

—Antonio Gramsci, Prison Notebooks

In entering Brown's monumentalized landscape, the Joneses (and *Joe's* readers) enter a realm of quirky (a)temporality, a sort of "prepost"-erous southern time in which a forgotten past (as opposed to the modernist southern over-remembered past) so saturates the land and the present and its language as to become unconsciously *of* it. Allen Tate's idea of southern literature as a "consciousness of the past in the present" seems irrelevant. If anything, Brown's characters have regressed from this vision rather than "advanced" into some rupturing postmodern beyond. While the elemental tableau—with its Steinbeckian outsize quality and Depression-era graininess—gestures toward (and potentially empties) the platitude that the essential pilgrimage of life remains the same, human identity in this scene constitutes itself within place figured as a form of temporality because place has absorbed time/history. Repeatedly, Brown's blistering landscapes overgrow or reclaim historical reading itself: thus, Joe stops to "run his hand over the old knife scars of names and dates healed almost unreadable in the bark of a giant beech" (111), or the landscape bears traces of erasures—"Fire had swept over it a long time ago, yet some of the trunks were still blackened" (110).

Rather than being ancestors of the Joads or Compsons, Brown's "Joneses" appear like fallout from time and tradition. They are the poorest white trash, unredeemed by positive qualities except Gary's pre-ethical loyalty to kin and those who help him. Similarly, the ruined cabin that the Joneses reclaim seems to predate the southern ancestral houses that have been collapsing prognostically since Poe's "Usher" and G. W. Cable's "Belles Demoiselles Plantation." The Joneses' cabin has been built by some unnamed "pilgrim," but the Joneses stagger onto the scene like historyless pseudo-pilgrims. They are not settlers but the unsettled, who seem to confirm Dainotto's notion of region as "an indestructible entity that transcends and survives history to remain everlastingly the same."[16] As the narrative proceeds, though, the reader learns that the

16. Dainotto, " 'All the Regions,' " 492.

cabin only seems historyless; Wade (Gary's monstrous father) lived in it before being driven from the region because of his involvement in a ghastly hanging: "It was Clinton Baker they hung. He was down there three days before they found him. Hangin' in a tree and buzzards eating on him" (207). Wade lives out the consequences of this action, and its effects are visited upon his family. In a world where misdeeds follow misdeeds, there is no easy way to break the cycle. Barker's hanging recalls ritual lynching and implies the psychic legacy that such events exert, which implicitly contribute to the (white male) southerner's reputed mood-swing problems. The lynching, associated with a debased frontier ethos as well as with slavery and Reconstruction, lingers over the land: when Joe enters a yard, he stops beside a "single tree, where a rope hung" (67).

Writing of various traditions, authors like Leslie Marmon Silko (Laguna Pueblo), Bruce Chatwin (on the songlines of aboriginal Australia), Denis Kawaharada (Hawai'i), William Butler Yeats (Ireland), Epeli Hau'ofa (Tonga), and Eudora Welty (Mississippi) have argued that knowledge of landscape is literally historical knowledge. In these traditions, however, relation to land differs; some have had land taken, others have been takers. In this sense, Welty's comment that "place is forever illustrative: it is a picture of what man has done and imagined, it is his visible past, result" emphasizes that connection to land may be a complex predicament.[17] In *Joe,* the disconnection of people from land suggests a perverse stake in a segment of the contemporary South living out the effects of violence. Their "forgetting" even expresses a latent desire to repeat history. Although Faulkner's Gavin Stevens may have been right in suggesting that at one time every southern boy carried around an image of Pickett's Charge, Brown portrays a generation of dirt-poor southerners whose "culture" is that of not knowing. His characters—with the exception of World War II veteran John Coleman, who sits around drinking and reading Civil War books, functioning as an archive of local lore—ignore history's monuments that, rigid and bespattered as they are, continue to signify: in the square of one town, "the stained marble soldier raised in tribute to a long dead and vanquished army went on with his charge, the tip of his bayonet broken off by tree pruners, his epaulets covered with pigeon droppings" (138–39). Lacking cultural memory, this South cannot feel nostalgia or feel that there is any former dignity to be upheld. Lacking a sense of place-history, these characters lack a sense of future direction.

17. Welty, "Place in Fiction," 129.

Thus, despite all the changes in the "outer" world that smuggle their ways into this text and the characters' homes and filling stations in the form of brand names, TV shows, and sporting events, more remains the same than otherwise. Whether or not Brown's characters fantasize about products ("I'd buy me one of them SS Chevelles with a automatic transmission and tinted windows" [83]), characteristically customizing them according to local taste, Brown's is still a world where one can speak of workers as virtually prehuman forms in a land that has forgotten time, "toiling shapes remorseless and wasted and indentured to the heat that rose from the earth and descended from the sky in a vapor" (248). It is their very unconsciousness of the forces that limit their consciousnesses that allows characters in *Joe* to retain the sense of being in control of their reckless destinies. They do not worry about being contained within a larger culture that is not like them, and they have no framework for identifying themselves as subjects within history, class struggle, or homogenizing mass culture. They retain a sense of freedom *from* that gives them a freedom *to* preserve their own order of things.

Balances shift slowly. If there is little meditation of how social movements like feminism are relayed from the national media back into specific sites, the book does imply a measure of changing consciousness. The few women characters in the book are sympathetically drawn and shown as increasingly independent, though they are still to some degree defined in relation to their need (or lack of it) for men or by their vulnerability before male violence. Blacks and whites seem locked together in a dysfunctional intimacy; the Civil Rights Movement may have changed things legally, but it seems to have had little effect on social organization. For the most part, blacks work for whites who work for someone else. Most of the time, Joe keeps up a light banter with workers he's known all his life and whom he is concerned about as people, so long as they pull their weight. At other times, Brown shows a deeply ingrained racial fear getting the better of Joe. He dreams of "stealthy blacks with knives" (11). Likewise, in a passage that shows racism mixing with the pop-culture of Oz, Joe jokes, "My niggers can't work in the rain. Afraid they gonna melt" (68).[18] Fixating on the present as if it had no context, racism here

18. These "phobias" or attitudes are of course Joe's. Brown makes the relation between a black and white southerner central and complex in his deeply affecting novel *Dirty Work* (Chapel Hill: Algonquin Books, 1989). A lengthy conversation between two badly maimed Vietnam veterans, with the war as an important backdrop, the book suggests a disfiguring legacy of racial division in the South as well as a moment of transcending those divisions.

centers on labor, on the fear that "others" may steal one's job and/or are too lazy to work. So Gary says that his own nomadic family moved because "wetbacks" (116) took their jobs, or Joe tells his workers, "You've laid on your goddamned ass all your life and drawed welfare and people like me's paid for it" (197). Such moments show history, race, and region knotted within the consciousness of a man presented as hard but decent within the shifting standards of his time-place—a man who differs essentially from Wade in the understanding and application of the values he has inherited.

In presenting Joe's consciousness, Brown favors a hyper-remniscient *being in the scene,* less a displayed knowledge of psychologies than a conveyed sense of motivational inner tides. We can almost predict how Joe will act, but though we are led to the edges of Joe's consciousness, Brown refuses to open out his thoughts. This stresses consciousness as deeply ingrained, not a matter of forebrain or analytical internal debate but of something residual within subjectivity that is constituted by a perpetual, imperceptible dialogue between received ideas and lived relations. The method is at its best in one of Joe's introspective moments as he reflects on his livelihood. By day, Joe heads a team involved in "deadnin timber." They spend their days shooting trees with poison guns. The forest will die slowly and be on the ground in six to eight years so Weyerhauser can plant pines. Although some might argue that Weyerhauser, having done impact studies, acts with an ecological conscience and creates valuable jobs, Brown's text presents what is happening to the anthropomorphized forest as a murder: the workers "kill" it; it looks like "the red ground [is] bleeding" (25). Brown lets us know that Joe reflects on what he is doing, though not specifically *what* or *how* he reflects about it:

> The whole party moved off into the deep shade with their poison guns over their shoulders, the merciless sun beating down. . . . The heat stood in a vapor over the land, shimmering waves of it rising up from the valleys . . . Joe stood in the bladed road with his hands on his hips and watched them go. He surveyed his domain and the dominion he held over them not lightly, his eyes half-lidded and sleepy under the dying forest. He didn't feel good about being the one to kill it. He guessed it never occurred to any of them what they were doing. But it had occurred to him. (202–3)

Brown emphasizes Joe's connection to the land by applying the same verb (*stood*) to him and the heat, and by suggesting that he dies out of consciousness as the forest dies. At the same time, his proprietary relation to the land is underscored and undermined by the attribution of similar

feelings to Wade, who has been described as "drinking a beer and looking off into the trees as if this magnitude of land were his and he was
wondering what it was worth" (92). Joe argues a relation between such
attitudes toward land and right living. Throughout, Brown contrasts images of hard-working farmers with inversions of that life, where characters like Wade "harvest" dumpsters for cans (51), think of ditches "rich
with cans" (155). In contrast, almost as a rebuke to characters like Wade
and Russell, who are presented as "burning" with "meanness ingrained"
(88), Brown presents idyllic pastorals: "They coasted to a stop beside the
growing cotton, where the honeysuckle blossoms hung threaded through
the hogwire in bouquets of yellow and white, the hummingbirds and bees
constant among them . . . riding the Summer air" (209). This is argument
by tone and juxtaposition. For authors like Wendell Berry and Gary Snyder, canny pastoralism inclines toward local activism and common cause
enables coalitions that might redistribute power within communities.[19]
Joe does not take the reader to this point. There are glimmers of eco-
consciousness in John Coleman, who is something of a critical regionalist
in taking what he likes from pop culture while retaining a sense of what
is primary to him: "Coleman would hear a song he recognized and, once
in a while, turn the radio up, then turn it back down when the song was
over." Watching a redtail, Coleman says, "I'm glad they protected them
hawks," to which Joe answers: "I sure like to watch them" (285–86).
The moment illustrates the difference between a conscious endorsement
of protective measures and an implicit recognition of their desirability.

For the most part, though, Brown rarely provides narrative distance
from the perspectives of his principals, and even in these moments it pulls
up suggestively short: "The owner sighed. Dealing with these people over
and over. With the depths of their ignorance. The white ones like this
were worse than the black ones like this. Where they came from he didn't
know. How they existed was a complete mystery to him. How they lived
with themselves. He tossed his list onto the counter without ever thinking
he might have helped to make them that way" (178). How, the passage
asks without answering (and not independently of its exposure of
pseudo-liberal racism), is every person in a community responsible for
and related to the development of every other person? Likewise, as sug-

19. See Wendell Berry, "Writer and Region," *Hudson Review* 40, no. 1 (1987): 15–30;
and Gary Snyder, "Poetry, Community, and Climax," in *Interchange: A Symposium on Regionalism, Internationalism, and Ethnicity in Literature*, ed. Linda Spaulding and Frank
Stewart (Honolulu: InterArts Hawaii, 1980), 47–59.

gested, Joe is placed in a position of "dominion" over the landscape, and thus over the community. If Joe doesn't feel good about being "the one to kill" the forest, it's partly because, in ways pressing at the edges of his sensibility ("half-lidded" implies that he half-sees and connects him again to Wade, who sees through "sloe-lidded eyes" [233]), he's performing a self-slaughter, poisoning his own "domain." The text suggests that the death he is spreading is catching up to him: "Joe raised his head and looked far down the tract to the dying trees they'd injected three days before. It was as if a blight had grown across the emerald tops of the forest and was trying to catch up to where they stood" (22). Metaphorically, to "stab" and "poison" the forest resembles allowing southern letters to become commodified in relation to outside consumption habits, to disengage it from its roots and sell transplanted versions of southern "tract." If this is one of *Joe*'s warnings, it is implicitly a call for critical regionalism, whether or not Brown, or Joe, or *Joe,* cares to be specific about what is at stake in bringing "blight" to the "emerald" trees.

Joe is finally neither redneck text nor simply backroads verisimilitude. What can at first seem reactionary in the book moves toward a cannily ambivalent sense of the degree to which the regional culture it represents must move beyond a self-defeating bigotry and exploitative relation to land. The book balances lyricism and humor with violence, avoiding at all costs a jaded Kmart realism; it at once endorses masculinist viewpoints and foregrounds their inadequacies. Although critical of some local attitudes, it maintains a strong sense of identification with its "time-place." *Joe* does not end, as Lee Smith's *Oral History* does, with a culture faced with its theme-park double; rather, it closes with birds headed toward "their ancient primeval nesting lands" being "swallowed . . . up into the sky and the earth that met it and the pine trees always green and constant against the great blue wilderness that lay forever beyond" (345).

In this, *Joe* finally warns against a reading that would make the regional text overly determined by the latest encroachments of economic forces; as Mike Featherstone argues, "not everyone is affected by, or conscious of . . . globalization processes to the same extent." Residually regional literatures have demonstrably flourished in America at moments when major changes in the modes of production threatened traditional patterns of life, but it is reductive to speak of sectional consciousness at any given juncture as primarily the product of changes in the structure of capital.[20] Economic or horizontal explanations must be balanced with more vertical cultural, historical, and ideological ones, including those reproduced through the institutions of literature. This is not to say that such institutions and the traditions they perpetuate or critique exist without translocal economic and cultural linkages, but to suggest that received cultural patterns exert imaginative pressures that operate in idiosyncratic ways through individual writers in particular locations.

✻   ✻   ✻

The bulldozing of an irregular topography into a flat site is clearly a technocratic gesture which aspires to a condition of absolute *placelessness*.
　　　　　—Kenneth Frampton, "Towards a Critical Regionalism"

In a discussion of "supermodernity," Marc Augé distinguishes between "places" and "non-places" as follows: "If a place can be defined as relational, historical and concerned with identity, then a space which cannot be defined as relational, or historical, or concerned with identity will be a non-place. . . . Supermodernity produces non-places, meaning spaces which are not themselves anthropological places and which . . . do not integrate with earlier places."[21] Critical regionalism opposes the de-differentiation of supermodernity, finding "in" place an important relational ground conductor to identity that implies with it a whole nexus of residual attitudes; it sees region as an appropriate frame both for renegotiating these attitudes and for positioning local cultures in relation to both contiguous locales that share family resemblances and political concerns, and to translocal systems. Supermodernity may suggest a utopian quality of "non-places" within which categories like race/gender/queerness no longer carry predetermining significances, but if standardized spaces accomplish egalitarian neutrality, it may be through reducing all relations to the casual and economic. In an age of increased nomadism, the critical regionalist thus envisions region as inevitably more polyphonic, inflected by newcomers, but one that keeps as a "bass line," to

---

20. Mike Featherstone, "Localism, Globalism, and Cultural Identity," in *Global/ Local*, ed. Wilson and Dissanayake, 46. For a traditional analysis of this sort, see Richard H. Brodhead on how "regionalism became the dominant genre in America at the moment when local-cultural economies felt strong pressures from new social forces, from a growingly powerful social model that overrode previously autonomous systems and incorporated them into translocal agglomerations," in *Cultures of Reading: Scenes of Reading and Writing in Nineteenth-Century America* (Chicago: University of Chicago Press, 1993), 119.

21. Augé, *Non-Places*, 77–78.

use Jean Starobinski's analogy, the ancient places and rhythms that undergird a "place." As Augé notes, these rhythms (intertwined with the clichés that go into every sectional hopper) are not obliterated by modernity but pushed "into the background," where they function as "gauges indicating the passage and continuation of time." As Walter Benjamin has it, to change the metaphor, the past illuminates present identities in "lightning flashes."[22]

Despite the prevalence in every historic U.S. section of centers for regional studies and sizable regional apparatuses, global/local theorists confronted with the superabundance of the present, the excess of information, and the collapse of space have had little use for "region" except as a micro-marketing term. They tend to dismiss "region" as the kind of nostalgic nationalism that sectional theorizing produces by sublimating both "global" and "local." But although the "local" may be the site of particular, crucial resistances to development and supermodernity, its relation to the sectional "regions" ingrained in individual and national American psyches cannot be overlooked by careful analysts, whatever the critical desire to do so. As "local" text, *Joe* refers to particular road junctions and a rhetorical country in which "the word travel[s] fast" (239) within a circumscribed location and reputation affects the practice of everyday life, whatever products one consumes. At the same time, *Joe* clearly perpetuates—in its modes of telling, its tropes, its landscapes and codes, its relation to history—a larger understanding of "region" as crucial to the formation of individual consciousness.

The "region concept" thus remains a more appropriate frame for books like *Joe* than local, national, or transnational frames, as it implicitly does for discussing relations among the peoples occupying its "postage stamp" of Mississippi. The book even suggests that global/local interactions figure in inverse proportion to the extent to which regional identity matters. Many of the diasporic notions of "location of culture" characteristic of major urban centers do not obtain in this rural culturalscape. At the same time, *Joe* demonstrates how contemporary regional fiction about the rural poor, which can be sloppily made to stand in for the (im)pure, authentic heart of the entire traditional section, cannot avoid involvement with postmodern problematics. The text builds toward recognition within its eponymous hero of the necessity for becoming more conscious about powers that molest the local from within and without. However, in its caught-betweenness, *Joe* remains a text that

22. Quoted ibid., 77.

dramatizes the resistance to overcoming a certain chauvinistic consciousness. If *Joe* presents people often choked by hate, their latent aggressions released by alcohol, it also presents a world in which perpetrators generally get something like what they deserve. The book both marks and gestures beyond its own limitations, suggesting abuses of the region concept as well as potential uses, not just for understanding contemporary subjectivities but for challenging them to inaugurate change.

Traditionally, sectionalists have heroicized the struggle of individual will (shaped by regional ethos) against incursion and poverty rather than analyzing the relays between global and national forces and regional self-understanding. In the South, this is in part because literary critics have tended to conceive of their vocation as a form of humanist praxis—as active upholding of values and forms of community—rather than as an intervention in the messy world of cultural politics. *Joe* certainly invites (and reflects) such humanist criticism, with its presentation of a "hero" who gives his life as "ransom" to repay conduct he abhors, implying an extralegal system of retributive justice. But, as Michael Kreyling puts it, such readings, like the formalism with which they are historically associated, "satisfy the desire . . . to avoid dealing with narrative on its own shifting, complex ground." Today, this shifting ground includes a sense of the connectedness of race and gender to notions of regions, and of the existence of counter-hegemonic claims on regional space. In no way does the continued significance of residual regionalisms preclude the great variety of alter/native narratives increasingly seen to cut across sectional lines, such as those discussed in Ramon Saldivar's exemplary *Chicano Narratives,* or those produced by diasporic movements. A look at regional anthologies from the Southwest and the West in particular suggests that a place-centered multiculturalism, in its simultaneous decentralizing and recentering, might avoid many of the problems with a nationalized multiculturalism. In *New Writers of the Purple Sage,* for instance, editor Russell Martin argues that the stories he selects are all identifiably "Western," but that, in selecting them, "diversity seemed the only consideration of much editorial merit. I wanted the collection to reflect the geographic, ethnic, and stylistic diversity of the region's writers." The region concept, that is, might embrace the contributions of newcomers while re-affirming the value of geographically and historically inflected cultural patterns and priorities. At the same time, although there are inevitable limitations to what metropolitan global theories contribute to discussions of residual regionalisms, it is also clear that "any version of the *local* or *regional* . . . will have to be spread upon the cognitive map of global postmodernity." A critical regionalism acknowledges these conditions and possibilities and cannot ignore the concept of historic "regions" in the U.S. as value-full, rich, sedimented cultural ground for working through the predicaments or possibilities of contemporary culture.[23]

23. Michael Kreyling, "*The Fathers*: A Postsouthern Narrative Reading," in *Southern Literature,* ed. Humphries, 186–87; Ramon Saldivar, *Chicano Narratives: The Dialectics of Difference* (Madison: University of Wisconsin Press, 1990); Russell Martin, ed., *New Writers of the Purple Sage: An Anthology of Contemporary Western Writing* (New York: Penguin, 1992), xx; Rob Wilson, "Blue Hawaii: *Bamboo Ridge* as 'Critical Regionalism,'" in *What Is in a Rim? Critical Perspectives on the Pacific Region Idea,* ed. Arif Dirlik (Boulder, Colo.: Westview Press, 1993), 286. Wilson's reading exemplifies the "striated" strategies of the critical regionalist in describing the emerging literatures of Hawai'i as sharing "a sustained commitment to articulating a shared *ground,*" which involves a complex relation to the indigenous peoples of Hawai'i. For a further illustration of the complexities attending competing claims to cultural geography in Hawai'i, see Candace Fujikane, "Between Nationalisms: Hawaii's Local Nation and Its Troubled Paradise," in *Critical Mass: A Journal of Asian American Cultural Criticism* 2 (1994): 23–57.

PART II **MAPPING THE REGION**

[in memory of my brother]

I'll Take My Land: Contemporary Southern Agrarians

Suzanne W. Jones

How can we have something better if we do not imagine it? How can we imagine it if we do not hope for it? How can we hope for it if we do not attempt it?
—Wendell Berry, "Writer and Region"

For many earlier southern white writers, the southern rural landscape was the repository of nostalgia for lost ways of life, whether it was the plantation fantasy that Thomas Nelson Page pined for in his stories *In Ole Virginia* (1887) or the segregated agrarian ideal that many contributors yearned for in *I'll Take My Stand* (1930). For modern southern white writers, beginning most prominently with William Faulkner, the rural landscape has conjured up unsettling guilt about a way of life that flourished on the backs of the black people who tilled that land. And not surprisingly, for many black writers the southern rural landscape has been the repository of troubled memories—"slavery's old backyard," as Eddy Harris terms it in *South of Haunted Dreams* (1993). African American writers such as Richard Wright and Ralph Ellison started their lives and their plots in the rural South and then fled its racism. During the Harlem Renaissance, writers such as Jean Toomer and Zora Neale Hurston found the rural South to be a storehouse of African American culture, a culture that Hurston's anthropology professor Franz Boaz thought might be lost during the Great Migration of blacks from the South, a culture that she reclaimed. Many contemporary African American writers, no matter their region of origin, have found that at some time in their writing lives they must go South in their fiction to understand their history, to confront old enemies, and to heal old wounds. For writers not native to the South, the turn South is often made in historical fictions recounting slavery or segregation—Charles Johnson's *Middle Passage*, Toni Morrison's *Beloved*, Sherley Anne Williams's *Dessa Rose*, and Bebe Moore Campbell's *Your Blues Ain't Like Mine*. In David Bradley's *The Chaneysville Incident*, Toni Morrison's *Song of Solomon*, Gloria Naylor's *Mama Day*, and Octavia Butler's *Kindred*, contemporary characters delve into their ancestors' southern rural past in order to understand their racial heritage.[1]

If the rapidly growing urban centers of the Sunbelt have somewhat overcome the stigma of a racist past and the gentrified picturesque coastal cities have mostly hidden evidence of de facto segregation from tourists,[2] the rural South still remains the repository of racism in the American imagination—a place where black churches smolder, paranoid militia men organize, white hate groups meet clandestinely, and Sons of Confederate Veterans congregate openly and fly their battle flag proudly. How to reclaim this landscape haunted by racism, how to rejuvenate the soil soaked with the blood, sweat, and tears of slavery and segregation, and how to make a space for white liberals and all African Americans to call themselves southerners and to return to the South has been the work of a number of contemporary novelists who grew up in the rural segregated South. As Nell Irvin Painter has pointed out, during the era of segregation, "*the South* meant white people, and *the Negro* meant black people. . . . *The South* did not embrace whites who supported the Union in the Civil War or those who later disliked or opposed segregation." For some today, these limited and limiting connotations of the word still hold. I think for example of the recently formed white reactionary political party that calls itself the Southern Party and the ultra-conservative magazine, *Southern Partisan*. Other southerners, both black and white,

---

1. After a trip to Africa, Eddy Harris, a black journalist from New York, discovered his cultural roots in the American South, during a motorcycle journey that he details in *South of Haunted Dreams: A Ride Through Slavery's Old Back Yard* (New York: Simon and Schuster, 1993).

2. Fred Hobson, *Tell About the South: The Southern Rage to Explain* (Baton Rouge: Louisiana State University Press, 1983), 352–54. In *Confederates in the Attic: Dispatches from the Unfinished Civil War* (New York: Pantheon, 1998), Tony Horwitz found that the Civil War continues to be fought through historical re-enactments, especially in the rural South, though not all re-enactors participate for neo-Confederate reasons.

are beginning to loosen the neo-Confederate stranglehold on the word *South,* especially the rural South. In her analysis of the recent, more racially inclusive definition of "southern" culture, Thadious Davis argues that the return migration of African Americans to the rural South is not just "flight from the hardships of urban life" but also "a laying claim to a culture and a region that though fraught with pain and difficulty, provides a major grounding for identity." My focus is to examine how contemporary white writers Madison Smartt Bell and Ellen Douglas have intervened in such rhetoric and how they have represented the contemporary agrarian South.[3]

In *Tell About the South,* Fred Hobson argues that for contemporary liberal white writers, "the literature of self-exploration, even of confession and shame and guilt, had become . . . somewhat stylized, had become in part a habit, an aesthetic ritual. The talented, sensitive Southerner who left his home, or even remained, wrote his obligatory self-study, his love-hate drama, in part because his predecessors had." If the white southern memoirists whom Hobson analyzes wrote and rewrote the confessions of Quentin Compson because they both loved and hated southern culture and history, the white agrarian novelists that I highlight here, Ellen Douglas and Madison Smartt Bell, revise another of Faulkner's fictions, the narrative of Ike McCaslin, because they love southern places. Desiring social change, they write with an intensity and urgency that Hobson argues is missing from the works of most of his latter-day Quentin Compsons. And unlike their most notable agrarian predecessors, whom Wendell Berry suggests had "a tendency to love the land, not for its life, but for its historical associations,"[4] Bell and Douglas

3. Nell Irvin Painter, " 'The South' and 'the Negro': The Rhetoric of Race Relations and Real Life," in *The South for New Southerners,* ed. Paul D. Escott and David R. Goldfield (Chapel Hill: University of North Carolina Press, 1991), 43; Thadious M. Davis, "Expanding the Limits: The Intersection of Race and Region," *Southern Literary Journal* 20, no. 2 (Spring 1988): 6. For further analysis of African Americans' return to the South, see also David L. Langford, "Going Back Home to the South," *Crisis,* 101, no. 3 (April 1994): 26, 35, 40; Carol Stack, *Call to Home: African Americans Reclaim the Rural South* (New York: Basic Books, 1996); James C. Cobb, "Searching for Southernness: Community and Identity in the Contemporary South," in *Redefining Southern Culture: Mind and Identity in the Modern South* (Athens: University of Georgia Press, 1999), 125–49; and Wes Berry's essay in this collection.

4. Hobson, *Tell About the South,* 306 (he discusses works by Harry Ashmore, Hodding Carter, Larry King, Ralph McGill, Willie Morris, and Pat Watters); Wendell Berry, "The Regional Motive," in *A Continuous Harmony: Essays Cultural and Agricultural* (New York: Harcourt, Brace, Jovanovich, 1970), 65–66.

desire both to conserve southern rural landscapes and to create new, more racially inclusive southern communities. Thus the question of what to do with the land itself—how to use it and who should own it—is of paramount importance in their fiction. But of equal concern are constructions of "southernness" because both writers are trying to dislodge the pejorative, racist connotation that the adjective *southern* carries for white people who live in the South, especially the rural South.

Madison Smartt Bell grew up literally in the laps of several contributors to *I'll Take My Stand*; Andrew Lytle and Allen Tate were his parents' friends. Bell's mother majored in English at Vanderbilt, while his father went to law school there. After college, they moved out of Nashville and bought a small farm in nearby Williamson County, where his mother ran a riding school and his father set up a law practice in the rural county seat of Franklin. There they lived the life of subsistence farmers that Andrew Lytle describes in "The Hind Tit": killing hogs, raising sheep, milking a cow, and canning fruits and vegetables from their large garden. Bell explains the effect on his psyche: "they gave me a childhood which was sufficiently atavistic that in some ways I entered the modern world as a stranger."[5]

As a young man, Bell dreamed of becoming an Agrarian novelist, like the writers he knew and admired. He read William Faulkner, Robert Penn Warren, and Flannery O'Connor in addition to Lytle and Tate and all of *I'll Take My Stand*. At Princeton, he wrote about Madison Jones and Harry Crews in his English classes. There, however, he also encountered Walker Percy's work, which led Bell to make a connection between Percy's apocalyptic vision and the Agrarians' concerns about industrialism. But fearful of "just turning out imitations of southern writings" that he admired, Bell set his early novels in New York City, where he lived after college. At the same time, he insists that he brought to that urban landscape and society "a southern literary approach and stylistic conventions and also some attitudes that I got from southern writers." Although

5. Twelve Southerners, *I'll Take My Stand: The South and the Agrarian Tradition*, (New York: Harper and Brothers, 1930), 201–45; Madison Smartt Bell, "An Essay Introducing His Work in Rather a Lunatic Fashion," *Chattahoochee Review* 12, no. 1 (Fall 1991): 2. But Bell is quick to explain that his country upbringing was far from simply a rural experience: "The way I grew up was curiously double from the very beginning. I belonged to a pair of working farmers who were also accustomed to the rights and privileges of the best education available. This meant that I would get up in the morning, feed the horses, or milk the cow, and then be driven ten or fifteen miles to what I might as well admit was a rather posh private school in Nashville."

one may question whether his attitudes are exclusively "southern," Bell's sensitivity to nature, his feeling that something is awry, and his sense of alienation from modern life certainly combine the early lessons he learned from southern Agrarians with the views he later discovered in Percy's work.[6]

Not until his fifth novel, *Soldier's Joy* (1989), did Madison Smartt Bell set a novel in the South, and despite his predilection for the urban scene, he chose a rural setting, very much like the place where he grew up. His plot involves two Vietnam veterans—one white, Thomas Laidlaw, and the other black, Rodney Redmon—and the narration is alternately filtered through their perspectives as each tries to make a place for himself in the Tennessee hills where they grew up together. In *Soldier's Joy,* most of Bell's sympathetic characters have a strong connection to the land: Laidlaw, who returns to his family's farm; Redmon's father, Wat, who had been employed by Laidlaw's father; and Mr. Giles, a neighboring farmer who helps Laidlaw plant a garden. To use the terms of Walker Percy that Bell most identifies with, these characters feel "at ease" with themselves and "at home" in their environment when they are in the Tennessee hills.[7] Bell's least sympathetic characters—the unctuous, greedy real-estate developer Goodbuddy and the bitter, racist Vietnam veteran Earl Giles—are neither in tune with nature nor in harmony with those around them. They represent the evil forces, development and racism, that Laidlaw must do battle with when he returns home. Goodbuddy tries to buy him out, and Earl Giles tries to run him out.

Laidlaw's battle with Goodbuddy over the future of his property is little more than a skirmish. Because Laidlaw does not need the money, he quickly dismisses Goodbuddy's offer to buy all, or even some, of his land. Bell depicts the new houses that Goodbuddy sells as inharmonious with the rural landscape; Goodbuddy's realty office fits "as naturally into the surrounding countryside as if it had recently been dropped from a plane" (139). Like the Nashville Agrarians before him, Bell makes it clear that development is not necessarily progress, especially if people forget the connection between human life and the natural world. But Bell is more interested in people's emotional and psychological responses to places

6. Madison Smartt Bell, *Soldier's Joy* (1989; New York: Penguin, 1990) (quotations from this novel will be identified parenthetically in the text); Mary Louise Weaks, "An Interview with Madison Smartt Bell," *Southern Review* 30, no. 1 (January 1994): 3, 1.

7. Weaks, "An Interview," 11. See also Bell, "An Essay Introducing His Work," 4–5, 12.

than in the pastoral ideal that so preoccupied his predecessors. He establishes this concern in the first chapter when Laidlaw returns from Vietnam to California and buys a used Chevrolet pickup so that he can cruise the Pacific Coast Highway. Almost inexplicably, he is drawn to the East Coast:

> There were girls on the beaches, whiskey in the bars; you could have whatever you wanted if only you knew what it was. Laidlaw couldn't make up his mind to stop. Maybe, he thought, it just wasn't his kind of country. He tore the map out of the front of a phone book in a gas station booth just south of San Francisco, and set out east with that as his only guide. . . . Halfway across Virginia he stopped at a crossroads store, one of the old style with dust-covered cans ranked on the shelves, its only brisk trade in saltines and slices of rat cheese slicked onto sheets of wax paper at the counter. . . . The road was quite familiar now, every bend and curve of it known to him from summer after summer in the back seat of the car, chin propped on the front-seat cushion, peering around his father's boxy head to see the highway signs. . . . However, when he reached Virginia Beach it became a little strange, altered, more built up than he'd remembered. There were clumps of condo towers that had mushroomed since he'd been there, and he couldn't seem to find the house they used to stay in. . . . By dark he had gotten away from the high-rises and was passing in front of a row of bungalows, which then fell away entirely behind a rise of sand. (6–7)

With his back against a dune, the sea oats waving over his head, and the waves lapping the sand with their "*hush, hush, hush*" sounds, "Laidlaw was quietening within himself and a restlessness that had been in him began to drain away into the expanse of the cloudy water" (7). Laidlaw is calmed in this scene by nature itself, but also because this less-developed stretch of Virginia Beach is similar to the landscape he had vacationed in as a child. However, not until he is back on his family farm outside Nashville does Laidlaw feel that he is in the right place, and it is the rural place he loved as a boy that helps heal the psychic wounds he received as a soldier in Vietnam.

In setting his first southern novel in the rural Tennessee hills of his youth, Bell emulates his mentor Andrew Lytle. But Bell is not so much recalling a lost rural culture as he is a lost psychological relationship with the land. Richard Gray has argued that the "lost land" that Lytle and his cohorts recall in *I'll Take My Stand* was "lost in part, certainly, because of history but also for the simple reason that they had grown up and shades of the prison-house had started to gather around them." Michael

O'Brien has argued that many of the contributors to *I'll Take My Stand*
were city dwellers with romantic yearnings for country life. Both arguments could be made about Bell, who has said that he began to feel like
an "expatriate" in New York City. The feeling he experienced there of
being in "a foreign country" is the one he gives Laidlaw at the beginning
of *Soldier's Joy*. But Bell has articulated an additional dimension to the
powerful draw of his rural place. He represents the relationship between
Laidlaw and his homeplace as one built on sensory interactions, but he
represents it as a complex reciprocal relationship. Psychologist Roger
Barker calls such a relationship "psychological ecology"; he argues that
places become "behavior settings" because "individuals and their inani-
mate surroundings together create systems of a high order that take on a
life of their own." Winifred Gallagher interprets this relationship in these
terms: "The basic principle that links our places and states is simple: a
good or bad environment promotes good or bad memories, which inspire
a good or bad mood, which inclines us toward good or bad behavior. We
needn't even be consciously aware of a pleasant or unpleasant environmental stimulus for it to shape our states." One situation in the novel
depends on a reader's understanding of this concept in order to make
sense of Laidlaw's behavior. While the farm brings him the feelings of
peace and security he experienced as a boy, the forest at night resembles
the landscape where he experienced guerrilla warfare in Vietnam. The
sight of a doe's crudely hacked-up carcass calls up "an acutely uncomfortable sensation which he seemed unable to control" (97). After Laidlaw finds this evidence of a deer poacher on his property, he stalks and
knifes the man much as he would have an enemy soldier in Vietnam. By
including such a scene, Bell suggests that the environmental particulars
of a place can, in Gallagher's words, "work their way into the nervous
system" and "incline us toward knee-jerk reactions." Bell weds Laidlaw's
respect for animal life, a philosophy he learned when growing up in the
country, with the ability to kill human beings that was required of soldiers by their experience in the Vietnam War, and he ties both to what
Barker would call "psychological ecology."[8]

8. Richard Gray, *Writing the South: Ideas of an American Region* (London: Cambridge
University Press, 1986), 142; Michael O'Brien, "A Heterodox Note on the Southern Renaissance," in *Rethinking the South: Essays in Intellectual History* (Baltimore: Johns Hopkins University Press, 1988), 157–78; Madison Smartt Bell, "A Stubborn Sense of Place,"
Harper's 273. (August 1986): 36; Winifred Gallagher, *The Power of Place* (New York: Po-
seidon Press, 1993), 127–28, 132. Gallagher summarizes Barker's theories and those of
other psychologists on pp. 127–38.

While Bell is interested in his characters' emotional and psychological responses to their environment, he is equally interested in their moral and ethical connection to the land. He told a reporter for the *Atlanta Constitution* that after listening to a smooth-talking Ku Klux Klansman on a radio show and hearing of the arrest of a friend who participated in an anti-Klan demonstration, he was so angry that he began a novel set in the South not just to denounce the Klan but to reclaim the South as a place for whites who were not racist: "I especially wanted to deny their pretense of representing me or the great majority of other white Southerners—rural or urban, rich or poor—for whom they do not speak and never have." Bell thinks that our society's persistence in thinking of racism as confined to the South not only results in stereotyping the region but also in ignoring the national scope of racism, a truth confirmed for him by living most of his "adult life in urban slums outside the South."[9]

Thus Madison Smartt Bell set out to tell a more complex story of white southerners and race relations as well as of southern agrarianism. Both of his protagonists are emotionally scarred by the war, but Laidlaw's task of reentering southern society is easier than Redmon's because he is white and because his father owned property. Although fire has destroyed the farmhouse, Laidlaw's land, outbuildings, and a tenant house remain for him to use as he sees fit. In contrast, Redmon's family owned no property but lived in the tenant house on the Laidlaws' farm. As a result, Redmon cannot return to his "home" or make money from the land his father, Wat, farmed. In returning to the rural area of his childhood, Redmon can only become a wage laborer or a real-estate agent. He chooses the white-collar job, only to be betrayed by his white colleagues, including Goodbuddy. They implicate him in a fraudulent land scheme, for which only Redmon serves time in jail and after which he can find only blue-collar work.

Thus it is the inequitable pattern of land ownership based on the plantation past as much as contemporary race relations that puts Redmon in his place when he returns home to the South.[10] The economic difference in Laidlaw's and Redmon's relationship to the same piece of land makes

---

9. Don O'Briant, "Anger at Klan Fuels New Novel," *Atlanta Constitution*, 12 June 1989, B1.

10. Laidlaw suggests that significant landownership would help poor whites as well as blacks. He attributes some of their bitterness to an inability to fall back on subsistence farming should they need to, as well as to the consumerism promulgated on television (285).

friendship back in the States more difficult than their comradeship in Vietnam. Because Laidlaw's father owned this small farm, Laidlaw can fall back on subsistence farming if the music career he hopes for does not earn him a living. In contrast, Redmon feels "stuck," "in a corner" at his dead-end warehouse job (390). In a passionate exchange in Book IV, Redmon reminds Laidlaw that his father, Wat, lived and worked on this land before Laidlaw's father bought it: "You all didn't do anything but buy it. And then you put him off it in the end" (378). This view is similar to the one Ernest Gaines advances in *A Gathering of Old Men* (1983), where he suggests that although his old men have not owned the Marshall plantation, they have had a more intimate relationship with the land than the Marshalls have, because they have tilled the soil. For the first time in his life, Laidlaw understands the full power and privilege of his whiteness. He immediately agrees with Redmon's point and generously, if impulsively, offers him half of the property, saying, "I'd do it for justice" (379). Laidlaw has already been thinking of the tenant house he now lives in as belonging to the Redmons. When Redmon first asks him where he is living, Laidlaw answers, "In you all's old house" (258). Laidlaw's guilt about the complexity of whites possessing southern land that has been farmed by blacks and is now threatened by developers takes him in a different direction from Faulkner's Ike McCaslin in "The Bear."

Determined never to repeat the sins of his grandfather, Ike tries to distance himself from his grandfather's treatment of slaves by renouncing his inherited land and by fulfilling his grandfather's will and paying off the mulatto offspring from his grandfather's union with a slave. But Ike never acknowledges his kinship to his mixed-race cousins or considers giving them any of the land, which he deeds to his white cousin McCaslin Edmonds.[11] Thus Ike foregoes any involvement in how his family's land is used, even as he bemoans the loss of southern woodland to logging companies. Unlike Ike, Laidlaw protects his farm from development and desperately wants an equal relationship with black people and a true friendship with Redmon. Laidlaw tries not to escape but to correct the sins of his southern fathers. However, the question of how he and Redmon will co-own the farm becomes a conflict that the two men never re-

---

11. In "Delta Autumn," Faulkner exposes the limitations of Ike's renunciation by having him repeat his grandfather's racism when confronted with the mulatto mistress and child of McCaslin's son Roth Edmonds. Furthermore, Roth's ignorance of his ancestor's shadow family has resulted in a version of his grandfather's sin of incest, because the mulatto woman, unbeknownst to him, is his own cousin.

solve. Laidlaw wants a joint ownership that would follow the agrarian philosophy of his father. Redmon pronounces such a deal in which Laidlaw calls the shots just as paternalistic as the one his father was engaged in with Laidlaw's father. But Bell is clearly on the side of Laidlaw as far as appropriate use of the land.[12] He depicts the half-built tract homes of the failed development scheme that landed Redmon in jail as a blight on the landscape. Bell even has Redmon, who admits he was "all for it at the time" (360), wish the land "back the way it was before" (154).

The novel includes an unexpected chapter from Wat Redmon's perspective, which Bell uses not only to emphasize Wat's kinship to the land but to suggest that the land is as much Redmon's birthright as Laidlaw's own. This dreamlike sequence is printed in italics and written in the beautifully lyrical style that Bell takes up throughout the novel when he is describing the landscape, but especially when he is representing the reciprocal relationship of a person in tune with nature's rhythms. In this respect, Bell is very much like the earlier generation of southern Agrarians, who wrote, as Bell said in an interview, about "the culture of small farms" and who were concerned "about the destruction of the natural rhythms of life in connection to the land."[13] Wat's animistic communion with the snake and the groundhog recall Ike McCaslin's first encounter with the buck in "The Old People" and later with Old Ben in "The Bear."

In *Soldier's Joy,* Bell harks back to his own southern agrarian roots, both emotionally and intellectually, but he goes beyond his Agrarian predecessors' preoccupation with the machine invading the southern garden by acknowledging the evil of the prejudice and discrimination that made that garden grow. At the same time that Bell would like to get back to agrarian relationships to the land, he knows they can never be the same as they were in his parents' day—a time when black labor was cheap and white men depended on and exploited black men like Wat. Because his earliest attempts to write about the rural South had been "dry and derivative," Bell says that he wrote about the urban North using "applications of the old vision to new subject matter."[14] But in *Soldier's Joy,* Bell, like Laidlaw in his relationship with Redmon, "wanted to make up something new" (310), and indeed he almost succeeds in creating a new vision with old agrarian subject matter. In the middle of the novel, when Redmon and Laidlaw spend their first companionable night together in Laid-

---

12. See Weaks, "An Interview," especially 5–10.
13. Ibid., 5, 18.
14. Bell, "A Stubborn Sense of Place," 37, 38.

law's cabin, which is the tenant house that Redmon grew up in, readers experience great expectations that the two men will succeed in creating "something new" on this land. As the sunlight streams down the next morning from "deep untrammeled blue sky," Bell writes that Redmon looks "at home there in the daylight" (304). This day that Laidlaw and Redmon spend together close to nature and to each other is Edenic.

But the genre Bell has chosen for *Soldier's Joy* is psychological realism, not pastoral idealism. The Klan targets Laidlaw as soon as he initiates a friendship with Redmon, and the Klan tracks the activities of Brother Jacob, who, in the style of an evangelical preacher, advocates interracial friendships in open meetings throughout the South. At this point in the novel, Bell marries the Agrarians' wishful thinking to Walker Percy's apocalyptic vision, and the result is a violent ending, which I have discussed elsewhere.[15] Here I am most interested in the agrarian ending Bell teased readers with, but did not choose. In discussing the idealistic approach that New Age cults take to the possibility of global destruction in "An Essay Introducing His Work," Bell could have been discussing his difficulty in writing *Soldier's Joy*: "The problem for New Age prophets and believers is to weave a plausible relationship between this optimism and the real, actual threat of the fairly imminent end to human life on earth." The violent ending of *Soldier's Joy* hints at another, happier outcome. Hit with submachine-gun fire in the chest during a shootout with the Ku Klux Klan, Laidlaw is certain he is going to die, but Redmon refuses to give in to his pessimism. He wills him to live with a tempting reminder of the offer Laidlaw has made to share the land: "Hey, we still got a house to build. Are you taking back all you said?" (465). This remark comes as a bit of a surprise to readers because the two men have never resolved their differences about joint land-ownership. Indeed, the last time the subject comes up, it does not seem as if Redmon is interested in Laidlaw's gift unless Laidlaw will give him full rights to half of the property (391), and Laidlaw is reluctant to do so because as long as he retains some control of the land, he can control how it will be used. Most important, he does not want Redmon to sell farmland and woodland to Goodbuddy "to put a mess of those little square houses on" (391). For a few brief moments, Bell tantalizes his readers with the possibility of a

---

15. See Suzanne W. Jones, "Refighting Old Wars: Race Relations and Masculine Conventions in Fiction by Larry Brown and Madison Smartt Bell," in *The Present State of Mind: Southern Identity in the 1990s*, ed. Jan Nordby Gretlund (Columbia: University of South Carolina Press, 1999), 107–20.

happy ending, southern agrarian style—but racially integrated as befits the contemporary South. In many ways, Bell's narrative technique—with its lyrical descriptions of the land, its dialogic working-through of racial misunderstandings between Laidlaw and Redmon, its two main characters providing readers with both black and white perspectives, and its psychological realism in the first four books—does not seem to add up to the sensational shootout with the Klan in Book V, although Bell certainly prepares his readers for his use of violence.[16]

Perhaps Bell saw interracial agrarianism as an "escapist fantasy" equal to the "New Age menu of magical solutions" he disparages. Perhaps this ending is Bell's realistic analysis of the older southern Agrarians' romantic longings to turn back the clock. Whatever the cause, Bell makes Laidlaw more interested in music than in farming, which is unrelenting in its demands, and gives his protagonist Andrew Lytle's belief that one cannot be a good artist and a good farmer at the same time. The more involved Laidlaw becomes with his music, the more he neglects his land. Yet the possibility of a happier ending to this novel cannot be dismissed so easily, for Bell has argued that "what maybe all my characters have always been after in all my books, is a visionary solution to the fatal problem which our collective consciousness is virtually unable to acknowledge." Bell glimpses a new vision of the rural South, which involves an animistic approach to life, if not an agrarian one.[17] But he cannot quite solve the old problem of how both blacks and whites can possess the same land or cultivate a harmonious relationship with nature unless they are farmers, nor can he imagine how such an interracial friendship is sustainable in a place where hate still lurks.

Ellen Douglas tackles the same problems as Madison Smartt Bell but works out different fictional solutions in *The Rock Cried Out*, which is set in rural Mississippi.[18] Like Bell, Douglas grew up in the South, but

---

16. Bell, "An Essay Introducing His Work," 8; Jones, "Refighting Old Wars."

17. Bell, "An Essay Introducing His Work," 8, 13. Bell's comments on this visionary solution are on p. 13.

18. See John Griffin Jones, "Interview with Ellen Douglas," *Mississippi Writers Talking, Volume II* (Jackson: University Press of Mississippi, 1983), 47–73. In writing *The Rock Cried Out* (1979; rprt., Baton Rouge: Louisiana State University Press, 1994), Douglas has said that she was struggling with how best to present "the sensibility of young people of her children's generation," which is Madison Smartt Bell's generation: "When I decided to do that, I then had to decide where to put them, and it occurred to me that the setting in rural south Mississippi would be extraordinarily fruitful in terms of producing the kinds of circumstances that I could use in making that exploration, particularly because that part of the country was violently involved in the civil rights movement. I also knew the isolated, rural world I wanted to use; I was at home there. I knew the kind of people I would use,

unlike him she has lived there all of her life, except for a very brief interlude in New York City. The rural area outside of her fictional Homochitto roughly corresponds to her own family farm near Natchez, property that she and her siblings own jointly, just as the McLaurin siblings own Chickasaw in *The Rock Cried Out*. Like Bell, Douglas seeks to intervene in the stereotypical definitions of the South and to revise old stories, but her novel is more self-consciously autoethnographic.[19] Her implied readers are both native southerners and outsiders to the South. To address this dual audience, she chooses a first-person narrator in his late twenties, a liberal white insider who has lived outside the South. In 1978, Alan McLaurin writes about his experiences in 1971, when he left college in Boston to move home to rural Mississippi for an extended vacation, only to decide to stay. His account is punctuated with comments addressed to naïve outsiders: "Winter in Homochitto County might sound to a man from Boston as if it would be pleasant; but south Mississippi is not Florida" (9). When his college girlfriend from Ohio visits him, Alan has many opportunities to comment on the stereotypical stories that outsiders tell about the South and to expose the generic lens through which they see all southerners. At the same time, the retrospective narrative technique allows Douglas to address insiders—by underlining how much Alan needed to learn about himself, his family, and his community, and by emphasizing how ill-suited Faulkner's approach is for the story that Alan, and she, must tell.

Douglas has said that on first reading Faulkner's fiction, she felt "the joyous sensation of *coming home*." Not only was Faulkner writing about a place and people she knew, but he was obsessed with moral issues that caught her attention: "the temptation to violence, the nature of heroism, the indissoluble marriage of love and hate between white and black, the pernicious nature of respectability, the obligations of the individual to society—and everything laid out in that rolling, hypnotic, irresistible language." Later, as an adult, her response to his fiction changed: "I began to feel, not drawn to, but repelled by the hypnotically repetitive, overblown, latinate language. . . . And the sentimentality, the romanticism of

---

both the young white people and the black families" (68). Quotations from *The Rock Cried Out* will be cited parenthetically in the text.

19. Here I am using Mary Louise Pratt's definition in "Arts of the Contact Zone," *Profession* (New York: Modern Language Association, 1991), 33–40: "a text in which people undertake to describe themselves in ways that engage with representations others have made of them" (35).

my adolescence was being tempered, radically altered by the beginnings of maturity. I read with impatience and irritation as well as with pleasure and awe *Go Down, Moses* and *The Hamlet.*"[20]

In *The Rock Cried Out*, Douglas gives Alan her own criticisms of Faulkner, and she rewrites Ike McCaslin's story—in both form and content. As if demonstrating her desire to free the southern landscape itself from the powerful epithets attached to the region, she foregoes Faulkner's elaborately figurative descriptions of place—"verbal constructs," as Richard Gray calls them, which emphasize that place is "a product of human creativity." By the time Ike inherits his father's land, he can see it only in terms of the injustice that occurred there, a fact so powerful that it overwhelms his ability to see the land in any other way. Part IV of "The Bear" begins with Ike telling his cousin McCaslin Edmonds of his decision to relinquish his tainted inheritance: "then he was twenty-one. He could say it, himself and his cousin juxtaposed not against the wilderness but against the tamed land which was to have been his heritage, the land which Old Carothers McCaslin his grandfather had bought with white man's money from the wild men whose grandfathers without guns hunted it, and tamed and ordered or believed he had tamed and ordered it for the reason that the human beings he held in bondage and in the power of life and death had removed the forest from it and in their sweat scratched the surface of it." While Douglas, like Faulkner, is quick to let readers know of the history that has been played out on the Mississippi landscape, she describes southwestern Mississippi's specific geological formations in an attempt to allow the landscape to reassert itself—not to suggest that one's sense of the landscape is ever unmediated but to unburden it of Faulkner's mythic figuration: "We had been whirling along the winding two-lane black-topped road deep between sheer loess bluffs, traveling as fast as the car would take the curves; and now we were climbing toward Chickasaw Ridge, narrow backbone of the hills, where straggling bands of Chickasaw Indians had made their camps before they crossed the river on the way westward, after the Treaty of Pontotoc Creek robbed them of their lands" (7).

Rather than describe a generalized setting with vegetation ubiquitous to southern literature (crepe myrtle, magnolias, wisteria), Douglas places the reader in a very specific southern place near Natchez (her Homo-

20. Ellen Douglas, "Faulkner in Time," in *"A Cosmos of My Own": Faulkner and Yoknapatawpha*, ed. Doreen Fowler and Ann J. Abadie (Jackson: University Press of Mississippi, 1981), 289, 290, 295–96.

chitto) and takes care to identify flora and fauna native to that locale. Take for example this passage, where she describes the sensory experience of Alan's winter homecoming: "the pervasive smell, not of boiling syrup and automobile exhaust fumes, but of cedar and pine; of smilax and jasmine twisting dark green up into the bare dogwood and walnut and cherry trees; of oaks under shawls of gray moss that turn out when you look closely to be throbbing with pale green life; of the winter silence, above all, broken only by the voices of birds that stay with us all year: the towhee, the crow, the mourning goatsucker" (10). With such specific localization, Douglas employs description as many of the earliest novelists did, to distinguish an individual place from the mythic landscapes used in epic forms. In so doing, she resists her readers' inclinations to mentally conjure a generic southern place without registering the words that make it a very specific geographic locale. When discussing the importance of "place" in her fiction, Douglas underlines this distinction by saying, "*place*, in the sense of the specific, is absolutely essential. . . . I don't think *regionalism* is important."[21]

The way Douglas depicts Alan's visceral feelings about his homeplace is interesting. Rather than attribute human feelings to nature, Alan expresses his intense emotions in terms of the natural world. For example, when he hears of his Aunt Lelia's affair with the McLaurins' black tenant Sam Daniels, "it was as if the house and everybody and everything in it shifted along a fault" (124). As Alan learns these new facts about his family and speculates about how they have shaped and will shape him, he says, "I feel mostly wonder at how our lives move, by twists and turns, as a creek moves, rippling in its bed, doubling around and shaping itself against the contours of rock and silt and fallen log, eating out a bank and appearing one day, after a rainstorm, flowing down a ravine that yesterday was half a mile from its course" (124). Douglas seems to suggest that nature can provide analogies that help people know themselves.

Douglas's mode of describing Alan's feelings underlines the fact that he has been more sensitive to the beauty of the natural world than to the feelings of other human beings, a situation that causes problems in his relationship with his girlfriend, Miriam. But this technique also reminds

---

21. Gray, *Writing the South,* 177; William Faulkner, *Go Down, Moses* (1942; rprt., New York: Vintage Books, 1990), 243; D. S. Bland, "Endangering the Readers' Neck: Background Description in the Novel," in *The Theory of the Novel,* ed. Philip Stevick (New York: Free Press, 1967), 316, 326; Jerry Speir, "Of Novels and the Novelist: An Interview with Ellen Douglas," *University of Mississippi Studies in English* 5 (1984–87): 236.

readers that although our experience of the natural world is mediated by our cultural perceptions, nature is not passive in the relationship. In *The Rock Cried Out*, the forces of nature take an active role in the working-out of the plot, reminding readers of nature's power and of the need for careful management of land and natural resources, but also that place is not just myth but also reality. These are matters that Alan has been oblivious of while he soothes his soul in the bosom of nature and rebuilds one of the tenant houses for his rural retreat. Alan barely pays attention when his Uncle Lester remarks that the dam is dangerously positioned above the farmhouse and that too much rain could cause a disaster. Alan thinks of his Uncle Lester, who works at J. C. Penney's, as incapable of appreciating nature's beauty and the farm's rejuvenating powers. What he finds out is that in judging Lester's practical point of view as beneath his own aesthetic and spiritual one, Alan has misjudged his own relationship to the land.

Near the end of the novel, Douglas includes just the sort of rainstorm Lester predicted. Sam and Lelia are the first to discover that Chickasaw and the community below are threatened by the weakening earthen dam that holds back the lake's now-overflowing waters. Preoccupied as usual with personal matters, Alan has just learned that his childhood friend Dallas Boykin is indirectly responsible for his adored cousin Phoebe's death, and Alan has followed Dallas to the lake to kill him in retribution, even though he knows Phoebe's death was an accident. In the midst of their fight, it is Dallas, not Alan, who helps avert disaster at the dam. Alan is too preoccupied with his own anger and grief to think about the welfare of the community. Dallas's confession makes the familiar ground of family history shift metaphorically beneath Alan's feet, but in this scene the "shift" (287) is literal as well,[22] thereby giving the storm both symbolic and thematic power. For as with most natural disasters, the storm causes a disparate group of contentious people to work together because they have an abiding love of the land and a passionate desire to save Chickasaw farm. The storm moves Alan beyond his self-centered approach to life. Thinking he has killed Dallas, he repents this action, and he risks his own life to save Dallas's body from being swept away. In saving the body, he saves Dallas's life and outgrows both his solipsism and his idealism. A conscientious objector in the Vietnam War, Alan has thought himself incapable of killing a fellow human. That night he learns the lesson Faulkner's Ike never learned, that no one is "pure" (295).

---

22. Lelia too feels that the earth "quaked underfoot" in the storm (286).

But this novel is not simply a sentimental story about how love of a place can bring people of different races and classes together. While Douglas is incredibly sensitive to the power of place, she also knows the power of fiction to shape perceptions of place and region,[23] and she uses Alan's college girlfriend Miriam to demonstrate this power. Although Miriam has never been in the Deep South until she visits Alan, she has seen plenty of moss-draped live oaks in the movies. However, she has difficulty processing the winter landscape with its unexpected "bare tangled vines" and "limp and frost-blackened" wood ferns: "What is this, anyhow, Alan? Could be the set for a bad movie. Faulkner? Tennessee Williams?" (91). Because movie images have etched long hot southern summers in her brain, Miriam cannot see what Alan sees—the stark beauty of the Mississippi countryside in winter. Because of her limited knowledge of the place, she misses the awesome sight of a soaring red-tailed hawk. Douglas shows the difficulty of dislodging outsiders' preconceptions, of adding unfamiliar images to the familiar ones. Even as Miriam imagines making a film of her own—shooting the southern winter vegetation, "stark, not leafy," getting "a shot of the house from the gate," and panning around "to the rusty tractor parts and falling-down sheds and back to the front porch"—she is unable to hold on to the sights she sees right in front of her. She concludes her imagined winter filming by unconsciously reverting to an image of the South fixed in eternal summer: Alan's aunt lazing "in a hammock with a box of chocolates" (92).

At times, Miriam knows that she is using clichés. For example, she playfully parodies a southern-belle accent and air when she admits to Alan, "I learned just about evahthin' I know at the movies" (92). But when interacting with the new people she meets, Miriam relies on clichés of "southernness" and stereotypes of southerners. She liberally peppers her speech with "y'all," unaware that the colloquialism is not used to refer to one person. She relates to southern women by talking about cooking and crocheting, never imagining, as Alan points out, that "most of the ones I know, like men, talk about sex and money and politics and movies and television and books and vice and crime and drugs and the vagaries of human nature and tragedies of human fate" (106). Through Miriam, Douglas critiques the very "obsession with idiom and idiosyncrasy" that historian James Cobb argues "threatens to turn the South of popular perception into caricature."[24]

23. Ellen Douglas, "Provincialism in Literature," *New Republic* 173 (5 and 12 July 1975): 23–25.
24. Cobb, *Redefining Southern Culture*, 142.

Perhaps most significantly, Miriam predictably simplifies the earlier unhappy outcome of Sam and Lelia's interracial love affair by reducing the causes to race alone, missing the very human emotions of jealousy and lust and revenge and love of place. Douglas uses Miriam's reductive language to construct a parodic representation of the outsider's perception of southerners' behavior. As Alan's Aunt Lelia histrionically lists what she had been willing to relinquish for her black lover, Sam— "friends, family, my country"—and bemoans Sam's refusal to leave Chickasaw with her, Miriam interrupts with "Weren't you, no matter what happened, an enemy? I mean, *white*? Wouldn't that enter into it?" (140). As readers get to know Sam, we see that the motivations for his refusal to leave are neither as simple as Miriam thinks (white racism) nor as simple as Lelia thinks (insatiable male sexual desire) nor as simple as Alan thinks (love of Chickasaw farm). Rather, the Sam that Douglas slowly reveals is a complex man, motivated by many strong feelings. Paradoxically, he is emotionally tied to the rural landscape of a region that has discriminated against him; ironically, he is a tenant farmer on the very land that his white lover's family owns.

It would be easy to dismiss Sam's emotional ties to the land as the product of his lack of training to do anything else but farm. However, Douglas uses another African American character with more options as a reminder that the temperament and personality traits that draw people to rural areas cross racial, class, and gender lines.[25] Calhoun Levitt, a man of mixed race, was educated in the North but chose to return South to his family's farm. Douglas makes certain she does not recreate that old dichotomy coupling South with rural and North with urban. A white union organizer tells Levitt that he too is burned out on cities, but they are southern cities—Nashville, Miami, and New Orleans.[26] Repeatedly,

25. See Winifred Gallagher's summary of recent scientific research into human temperament in chapter 6, "Different People, Different Worlds" of *The Power of Place*. These scientists regard "behavior as the product of an individual's effort to match his physiological and psychological makeup with settings that can help him maintain an optimum level of arousal" (161).

26. Here I differ from John L. Grigsby in "The Agrarians and Ellen Douglas's *The Rock Cried Out* and *Can't Quit You, Baby*: Extending the Tradition While Expanding the Canon," *Southern Quarterly* 34, no. (Fall 1995): 41–48, who sees Douglas as employing the conventional opposition between "industrial-urbanized North and Agrarian-rural South" (42). Although he points out some of her differences from the Agrarians, his purpose is to show the "centrality" of their concerns in her work (41). As a result, I think he sometimes over-reads the connections.

Douglas's characters, like Madison Smartt Bell's, declare their emotional responses to places. Alan says, "I had begun to feel a pull—like gravity, maybe, whatever it is that makes one sure . . . that one's own part of [the world] is a necessary spiritual terrain, as much one's own as a cast in the eye—that drew me southward again" (57).

Thus Alan sees Miriam not only as an outsider to the South but as a person who is detached from place. He contrasts her "uprooted life," moving from one college town to another, with his own attachment to Chickasaw farm, which "holds his past and considerable of the past of his parents and grandparents, and even his great-grandparents, the landscape of his nightmares and of all those dreams so sweet" (127). He conceives of the difference in their relationship to place as a dichotomy between place as ideology and politics, and place as land and people. For example, to Miriam the South is the Klan, George Wallace, the Citizens' Council, *Brown v. Board of Education;* to him, the South is Chickasaw, his relatives, and the black tenants Sam and Noah with whom he hunts and fishes. Like Ike McCaslin, Alan uses the land for his pleasure and spiritual rejuvenation; like Ike McCaslin, Alan has as mentor a mixed-race man of the earth named Sam, who owns a mongrel dog and who has tutored Alan in his reverent relationship with the land.

Also like Ike McCaslin, Alan is naïve. Although he is not unaware of the Civil Rights Movement in Mississippi, he remembers the sixties as a time of bad news on television, a period during his adolescence when he was obsessed with his beautiful cousin Phoebe. As an adult, he harbors no guilt about prejudice against blacks because he is protected by the cloak of his parents' liberalism—although in the sixties it made him an outsider in his community. But while *The Rock Cried Out* begins as a novel of education about the South for outsiders and people detached from the land, like Miriam, it ends as a novel of education for insiders like Alan, who thinks he knows his family and Chickasaw farm like the back of his hand. The novel opens with broad hints of what Douglas sees is Alan's problem in thinking about place—the idea that he can divorce geographical location from "moral climate."[27] Fleeing Boston, factory work, and his girlfriend Miriam to romance nature and create poetry in solitude at Chickasaw, he runs smack into the disconcerting effects of southern race relations when black college students and their graduate instructor pick him up as he is hitchhiking the last leg home. A young black woman in a passing car throws a Coke bottle that shatters against

27. Speir, "Of Novels and the Novelist," 236.

the sign near him. When the driver comes back to give Alan a ride, he assures him that what looked like a racial incident was a coincidence, but just as Alan gets out of the car, the young woman says she meant to hit him. Alan's response to this ambiguous encounter, "This was not what I had meant my arrival to be like, not at all" (7), shows the extent to which in Boston he has made Chickasaw into a pastoral ideal, just as another generation of southern Agrarians did before him. Much like Bell's Thomas Laidlaw, Alan looks to nature for redemptive recovery and to rural solitude for creative inspiration. What Douglas gives him is "the empty-bed blues" (181), bad lyric poetry about welding a bush hog, and some surprising encounters with his neighbors. Alan's attempt to interpret the rural landscape fails him as surely as Miriam's because both perceive the place through interpretive lenses that precede their present experience there and neither knows all of the local stories, or even the whole truth of familiar stories.

Before Alan can write successfully about his homeplace, Douglas shows that he must open himself up to the repressed stories that reside there. Like Ike McCaslin, Alan learns of interracial sexual relations within his family, but with an important twist. His Aunt Lelia's secret is the South's most repressed story and most tabooed relationship—one of mutual desire and illicit sex between a white woman and a black man. As a device to unearth other repressed southern stories, Douglas has Alan and his childhood friend Lee Boykin, a hippie photographer, team up to write about the South—human-interest stories about old times for the popular magazine *Southern Life* and stories about the Civil Rights movement and the pulpwood cutters' union for the more progressive *New York Times* and *The Speckled Bird*.[28] Alan, Lee, and Miriam collect oral history from Sam's father, Noah Daniels, and Calhoun Levitt.

Noah's stories reveal a narrative that southern liberals sometimes repress, the fact that they or their families may be implicated in the racism that produced inequitable land distribution in the South. One definition of *agrarian* is "a person who favors equitable distribution of land,"[29] which is not a definition associated with the Nashville Agrarians. Nor is it a concept that Ike McCaslin thinks of when he gives his family land to

28. The title *Southern Life* is surely either Lee's failure to remember the title of *Southern Living* or Douglas's veiled reference to that lifestyle magazine, and *The Speckled Bird* is probably a reference to the *Great Speckled Bird*, an Atlanta underground newspaper of the 1960s and 1970s.

29. *American Heritage Dictionary.*

McCaslin Edmonds instead of distributing it equally among all his relatives, both black and white. From Noah, Alan learns that his great-uncle Dennison never gave Noah the oil well he promised him as payment for Noah's advice about where to drill on Chickasaw farm. Alan also learns that this betrayal was one in a string that stretched back to Alan's great-grandfather, who never deeded Noah's father the promised sixty acres of Chickasaw land that he had allowed him to build a house on and farm rent-free. This breach of trust is reminiscent of the black freedmen's expectations during southern Reconstruction that they would receive forty acres and a mule.[30] Thus Alan learns that his family, which he takes such pride in thinking has a close relationship to the Daniels family, has violated their trust repeatedly. Later, insult is added to injury when Alan's Uncle Lester discloses that Lelia contracted with the U.S. Navy to set up the satellite-tracking station on a portion of the family farm as revenge for Sam having jilted her. Alan had always placed the blame for this high-tech use of the land on his boring, bourgeois Uncle Lester. Leasing land to the government has been financially beneficial to the McLaurins but devastating to the Danielses, who had used that acreage to graze their cattle. Given this history between the black and white families of Chickasaw, it is no wonder that, for the Daniels family, trusting the McLaurins is no easy matter. Noah sets Alan straight when Alan upbraids him for not telling the whole truth earlier and for trying to making him feel guilty now: " 'You're still thinking only about yourself, ain't you, son?' Noah said. 'Stop and consider. When you come down here this winter, what I actually *know* about you—now you're a man? If you expect somebody to talk to you, you got to tell them who you is. Teach 'em to trust you. All you ever done with me was throw me a bone every now and then— show me off to your girl friend' " (298).

The oral history that Alan, Lee, and Miriam collect from Calhoun Levitt contains similar suppressed truths about race relations and land ownership in the South. Both Calhoun's grandparents and his parents were interracial couples who could not live together openly; his grandparents' story is one of publicly segregated housing and a privately integrated home. His white grandfather willed Calhoun's mother three hundred acres of land, which Calhoun now farms. He provides an inter-

---

30. This proposal was made by Congressman Thaddeus Stevens. He wanted to seize land owned by slaveholders and redistribute it to former slaves, but Congress never acted on his belief that the vote was not enough to uplift southern blacks. After he died in 1868, the idea was no longer discussed.

esting contrast both to Douglas's Noah and Sam Daniels and to Bell's Rodney Redmon. The fact that Calhoun owns land gives him more choices than Noah, Sam, or Redmon; landownership allowed Calhoun to leave the cold northern city he hated and to make ends meet during the Depression. But the bulk of Calhoun's story concerns another buried southern tale about a liberal southern white union organizer who learned his socialism and his racial tolerance at Vanderbilt Divinity School. With this story, Douglas excavates the small but not insignificant southern liberal movement in the 1930s.[31] This story puts Lee in the same position that Noah's story puts Alan, because it leads to the revelation that Lee's father was a Klan member who took Lee to meetings, a memory Lee has repressed. Unlike Alan, Lee reacts to the incriminating facts about his father's racism by pronouncing Calhoun's "truth about Homochitto County" (198) a "lie" (229) and then abandoning the oral history project and fleeing to New Orleans. Lee's inability to admit to participating in his society's evils leads to his failure to do the work necessary to correct them.

Alan's assessment of their oral history project is that "none of these stories lent themselves to the needs of The New York Times—or The Speckled Bird. I doubt they would have borne out anybody's theories—economic, political, moral—or mythological" (145). But their very failure to meet outsiders' expectations about Mississippi is precisely Douglas's point for including these stories in her novel. If audience expectations determine publication, how will the repressed southern stories get told? Who will publish them? How to get a truthful story and how to hear it accurately are issues embedded in the way Douglas sets up these chapters on storytellers and listeners. Lee attempts to elicit answers from the storytellers by asking leading questions, but both Noah and Calhoun resist the pattern that Lee tries to impose on their narratives. As Calhoun says, "The problem is, my answers may not be the answers to your questions. . . . But that's their problem, I said to myself. Maybe they can think up some questions to fit my answers" (198). Unlike Lee, Alan opens himself up to the possibility that Noah's and Calhoun's stories are true. In seeking further verification from many sources, Alan's understanding of both family and local history changes. Douglas suggests that these new

31. One example is Herman C. Nixon, a leader in the Southern Conference on Human Welfare, whose writings emphasized class conflict and pointed to how southern landowners and businessmen exploited both poor whites and poor blacks. See Morton Sosna, In Search of the Silent South (New York: Columbia University Press, 1977).

stories make his sense of place more complex because the history of southern people and their relationship to the land is more integrated than southerners themselves know, particularly white southerners. The suppressed stories reveal the false dichotomy between Miriam's notion of place as ideology and politics, and Alan's of place as land and people. Interestingly, they drive Alan to give up pastoral poetry and journalism in favor of modernist fiction, a better literary vehicle for bringing all these stories into the open and all the perspectives into dialogue.

Like Ike McCaslin, Alan eventually takes up a simple trade to support his writing, but it is welding, not carpentry work; Alan does not fancy himself a Christ figure the way Ike does. In "The Bear," Ike's wife begs him to keep his land; in *The Rock Cried Out,* Alan's girlfriend Miriam begs him to do the opposite—to give up his tainted land and go to New Orleans with her and Lee. Unlike Ike, Alan does not put his ideals above his humanity. He promises to leave the farm if Miriam wants to be with him and if she will end a sexual relationship she has begun with Lee, but he will not promise to renounce his portion of his beloved land for Miriam, although he does promise to give Noah and Sam the oil wells that are their due. In vowing to hold on to his share of the family farm—even though Chickasaw is planted in trees and derricks, not cultivated in traditional crops—Alan is vowing to preserve the rural landscape in a way that Ike did not when he relinquished his property to McCaslin Edmonds. Like Bell's Laidlaw, Alan learns from the sins and mistakes of his fathers; in "Delta Autumn," Ike repeats their sins because he tries to escape the moral responsibility of the past. For Bell and Douglas, unlike Faulkner, the southern landowner's crime is not so much possession of the land as it is inequitable possession. At the end of *The Rock Cried Out*, Alan criticizes Faulkner as romantic: "It is only in certain kinds of stories that you can pull off the kind of sacrifice Faulkner used in *The Bear* when he had Ike McCaslin give away his tainted inheritance and become a humble carpenter" (295). Another of Alan's closing remarks reveals how naïve Douglas thinks some of the southern Agrarians were in creating such a sharp dichotomy between agriculture and industrialism: "So I've joined the human race in its despoliation of the earth. Because, although the pulpwood trucks I work on belong mostly to poor men, ultimately, like them, I'm working for the International Paper Company and the Georgia Pacific. Or, if I'm in the oil fields, for Exxon and Cities Service" (295). In talking about this passage in an interview, Douglas said, "Until you can do without gas and paper, you can't present yourself to yourself as a person who is so pure that he is not involved in these things."[32] Maybe a good writer cannot be a good subsistence farmer, as Bell's Laidlaw determined once and for all, but Douglas shows that a writer can be a good tree farmer, which, with a little part-time welding on the side, makes "it possible to spend considerable time writing" (294) and enjoying rural life. Unlike Madison Smartt Bell, Douglas not only allows Alan to stay on the land but to live something of an integrated communal life with Noah and Sam, albeit in separate houses on the farm.

Unlike Faulkner, Douglas moves her characters beyond the South's ignoble past to what she terms "its misunderstood past." As a result, for her characters she creates the possibility that the future can grow out of the past, rather than be overshadowed by it.[33] However, readers do not know whether Alan will ever give Sam and Noah the promised oil wells or talk with his relatives about deeding them the sixty acres they worked so hard to cultivate and preserve. Thus Ellen Douglas, like Madison Smartt Bell, fails to resolve the troubling issue of making restitution for inequitable land distribution in the South. However, both writers acknowledge this problem, which was caused by slavery and continued by racism, and which the United States government did not begin to face until very recently. In 1999, the Department of Agriculture settled a class-action lawsuit brought by black farmers, many of whom were southerners, who were denied government loans and disaster assistance simply because of their race.[34] Given the racially different relationship to

32. Speir, "Of Novels and the Novelist," 247. In "The Enduring Soil," Hamilton C. Horton Jr. argues that the location of factories in the rural South, which have provided much-needed jobs for rural people, has actually "*saved* the family farm" since income from most family farms alone is insufficient. Fifteen Southerners, *Why the South Will Survive* (Athens: University of Georgia Press, 1981) 61–62. Writing almost twenty years later in "Agriculture in the Post–World War II South" (in *The Rural South Since World War II*, ed. E. Douglas Hunt [Baton Rouge: Louisiana State University Press, 1998]), Donald Winters agrees that nonagricultural employment has preserved agrarian life for some part-time farmers, but he points out that "farming as a business has, for the most part, undermined farming as a way of life" (26). In 1981, Horton optimistically predicted that "the South may well be the first major region of this world to be industrialized and yet preserve the human dimension" (62). For an analysis of this prediction, see David R. Goldfield, "Urbanization in a Rural Culture: Suburban Cities and Country Cosmopolites," in *The South for New Southerners*, ed. Paul D. Escott and David R. Goldfield (Chapel Hill: University of North Carolina Press, 1991); and David R. Goldfield, *Promised Land: The South Since 1945* (Arlington Heights, Ill.: Harlan Davidson, 1987).

33. In "Faulkner in Time," Douglas reiterates Jean-Paul Sartre's point that in Faulkner's metaphysic, "the future does not exist" (298).

34. In Douglas's *Can't Quit You, Baby* (1988; New York: Penguin Books, 1989), Tweet, a poor black woman, loses her small family farm because of white greed and white manipulation of the legal and banking systems. For analysis of how the lives of southern

landownership in the South, it is not surprising that while contemporary white agrarians such as Bell and Douglas are preoccupied with the beauty of southern places, even as they criticize the white privilege that predominates, many southern black agrarians such as Ernest Gaines, Randall Kenan, and Dori Sanders focus primarily on the power that comes from landownership and the problems that still arise based on a legacy of mistrust across the color line.

In *A Gathering of Old Men,* because Ernest Gaines's old men do not own the land they once farmed, they lose a way of life. In contrast, in Randall Kenan's "The Foundations of the Earth," because Miss Maggie does own her own land, she not only has financial independence but the freedom to rebel against the prejudice, homophobia, and religiosity of her black neighbors, even her minister. But continued wariness about trusting white people is a subject of primary importance in agrarian fiction by contemporary African American writers. In Kenan's "Run, Mourner, Run," a black landowner, who is an undeclared homosexual, is blackmailed by a greedy white landowner into selling his land so that he can remain in the closet, thereby protecting his reputation in his conservative rural community. In Dori Sanders's *Clover,* a black peach farmer predicates his dealings with whites on the belief that "a white man never gets enough land or money," a racial generalization that causes unfortunate misunderstandings and that Sanders attempts to undermine. In *Her Own Place,* Sanders represents the past inequities from which such present generalizations arise: Mae Lee Barnes has the money to buy land, but until she finally identifies the one white landowner in her county willing to sell to a black person, she despairs of ever fulfilling her desire to farm, for none of her black neighbors own property.[35]

In *The Rock Cried Out,* Douglas finesses her failure to resolve the ongoing McLaurin/Daniels landownership saga by having Alan resist the storyteller's urge "to tie up loose ends" (303). But if Douglas has no solu-

---

rural blacks continue to be shaped by the "legacy" of "slavery, sharecropping, segregation, marginal employment opportunities, and limited educational choices," see Louis E. Swanson et al., "African Americans in Southern Rural Regions: The Importance of Legacy," in the special issue, "Blacks in Rural America," of *Review of Black Political Economy* 22, no. 4 (Spring 1994): 109–24. See also Daniel T. Lichter, "Race, Employment Hardship, and Inequality in the American Nonmetropolitan South," *American Sociological Review* 54 (June 1989): 436–46.

35. Stories by Randall Kenan in *Let the Dead Bury Their Dead* (New York: Harcourt Brace and Company, 1992); Dori Sanders, *Clover* (1990; New York: Fawcett Columbine, 1991), 137; Dori Sanders, *Her Own Place* (Chapel Hill: Algonquin Books, 1993).

tion to the thorny problem of inequitable land distribution in the South, the conclusion of her novel both shows why liberal southerners can and must go home again and suggests how they should write about the South. Alan reveals that his strategy in writing the novel, which we have just read, has been to tell all: "adding a sentence here, a paragraph there, trying to put in everything, to ask and answer as many questions" as he can (302). Although Alan resists the moralist's urge "to make his point," the ending that he writes—simply stating that he cannot tie up loose ends because "the shape [of his story] is still changing" (303)—reverberates beyond his narrative to become a comment on contemporary southern fiction. Jan Gretlund has proclaimed Madison Jones's characters the "last southern agrarians," and although the fate of Bell's Laidlaw seems to bear him out, Douglas's McLaurins and Danielses suggest that this southern species has not died out yet. However, their stories are changing along with their new relationships to the land and to each other. The enemies of the contemporary southern agrarians are no longer specialization and mechanization but racism and self-deception. Both *Soldier's Joy* and *The Rock Cried Out* enact Wendell Berry's warning that any attempt "to redefine Southernness without resort to geography" in a regional attempt to escape American homogenization is problematic. Berry suggests that such "a regionalism of the mind" creates "a map without a territory, which is to say a map impossible to correct, a map subject to become fantastical and silly like that Southern chivalry-of-the-mind that Mark Twain so properly condemned." Madison Smartt Bell and Ellen Douglas suggest that such "a regionalism of the mind" homogenizes the South and its people.[36]

36. Jan Nordby Gretlund, *Frames of Southern Mind: Reflections on the Stoic, Bi-Racial and Existential South* (Odense: Odense University Press, 1998), 47, 48; Wendell Berry, "Writer and Region," *Hudson Review* 40, no. 1 (spring 1987): 25. The phrase "to redefine Southernness without resort to geography" is quoted by Berry from the *New York Times Book Review* article by Marc K. Stengel, "Modernism on the Mississippi: *The Southern Review* 1935–1985" (24 November 1985, 3). In this article, Stengel reports that during a symposium to honor the *Southern Review*, the participants agreed that definitions of regionalism had been too limiting and that since the material South was disappearing, they should "redefine Southernness without resort to geography." Berry's immediate response is a reminder that the natural world is not subject "to limitless homogenization" (25).

Toni Morrison's Revisionary "Nature Writing": *Song of Solomon* and the Blasted Pastoral

Wes Berry

African American contributions to the genre of nature writing have been few.[1] As Elizabeth Dodd points out in the recent *PMLA* forum on literatures of the environment, "African Americans seem largely absent from this burgeoning literary, cultural, and critical movement." Exceptions include Alice Walker, whose collection *Living by the Word* contains several essays dealing with ecological issues, and Eddy Harris, whose travel narrative *Mississippi Solo* offers some of what one expects from the genre: attention to the details of landscape, excursions into spaces distanced from human population centers, and philosophical reflections about the relationships between humans and other-than-human nature.[2] Furthermore, Toni Morrison expands the possibilities of African American environmental writing by exploring through a black male protagonist the healing potential of southern woodlands; she accordingly forces a reeval-

1. Gracious thanks to Ann Fisher-Wirth and Jay Watson for reading drafts of this essay and offering skillful criticism.

2. Elizabeth Dodd, "Forum on Literatures of the Environment," *PMLA* 114 (1999): 1094; Alice Walker, *Living By the Word* (San Diego: Harcourt, 1988); Eddy L. Harris, *Mississippi Solo: A River Quest* (New York: Harper, 1988).

uation of African American attitudes toward "wilderness" and "wild-life." Her novel *Song of Solomon* examines the complicated interactions of an African American protagonist with southern fields and woodlands, as do texts by Zora Neale Hurston, Richard Wright, Eddy Harris, and others. The significant difference is that Morrison's portrayal of a black man returning to the South, learning his family history and experiencing a newfound sense of rootedness in the place, relates an affirmative relationship of African Americans with landscape in a language recalling narratives of regeneration through wilderness in the American nature-writing tradition.

Many of the standard texts we consider to be "nature writing" are informed by what critic John Tallmadge calls the "excursion": "a simple neighborhood walk during which the curious naturalist merely records observations." Tallmadge cites Gilbert White's *Natural History of Selbourne* as an early text structured by this framework. Other practitioners of the mode include William Wordsworth, "for whom nature provided lessons in the conduct of life and the motions of the mind," Ralph Waldo Emerson, Henry Thoreau, Edward Abbey, John Muir, Aldo Leopold, Annie Dillard, Terry Tempest Williams, and other Anglo-American writers. Eddy Harris's memoir of his Mississippi River quest is structured by such an excursion, going beyond the "neighborhood walk" by venturing within a riparian landscape packed with natural history, myth, more-than-human life, and unique human settlements. Most African American writing that gives intensive treatment to the nonhuman environment does so within the context of human communities. Jean Toomer's *Cane* paints detailed scenes of the Georgia landscape, but Toomer seldom writes about landscape for landscape's sake, chronicling instead how the nonhuman environment and human actions share a mutual influence. Zora Neale Hurston's *Their Eyes Were Watching God* likewise deals with how human communities interact with southern landscapes, her primary topography being the "Glades" of Florida. Other examples include Dori Sanders's *Her Own Place,* chronicling the life of hard-working African American farmers in South Carolina, and Gloria Naylor's *Mama Day,* a novel set in an island community between South Carolina and Georgia. These texts satisfy one of the tenets for an environmentally oriented work that Lawrence Buell outlines in his book *The Environmental Imagination*: "The nonhuman environment is present not merely as a framing device but as a presence that begins to suggest that human history is implicated in natural history." "Nature" is more than a mere backdrop; it is a force shaping and being shaped by human action. Accordingly, African American writing about the more-than-human environment is seldom separated from cultural and historical contexts.[3]

In canonical nature writing, wilderness is often a destination, a playground where a person can be freed for a while from the mathematical progression of modern civilization. In the words of environmental historian William Cronon, wilderness generally "represents a flight from history": "Seen as the original garden, it is a place outside of time, from which human beings had to be ejected before the fallen world of history could properly begin. . . . Seen as the bold landscape of frontier heroism, it is the place of youth and childhood, into which men escape by abandoning their pasts and entering a world of freedom where the constraints of civilization fade into memory. . . . No matter what the angle from which we regard it, wilderness offers us the illusion that we can escape the cares and troubles of the world in which our past has ensnared us." Richard Slotkin concurs: "The characteristic American gesture in the face of adversity is . . . immersion in the native element, the wilderness, as the solution to all problems, the balm to all wounds of the soul, the restorative for failing fortunes." This motif of an individual recuperating from adversity and loss through immersion in "wild" or "natural" landscapes recurs often in contemporary Anglo-American writing. In nonfiction and autobiography about southern places, this pattern is manifest in *The Horn Island Logs of Walter Inglis Anderson,* in which the narrator, who has suffered from mental disease, undergoes a recuperative experience by immersing himself in the elements of an island off the Gulf Coast; and in *Crossing Wildcat Ridge: A Memoir of Nature and Healing,* Philip Lee Williams shares how North Georgia woodlands—trees, birds, insects, water, and other nonhuman life—advance his recuperation from openheart surgery and depression. Environmental philosopher Barry Lopez writes: "That wilderness can revitalize someone who has spent too long in the highly manipulative, perversely efficient atmosphere of modern life

---

3. John Tallmadge, "Beyond the Excursion: Initiatory Themes in Annie Dillard and Terry Tempest Williams," in *Reading the Earth: New Directions in the Study of Literature and Environment,* ed. Michael P. Branch et al. (Moscow, Id.: University of Idaho Press, 1998), 197; Jean Toomer, *Cane* (1923; rprt., New York: Norton, 1988); Zora Neale Hurston, *Their Eyes Were Watching God* (1937; rprt., New York: Harper, 1990); Dori Sanders, *Her Own Place* (New York: Fawcett Columbine, 1993); Gloria Naylor, *Mama Day* (New York: Vintage, 1988); Lawrence Buell, *The Environmental Imagination: Thoreau, Nature Writing, and the Formation of American Culture* (Cambridge: Harvard University Press, 1995), 7.

is a widely shared notion." These southern texts by Anglo writers testify to this belief.[4]

In novels and memoirs by minority writers, however, "wilderness" is bound up with cultural memory to an extent that it is seldom just a place to escape to. In *Mississippi Solo,* Harris makes clear that his canoe voyage on the Mississippi River is more than a jaunt through the countryside to explore its natural history. He is also concerned with the human history of the river, including the settlements dotting its banks. Other texts written by African Americans represent the complexities that individuals may confront in realizing "healing potential" in landscapes fraught with historic violence. In Richard Wright's *Uncle Tom's Children,* for instance, chirping night crickets (a pleasant music for some who live in rural households where windows are left open on summer nights) become for minority protagonist Big Boy a surprising sound: at once a part of a pastoral imagery of butterflies, bees, sweet-scented honeysuckle, and twittering sparrows, but also a sound intermixed with the shouts of a lynching mob. Additionally, Harris's *South of Haunted Dreams* offers an account of "fronting" southern landscapes that, from the perspective of black history, pose both physical and psychological challenges. This travel narrative operates under the rubric of masculine exploration, with Harris, the solo quester, traveling into exotic southern landscapes that he imagines as potentially threatening, a type of *Heart of Darkness* on a BMW motorcycle. Harris brings along with him his cultural memory, which shapes how he experiences the physical environment.[5]

Likewise, in Hurston's *Their Eyes Were Watching God* and Toni Morrison's *Beloved,* undomesticated spaces are a mixed blessing. In Hurston's novel, when the matriarch of a plantation threatens to whip Nanny and sell her child, Nanny flees into a swamp. She recalls her fright to Janie: "Ah knowed de place was full uh moccasins and other bitin'

---

4. William Cronon, "The Trouble with Wilderness: or, Getting Back to the Wrong Nature," in *Uncommon Ground: Toward Reinventing Nature,* ed. William Cronon (New York: Norton, 1995), 79–80; Richard Slotkin, *Regeneration Through Violence: The Mythology of the American Frontier, 1600–1860* (Hanover, N.H.: Wesleyan University Press, 1973); Walter Inglis Anderson, *The Horn Island Logs of Walter Inglis Anderson,* ed. Redding S. Sugg Jr. (Rev. ed.; Jackson: University Press of Mississippi, 1985); Philip Lee Williams, *Crossing Wildcat Ridge: A Memoir of Nature and Healing* (Athens: University of Georgia Press, 1999); Barry Lopez, *Crossing Open Ground* (London: Picador, 1989), 82.

5. Richard Wright, *Uncle Tom's Children* (1940; rprt., New York: HarperPerennial, 1993), 28, 55; Eddy Harris, *South of Haunted Dreams: A Ride Through Slavery's Old Back Yard* (New York: Simon and Schuster, 1993).

snakes, but Ah was more skeered uh whut was behind me. . . . Ah don't see how come mah milk didn't kill mah chile, wid me so skeered and worried all de time. De noise uh de owls skeered me; de limbs of dem cypress trees took to crawlin' and movin round after dark, and two three times Ah heered panthers prowlin' round." Nanny perceives this swamp with complicated emotions; it terrifies her but also offers her sanctuary from the wrath of the "Mistis." Morrison's *Beloved,* furthermore, explores how Paul D. constructs an imaginary barrier between himself and rural southern landscapes—both "wild" and domesticated—as a means of coping, of staying sane in places where he lacks the freedom to own a piece of land. He escapes from slave bondage several times and travels in Georgia, Alabama, North Carolina, Kentucky, Delaware, "and in all those escapes he could not help being astonished by the beauty of this land that was not his. He hid in its breast, fingered its earth for food, clung to its banks to lap water and tried not to love it. On nights when the sky was personal, weak with the weight of its own stars, he made himself not love it. Its graveyards and low-lying rivers. Or just a house— solitary under a chinaberry tree; maybe a mule tethered and the light hitting its hide just so. Anything could stir him and he tried hard not to love it." By emphasizing Paul D.'s schizoid attraction to and dissociation from the land, Morrison forces us to consider how the impulse to possess land may be more complex for historically marginalized people.[6]

Paul D. reminds one of Ralph Kabnis, a character in Toomer's *Cane.* Toomer's Georgia is a place of "pain and beauty," a "land of cotton" where the white folks get the boll and blacks get the stalk. Southern nights entice northern intellectual Kabnis. The hills and valleys are "heaving with folk-songs," "a radiant beauty in the night that touches and tortures." He is attracted to the deep-rooted African culture and simultaneously repulsed by a place where humans burn and hang other humans. Rural Georgia offers "the serene loveliness of . . . autumn moonlight," but also "loneliness, dumbness, [and] awful, intangible oppression" that can drive one to insanity. Eldridge Cleaver summed up such African American ambivalence to rural landscapes thirty years ago in an essay entitled "The Land Question and Black Liberation":

> From the very beginning, Afro-America has had a land hang-up. The slaves were kidnapped on their own soil, transported thousands of miles across the ocean and set down in a strange land. They found themselves in

---

6. Hurston, *Their Eyes Were Watching God,* 17–18; Toni Morrison, *Beloved* (New York: Plume, 1988), 268.

a totally hostile situation and America became a land from which black people wanted only to flee, to escape such evil soil and those vicious creatures who had usurped it.

During slavery itself, black people learned to hate the land. From sunup to sundown, the slaves worked the land: plowing, sowing, and reaping crops for somebody else, for profit they themselves would never see or taste. This is why, even today, one of the most provocative insults that can be tossed at a black is to call him a farm boy, to infer that he is from a rural area or in any way attached to an agrarian situation. In terms of seeking status in America, blacks—principally the black bourgeoisie—have come to measure their own value according to the number of degrees they are away from the soil.

Security and terror, sublimity and alienation—African American attitudes toward southern landscapes are packed with conflict.[7]

*   *   *

Literary critic Gurleen Grewal notes that *Song of Solomon* resonates alongside novels "that have documented and refashioned ethnic identities in the United States since the 1970s": Louise Erdrich's *Love Medicine,* Maxine Hong Kingston's *China Men,* Leslie Marmon Silko's *Ceremony,* and Peter Najerian's *Voyages.* In such novels, "characters' self-hatred and angry confusion are related to a historic dispossession and to a psyche cut off from ancestral or communal wellsprings; their narratives chart a moving and powerful repossession of selfhood, articulating personal well-being in terms of the collective." *Song of Solomon* examines a similar theme through the character of Milkman Dead, a young midwesterner who travels alone to a rural community in the Blue Ridge Mountains, the locus of his paternal ancestry. Milkman's trip to the South has been the subject of a significant amount of critical inquiry. Most critics have focused on the final section of the novel, framed by Milkman's searching for mythical gold and his ultimate enthusiasm for discovering the oral history of his family. Stephanie A. Demetrakopoulos views Milkman's flight to the South in quest of gold as an "archetype of the hero leaving home to seek his fortune," and his subsequent "ego

---

7. Toomer, *Cane,* 107, 84–86; Eldridge Cleaver, *Eldridge Cleaver: Post-Prison Writings and Speeches,* ed. Robert Scheer (New York: Random House, 1967), 57–58. Granted the apparent shortage of African American narratives of regeneration through landscape, if landscape is understood in the traditional sense of wilderness, still there is another subgenre where regeneration is achieved through what Wendell Berry calls "kindly use" of the land. Here the pattern is not so much one of escape and relinquishment as it is one of "settling in," of domestic cultivation and farming. Dori Sanders's *Her Own Place,* a novel tracing the life of Mae Lee Barnes, a female farmer in South Carolina who is loyal to her farm and community, is one contemporary African American novel modeling this alternate mode of regeneration through work and benevolent use of the land.

death" as a point of maturation. She writes, "Milkman can connect authentically and deeply with women and his own anima only through and after this ego death." Gurleen Grewal points out that Milkman is raised with little historical perspective and is thus "representative of every person's existential predicament: that of being born to a time and place in medias res. . . . Milkman has grown up within the specific cultural discontinuity created by migration from the South to the urban north and by the black middle-class's repudiation of a stigmatized past." His trip to Virginia brings a reversal of this existential condition through a newfound awakening to family history and through his connection to a human community. "The entire novel is about the interdependence of individuals and the insurance of mutual life; redemption cannot be individual," Grewal writes. This statement brings to mind farmer-writer Wendell Berry's emphasis on holistic health care, his belief that "the community—in the fullest sense: a place and all its creatures—is the smallest unit of health and that to speak of the health of an isolated individual is a contradiction in terms."[8]

Milkman Dead certainly undergoes a change in attitude while visiting his ancestral homeland, and yes, this shift is linked to his establishing roots—an understanding of familial cultural continuity—where none existed before. My intrigue, however, lies in the echoes of American "nature writing" that I detect in Morrison's prose. To what extent is Milkman's "regenerative moment" in the Virginia woodlands a sincere expression of natural mysticism or, conversely, a parody of the American gesture of escaping into the wilds to soothe the wounds of the soul?[9]

Milkman is a dynamic character whose growth Morrison charts by illustrating his progressive awareness of the landscapes he moves within. Scenes that immerse Milkman in unfamiliar territory, that show him struggling as an uninitiated visitor to sylvan lands, are reminiscent of literature in the American naturalist tradition. Like ecologist Anne La-

8. Gurleen Grewal, *Circles of Sorrow, Lines of Struggle: The Novels of Toni Morrison* (Baton Rouge: Louisiana State University Press, 1998), 63, 66, 73; Karla F. C. Holloway and Stephanie A. Demetrakopoulos, *New Dimensions of Spirituality: A Biracial and Bicultural Reading of the Novels of Toni Morrison* (New York: Greenwood, 1987), 93; Wendell Berry, *Another Turn of the Crank* (Washington, D.C.: Counterpoint, 1995), 90.

9. Ann E. Imbrie, " 'What Shalimar Knew': Toni Morrison's *Song of Solomon* as a Pastoral Novel," *College English* 55, no. 5 (1993): 473–90, addresses how the novel develops patterns of such archetypal pastoral literature as *The Winter's Tale* and *As You Like It*, and thus is likewise concerned with the excursion motif—the restorative sojourn from the "civilized" place and into the "natural" world.

Bastille—who details in her memoir *Woodswoman* how she fronts harsh, dangerous winters while relocating to a remote cabin in the Adirondack National Park, gaining a heightened awareness of her own limitations and strengths[10]—Milkman becomes more self-aware through his encounters with the "other" realm of woods, streams, and caves. During the early stages of Milkman's southbound journey, he is a passive observer of his surroundings. On a Greyhound bus approaching Danville, Pennsylvania, Milkman tries to appreciate the scenery he has heard his father rave about, "but Milkman saw it as merely green, deep into its Indian summer but cooler than his own city, although farther south. . . . For a few minutes he tried to enjoy the scenery running past his window, then the city man's boredom with nature's repetition overtook him. Some places had lots of trees, some did not; some fields were green, some were not, and the hills in the distance were like the hills in every distance. . . . His eyes were creasing from the sustained viewing of uneventful countryside."[11] A few pages earlier, at the beginning of the second section of the novel, Morrison emphasizes the disjunction or radical shift from urban space to rural by showing Milkman bungling through this strange territory, blind to the multiple species and local life surrounding him. In the countryside outside of Danville, Milkman "was oblivious to the universe of wood life that did live there in layers of ivy grown so thick he could have sunk his arm in it up to the elbow. . . . Life that burrowed and scurried, and life so still it was indistinguishable from the ivy stems on which it lay. Birth, life, and death—each took place on the hidden side of a leaf" (220). But of course, Milkman is not concerned about what occurs on the underbelly of a leaf, the "universe" of wood life—insect and animal communities—because he is forever moving, negligent of even the human communities he encounters.

We first encounter Milkman's lack of interest in the landscape early in Part II of the novel as he rides the bus into Danville, and we appropriately perceive the first stages of his heightening perception as he rides the Greyhound bus away from that place. After his uncomfortable experience in the country, Milkman has a changed vision: "The low hills in the distance were no longer scenery to him. They were real places that could split your thirty-dollar shoes" (256). Milkman's excursion through the fields and woodlands of Pennsylvania in quest of gold provides substantial comic

10. Anne LaBastille, *Woodswoman* (New York: Penguin, 1976).

11. Toni Morrison, *Song of Solomon* (New York: Plume, 1987), 226–27. Subsequent references to this work are given parenthetically in the text.

relief. He falls into a creek, tears the sole of a leather dress shoe, agitates bats in a cave with his "hollering," and is thereafter driven, shoe sole flapping, from the cave. This disjunction between the protagonist and the landscapes he encounters forces him to reevaluate his character and opens him to new possibilities. Or, as ecocritic Scott Slovic writes about literary naturalists, "it is only by testing the boundaries of self against an outside medium (such as nature) that many nature writers manage to realize who they are and what's what in the world."[12]

Milkman's rejuvenation involves much more than a bonding with so-called "nature"; it also involves his growing respect for a human community and its history. Before making the trip to Pennsylvania, Milkman "had never had to try to make a pleasant impression on a stranger before, never needed anything from a stranger before, and did not remember ever asking anybody in the world how they were" (229). His compassion for human others has been slight, as evidenced by his careless attitude toward members of his family. For example, he breaks his long-term relationship with Hagar by sending her a terse note and some money. He steals from his aunt Pilate. He has been the recipient of a privileged childhood, without having to give much in return. His older sister Magdalene chastises him for his selfishness, suggesting that he has "peed" on people since childhood: " 'You've been laughing at us all your life. Corinthians. Mama. Me. Using us, ordering us, and judging us: how we cook your food; how we keep your house. . . . You have yet to wash your own underwear, spread a bed, wipe the ring from your tub, or move a fleck of your dirt from one place to another. And to this day, you have never asked one of us if we were tired, or sad, or wanted a cup of coffee. You've never picked up anything heavier than your own feet, or solved a problem harder than fourth-grade arithmetic' " (215). Milkman's southbound journey places him in difficult situations—for instance, his bungling excursion into the Pennsylvania countryside—that force him to reevaluate his attitudes toward others.

After his initiation into the rugged Pennsylvania countryside, Milkman travels to the Blue Ridge Mountains. The journey ultimately liberates Milkman, allowing him a sense of independence from the long arm of his wealthy, domineering father. Before he adopts a newfound responsibility to self and others, however, Milkman encounters and overcomes

12. Scott Slovic, *Seeking Awareness in American Nature Writing: Henry Thoreau, Annie Dillard, Edward Abbey, Wendell Berry, Barry Lopez* (Salt Lake City: University of Utah Press, 1992), 4.

multiple challenges. For instance, upon arriving in the town of Shalimar, Virginia—a "no-name hamlet . . . so small nothing financed by state funds or private enterprise reared a brick there" (259)—Milkman confronts economic need and the violence stemming from it. He is a conspicuous stranger: "His manner, his clothes were reminders that they [the poor locals] had no crops of their own and no land to speak of either. Just vegetable gardens, which the women took care of, and chickens and pigs that the children took care of. He was telling them that they weren't men, that they relied on women and children for their food. And that the lint and tobacco in their pants pockets where dollar bills should have been was the measure" (266). Shalimar is not the "home" that Milkman expects. He assumes the locals will treat him with respect, as they have in other small towns en route to Shalimar. Indeed, his positive experiences with people in the early stages of his journey prompt him to wonder why black people ever left the South: "Where he went, there wasn't a white face around, and the Negroes were as pleasant, wide-spirited, and self-contained as could be" (260). In the impoverished hamlet of Shalimar, however, Milkman encounters men who challenge him to a knife fight. His ancestral "home" appears to offer little more than a dilapidated service station and easily offended, unemployed rustics.

Some local men invite Milkman on a nighttime hunting trip, an episode that sets up the ego dissolution that several critics associate with growth or maturity.[13] Morrison seems to be intentionally pushing readers to connect Milkman's experience with the motif of relinquishment common in American literary naturalism, by using a language of land-based mysticism familiar to the genre. Before examining a key passage, however, I wish to consider for a moment Annie Dillard's discourse on "seeing" in her staple of American nature writing, *Pilgrim at Tinker Creek*. Like Wordsworth in his poems on childhood, Dillard romanticizes infancy as a time of hypersensitive perception. She accordingly la-

---

13. In addition to Stephanie A. Demetrakopoulos's psychoanalytic reading of Milkman's "ego death," Joyce Irene Middleton's "From Orality to Literacy: Oral Memory in Toni Morrison's *Song of Solomon*," in *New Essays on "Song of Solomon*," ed. Valerie Smith (Cambridge: Cambridge University Press: 1995), focuses on how the scene highlights Milkman's initiation into African American "cultural oral memory": "Milkman's immersion in this auditory experience awakens his dormant listening skills to new language experiences and ways of knowing." His experience in the woods "move[s] him to use his preliterate imagination to reclaim his unlettered ancestors' skill for listening," an ability that saves his life by enabling him to sense Guitar's presence and thus avoid being strangled by him (35).

ments the passage of innocence that accompanies adult knowledge and the consequent loss of "newly sighted" vision that follows our immersion in language systems. "Form is condemned to an eternal danse macabre with meaning," she writes. Dillard therefore desires to see "the world unraveled from reason, Eden before Adam gave names." She is unable as an adult to see the "color patches" she believes she saw as an infant. "My brain then must have been smooth as any balloon," she reflects. "I'm told I reached for the moon; many babies do. But the color-patches of infancy swelled as meaning filled them. . . . The moon rocketed away." To be able to reclaim this rare privileged vision, one must relinquish one's ego, Dillard suggests. One must "hush the noise of useless interior babble." But of course few individuals are privy to this gift, because "the mind's muddy river, this ceaseless flow of trivia and trash, cannot be dammed. . . . Instead you must allow the muddy river to flow unheeded in the dim channels of consciousness. . . . The secret of seeing is to sail on solar wind. Hone and spread your spirit till you yourself are a sail, whetted, translucent, broadside to the merest puff." Dillard's prose is fanciful—the skeptical reader may call it ridiculously abstract, akin to Emerson's metaphor of the transparent eyeball—but nevertheless it conveys the idea that dissolution of the ego is a necessary stage toward an experience of natural mysticism.[14]

Bearing in mind Dillard's words, consider Toni Morrison's description of Milkman when he falls behind on the nighttime hunting trip in the Blue Ridge Mountains. The other hunters, in pursuit of a bobcat, leave Milkman behind. He is winded. He cannot keep up with their pace. He wants to rest a while under a sweet gum tree, long enough at least to allow his heart to drop back down into his chest. There he rests, his mind filled with existential ponderings, when suddenly, without warning, he experiences a momentary reprieve from his ego: "Under the moon, on the ground, alone, with not even the sound of baying dogs to remind him that he was with other people, his self—the cocoon that was his 'personality'—gave way. He could barely see his own hand, and couldn't see his feet. He was only his breath, coming slower now, and his thoughts. The rest of him had disappeared" (277). Milkman's thoughts, however, remain. Indeed, unlike with Dillard, who views spiritual perception as the world detached from language and reason, Milkman's mystical moment is bound up with language. It is for him a new language—the voices of people and animals tied to their regional landscape.

14. Annie Dillard, *Pilgrim at Tinker Creek* (1974; Toronto: Bantam, 1975), 31–32, 34, 35.

As with Ike McCaslin in Faulkner's "The Bear," Milkman's material possessions will not help him in the woods, but hamper him. "His watch and his two hundred dollars would be of no help out here, where all a man had was what he was born with, or had learned to use. And endurance." Like young McCaslin, Milkman must abandon his material possessions before he can learn the language of the woods—the distinctive, complicated communications between hunting dogs and men, and the subtle tracks on tree bark and the ground that hunters read. He thinks there may be an ur-language shared by rustics, "[l]anguage in the time when men and animals did talk to one another, when a man could sit down with an ape and the two converse; when a tiger and a man could share the same tree, and each understood the other; when men ran *with* wolves, not from or after them" (278). Milkman feels a sudden rush of brotherly love under the sweet gum tree in the Blue Ridge, and believes he may finally understand his country companions and his friend Guitar's nostalgia for the South. He admires for the first time these bobcat hunters, men like Calvin who can communicate with dogs and "read" the earth: "It was more than tracks Calvin was looking for—he whispered to the trees, whispered to the ground, touched them, as a blind man caresses a page of Braille, pulling meaning through his fingers" (278).

Withdrawing from the hunt for just a brief time opens Milkman to this flood of thoughts and raises his awareness of these alternate modes of perception; Milkman therefore reminds one of Thoreau, Dillard, Edward Abbey, Barry Lopez, and other naturalists who believe one may discover rare perception when distancing oneself from the white noise of dominant society. Lopez, for instance, suggests that places like the Inner Gorge of the Grand Canyon offer incomparable respite from the pain of the world. Down in the belly of the canyon, an individual may experience a "stripping down, an ebb of the press of conventional time, a radical change of proportion, an unspoken respect for others that elicits keen emotional pleasure, a quick, intimate pounding of the heart."[15] In like manner, while alone in the bucolic quiet of the Virginia night, Milkman begins to "merge" with the woodlands of his ancestors: "Down either side of his thighs he felt the sweet gum's surface roots cradling him like the rough but maternal hands of a grandfather. Feeling both tense and relaxed, he sank his fingers into the grass" (279).

However, for Milkman there is no escape to the "original garden," for his moment of "union" with the dirt and sweet gum is interrupted when

15. Lopez, *Crossing Open Ground*, 52–53.

a man tries to strangle him. Morrison bursts Milkman's pastoral moment with violence: "He tried to listen with his fingertips, to hear what, if anything, the earth had to say, and it told him quickly that someone was standing behind him and he had just enough time to raise one hand to his neck and catch the wire that fastened around his throat" (279). Milkman's childhood friend Guitar, having tracked him from the city, unleashes on Milkman his history of racial frustration. As Grewal notes, "Guitar's problem is a baneful race politics sowing discord with hate." Earlier in the novel, we learn how Guitar attempts to check hate crimes against black people by murdering white people. He wants to keep the ratio of black to white in balance. Before Milkman begins his trip south, Guitar reminds him about the links between racial oppression and the control of land holdings: "The earth is soggy with black people's blood. And before us Indian blood . . . and if it keeps on there won't be any of us left and there won't be any land for those who are left. So the numbers [the ratio of black to white people] have to remain static" (158). Guitar's statement recalls Eldridge Cleaver's point about the "deep land hunger" of African Americans: "Suffice it to say that Afro-Americans are just as land hungry as were the Mau Mau, the Chinese people, the Cuban people; just as much so as all the people of the world who are grappling with the tyrant of colonialism now, trying to get possession of some land of their own." Both Guitar's and Cleaver's remarks remind us that unbuilt landscapes and "wild" places are far from being ahistorical. Morrison seems to be emphasizing this point, forcing readers to consider Milkman's potential regeneration in the woods within the context of black-on-black crime, or, perhaps, to connect the wire around his neck with the lynchings that have bloodied southern ground.[16]

In *Ride Out the Wilderness: Geography and Identity in Afro-American Literature,* Melvin Dixon reads Milkman's experience with the southern landscape as authentic regeneration. He believes Milkman "develops a more effective relation to the land when he confronts the wilderness. . . . Milkman's participation in the hunt gains . . . fraternity and friendship [of local men]. . . . Milkman has to earn kinship by enduring the woods, the wilderness. Like the fugitive in slave narratives, he has to renew his covenant with nature to secure passage out of the wilderness that had invited him in." Dixon reads the southern woodlands he calls "wilderness" as a proving ground for meaningful livelihood. Similarly, in *Reclaiming Community in Contemporary African American Fiction,*

16. Grewal, *Circles of Sorrow,* 71; Cleaver, *Eldridge Cleaver,* 63.

Philip Page notes that Milkman's night in the woods serves the function of connecting him with his heritage: "Milkman is guided not only by ancestor figures but also by Calvin, Small Boy, Luther, and Omar, who initiate him during the hunt and offer him the bobcat's heart, thereby inducting him into his past and his racial identity and midwifing his rebirth in harmony with himself, his family, his community, and nature." These evaluations seem apt, for after Milkman's interrupted merging with the southern woodlands, he appears renewed. Walking along with the local hunters, Milkman "found himself exhilarated by simply walking the earth. Walking it like he belonged on it; like his legs were stalks, tree trunks, a part of his body that extended down down down into the rock and soil, and were comfortable there—on the earth and on the place where he walked" (281). Perhaps the exhilaration he feels is a case of "death makes life sweet," a type of euphoria expressed by those who have recovered from life-threatening cancers and car wrecks, or even by those awakening from realistic nightmares to find their bodies warm and breathing; or maybe Milkman's elation is the result of a real transformation, a shift in attitude from one who feels disconnected from other people and places to one who, for the first time in his life, understands a sense of membership in a community. In the land of his ancestry, Milkman appears to experience rootedness, a sense of connection with the locals "as though there was some cord or pulse or information they shared. Back home [in the city] he had never felt that way, as though he belonged to anyplace or anybody" (293). One cannot, of course, neatly separate from "culture" to escape into "wilderness." Morrison recognizes this and accordingly brings Guitar, a stalking history of racial bigotry who confounds the archetypal moment of ego dissolution in the wilderness, back into the story.[17]

Is Morrison parodying conventional nature writing by suggesting that the archetypal "flight" into the woods and wilderness is much more complex for historically oppressed people? Consider, furthermore, how early in his travels Milkman hears from the local men in Pennsylvania stories about his grandfather, the magnificent Macon Dead—a model example of one who turned a piece of land into a profitable farm and therefore strived to establish a sense of history where none existed before. The farm

17. Melvin Dixon, *Ride Out the Wilderness: Geography and Identity in Afro-American Literature* (Urbana: University of Illinois Press, 1987), 167; Philip Page, *Reclaiming Community in Contemporary African American Fiction* (Jackson: University Press of Mississippi, 1999), 15.

owned and worked by Milkman's grandfather served as an inspiration for how to establish a sense of place and worth. It spoke "like a sermon" to the other poor men in Montour County:

> "You see?" the farm said to them. "See? See what you can do? . . . Here, this here, is what a man can do if he puts his mind to it and his back in it. Stop sniveling," it said. "Stop picking around the edges of the world. Take advantage, and if you can't take advantage, take disadvantage. We live here. On this planet, in this nation, in this country right here. *Nowhere else!* We got a home in this rock, don't you see! Nobody starving in my home; nobody crying in my home, and if I got a home you got one too! Grab it. Grab this land! Take it, hold it, my brothers, make it, my brothers, shake it, squeeze it, turn it, twist it, beat it, kick it, kiss it, whip it, stomp it, dig it, plow it, seed it, reap it, rent it, buy it, sell it, own it, build it, multiply it, and pass it on—can you hear me? Pass it on!" (235)

For these newly freed ex-slaves, the land is a commodity, property with which one needs to forge an identity and family history rather than to escape it. Furthermore, after this "sermon" on the land, in a descent from the sublime moment that is even more poignant than Milkman's interrupted merging with the sweet gum tree, the narrative shifts. In the next paragraph following the command to "Pass it on!" we read: "But they shot the top of his head off and ate his fine Georgia peaches. And even as boys these men began to die and were dying still" (235). White men murder Milkman's grandfather and take his farmland, thereby destroying not only a family's longevity in the place but also the will of the male progenitors who would shape the future of African American existence in that particular region. These African American subjects are deprived of agency unwillingly, in contrast to the tradition of ego dissolution in American nature writing, where subjects *desire* relinquishment of selfhood.

Where does Milkman's experience of "self" giving way under the sweet gum tree stand in relation to these violent, involuntary removals of selfhood? Where does his potential regeneration stand vis-à-vis the "classic" dissolutions of ego in American wilderness writing? Milkman's ego dissolution in/on unowned land provides a marked contrast to his father's attitude toward property as the material to confirm one's societal status. Macon Dead promises to Milkman an inheritance of property: "You'll own it all. All of it. You'll be free. Money is freedom. . . . The only real freedom there is" (163). Milkman's journey southward begins as a quest for such material prosperity, before he realizes spiritual benefits from intense interaction with a local culture and undeveloped wood-lands. In place of his father's version of freedom, Milkman discovers he can be rejuvenated through nonmaterial means, or as Valerie Smith puts it, "through [Milkman's] story, Morrison questions Western conceptions of individualism and offers more fluid, destabilized constructions of iden-tity."[18]

The quest for a destabilized or alternative mode of identity from that offered by dominant Western culture is shared by writers of American naturalism. I have noted how Annie Dillard seeks to experience "the world unraveled from reason." In *Desert Solitaire,* Edward Abbey de-scribes a kindred desire to escape Western modes of perception. About his self-imposed isolation in a Utah wilderness area, Abbey claims: "I want to be able to look at and into a juniper tree, a piece of quartz, a vulture, a spider, and see it as it is in itself, devoid of all humanly ascribed qualities, anti-Kantian, even the categories of scientific description. To meet God or Medusa face to face, even if it means risking everything human in myself. I dream of a hard a brutal mysticism in which the naked self merges with a nonhuman world and yet somehow survives still in-tact, individual, separate. Paradox and bedrock."[19] Milkman's climactic moment of "merging" with the sweet gum is just that—a "moment" of ego-dissolution, after which he must mobilize his mental and physical ca-pacities to repel/thwart his would-be murderer. Abbey's merging with the desert landscape is likewise tentative. Perhaps he drops some of his civi-lized mannerisms during his season in the wilderness, while getting closer to the more-than-human world, as when he crawls on his belly in an at-tempt to observe two gopher snakes entwined together in a courtship dance; but Abbey nevertheless remains intact, of (arguably) sane mind, or as he puts it, "individual, separate." Even though the experience with more-than-human nature is temporary, it nevertheless seems worthwhile to consider, as Abbey, Dillard, and Morrison do, these moments when an individual can sample a mode of "being" not grounded in material culture.

Interesting questions arise when we consider a hybrid literature such as *Song of Solomon* that illuminates the lives of African American subjects while making use of British and Anglo-American narrative conventions,

---

18. Valerie Smith, "Introduction," in *New Essays on "Song of Solomon,"* 13.
19. Edward Abbey, *Desert Solitaire: A Season in the Wilderness* (1968; New York: Touchstone, 1990), 6.

or, conversely, literature by writers of the dominant culture that appropriates the conventions of, say, Native American or African American art.[20] We may ask such questions as: How innocent (or not) is a writer's use of the themes, subjects, and narrative forms of the other culture? To what extent does a writer appropriate the conventions of the other uncritically? Is the writer sincere in the use of these conventions, or is she merely co-opting them for parodic effect? Lawrence Buell raises such questions when he notes how Native American poet Simon Ortiz mixes both "Native" and "Anglo" narrative conventions in his verse and therefore practices a "hybridized art." It would be wrongheaded, Buell asserts, to think of Ortiz as having been "colonized" by the time he spent at a writing program at Iowa or as "using western lyric conventions of persona and aesthetic distance to deconstruct them."[21] My initial reading of *Song of Solomon* was, perhaps, wrongheaded in this sense: I believed Morrison's use of such conventions as the moment of ego dissolution in the woods to be a parody of the mystical "nature writing" dominated by Anglo-American writers. A more constructive approach to Morrison's fiction, however, may ask how her "hybrid" art takes risks by placing an African American protagonist in a situation where he "finds" himself after losing his material well-being, after his magnificent ego is broken down, and is therefore a shift from what we expect from African American writers—namely, narratives that reinforce the importance of asserting and gaining subjectivity.[22] By echoing emphatically the language of

20. Writing about Third World literary traditions, particularly those of the Maori of New Zealand, C. Christopher Norden in "Ecological Restoration and the Evolution of Postcolonial National Identity in the Maori and Aboriginal Novel," in *Literature of Nature: An International Sourcebook*, ed. Patrick D. Murphy (Chicago: Fitzroy Dearborn, 1998), notes the critical richness of cross-cultural intertextuality. Noting that Maori writer Witi Ihimaera's novel *Tangi* may evoke in some readers echoes of Emerson, Whitman, and other American transcendentalists, Norden writes: "An interesting question regarding Native novelistic and poetic traditions concerns the degree to which particular writers have intentionally evoked and played off of either transcendentalist rhetoric, for models of spiritual connectedness, or . . . Anglo-American modernist writers for models of alienation from nature, community, and traditional culture" (274). Inquiries about the extent of such intertextual influences may, as I hope this essay has, continue to reveal fresh ways of viewing nature writing and the position of minority writing against or within it.

21. Buell, *The Environmental Imagination*, 20.

22. Demetrakopoulos's affirmative reading of Milkman's "ego death" in *Song of Solomon*, for instance, deviates from the focus upon ego consolidation often emphasized in African American literature and scholarship. Consider *Their Eyes Were Watching God*, which foregrounds the growth of Janie into a confident, independent woman. Through her oral autobiography to Phoeby, Janie affirms the value of her sexuality, voice, and sense of self-

ego dissolution in such canonical environmental texts as *Desert Solitaire* and *Pilgrim at Tinker Creek,* Morrison may be giving voice to a progressive "nature writing"—one that sincerely considers the spiritual possibilities of human interaction with more-than-human life-forms, but that does so within a complex web of cultural and historical contexts.[23]

worth. Likewise, a primary concern of Alice Walker's *The Color Purple* is Celie's acquisition of voice, her ability to assert her selfhood after years of forced silence and abuse by violent men. With the help of Shug, Celie realizes she is a valuable inhabitant of this earth.

23. Rachel Stein's *Shifting the Ground: American Women Writers' Revisions of Nature, Gender, and Race* (Charlottesville: University Press of Virginia, 1997) is one of a growing body of texts offering provocative criticisms of minority literature and its position in relation to canonical American nature writing. Stein's study includes discussions of textual production by Emily Dickinson, Zora Neale Hurston, Alice Walker, and Leslie Marmon Silko, as she explores her fundamental question: "[H]ow do their revisions of the intersections of nature, gender, and race shift the ground of problematic aspects of American identities and allow the writers to reimagine more fertile social/natural interrelations?" (4). Other texts considered to be a "new wave" of American literary ecology—shifting the focus of nature writing from the "pastoral impulse" to considerations of complex social problems bound up with our conceptualizations and use of what we call "nature"—include Karen J. Warren, ed., *Ecofeminism: Women, Culture, Nature* (Bloomington: Indiana University Press, 1997) and Greta Gaard and Patrick D. Murphy, eds., *Ecofeminist Literary Criticism: Theory, Interpretation, Pedagogy* (Urbana: University of Illinois Press, 1998).

Native American Literature, Ecocriticism, and the South: The Inaccessible Worlds of Linda Hogan's *Power*

Eric Gary Anderson

Chickasaw writer Linda Hogan's turn to Florida in her most recent novel, *Power* (1998), serves as a welcome reminder that the American South figures prominently in the literary as well as the larger multicultural history of Indian Country.[1] Of course, that such a reminder is needed at all also calls sharply to mind the various ways in which American Indians of the South have been colonized, dispossessed, and erased. They have been marginalized in highly visible ways (as, for example, mascots—Florida State University Seminoles) and have also been made to seem invisible; Spanish colonial forces, United States government officials, and other more local agents and agencies have expended a great deal of energy in their efforts to remove, reserve, assimilate, and/or terminate southern Native peoples.[2] At the same time and as one offshoot of

1. Linda Hogan, *Power* (New York: Norton, 1998). Further citations of *Power* are made parenthetically in the text.

2. On the Spanish colonial presence in the Southeast, see David J. Weber, *The Spanish Frontier in North America* (New Haven: Yale University Press, 1992). Of the many studies of Indian Removal, dispossession, assimilation, and/or termination, the following provide useful starting points: M. Annette Jaimes, ed., *The State of Native America: Genocide, Col-*

these struggles for land and power, non-Native writers and other custodians of southern literature and history often downplay the longstanding indigenous presence in, as it were, their own backyard. As Thadious M. Davis observes, "[t]he traditional southern world is divided into two parts, one white and the other black. Granted, there are other divisions within each part (class, caste, family, sex among others) but black and white are the two major divisions."[3] Given this traditional bicultural state of affairs, it is not surprising that the broader southern spectrum of multicultural interactions has received limited attention. In presenting her readers with an invented tribe of Florida Indians, the Taiga, whose lives are entirely predicated and centered on their intimate, knowing experiences of particular southern homeplaces, Hogan reminds us of how much we don't know, and how decentered, how inaccessible, how fictive, indeed how absent such lives and experiences can be in non-Native cultural histories of the South.

But in large part because the present-day Florida Indians of *Power* are so keenly and inescapably aware of their own cultural losses and their own marginalization, Hogan suggests that even an Indian-centered, Indian-narrated history of the American South will be incomplete: the elements of Florida Indian history that she transmits remain inaccessible, or grow increasingly so, even to the Florida Indian characters in question. And, by packaging this construction of history in the form of a novel,

---

onization, and Resistance (Boston: South End Press, 1992); Brian W. Dippie, *The Vanishing American: White Attitudes and U.S. Indian Policy* (Middletown, Conn.: Wesleyan University Press, 1982); Ronald Satz, *American Indian Policy in the Jacksonian Era* (Lincoln: University of Nebraska Press, 1975); Anthony F. C. Wallace, *The Long Bitter Trail: Andrew Jackson and the Indians* (New York: Hill and Wang, 1993); Frederick E. Hoxie, *A Final Promise: The Campaign to Assimilate the Indians, 1880–1920* (Lincoln: University of Nebraska Press, 1984); Donald L. Fixico, *Termination and Relocation: Federal Indian Policy, 1945–1960* (Albuquerque: University of New Mexico Press, 1986); and Robert Bensen, ed., *Children of the Dragonfly: Native American Voices on Child Custody and Education* (Tucson: University of Arizona Press, 2001).

3. Thadious M. Davis, *Faulkner's "Negro": Art and the Southern Context* (Baton Rouge: Louisiana State University Press, 1983), 3. Also see Doreen Fowler and Ann J. Abadie, eds., *Faulkner and Race* (Jackson: University Press of Mississippi, 1987), in which "race" almost exclusively signifies "African American." Of the fifteen contributors to this volume, only one makes even a glancing reference to the Chickasaw (and African American) character Sam Fathers; see Blyden Jackson, "Faulkner's Negroes Twain," in *Faulkner and Race*, 66–67. Fathers appears in William Faulkner, *Go Down, Moses* (1942; rprt., New York: Vintage, 1990) and elsewhere. See Howard C. Horsford, "Faulkner's (Mostly) Unreal Indians in Early Mississippi History," *American Literature* 64, no. 2 (June 1992): 311–30.

she raises additional, poststructuralist questions about the historicity of fiction and the fictionality of history. "Insider" knowledge and readerly knowledge come to seem ironically similar in that both can go only so far. For example, Omishto, the Taiga first-person narrator of *Power,* is well aware of the fragile, elusive presence of an "ancient" Indian world in the South, a world still visible at times to her: "Sometimes I see things as they were before this world, in the time of first people. Not just before the building of houses, the filling in of land, the drying up of water, but long ago, before we had canoes and torches and moved through the wet night like earthbound stars, slow and enchanted in our human orbit, knowing our route because . . . it had always been our route" (83). The lyric power of this passage evokes the narrator's own deep sense of connectedness to both her ancestors and the natural place she and they share. But, as her use of past-tense verbs indicates, the route has changed, and changed hands, to a significant extent within the much more recent history of the American Indian South. What she glimpses here and elsewhere, a few others of her very small tribe see more clearly and more frequently, but those who can "see things as they were before this world" live apart from the rest of their people as well as from the larger Euro-American world that is generally blind to such ways of seeing. *Power,* then, is less a novel about recovering the old ways and returning to the old routes than it is a novel about how these old ways are one teenaged Indian girl away from being not only relinquished but also extinguished. Access to the old ways, to the natural world that drives them, to the small Florida tribe that still bears responsibility for both, and to the American Indian South writ larger, is a form of literary and multicultural power— but power, as Hogan understands it, is a deeply fraught, deeply ambiguous entity that defies all desires—characters' and readers'—for instant gratification and confident cultural authority. Her welcome reminder of an Indian presence in the South carries with it a number of unwelcome, or at the very least vexing, complexities.

Of course, some of the complexities of American Indian experiences in the South are not exclusively "southern" in nature or import. As one result of European and Euro-American colonization, the South has become one of many key sites of legal contestations between Indian nations and the United States, and southern Indians are among the hundreds of Indian cultures that have been and continue to be lethally affected by colonial and federal policies and practices. Analogously, some of the general issues that Hogan investigates in *Power*—such as the tensions between resistance and assimilation and the pressures faced by younger

Native generations—will be recognizable to readers of American Indian literary texts not grounded in the South.[4] Like most Native texts, *Power* signifies both intertribally and intertextually; it is not an example of Native American literary isolationism. For the purposes of this essay, however, I am interested in mapping some of the particularities of Hogan's work—the elements that, perhaps subtly, distinguish it as southern, ecocritical, and inaccessible—as well as a few of the particularities of Indian-white arguments about the place and identity of indigenous cultures in the South. In 1830, for example, the Cherokee presented "memorials" to the United States Congress, petitioning that body to rethink its anti-Indian policies; then, in 1831, the Cherokee were famously and puzzlingly defined by U.S. Supreme Court Chief Justice John Marshall as a "domestic dependent nation." As one result of what Timothy Powell has called a "crisis of white entitlement," the South remains notorious as one of the places from which American Indians were, beginning in the 1830s, "removed" with brutal force by dictate of President Andrew Jackson. Chickasaws and Florida Seminoles, Cherokees, Creeks, and Choctaws, along with Quapaws and Caddoes, were forcibly removed to Indian Territory (Oklahoma, the place of Hogan's birth) and elsewhere. And in the mid-twentieth century, to cite but one more example, the Seminole Land Claims Case stands as an important and successful defense of Florida Seminole tribal sovereignty against the Indian Claims Commission and, by extension, the federal government—but, in one of the complexities of this case, the Florida Seminoles found themselves challenged by Oklahoma Seminoles who, as Harry A. Kersey Jr. explains, "made additional claims based upon their experiences after removal to Oklahoma."[5]

4. Both of these issues figure prominently in a number of contemporary works of American Indian fiction. See Leslie Marmon Silko, *Ceremony* (New York: Viking, 1977); James Welch, *Fools Crow* (New York: Viking, 1986) and *The Heartsong of Charging Elk* (New York: Doubleday, 2000); Louise Erdrich, *Tracks* (New York: Harper and Row, 1988) and *Love Medicine* (New and expanded ed.; New York: HarperCollins, 1993); and Sherman Alexie, *The Lone Ranger and Tonto Fistfight in Heaven* (New York: Atlantic Monthly Press, 1993).

5. The Cherokee memorials are reprinted in *The Norton Anthology of American Literature*, Vol. 1, ed. Nina Baym (5th ed.; New York: Norton, 1998), 998–1005. On Marshall's definition of the Cherokee, see Satz, *American Indian Policy*, 45. Timothy B. Powell, *Ruthless Democracy: A Multicultural Interpretation of the American Renaissance* (Princeton: Princeton University Press, 2000), 37. On Indian Removal, see Satz, *American Indian Policy*; Wallace, *The Long Bitter Trail*; and Michael Rogin, *Fathers and Children: Andrew Jackson and the Subjugation of the American Indian* (New York: Knopf, 1975). Harry A. Kersey, Jr., *An Assumption of Sovereignty: Social and Political Transformation Among the Florida Seminoles, 1953–1979* (Lincoln: University of Nebraska Press, 1996), 135–53, 138.

Hogan herself is, in a different sense, several times removed from the South. Although *Power* is set entirely in the southern reaches of Florida, its author is not necessarily or automatically a "southern writer" simply because she has written this novel: her family is from Gene Autry, Oklahoma; she has spent considerable amounts of time in Minnesota and in Boulder, Colorado, where she currently teaches; and her two other novels—*Mean Spirit* (1990) and *Solar Storms* (1995)—are set in Oklahoma and on the Canada–United States border, respectively. Compared to Eudora Welty's or Flannery O'Connor's or William Faulkner's long-term residency in very particular southern places, both actual and imagined, Hogan's act of just visiting and then finding herself writing a novel about her visit strikes a distinctly different southern literary chord. In focusing on a place where she feels at home without necessarily *being* at home, Hogan in *Power* revises received notions of the American South, of American regionalism, and of American Indian interrelationships with particular places. As Scott Romine points out, "a central feature of regionalism and the 'sense of place' attendant upon it [is that] both are embedded in oppositional relationships with locations that are not regions or even places." One of the ways Hogan enters imaginatively into the South in *Power* is through her planetary understanding of herself as a part of something much larger than any American region *and* still very definitely a place. As she tells interviewer Phebe Davidson, "[t]he more I observe the world, the more I learn about it, the more I think that there's a vast terrestrial intelligence all around us," an intelligence that Hogan articulates not only in *Power* but also in several volumes of poetry and in her essay collection *Dwellings: A Spiritual History of the Living World* (1995). This understanding of global natural power permits her to respect but also to rethink the longstanding and often noted regionalist tensions between the local and the national, the country and the (sub)urban, the "native" and the alien. In other words, Hogan shifts the nature and place of the "oppositional relationships" that Romine discusses; they are certainly matters of regional location, but because Hogan sees the local and the global as interconnected more than dichotomized, familiar regionalist binaries do not apply. Instead of pitting place against place, for example, Hogan examines intraregional conflict—Taiga Indians who maintain the old ways stand in opposition to Taiga Indians who spurn tribal traditions; Floridians clash over animal-protection laws—and gender troubles that do not necessarily hinge on regional identity: Omishto receives stronger mothering from her surrogate Aunt Ama than from her biological mother, and must also fend off an abusive, sexually predatory stepfather.[6]

Granted, when Hogan, a Chickasaw, writes a Florida Indian story, if not a story she directly identifies as Seminole or Miccosukee, she in a sense contributes more specifically to the already intertwined cultural histories of the Seminoles and the Chickasaws in the Southeast.[7] In the same gesture, though, her respectful decision not to risk appropriating another tribe's stories and cultural history—particularly in light of the sharp criticism she received for her construction of Osage characters and perspectives in her first novel, *Mean Spirit*—further intensifies and complicates the already complex issue of inaccessibility.[8] In inventing the Taiga, she removes or throws into question all the usual deceptively reliable Euro-American sources of knowledge about a given American Indian culture, foregrounding the complex entanglements of "fact" and "fiction" when it comes to Indian-white *and* Indian-Indian relations, and thereby challenging her readers to come face to face with how much they do not and cannot know about this Indian culture.[9] What is also clear is that although, as Omishto says, "[m]ost of the other [Florida] tribes, Seminoles, Mikosukkes,[10] do not remember us now . . . the old people say that, like them, we are related to the panther, Sisa, one of the first people here" (85). The point is that Hogan brings "history" and "fiction" into productive convergence—the Seminoles really do have a Panther Clan, but the Taiga don't actually exist—without allowing either to threaten the truths

6. Linda Hogan, *Mean Spirit* (New York: Ivy Books, 1990) and *Solar Storms* (New York: Scribner, 1995); Scott Romine, "Where Is Southern Literature? The Practice of Place in a Postsouthern Age," in this volume; Phebe Davidson, "An Interview with Linda Hogan," *Writer's Chronicle* 31, no. 4 (February 1999), 40; Linda Hogan, *Dwellings: A Spiritual History of the Living World* (New York: Touchstone, 1995); Eric Gary Anderson, *American Indian Literature and the Southwest: Contexts and Dispositions* (Austin: University of Texas Press, 1999), 4–5.

7. In fact, in 1983, Seminole tribal chairman James Billie shot and killed a Florida panther and, like Ama in *Power,* was tried for killing an endangered species. See John A. Murray, "Of Panthers and People: An Interview with American Indian Author Linda Hogan," *Terrain: A Journal of the Built and Natural Environments,* http://www.terrain.org/Archives/Issue_5/Murray-Hogan/murray-hogan.html, 8.

8. Eric Gary Anderson, "States of Being in the Dark: Removal and Survival in Linda Hogan's *Mean Spirit,*" *Great Plains Quarterly* 20, no. 1 (Winter 2000), 55–60.

9. For incisive commentary on the issues raised here, see Vine Deloria Jr., *God Is Red: A Native View of Religion* (1973; rprt., Golden, Colo.: Fulcrum, 1994) and *Custer Died for Your Sins* (1969; 2nd ed., Norman: University of Oklahoma Press, 1988).

10. "Mikosukkes" is Hogan's choice of one of several acceptable variant spellings of the tribal name.

conveyed by a narrator who is herself in some ways knowable and in some ways inaccessible, unknowable. As this narrator points out, "We are Taiga Indians and no one has heard of us" (85), and this, even as it contradicts the previous quotation, appears to be the point. Hogan challenges her readers to believe in this representation of American Indian experience in the South, and she challenges us to disbelieve.

As Craig Womack notes, the title of Angie Debo's 1941 study of Removal, *The Road to Disappearance,* is "unfortunate" precisely because the Indians in question have *not* disappeared, and indeed, as Hogan and various other Native writers make plain, not all Indians have left the South, let alone the plane of conscious, visible, bodily existence. Neither has Native literature of the South flagged or disappeared since its "beginnings" in the early nineteenth century. Granted, Daniel F. Littlefield Jr. and James W. Parins point out, "some [southeastern] tribes carried on little literary activity and others none that is presently known"; Seminoles, and other Florida tribes, are among those who produced significantly less written literature than, say, the Cherokees and Creeks. But Littlefield and Parins also observe, in the introduction to their 1995 anthology *Native American Writing in the Southeast,* that "The period from 1875 to 1935 was marked by tremendous literary energy and extensive production of a rich literature, which blossomed in the late nineteenth century and bore fruit in the twentieth. Literary expression conformed to various genres: nonfiction in the form of essays, letters, addresses, historical narratives, and biography; fiction in the form of short stories, novels, and dialect humor; poetry; and drama." Moreover, in commenting on the historical boundaries of their anthology, the editors acknowledge that southeastern Native American writers did not suddenly stop writing in 1935. Some, such as Cherokees Marilou Awiakta and Marijo Moore, make their homes in the South as of this writing. Other living contemporaries—such as Robert Conley (United Keetoowah Band Cherokee), Leslie Marmon Silko (Laguna Pueblo), Louis Owens (Choctaw/Cherokee), and Joy Harjo (Muscogee Creek)—are not themselves currently residents of the Southeast but have written incisively about the southeastern experiences of southeastern Indian nations.[11]

11. Craig S. Womack, *Red on Red: Native American Literary Separatism* (Minneapolis: University of Minnesota Press, 1999), 29; Daniel F. Littlefield Jr. and James W. Parins, "Preface," in *Native American Writing in the Southeast: An Anthology, 1875–1935,* ed. Daniel F. Littlefield Jr. and James W. Parins (Jackson: University Press of Mississippi, 1995), x; Littlefield and Parins, "Introduction," in *Native American Writing in the Southeast,* xviii. For examples of Native American writers with southeastern associations, see

But even so, for reasons that have not yet been adequately acknowledged and discussed, the fact remains that the American Indian South is very much a new place—or, more precisely, very much an underinvestigated place—within the critical-academic confines of Native American literature, let alone of southern literature. In the contexts of both these fields of literary study, then, Hogan's detailed portrayal of a swampy, hurricane-ridden part of Florida significantly reinforces (if not expands) our sense of the natural and textual environments of Indian Country as well as of the South. Among all the snakes, 'gators, humid swamps, dented aluminum trailers, tightly curled perms, snake-handling Pentecostal Indians, and tenacious Indian elders lives the narrator of *Power,* Omishto ("The One Who Watches"), a sixteen-year-old who is a Taiga, a self-described good student and obedient daughter, and a sort of ambivalent rebel who, in the process of discovering and articulating her own power, finds herself turning more and more toward Taiga women elders. In the wake of a powerful hurricane, Omishto and her Taiga "Aunt" Ama Eaton track and kill a sacred and endangered (and, as it turns out, sickly and hungry) female Florida panther. Ama believes that this complex and ambiguous act will help the Taiga survive and will help restore balance to the natural world. But given both the tribal-cultural and the federal status of the panther, most of the others who involve themselves or are otherwise brought into the discussion disagree with Ama, and even Omishto says, repeatedly, that "what Ama did was wrong, and it was right" (115); "[i]t isn't that she was innocent . . . it's just that she was not guilty" (198). After the killing of the panther, the novel plays out the consequences of the act: how it affects the natural environment, how it affects all who inhabit and mark these environs, how it enters into memory and story, how it redefines *and* reaffirms a variety of transcultural ambivalences. Here, for example, is Omishto, late in the novel: "And when I come to the house, I hear someone inside, rummaging, but when I open the door, it is silent. No one is there. I go to open the window, look out, see nothing. I try to make out a shape, but nothing moves. . . . In the house nothing is disturbed or taken, but all night I sit in darkness and listen, at times afraid it is an intruder, at times hopeful it is Ama" (193).

Robert Conley, *Mountain Windsong: A Novel of the Trail of Tears* (Norman: University of Oklahoma Press, 1992); Leslie Marmon Silko, *Almanac of the Dead* (New York: Simon and Schuster, 1991); Louis Owens, *Bone Game* (Norman: University of Oklahoma Press, 1994); Joy Harjo, "New Orleans," in *She Had Some Horses* (New York: Thunder's Mouth Press, 1983), 42–44.

The chapter ends here, with this almost tangible, audible experience of absence and presence, fear and hope. Hogan has said that *Power* is "about a young woman . . . who is having to make some of the most important decisions anyone has to make in their lives. . . . It's about a young Indian woman who has to make these serious decisions when she's very young."[12] As Omishto herself says, again near the close of the book: "Do I believe the old stories, the things I've heard? Do I believe in things I can't see but know are there like fish inside the depths of dark water? Do I believe I am composed of muscle, nerve, skin, or that a heart I've never seen is beating beneath my chest? These are all questions of trust and faith" (193). Coming to this powerful understanding of faith and trust involves an open acknowledgment of all that cannot be seen, touched, empirically known: in arriving at this sense of the radical and simultaneously traditional equivalences between human physiology, the invisible world, and the old stories, Omishto importantly leaves things unresolved. Some questions remain questions, and a respect for the inaccessible paradoxically drives her toward a more accessible (and, in the terms of the novel itself) a more traditional way of seeing and believing. But Hogan refuses to fall back on anything like a clearly and easily resolved conclusion to this narrative; trust and faith and tradition remain processes rather than achievements, and they remain marginal if not dismissed or forgotten processes for most of the characters in the novel. Issues and problems of community therefore haunt the book: who and what makes communities form, survive, stay available to those who would take their place or be granted a place within the community?

Indeed, especially in light of the various ways Hogan challenges and complicates notions of "region" and "the South," where exactly can *Power* be located on a map of southern literature? What is "southern" about *Power,* beyond the simple narrative fact that its setting is Florida and its terrain includes a swamp, water moccasins, a stand of bamboo, and some black Spanish moss? One way of beginning to develop responses to these questions is to read Hogan's novel alongside a canonical example of southern literature, one that parallels it in various striking ways. Both *Power* and Faulkner's "The Bear" (1942) feature main characters who go into the "wilderness" at the age of sixteen to participate in a ritual and in some ways sacramental hunt that both teenagers understand as transitional. The experience helps bring about a personal transition from youth to greater maturity, and it helps both characters

12. Murray, "Of Panthers and People," 8.

construct this maturity as oppositional, in part because they regret the ways the hunted and the hunting ground are also in transition, their mythic qualities pressured by technology and sliding toward anachronism: the bear resembles a locomotive, and Florida panthers die accidentally at the hands of biologists and Florida drivers. Ike McCaslin rejects his patrimony and, by implication, all that he believes it represents, while Omishto leaves the white world—and her own particular experience of what Linda Wagner-Martin calls "the abusive family romance plot" of southern literature—for Kili Swamp, which she comes to see as home. Of course, the hunters (including the part-Chickasaw Indian Sam Fathers) and the bear in Faulkner's narrative are all male, whereas the various main characters (including the panther) in Hogan's novel are all female. Gender matters in each text, not least in the ways the shadowy, marginalized women in "The Bear" and men in *Power*—figures that both texts associate with the realm of linear-historical time—influence both main characters' eventual oppositional stances.[13]

But perhaps more important still, the "timeless" natural world of each narrative is also a single-gender world under some duress. In Faulkner, different races can participate in that world (although all the men are deeply culturally marked as southern), and in Hogan, diverse species have more or less equal standing. But still, in each text the assumed "universal" he or she does not ever strongly manifest itself as a he *and* she, a *they* or, more to the point, a diverse *us*. And this inclination to construct communities that, for whatever reason, exclude or strongly downplay some rather large part of the local population, thereby troubling if not diminishing or outright rejecting the possibility of this more diverse *us*, is a characteristic burden of southern literature.[14] Whether these limitations

13. William Faulkner, "The Bear," in *Go Down, Moses; Linda Wagner-Martin, "Introduction," in *New Essays on "Go Down, Moses,"* ed. Linda Wagner-Martin (New York: Cambridge University Press, 1996), 6. For further discussion of Sam Fathers as Chickasaw Indian, see Lewis M. Dabney, *The Indians of Yoknapatawpha: A Study in Literature and History* (Baton Rouge: Louisiana State University Press, 1974); Horsford, "Faulkner's (Mostly) Unreal Indians"; and Mick Gidley, "Sam Fathers' Fathers: Indians and the Idea of Inheritance," in *Critical Essays on William Faulkner: The McCaslin Family,* ed. Arthur F. Kinney (Boston: G. K. Hall, 1990), 121–31.

14. Although she emphasizes "commonality and points of connection among the many voices that make up the wealth of southern literature," perhaps at the expense of the diversity she celebrates, Linda Tate's interest in "multiple Souths" and in "concerns, issues, and priorities that cut across racial, class, and subregional lines" roughly corresponds with my notion of a "diverse *us*." See Linda Tate, *A Southern Weave of Women: Fiction of the Contemporary South* (Athens: University of Georgia Press, 1994), 5–6. And for another take

are racial or ethnic or gendered or class-based or otherwise delineated, the point is that they signify as powerfully in a southern Native text as in a text by the most canonical non-Native southern writer. In both texts, then, the races and to a great extent the genders cannot mix; Ike spurns his patrimony because of its history of miscegenation, while Omishto stops trying to live in two worlds and instead chooses the Indian world of Kili Swamp. The ending of *Power* appears to be more positive and hopeful than the conclusion of "The Bear," but perhaps at a cost, since Hogan's ending can be understood as both a needed return to traditional ways and a self-progenitive retreat from multicultural engagement.

At the same time, *Power* (more than "The Bear") conducts a sort of running debate, involving a variety of Native, non-Native, and nonhuman points of view, on the cultural role and proper maintenance of particular southern ecosystems, and this debate, especially when considered in the context of the catastrophic cultural dispossessions mentioned above, focuses attention on another kind of removal: the gradual extinction of the Florida panther, which has been on the United States government's endangered species list since 1967.[15] Linking Florida Indians and panthers by what both have lost and by what both struggle to maintain, Hogan presents an ecocritical perspective that is largely predicated on unromanticized accounts of contestations over particular ecosystems and deeply aware of the gaping divides within as well as between particular implicated groups. She maintains that real and viable survival—of particular Florida Indian peoples, places, and philosophies—is possible but extremely difficult, often complicated by the ambiguous and even inaccessible nature of interrelationships between humans and their relatives (be these relatives human or animal, living or dead).

Hogan's cautiously particularized attention to the use and abuse of a particular ecosystem helps open up connections between two fields of study that have thus far been somewhat surprisingly disconnected from each other: Native American literature and ecocriticism. Perhaps part of the difficulty associated with bringing these fields into reasonable interchange is, as Philip Deloria argues, the persistence with which white Americans have latched onto "the practice of playing Indian," "reinterpreting the intuitive dilemmas surrounding Indianness to meet the cir-

---

on the matter of southern community, see Scott Romine, *The Narrative Forms of Southern Community* (Baton Rouge: Louisiana State University Press, 1999).

15. Charles Fergus, *Swamp Screamer: At Large with the Florida Panther* (Gainesville: University Press of Florida, 1998), 9.

cumstances of their times." For my purposes in writing this essay, the prospect of linking Indians and ecocriticism is fraught with problems, not least among them the power of white American desires for and expectations of Indian environmental wisdom. Take, for instance, the notorious television advertisement from the mid-1970s in which a middle-aged man wearing a full headdress paddles a canoe down a seemingly pristine river, only to arrive at an overcrowded, smog-ridden highway, at which point an aluminum can strikes him on the head and a single tear courses down his tragic cheek. This "Keep America Beautiful" ad reasserted the venerable non-Indian stereotype that American Indians are exceptionally, even mystically natural beings—even though the actor playing the Indian was, according to some sources, Italian and the image of the stoic Indian who bears a silent, simplistic relationship to nature is a romantic as well as a colonial and postcolonial Euro-American construction, not an Indian assertion of national, nationalist, or otherwise place-based identity.[16] This is of course not to say that Indians have been, or continue to be, somehow separate from nature—to assert such a thing would be a grave error—but it is to urge caution when thinking about how such relationships both work and misfire, as well as about how they get represented, often by non-Indians. As Hogan and other Native writers have strongly indicated, when it comes to the topic of Indians and the environment, the knowledge that has been lost, destroyed, kept within a particular culture, or not yet fully attained is significantly different from the knowledge that non-Indians (especially) can claim that they have. That is, despite the readiness with which some white Americans "play Indian" and appropriate "Native wisdom" about the environment, actual Native thinking about land and place is much more complex and much more inaccessible than those white Americans appear to believe.

To complicate matters further, ecocritical thinking about literature in general is very much a work in progress that sometimes, as Krista Comer points out, overlooks important complexities. She argues that it "focuses a good bit, though not exclusively, on nature writing" and on a short list of preferred western places, chiefly the Rocky Mountains and the Ameri-

16. Philip J. Deloria, *Playing Indian* (New Haven: Yale University Press, 1998), 7; Gretchen M. Bataille, "Jay Silverheels, Iron Eyes Cody, and Chief Dan George: Native Americans and the Imagined West," in *The Hollywood West: Lives of Film Legends Who Shaped It,* ed. Richard W. Etulain and Glenda Riley (Golden, Colo.: Fulcrum, 2001), 166. For a useful survey of this large topic, see Robert Berkhofer, *The White Man's Indian: Images of the American Indian from Columbus to the Present* (New York: Vintage, 1978).

can (much more often than the Mexican) Southwest. Its "view of nature . . . is holistic . . . 'innocent,' and transparent, while it simultaneously sums up a vague environmentalists' agenda: the desire for a more 'real' or environmentally sane life can be found in simpler living and a retreat from a postmodern world that decenters what ideally should be the 'whole' self." In other words, ecocritics favor "pure" wilderness and "a love of wide-open, 'wild' spaces; a penchant for the mystical, which is also the 'natural,' American Indian; the suggestion of redemptive possibility; a disavowal of the industrial or technological; and representations of woman as nature." I would add that both nature writing and ecocriticism sometimes presume a sort of unlimited access, whether imaginative or physical or both, to these "pure" spaces; nature writers, ironically, sometimes figure that they can go wherever they wish to go, escape whenever and wherever they wish to escape. However much they may be aware of the paradoxes and dangers inherent in writing about and thereby publicizing places they hope to preserve or conserve, they trust themselves implicitly.[17] And, as Comer suggests, ecocritics have, until very recently, by and large upheld a predominantly male canon of reflectively potent outdoorsmen. These tides are turning, though; critics such as Patrick Murphy have begun to argue for "an inclusivist ecocriticism," a more diverse, more multiethnic, more transnational, and perhaps more flexible approach to "nature-oriented literature." Scott Slovic agrees and, from a different angle than Murphy, asserts that "not a single literary work anywhere utterly defies ecocritical interpretation, is off-limits to green reading."[18] Given this recognition, the onus is on ecocritics to explain the boundaries between the ecocritical and the nonecocritical—to continue the hard work of determining what ecocriticism cannot do as well as what it can. As various ecocritics acknowledge, it seems important to balance any rush to ecocritical globalism with a healthy attention to local environments, and to understand the struggles over land in the

17. Krista Comer, *Landscapes of the New West: Gender and Geography in Contemporary Women's Writing* (Chapel Hill: University of North Carolina Press, 1999), 126–27. One interestingly egregious practitioner of this strain of ecocriticism is Edward Abbey. See, for example, *Desert Solitaire: A Season in the Wilderness* (New York: Touchstone, 1968).

18. Patrick D. Murphy, *Farther Afield in the Study of Nature-Oriented Literature* (Charlottesville: University Press of Virginia, 2000), 95; Scott Slovic, letter in "Forum on Literatures of the Environment," *PMLA* 114, no. 5 (October 1999), 1102. In addition to this *PMLA* forum, another very useful collection of ecocritical writing is Cheryll Glotfelty and Harold Fromm, eds., *The Ecocriticism Reader: Landmarks in Literary Ecology* (Athens: University of Georgia Press, 1996).

Americas as political, colonial, and imperial—as well as ecological—struggles.

Linda Hogan's turn to Florida, with its enclosed, swampy spaces, is in and of itself an interesting ecocritical move. For one thing, she writes of places within a state that has thus far been somewhat peripheral to the field of southern literature, Marjorie Kinnan Rawlings and Zora Neale Hurston notwithstanding (although Hogan's description of a powerful hurricane might remind some readers of a similar account in Hurston's 1937 novel *Their Eyes Were Watching God*, also set in Florida).[19] For another, she not only articulates ecocritical struggles such as those sketched in the previous paragraph, but also describes important literal and figurative boundaries: the places, peoples, and things that are difficult if not impossible to reach and know. Then again, she also creates Indian characters who *are,* we are told, rather mystical, particularly when it comes to their relationship with the Florida panther, which in her cultural role as creator and helper *is* in fact a representation of feminized nature. The narrator, for instance, says things like "As if the panther is a place and it holds her, as if they've always known and lived inside one another" (67). In other words, Hogan's novel meets several of Comer's categories and allows ecocritics to discuss precisely the sorts of things Comer criticizes them for emphasizing in their discussions of nature writing. But as I have also been suggesting, Hogan's insistence on, and enactment of, a complex notion of inaccessibility helps distinguish her work from that of various other nature writers.

For example, while tracking the panther with Ama, Omishto observes that "we are in wild nature this way, we are caught up in something that is driving and pushing at us like invisible hands at our backs" (59); "wild nature" feels sentient, active, and volitional, but this power cannot be named and to an important extent remains invisible, though powerfully physical. It tantalizes Omishto to the extent that she perceives it as both threatening and trustworthy, both inaccessible and potentially available; it urgently drives her and Ama forward on an errand they know to be complex, ambiguous, and in some ways against their judgment. In *Power,* these sorts of interconnections are central to a few characters but marginalized by many, who are marginalized in turn, in an ecocritical sense, by their inability or failure to enter into such risky but vital reciprocities with nonhuman forces that prove difficult and dangerous to de-

19. Zora Neale Hurston, *Their Eyes Were Watching God* (1937; rprt., New York: Harper and Row, 1990).

fine as "other," yet not easy to understand as "self," either. Hogan presents interconnection as more an uncertain possibility than an experience easy to represent, let alone to explicate; though often seen by eco-critics as a touchstone of their theory and practice, interrelatedness in the world of *Power* is both pressing and fragile, both desired and resisted, both intuited and not readily articulated or understood—even by the Indian characters who most powerfully experience and wish for it. Both celebrating and critiquing these complex, frequently inaccessible convergences of "nature" and "Native," Hogan suggests that in the American Indian South, where dispossession and genocide have been catastrophic facts of indigenous life since long before Jackson's Indian Removal Act of 1830, "nature writing" is, at best, a mixed blessing. It is a way of registering loss, struggle, ambivalence, and perhaps cautious hope; it is a way of articulating ambiguities such as those active in the title of the novel's final chapter: "What I Have Left."

Ancient as the Panther Clan in *Power* is, Hogan's very act of writing a novel about it brings her readers, in many different though related ways, South to a new place. As I have suggested, no one associated with *Power*—author, narrator, readers, or any of the characters—truly has anything like "full access" to the natural and cultural power her title evokes; indeed, the title of the book ironically misdirects readers seeking some sort of accessible if not instantly gratifying and exploitable "wilderness" or "Indian" or "southern" or even "southern Indian" experience. The power Hogan has in mind has existed and may still be available in the world(s) this novel centers on, but its very nature is such that it cannot be easily, quickly, smoothly acquired or even known: as the novel's epigraph puts it, "Mystery is a form of power." And so, in *Power,* Hogan investigates the related problems, more than the possibilities, of access and power: Who has proper access to natural places and properly "Native" world views? Who defines, interprets, maintains, obstructs, and/or destroys both Native and natural forms of power? And how do the Taiga Indians negotiate the tensions between human law and a natural law that is "older than human history" (114)? In the Euro-American courtroom where Ama is tried for killing an endangered species, Omishto perceives that the "black and white law" practiced there will fall short of comprehending the murky complexities of an act that is both right and wrong, both traditional and revisionist (129). "My words seem lost inside this room," she says. "My words have fallen like dust in the corners. And the beauty Ama has, no one can see" (129). In the hands of a white Western legal system that cannot possibly understand Ama's actions yet will not refrain from judging her anyway, Ama can only subvert "due process" by openly declaring herself guilty—and, precisely because she wants to be convicted, the judge declares a mistrial and thereby does not convict her. During the trial, the Indians in the room generally withhold information from the lawyers, judge, and jury, seeing no valid reason to communicate all that they know, and finding silence (or, at best, guarded speech) preferable to throwing themselves—and all that "themselves" entails—on the mercy and judgment of this alien realm.

But, as I have been contending, Hogan nevertheless refuses to see power as polarized; that is, she does not suggest, for example, that all or most of the Florida Indians in the novel are "good" and have "true," legitimate power, while all or most non-Indians are "bad" and powerless, or power-mad, or illegitimately empowered. Indeed, it is more accurate to say that Ama and the white participants in the trial are alien to each other: "Ama . . . is nothing they can imagine. The jury, the judge, the lawyers have never been in the wild places that are the places of Ama. In this way, it, this event, is not their affair. . . . And likewise, this world of theirs is none of her affair. Their lives are too narrow and brief for her. It is nothing she can understand or know or imagine. She has rarely been in the bleached and tamed confines of their world" (130).

Omishto, and by extension Hogan, appears willing to identify these worlds as mutually inaccessible to each other and to leave them at that. To underscore this state of affairs, the white courtroom trial is juxtaposed with another trial, this one conducted by Taiga elders at Kili Swamp, which is (to the extent possible) apart from the white world. And at Kili Swamp, Ama and Omishto, unimpeded by the white legal system, tell a quite different story about their tracking and killing of the panther, a story that can be told much more freely and fully because it is being told within Native narrative and cultural coordinates. Its complexities emerge even more richly, and the Taiga, Hogan is quick to point out, do not come to a comfortable consensus about how Ama should be judged. Indeed, as will be evident by now, Hogan does not see a clear-cut way of resolving most of the cultural and environmental issues her novel raises, issues that place various forms of power into productive as well as destructive convergence. The nature of power in *Power* is that it is often confusing, paradoxical, and hard to articulate.

I have argued in this essay that, like the endangered, respected Florida panthers who inhabit these ecosystems, some of the Taiga hang on to a fragile power that even other Taiga don't fully comprehend and can't fully know. "We [Taiga] barely have a thing, a bit of land, a few stories, and the old people that live up above Kili Swamp" (6), says the narrator of the novel, by way of introducing her people; "silent and nearly invisible," they have been "pushed up against the wild places" (8). Hogan's ecocriticism, then, like her self-positioning as a Native writer, is predicated on the productive tensions between telling and not telling, seeing and not seeing, knowing and not knowing, entering and not entering southern worlds both natural and Native. As a way of registering these complexities, Hogan seems intent on dismantling either/or approaches to places and peoples. Killing the panther is both right and wrong; the tribal elders who judge Ama guilty of killing the cat and punish her are both right and wrong (and, importantly, not diluted into a single, simplistically "Indian" point of view); the animal-rights activists who protest the killing of an endangered species but not the various ways in which the Taiga themselves are endangered are both right and wrong. (Since there are so few Taiga left in and around the community, they themselves very much feel the pressures of being as endangered as the Florida panther, and these pressures often make them inaccessible to each other, let alone to non-Taiga Indians. Omishto, for example, struggles to understand and embrace her mother, who is an ambivalent Taiga and a very demonstrative Christian.) Hogan makes it very difficult for any one character or culture or species or reader to find a secure foothold, an uncontaminated and unambivalent manifestation of power, an easily accessible place and position. In a section written from the point of view of Sisa the Panther, Hogan writes that Sisa believes she is doomed, "that humans have broken their covenant with the animals, their original word, their own sacred law" (190), and that "humans have lost the chance to be whole and joyous, reverent and alive" (191). With this splintering of humans into incomplete beings, both they and the panther lose place and power; both suffer. And neither appears to be strongly positioned to assuage that suffering. Emphatically voicing her knowledge that the specific natural world she inhabits has natural and sacred histories that are both inextricable and distinct from the narrative present, Omishto makes readers aware of this fragile and powerful, remembered and experienced world. It has been real for a long time, and its reality may still be recoverable. But its reality is predicated not on the ecocritical tenets that Comer critiques, with their presumption of unlimited imaginative access, but rather on delicate, shifting balances of knowing and not knowing and telling and not telling.

Extending my argument a bit further, I'd like to suggest that Linda Hogan's vested interest in writing both to persuade and to distance warrants further critical examination. In a variety of ways, she makes it very difficult for readers to inject themselves into the natural (and built) environments she describes, let alone into the tribal workings and experiences of a nearly extinct and, by Omishto's own admission, a largely unknown Florida Indian tribe. Hogan *does* at times present accessible, ecocritical world views, and she *does* create a narrator whose telling of this story doubles as an emergence into an increasingly powerful and complex understanding and practice of interrelatedness, and she *does* want readers to think ecocritically. She clearly enters into debates about the endangerment of Florida panthers, Florida Indians, and Florida ecosystems, and she boldly distributes responsibility for this endangerment. In all of these ways and more, she brings her readers South to a new place that is at the same time rich with respect for what Omishto frequently refers to as "the old days" and urgent in arguing against the contemporary tendency of both Indians and non-Indians to "believe, falsely . . . that all this ["the old days"] can no longer be so" (229). But Hogan also distinctly and interestingly finds various ways of making this Florida place and these Taiga people inaccessible. This assertion might appear to be a bit thickheaded, given that Hogan, in publishing *Power* with W. W. Norton and earning blurbs from such luminaries as *Booklist* and Barbara Kingsolver, makes the people and places of the book nothing if not accessible to a potentially broad range of readers and venues. My edition of the novel even features a "Reading Group Guide," with fifteen "Discussion Questions" provided to help imagined communities of enthusiastic readers find inroads into the narrative. My point, though, is that this narrative does not function primarily as a popular introduction to the Taiga, or to Florida or southeastern Indians in general, or as a sort of tourist-recruitment package luring readers into a desirable, romanticized South. Even for Hogan's narrator and for some of the Taiga elders, the stories they tell muddy the already muddy waters much more than they clear things up; even for various characters in the book, active engagement with natural environments and processes is at least as dangerous as it is vital. Even Omishto's fragile sense of other (ancestral, natural) voices, other presences, other realms does not distract her from what the hurricane does to South Florida: "Street signs are bent, trees thrown down. . . . Fences are down, balconies torn away, cars are twisted wreckage," and everything seems to reflect "the despair of the broken world" (89). A set of discussion questions, in other words, is probably not going to allow readers to crack effectively uncrackable worlds and powerfully complex world views. *Power* does not encourage readers to play Indian.

The notion of inaccessibility puts an intriguing spin on contemporary Native arguments for Native sovereignty and self-determination[20]; it also helps forward an ecocritical argument about preserving the fragile yet powerful environmental and cultural complexities of the place in question: a flawed or untold power, Hogan suggests, is preferable to extinction. Similarly, Hogan's depiction of a South that points ambiguously or inconclusively to new places helps readers recognize and situate a variety of Souths that point to the same old places in the same old ways, or a South that points nowhere at all. Perhaps such a notion of inaccessibility is not, after all, so different from what we have come to understand as a central tenet of southern literature: its often relentless obsession with a flawed but remembered past intertwined with a dysfunctional or otherwise malformed understanding of community. But simply by including discussion of a novel by a Chickasaw Oklahoma-Colorado Indian woman such as Linda Hogan in a collection of essays on southern literature, we are better positioning ourselves to stretch and complicate our understanding of both community and history, both American Indian literature and the South, both right ecological relations and wrong thinking. In the very last sentence of *Power,* Omishto tells us that she dances "and as the wind stirs in the trees, someone sings the song that says the world will go on living" (235). Hogan does not say who sings the song, or what the song specifically says; she also raises questions about her main character's efforts to leave one world and one history in favor of another. But in powerfully reassuring us that someone *does* sing the song, and that the world *will* survive, she also reassures us about the generous power of what we don't know as well as the abiding power of what we do.

20. See, for example, Robert Allen Warrior, *Tribal Secrets: Recovering American Indian Intellectual Traditions* (Minneapolis: University of Minnesota Press, 1995) and Womack, *Red on Red.*

Queer Locations, Queer Transformations: Randall Kenan's *A Visitation of Spirits*

Robert McRuer

Vito Russo pointed out in cinema . . . that historically, the gay character always had to end up with his head in the oven or in some similar state. It was like a Hays rule that you had to come to a bad end. *Giovanni's Room* isn't really an exception to this; and in Randall Kenan's book you get a brilliant tormented homosexual, Horace, who commits suicide. . . . There's another way of reading this [suicide]: which is just as a way of registering some pretty tragic facts of history. . . . But I want Randall Kenan to, as it were, take Horace to the big city in his next novel.
—Henry Louis Gates Jr., interview with Charles Rowell, 1991

Randall Kenan's *A Visitation of Spirits* (1989) is set in the fictional fundamentalist Christian, rural, African American community of Tims Creek, North Carolina. The novel is organized around two days in the life of the Cross family of Tims Creek: December 8, 1985, and April 29–30, 1984. *A Visitation of Spirits* moves back and forth between these two days, and each section heading further specifies the exact placement of events in time: e.g., "December 8, 1985; 8:45 A.M. . . . April 30, 1984; 1:15 A.M." This temporal precision gives each section of the novel the appearance of measurable, scientific "fact"; the events of *A Visitation of Spirits*, however, belie any easy distinction between "fact" and "fiction." Dissatisfied with his life, Horace Cross attempts to use a magic spell to transform himself into a bird. When the transformation fails, "spirits" and "demons" reveal themselves to Horace in order to lead him on a whirlwind journey through his own life. Past, present, and future blur together as freely as "fact" and "fantasy" as Horace's journey progresses. Even Horace himself is confused as to whether what he is seeing is "real" or not. One of the demons attempts to explain: "Ghosts? Yeah, you might call them ghosts. Ghosts of the past. The presence of the present. The very stuff of which the future is made. This is the effluvium of souls that surround men daily." The echoes here are of the humanistic, transformative experience of Ebenezer Scrooge in *A Christmas Carol*; Horace, however, is not in a position to experience the same sort of happy ending in *A Visitation of Spirits*. In contrast to the miserly gentleman of Dickens's tale, Horace, after observing the constraint and confusion that he has endured throughout his young life, does not undergo some humanistic "redemption" but instead commits suicide.[1]

Henry Louis Gates's prescription for this tragedy, and for Kenan, is in many ways predictable; the "migration to the big city" is a widely available trope in contemporary lesbian and gay literature, with a long and illustrious history.[2] And yet I find the need to transport characters like Kenan's Horace Cross off to "the big city" symptomatic of a regional elision in queer theory generally. What Gates elides in his suggestion to Kenan is the fact that taking Horace *to* anywhere also entails taking him *from* somewhere. In this case, the unmentioned "somewhere" is the religious community of Tims Creek, North Carolina. Not the most conducive atmosphere for the expression of queer desire, certainly; but as

---

1. This essay is excerpted from a much longer chapter, "Queer Locations/Queer Transformations," in Robert McRuer, *The Queer Renaissance: Contemporary American Literature and the Reinvention of Lesbian and Gay Identities* (New York: New York University Press, 1997). My thanks to New York University Press for permission to reprint this selection here. Randall Kenan, *A Visitation of Spirits* (New York: Doubleday, 1989), 3, 66, 73. Subsequent references to this work are given parenthetically in the text.

2. "Widely available" is an understatement; migration-to-the-big-city novels could compete against coming-out stories for the title of "Most Common Lesbian/Gay Genre." Pre-Stonewall works that turn upon migrations to the city include Ann Bannon's Beebo Brinker series—for example, *Beebo Brinker* (1962; rprt., Tallahassee: Naiad Press, 1986), the back cover of which declares, "She landed in New York, fresh off the farm"; and John Rechy's *City of Night* (New York: Ballantine Books, 1963). Post-Stonewall explorations of the trope include Armistead Maupin's Tales of the City series—for example, *Tales of the City* (New York: Harper & Row, 1978)—the front cover of the first paperback edition depicts a female figure with luggage, awed by the immensity of the Golden Gate Bride; Andrew Holleran's *Dancer from the Dance* (New York: Plume, 1978); and Edmund White's *The Beautiful Room Is Empty* (New York: Knopf, 1988). Ethan Mordden's *I've a Feeling We're Not in Kansas Anymore* (New York: St. Martin's, 1985) explicitly thematizes the disjunction between the city and the "provinces."

Of course, as Gates himself notes, the migration from South to North (and the corresponding shift from rural to urban) is also a trope in the African American literary tradition (*The Signifying Monkey: A Theory of African-American Literary Criticism* [New York: Oxford University Press, 1988], xxv). In a way, suggesting that Randall Kenan replicate this trope precludes him from signifying on it.

liberal lesbian and gay thought likes to remind us, "we are everywhere," and rather than concede that "everywhere" actually means New York and San Francisco, I am interested in the (perhaps more radical) implications of recognizing that "everywhere" includes such an apparently marginal and inhospitable place.

Contemporary gay fiction that deals with "family" or "community" often exposes the ways those concepts cover over difference: the group achieves a cohesive identity through disavowal of "aberrant" individual identities. Thus, as Gates suggests, "one thing that a good deal of contemporary fiction that deals realistically with gay themes achieves, which I think is very important, is to desentimentalize the notion of 'community' as an unadulterated good."[3] In my mind, this is precisely what Kenan does with the story of Horace in *A Visitation of Spirits*; yet Gates is uncomfortable enough with Horace's suicide to envision *another* community in "the big city." Certainly, the narrative in which Gates places Horace allows for the possibility of an *alternative*, perhaps more sustaining, community. Difference, however, is again suppressed by transporting Horace off to a community of others "like him," and away from the community he threatens. Locating Horace in an urban area where, presumably, a "black gay identity" is more developed and secure[4] effaces the possibility of transforming the community in which Horace is already located and—more important—undermines Kenan's critique of the "regime of sameness" embodied by the people of Tims Creek.

The term *regime of sameness* is Marcos Becquer's, and before I proceed with my reading of Horace and Tims Creek, North Carolina, I want to use Becquer's analysis to center my own. Becquer analyzes "snapping" and "vogueing," two of the black gay discursive practices celebrated in and by Marlon Riggs's critically acclaimed film *Tongues Untied*. Since the discursive practices in Riggs's film "emerge both from within and against the cultural and historical discourses operating around them," Becquer argues that "*Tongues Untied* can confront and condemn the regime of sameness which alienates black gays from the black community, the white gay community, and discourse/representation in general."[5] In

---

3. Charles Rowell, "Interview with Henry Louis Gates, Jr.," *Callaloo* 14 (1991): 454.

4. This presumption, of course, may be a bit hasty. Gates, himself, earlier in the interview I have been citing, notes that " a lot of gay black men in Harlem . . . are tired of being used for batting practice." Ibid.

5. "Vogueing," developed by black and Latino gay men in New York City, is a form of dance in which dancers imitate and implicitly critique "high-fashion" styles and poses, such as those depicted in *Vogue* magazine. "Snapping" is a gesture of pride and defiance used to

other words, black gays, confronted by black heterosexual or white gay communities with the compulsion to be "the same," can, in turn, use the discourses made available by those very communities to contest such a compulsion.[6] Becquer's analysis thus foregrounds "difference" while nonetheless arguing for the connective, political importance of a subverted and subversive "sameness": "It is, then, however ironically or heroically, just that differentiated voice within sameness which *Tongues Untied* attempts to distill, so as to ensure not only that black gays speak up, but that they remain audible in discourse. It proceeds, then, not by nullifying the value of sameness within difference . . . but by acknowledging its political importance and admitting, within the logic of 'constructed identity,' that sameness is always already a part of difference, as well as vice versa."[7]

Becquer's theory, with its focus on snapping and vogueing, is particularly relevant when discussing the tremendous outpouring of urban and secular black gay cultural production represented in films such as Riggs's *Tongues Untied* and Jennie Livingston's *Paris Is Burning*. Indeed, Becquer explicitly elaborates on "black gays' *secular* use of snapping as a means by which to metaphorically awaken one out of the codes of (discursive) domination" and on vogueing's "reconstitut[ion of] the literal *urban* battlefield of bloody violence . . . into a figurative arena upon which these confrontations between images are played out."[8] In this urban and secular context, snapping and vogueing address the exclusionary practices of black heterosexual and white gay communities: Becquer concludes, for instance, that the segment on snapping in *Tongues Untied* "depicts the snap precisely in its ability to overcome the discursive mechanisms which position black gays beneath both black heterosexuals and white gays." Through the snap, black gays reposition themselves as apart from and yet a part of, on the one hand, white gays, and on the other

---

"read," punctuate, or invalidate another's discourse (Marcos Becquer, "Snap!thology and Other Discursive Practices in *Tongues Untied*," *Wide Angle* 13 [1991]: 6–17).

6. Michel Foucault's famous formulation is relevant here: "There is not, on the one side, a discourse of power, and opposite it, another discourse that runs counter to it. Discourses are tactical elements or blocks operating in the field of force relations; there can exist different and even contradictory discourses within the same strategy; they can, on the contrary, circulate without changing their form from one strategy to another, opposing strategy" (*The History of Sexuality*, Vol. 1, trans. Robert Hurley [New York: Random House, 1978], 101–2).

7. Becquer, "Snap!thology," 15.

8. Ibid. (my emphasis), 9, 12.

hand, black heterosexuals, and "the very binarism of sameness/differ-
ence" is thereby deconstructed. In other words, snapping (and elsewhere
in Becquer's article, vogueing) works as an empowering and signifying
difference for black gays, but this signifying difference nonetheless forges
connections with the groups it critiques. With this revised idea of sameness in mind, Becquer concludes, "*Tongues Untied* is not a separatist
film."[9]

Becquer's analysis is fueled by "recent revisions of identity politics,"
which understand identity as a construction and thus allow for "the hope
of deconstructing the binarism of otherness which marks discursive alienation and domination by acknowledging that the other is always already
a part of ourselves and vice-versa." Yet, although putting sameness back
into difference forges connections and hence undermines, as Becquer argues, black homophobia and white gay racism, this queer theoretical
move should not overshadow the ongoing need for a queer theory that
challenges the "regime of sameness," even when that regime is reproduced *inside* the cultural category "black gay." Despite Becquer's best efforts, indeed, his article concludes with the inscription of a fairly
monolithic, snapping and vogueing "black gay identity" singular. Although he begins the article decrying "the essentialism inherent in notions of *the* black subject or *the* gay sensibility," Becquer himself subtly
moves from plurality to singularity in his discussion of black gay identities: *Tongues Untied* is, at the beginning, "a condensed version of black
gay (collective) experiences" but has become, by the end, a celebration of
"the emergence of a black gay difference that is unique."[10]

This slippage does not invalidate Becquer's argument; it simply demonstrates, as Ed Cohen suggests, that "no matter how sensitively we go
about it, 'identity politics' has great difficulty in affirming difference(s)."
Becquer's article, with its critique of white gay and black heterosexual
hegemony, recognizes the difficulty of affirming difference but simultaneously affirms the "sameness" that is always already present within "difference." Cohen argues, with a nod to Diana Fuss, that "identity politics
is predicated on denying the difference that is already there in 'the
same.'"[11] This predication ensures that difference can be denied or re-

---

9. Ibid., 9, 15.

10. Ibid., 7, 16, 7, 8, 15.

11. Ed Cohen, "Who Are 'We'? Gay 'Identity' as Political (E)motion: A Theoretical
Rumination," in *Inside/Out: Lesbian Theories, Gay Theories,* ed. Diana Fuss (New York:
Routledge, 1991), 76.

pressed even when identity politics is grounded in sophisticated post-structuralist attempts, such as Becquer's, to move beyond the sameness/difference binarism.

While black gays are undeniably marginalized by black heterosexuals and by both heterosexual and gay whites, and hence are strategically positioned to disrupt and decenter heterosexual and white hegemony, a focus on *urban* black gays will always, in turn, produce other margins. Still, I want to extend rather than disarm Becquer's analysis. By pushing his ideas further, I hope to create a space in which to consider black gay cultural production (and perhaps queer cultural production generally) *outside* an urban, secular arena. It was no accident that I used Becquer's analysis to "center" my own. Until quite recently, queer theory has predominantly "centered" on urban areas. Such a focus is in some ways inevitable: after all, as John D'Emilio and Estelle B. Freedman explain, it was initially in American cities that a gay subculture flourished in the middle of the twentieth century. The urban "center" that D'Emilio, Freedman, and other queer theorists and historians have analyzed, though, might be productively understood as part of a complex array of "centers" and "margins," since both concepts emerge relationally. Moreover, critical interrogation of the processes of marginalization proceeds hand in hand with the establishment of unexpected, even unlikely, new centers. Thus we would do well to consider—before placing Kenan's Horace "safely" (or more "appropriately"?) in an urban "center"—just what black queer desire is doing in, or does to, rural North Carolina. Essex Hemphill's words, with their subtle promise/threat that black gays will transform *whatever* community they are in, seem appropriate to me here: "I ask you brother: Does your mama *really know* about you? Does she *really* know what I am? . . . I hope so, because *I am* coming home."[12]

12. John D'Emilio and Estelle B. Freedman, *Intimate Matters: A History of Sexuality in America* (New York: Harper & Row, 1988), 288. The theme of "coming home" runs throughout Hemphill's work. This quotation comes from his essay "Does Your Mama Know About Me?" in Essex Hemphill, *Ceremonies* (New York: Plume, 1992), 42. Later, in "Loyalty," Hemphill makes a similar point: "We will not go away with our issues of sexuality. We are coming home" (ibid., 64). Consider also Joseph Beam, who writes, "When I speak of home, I mean not only the familial constellation from which I grew, but the entire Black community: the Black press, the Black church, Black academicians, the Black literati, and the Black left. Where is my reflection? I am most often rendered invisible, perceived as a threat to the family, or am tolerated if I am silent and inconspicuous. I cannot go home as who I am and that hurts me deeply" ("Brother to Brother: Words from the Heart," in *In the Life: A Black Gay Anthology*, ed. Joseph Beam [Boston: Alyson, 1986], 231). Hemphill's work, with its insistence that "*I am* coming home," explicitly responds to Beam's lament here.

Near the end of *A Visitation of Spirits*, Horace's voice is presented directly for the first time in a section called "Horace Thomas Cross: Confessions" (245–51). Almost every sentence of this section in which Horace meditates on his life in Tims Creek begins with the phrase "I remember": "I remember the first time I saw Granddaddy kill a chicken. I remember it, dirty-white and squawking, and Granddaddy putting it down on a stump" (245). Similar vignettes fill out this representation of life in rural North Carolina as Horace's "confessions" continue. It quickly becomes clear, however, that despite the hardships Horace endured, this rural setting is not simply the site of "backwardness" or "repression." Like other communities in which black gay men find themselves, Tims Creek, North Carolina, is a site of struggle and possible transformation. And like the snapping and vogueing black gay men of Becquer's analysis, Horace's own queer sense of self emerges both from within and against the community around him:

> I remember my Aunt Ruthester's chocolate-chip cookies and how she would make an extra batch for me. . . . I remember the way it made my mouth happy, dissolving almost as soon as I ate it, buttery and hot.
>
> I remember finally touching a man, finally kissing him. I remember the surprise and shock of someone else's tongue in my mouth. I remember the taste of someone else's saliva. I remember actually feeling someone else's flesh, warm, smooth. . . . I remember being happy that I was taking a chance with my immortal soul, thinking that I would somehow win in the end and live still, feeling immortal in a mortal's arms. I remember then regretting that it was such a sin. I remember the feeling I got after we climaxed, feeling hollow and undone, wishing I were some kind of animal, a wolf or a bird or a dolphin, so I would not have to worry about wanting to do it again; I remember worrying how the other person felt.
>
> I remember church and praying. I remember revival meetings and the testifying of women who began to cry before the congregation and ended their plea of hardships and sorrow and faithfulness to the Lord with the request for those who knew the word of prayer to pray much for me. I remember taking Communion and wondering how the bread was the body and the grape juice was the blood and thinking how that made us all cannibals. . . . Then I remember the day I realized that I was probably not going to go home to heaven, cause the rules were too hard for me to keep. That I was too weak.
>
> I remember me. (250–51)

Clearly, Horace's desire arises in opposition to the mores of this community; as far as they are concerned, queer desire is simply "sinful." Because of their stringent moral codes, Horace feels like an outcast and wants to escape by transforming himself into an animal. At the same time, however, Horace's desire emerges from *within* this community. The very language of the fire-and-brimstone sermons he has endured ("I remember being happy that I was taking a chance with my immortal soul") heightens the eroticism of his encounters and helps solidify his developing queer identity. Moreover, despite the fact that Horace ultimately feels weak in the face of such a powerful religious institution, his confessions highlight his attempts to appropriate and re-signify the language of that institution (e.g., "feeling immortal in a mortal's arms"). In short, this may be a sin, but it is also, nonetheless, a contestation—however temporary—of the community's ideas about "sin" and "mortality." As Lisa Duggan writes, the "project of constructing identities" is "a historical process in which contrasting 'stories' of the self and others—stories of difference—are told, appropriated, and retold as stories of location in the social world of structured inequalities."[13] In the fictional social world that is the First Baptist Church of Tims Creek, North Carolina (a "social world of structured inequalities," certainly), Horace must learn, somehow, to make sense of his identity, and he does so by appropriating the language of this institution for his own queer uses.

Other elements of this passage underscore the extent to which Horace uses this particular location to construct and make sense of his own identity. A description of the sumptuous tastes and smells of a country home, for example (the batch of cookies "made my mouth happy . . . buttery and hot"), immediately precedes and influences Horace's attempt to find a language for making sense of his erotic encounters with men ("I remember the surprise and shock of someone else's tongue in my mouth. I remember the taste of someone else's saliva"). And if this sharp juxtaposition were not enough to demonstrate how intertwined the various elements of Horace's life are, food and flesh come together yet once more in the Communion, as Horace muses on the "cannibalism" of that familiar ritual.

Immediately before the final sentence, Horace asserts "I was too weak." And yet, his "I remember me," with its placement in a paragraph of its own at the very end of his confessions, overrides such an assertion of "weakness." The sentence "I remember me" solidifies the confessions

---

13. Lisa Duggan, "The Trials of Alice Mitchell: Sensationalism, Sexology, and the Lesbian Subject in Turn-of-the-Century America," *Signs: Journal of Women in Culture and Society* 18 (1993): 791–814.

that have preceded it as ineradicable parts of Horace's identity; despite his difference(s), the community of Tims Creek, North Carolina, has shaped Horace's identity, and his staunch refusal to relinquish the various parts of this identity suggests forcefully that it is the community, and not Horace, that is in need of transformation.

This is not to deny that Horace's story is a tragedy.[14] None of the subcommunities of which Horace is a part in Tims Creek is comfortable with "difference" within its ranks; thus, in none of the locations in which Horace finds himself is he able to be wholly comfortable with "sameness." The compulsion to be "the same," even as it is reproduced within the cultural category "black gay," invalidates any of Horace's attempts to come to terms with his own identity. "You black, ain't you?" Horace's aunt asks him (186). One of Horace's lovers from the community theater where he works taunts him: "Faggot. . . . What's the matter? Don't like to be called what you are?" (225). Even Gideon, another black gay character who is Horace's first lover, says to Horace in the heat of an argument, "But remember, black boy, you heard it here first: You're a faggot, Horace. . . . At least I know what I am" (164).

In each confrontation, it is not that the labels are wholly inappropriate for Horace; it is just that every question of identity in *A Visitation of Spirits* needs to be followed by a "yes, but . . ." Judith Butler's comments are particularly relevant to Horace's situation here: "The prospect of being anything . . . seems to be more than a simple injunction to become who or what I already am."[15] Throughout *A Visitation of Spirits*, the discordant and demanding chorus of voices surrounding Horace immobilizes him, apparently preventing any strategic resistance of the compulsion to be the same.

As a black gay teenager in Tims Creek, Horace always finds himself embodying what are—at least, to the other members of the groups of which he is a part—contradictory identities: in his own family, as in the church, he is "black," but not "gay"; at the community theater where he works, he (along with many other actors) is openly "gay," but his blackness is rendered invisible (particularly by the production itself, which is about the history of the Cross family—the *white* Cross family—in North Carolina); with his "alternative" and white high-school friends, he is

---

14. In the longer version of this essay, I focus more thoroughly on the comedic aspects of *A Visitation of Spirits*, reading the novel through Gates's theories of signification.

15. Judith Butler, "Imitation and Gender Insubordination," in *Inside/Out*, ed. Fuss, 13.

"smart and black" (237), but he is not "gay," and he feels his "black-ness" is tokenized. Only with Gideon does Horace find a "niche," where he should "fit" exactly. But although their relationship is consummated, Horace and Gideon do not embrace a "black gay identity" together, an identity with which they subvert and expose the contradictions of the various communities of which they are constituents. Instead, the pressure from each of these communities precludes the possibility of Gideon and Horace coming together.

Much more effectively than a migration to the big city, Horace's subsequent suicide demonstrates what the compulsion to be the same has done to Horace. Indeed, in the context of all the demands put on him by various communities, Horace's suicide can be seen as an apt re-presentation of the violence involved in the attempt to "alienate con-clusively, *definitionally*, from anyone on any theoretical ground the au-thority to describe and name their own sexual desire,"[16] or indeed, any component of their identity. That *A Visitation of Spirits* appeared in the same year (1989) that right-wing religious and political leaders attempted to suppress the findings of the Department of Health and Human Ser-vices' Report of the Secretary's Task Force on Youth Suicide, which claimed that gay teenagers account for 30 percent of all teenage suicides, only underscores the validity of representing the compulsion toward sameness as violence.[17] Horace's suicide is detailed in stark, scientific (and hence "real") prose and is juxtaposed to the "fantastic" events in this postmodern, magical realist text. The realness of the suicide moves the theoretical opposition "Is It Real?"/"Is It Fantasy?" to a more urgent level and, in the process, starkly confronts and condemns the community where Horace is located: What if it is real? How is the community impli-cated in such violence?

Immediately after the suicide, the question of what queer desire (and its violent extermination) is doing in and to rural North Carolina is fore-grounded. As the novel concludes, the narration shifts to the second per-

16. Eve Kosofsky Sedgwick, *Tendencies* (Durham: Duke University Press, 1993), 26.

17. Suzanne Ruta, "On Why Gay Teenagers Are Committing Suicide," *Wigwag*, March 1990, 12–14. Sedgwick discusses the Department of Health and Human Services report in her essay "Queer and Now": "I think everyone who does gay and lesbian studies is haunted by the suicides of adolescents. To us, the hard statistics come easy: that queer teenagers are two to three times likelier to attempt suicide, and to accomplish it, than oth-ers; that up to 30 percent of teen suicides are likely to be gay or lesbian; that a third of lesbian and gay teenagers say they have attempted suicide; that minority queer adolescents are at even more extreme risk" (in *Tendencies*, 1).

son in a nostalgic section called "Requiem for Tobacco": "You remember, though perhaps you don't, that once upon a time men harvested tobacco by hand. There was a time when folk were bound together in a community, as one, and helped one person this day and that day another, and another the next, to see that everyone got his tobacco crop in the barn each week, and that it was fired and cured and taken to a packhouse to be graded and eventually sent to market. But this was once upon a time" (254). The section continues, lamenting the tragic loss of this idyllic way of life. But this section is already and inescapably in dialogue with the suicide that immediately precedes it. Because of this dialogue, the "time when folk were bound together in a community, as one," is exposed even as it is being constructed. The mythical, pastoral wholeness of this "community" is ripped apart as surely as "the bullet did break the skin of his forehead, pierce the cranium, slice through the cortex and cerebellum, irreparably bruising the cerebrum and medulla oblongata, and emerge from the back of the skull, all with a wet and lightning crack. This did happen" (253). Mikhail Bakhtin argues that "sexuality is almost always incorporated into the idyll only in sublimated form," since the idyllic form in literature demands a unity of time and place that smooths over differences and avoids the "naked realistic aspect" of life. Kenan's juxtaposition here of idyll and suicide foregrounds the murderous consequences of such a sublimation. Kenan himself insists, in an interview, "It seemed, and it seems . . . that for that community to change they have to understand the devastation that they're wreaking on certain people." In the end, Horace's story highlights the need for transformation of this community on the margins of the queer world. Kenan's shift to second-person narration in the conclusion further emphasizes this need: although "you remember" what this community was like, you should not, after *A Visitation of Spirits*, be able to consider this or any community without a queer sense that something is amiss.[18]

Queer theory, according to Michael Warner, must "confront the default heteronormativity of modern culture with its worst nightmare, a queer planet." Of course, such a queer planet will ultimately infiltrate more places than New York and San Francisco. Indeed, the term *queer* should suggest that this desire will continue to turn up and transform even the most apparently "inappropriate" places. To Gates's credit, he

18. Mikhail M. Bakhtin, *The Dialogic Imagination*, trans. Caryl Emerson and Michael Holquist; ed. Michael Holquist (Austin: University of Texas Press, 1981), 226; V. Hunt, "A Conversation with Randall Kenan," *African American Review* 29 (1995), 416.

provides a hearty endorsement on the back cover of *Let the Dead Bury Their Dead and Other Stories*, Kenan's 1992 collection of short stories. In this collection, not surprisingly, Kenan does not hustle Horace off to New York City. There is still too much cultural work to be done in Tims Creek, North Carolina, where (as elsewhere) "[n]othing like talk of crimes against nature gets people all riled up and speculating and conjecturing and postulating." Although no one in *Let the Dead Bury Their Dead* is reducible to cultural categories such as "black," "gay," or "black gay," queer desire (in its many different manifestations or "visitations") permeates the collection. Michael Berube, writing about Melvin Tolson, describes Tolson as "an African-American literary version of the maroon, the escaped slave living on the frontier, imperialism's margin, raiding the nearest plantation periodically for supplies and planning the long-term offensive in the meantime." Kenan, likewise, explains in one story from *Let the Dead Bury Their Dead* that the town of Tims Creek was founded by "the Former Maroon Society," a community of ex-slaves who lived on the "margins" but constantly worked to pilfer and disrupt the hegemonic white "center." Like these fictional forebears, Kenan refuses to capitulate to already delimited notions of what is "central" and what is "marginal." Gates, in his endorsement, calls Kenan, with his "generous moral imagination," a "fabulist for our times." Queer transformations can begin in the queerest of locations; as fabulist for our times, Kenan transforms a place on the so-called margins into a center of the queer world.[19]

19. Michael Warner, "Introduction: Fear of a Queer Planet," *Social Text* 9 (1991): 5–17; Randall Kenan, *Let the Dead Bury Their Dead and Other Stories* (New York: Harcourt Brace Jovanovich, 1992), 19, 271; Michael Berube, *Marginal Forces/Cultural Centers: Tolson, Pynchon, and the Politics of the Canon* (Ithaca: Cornell University Press, 1992), 145.

Into the Suburbs: Richard Ford's Sportswriter Novels and the Place of Southern Fiction

Matthew Guinn

"If you don't know who you are or where you come from, you will find yourself at a disadvantage. The ordered slums of suburbia are made for the confusion of the spirit. Those who live in units called homes or estates—both words do violence to the language—don't know who they are."
—Andrew Lytle, *A Wake for the Living*

"I wanted to write about a certain stratum of life that I knew, which was life in the suburbs."
—Richard Ford, interview with Kay Bonetti, 1987

It seems natural that the issue of place should be near the center of most discussions of southern literature, yet just how the construct of "southern place" may be defined has become a complicated business in the postmodern era. The traditional rural community that the first critics of Renascence fiction saw as a vital component of southern place has been nearly consumed by mass culture, as the South of the late twentieth century and early twenty-first becomes increasingly modernized and urban. Those writers born in the region from midcentury onward have not inherited the same milieu as their predecessors; *their* South is, in Fred Hobson's phrase, "no longer the defeated, failed, poor, guilt-ridden, tragic part of America," but rather a place much the same as others in the country.[1] In addition to these sociological factors, the dynamics of literary influence have contributed to the present disposition toward place. As the

---

1. Fred Hobson, *The Southern Writer in the Postmodern World* (Athens: University of Georgia Press, 1991), 8.

work of many younger writers demonstrates, the traditional southern setting can be a handicap to the contemporary fiction writer from the
South—a writer today might find the Mississippi Delta, for example, too
crowded by the presence of Welty, the piney woods and small towns
fraught with the shadow of Faulkner, the red-clay hills O'Connor-
haunted. What was exotic, densely complex, and mysterious about the
region for Renascence writers has become, through extensive fictional
mapping of the region, almost too familiar, an emptied signifier on the
one hand, a cliché on the other.

Richard Ford's work is fully embroiled in these concerns. Ford has not
only situated his latest fiction entirely outside the South—in locales as
varied as Montana, New Jersey, and Paris—he has also chronicled
through several protagonists a truly exiled sensibility that is more profoundly rootless than the delineations of geographical boundaries would
indicate. The avatar of this postmodern detachment from place is Frank
Bascombe, the protagonist of *The Sportswriter* (1986) and *Independence
Day* (1995). Ford's chronicle of Frank Bascombe—a former fiction
writer who has left the South to live in New Jersey—deconstructs the supposed bedrock sense of place in southern culture and reveals how firmly
our common definition of southern place is bound up with modernist
tropes. These novels not only concern an ambivalent protagonist leaving
the South; they also subject the South to the anti-essentialist scrutiny of
postmodern evaluation.

An apt starting point is Frank's discovery of a battered copy of his first
and only book of fiction in the library of a bed and breakfast at which he
is staying. The fiction career Frank has relinquished was replete with such
staple themes as "bemused young southerner[s]" attempting to reconcile
"the vertiginous present" with the guilt-ridden past. History and place
were central to Frank's fiction; his technique relied heavily on flashback,
and one story concerns "a violent tryst with a Methodist minister's wife"
consummated "in an abandoned slave-quarters." As Frank admits, "I
seemed . . . to have been stuck in bad stereotypes."[2] His description of
the book's jacket, then, allows Ford the opportunity for sardonic commentary on the topos of the traditional southern novel: "And to my won-
derment and out of all account . . . here is a single copy of my own now-
old book of short stories, *Blue Autumn*, in its original dust jacket, on the
front of which is a faded artist's depiction of a 1968-version sensitive-

2. Richard Ford, *The Sportswriter* (New York: Vintage Contemporaries, 1986),
36, 46.

young-man, with a brush cut, an open-collared white shirt, jeans, and an uncertain half smile, standing emblematically alone in the dirt parking lot of a country gas station with an anonymous green pickup (possibly his) visible over his shoulder. Much is implied."[3]

As Charles Michaud has noted, the cover that Frank describes is the dust jacket of Ford's own first novel, *A Piece of My Heart* (1976).[4] The first edition of Ford's novel indeed bears the image of a solitary young man in a dirt parking lot (looking very much the part of a bemused young southerner), with a green pickup truck and a country store in the background. The description of the fictitious *Blue Autumn* cover corresponds in every detail with *A Piece of My Heart,* save only the name of the gas station—Goodenough's—which is visible on the cover of Ford's novel. This confluence of fiction and reality is a gloss of Ford's own start as a southern author: those who have read *A Piece of My Heart* know that it suffers from the same gothic excesses as Frank's *Blue Autumn*. The episode reveals clearly how southern place could stifle a writer of the postmodern era such as Ford. The South as depicted here is rural, agrarian—it belongs to an earlier generation of writers. The dust jacket could be the cover of any number of southern novels, from one of several decades.

The sportswriter novels are Ford's protest against such a South, which he and many of his contemporaries have found to be so firmly established by the Renascence, so familiar and looming, as to subsume those who have come after. The stereotypical ease with which *Blue Autumn / A Piece of My Heart* could be packaged, marketed, and sold in the Traditional Southern Novel Niche underscores Ford's awareness of this fact. In response, his sportswriter novels leave the southern setting for the New Jersey suburbs. As Noel Polk has observed, such a geographical relocation does not immediately disqualify a work as southern fiction; Faulkner's *A Fable* and Welty's *The Bride of the Innisfallen* retain a southern sensibility despite their nonsouthern settings.[5] But the sportswriter novels carry emigration a step further. They flout modernist conventions by positing an expatriate southerner in a landscape antithetical

3. Richard Ford, *Independence Day* (New York: Alfred A. Knopf, 1995), 319.

4. Charles Michaud, "Richard Ford: What a Difference a Pulitzer Makes," *Firsts* 7 (February 1997): 50–55.

5. Noel Polk, "The Southern Literary Pieties," in *Southern Literature in Transition: Heritage and Promise,* ed. Philip Castille and William Osborne (Memphis: Memphis State University Press, 1983), 30–32.

to the South, where he thrives on the currents of contemporary consumer culture. And in the process of subverting the modernist expectations of southern fiction such as the dust jacket embodies, Ford has helped to bring southern fiction into the postmodern era.

The sportswriter novels unfold in a welter of settings that might be termed antisouthern, at least according to the traditional definitions. These range from New Jersey and Michigan to New York and Florida—settings which, despite their geographical differences, share a common denominator: all are marked by the presence of a pervasive commercialism that exerts a homogenizing effect on the local culture, rendering one locale hardly distinguishable from another. Ascendant throughout is the architectural disposition that Fredric Jameson calls "aesthetic populism," and in rendering this postmodern tendency Ford treats the concept of place in anti-essentialist terms, through a constant focus on mass culture that is at odds with conventional regionalism. What defines a place is not its unique characteristics but the strength of its adherence to the middle-class Zeitgeist of progress, utility, and comfort. Consequently, the place of the sportswriter novels offers little assistance in the quest for individual self-definition; the settings in which Frank finds himself do not facilitate the traditional bond between the southern self and its surroundings. If Jameson is correct in asserting that the postmodern era is at ease with the " 'degraded' landscape of schlock and kitsch, of TV series and *Reader's Digest* culture, of advertising and motels," then Ford's astutely realistic chronicle of his age puts him at odds with tradition.[6]

The eclecticism of mass culture is evident in nearly all the physical fixtures of the novels. Frank navigates through a landscape of "strange unworldliness" in which authenticity appears to have been banished, in which the local and the regional have been subsumed by an anarchic mix of architectural references.[7] None of the structures in Frank's environment is indigenous to its surroundings; instead, each building seems to draw on a number of heterogeneous and distant references. Frank, for example, lives in a neighborhood of "historical reproductions" and passes through a New Jersey subdivision called—in a misguided attempt at euphony—Sherri-Lyn Woods, a place where "there are no woods in

6. Fredric Jameson, *Postmodernism, or, The Cultural Logic of Late Capitalism* (Durham: Duke University Press, 1991), 2.

7. Ford, *The Sportswriter*, 7. Subsequent references to this novel are cited parenthetically within the essay as *S*.

sight" and "all the houses down the street look Californiaish and casual"
(*S*, 51, 243). In Detroit, he views an anomalous scene of "flat, dormered
houses and new, brick-mansard condos" juxtaposed in a "complicated
urban-industrial mix" (*S*, 115). Like the carefully manufactured authenticity of Nathanael West's suburbs in *The Day of the Locust*, nothing in
Frank's environment is as genuine as it appears; the prevailing architectural mode might be termed Generic Indigenous.

The apotheosis of this mode is a pretentious condominium development that exemplifies an ersatz blending of high and low culture, and that
could only be described as postmodern in its chaotic mixture of rural and
urban, old and new:

> I make the turn up the winding asphalt access that passes beneath a great
> water tower of sleek space-age blue, then divides toward one end or the
> other of a wide, unused cornfield. Far ahead—a mile, easy—billowing
> green basswoods stand poised against a platinum sky and behind them the
> long, girdered 'Y' stanchions of a high-voltage line, orange balls strung to
> its wires to warn away low-flying planes.
>
> Pheasant Run to the left is a theme-organized housing development
> where all the streets are culs-de-sac with 'Hedgerow Place' and 'The This-
> tles' painted onto fake Andrew Wyeth barnboard signs. All the plantings
> are young, but fancy cars sit in the driveways. . . .
>
> Pheasant Meadow sits at the other lower end of the stubble field—a
> boxy, unscenic complex of low brown-shake buildings overlooking a shal-
> low man-made mud pond, a yellow bulldozer, and some other apartments
> already half-built. (*S*, 53)

Here is a place in which a quest for self-definition will prove problematic.
There is nothing *authentic* in Frank's surroundings—nothing with connections to a genuine tradition. The Andrew Wyeth signs and the pond
are "fake" and "man-made," not autochthonous or local. They represent
an environment that is untraditional and commercial, despite its pretensions to venerable gentility. High and low architectural styles are mixed
together disingenuously in a perfect display of the conflation (in Jameso-
nian terms) of aesthetic and commodity production. What Jameson calls
the "frontier between high culture and so-called mass or commercial culture" is obscured in the appropriation of Wyeth's techniques to decorate
street signs whose very anglophilic names indicate a tradition that was
never present in this New Jersey cornfield—a fact that the high-voltage
lines underscore with irony.[8] The landscape might be described as faux-
pastoral.

8. Jameson, *Postmodernism*, 4, 2.

Perhaps the single best example of the postmodern commercial aesthetic is Frank's hotel room in Detroit. It thoroughly displays what Robert Venturi calls "the commercial vernacular"—the characteristically postmodern approach of blending the motifs of high culture with the less-lofty aim of commercial gain: "It is four-thirty by the time we get to our room, a tidy rectangle of pretentious midwestern pseudo-luxury—a prearranged fruit basket, a bottle of domestic champagne, blue bachelor buttons in a Chinese vase, red-flocked whorehouse wall décor and a big bed. There is an eleventh-story fisheye view upriver toward the gaunt Ren-Cen and gray pseudopodial Belle Isle in the middle distance—the shimmer-lights of suburbs reaching north and west out of sight" (*S*, 120). This "pseudo-luxury" is a populist appropriation of high culture writ large. And what Frank can see from the window is a landscape that Venturi would find congenial: not only Belle Isle, with its mismatched zoo and casinos, but also the Renaissance Center, the "city within a city" designed by John Portman, a paragon of self-referential architecture whose work Jameson describes as the epitome of "postmodern hyperspace." It is an eminently postmodern milieu.[9]

Frank does not object to occupying such an environment, and in his reaction to the materialism around him one detects the emergence of a new kind of southern expatriate. He revels in the materialism of consumer culture and seems to enjoy the self-indulgence of "pretentious midwestern pseudo-luxury" even as he denigrates it. Rental cars, for example, provide a "stirring" kind of exhilaration in their very interchangeable anonymity: "New today. New tomorrow. Eternal renewal on a manageable scale" (*S*, 148). His affinity for mass culture affects his conception of place to such an extent that it could hardly be termed southern in any traditional sense. He interprets adherence to the generic, not the local, as the best means of assessing the value of a place. He abjures what he calls the pretentious mystery of places such as New Orleans, along with the "genuine woven intricacy" of cities like New York and Los Angeles (*S*, 48, 103). What he seeks, instead, is a *knowable* setting, one without mystery or contingency. He admires Detroit because "so much that is explicable in American life" is made there, and he lives in New Jersey because "an American would be crazy to reject such a place, since it is the most diverting and readable of landscapes, and the language is always American" (*S*, 115, 52). He even praises contemporary society's

9. Robert Venturi et al., *Learning from Las Vegas* (Rev. ed.; Cambridge: MIT Press, 1996), 6; Jameson, *Postmodernism*, 44.

drift toward homogenization: "I have read that with enough time American civilization will make the midwest of any place, New York included. And . . . that seems not at all bad" (S, 115). These are hardly the sentiments of the unreconstructed southerner. And Frank's song of the suburbs may be interpreted as the death-knell of Donald Davidson's autocthonous ideal: "We all need our simple, unambiguous, even factitious landscapes like mine. Places without change or double-ranked complexity. Give me a little Anyplace, a grinning, toe-tapping Terre Haute or wide-eyed Bismarck, with stable property values, regular garbage pickup, good drainage, ample parking, located not far from a major airport, and I'll beat the birds up singing every morning" (S, 103–4).

It is difficult to imagine a landscape in Renascence fiction that could be described as "simple," "unambiguous," or "factitious"—or indeed to imagine any southern modernist novel with a setting not fraught with change and complexity. It is perhaps even more difficult to conceive of a modern southern protagonist *yearning* for such a place. The type of landscape Frank desires is in fact an antimodernist one, one in which the quest lies almost entirely on the surface of things, unencumbered by the "double-ranked complexity" inherent in narratives such as Faulkner's. Frank's comments about the dubious "mystery" of certain places reveal an anti-essentialist conception of place, a notion of setting as empty of transcendent or definitive character. He is suspicious of the type of abstraction that would construe a place as vital to human character, a sentiment evident in his praise of his own town, Haddam, as "straightforward and plumb-literal as a fire hydrant, which more than anything makes it the pleasant place it is" (S, 103). For the postmodern individual such as Frank, a new conception of place is in order: a sense of place as literal, straightforward, and knowable—with no mystery to complicate things beyond the tangible, no character beyond the commercial. In short, a postregional landscape.

One may feel tempted to dismiss Frank as an anomaly, an individual case of defection from the South. The South, after all, is supposed to stand in sharp contrast to the type of urban anonymity depicted here, and a true southerner would recognize this. How, then, may we define who is "southern" in the novels? Ford offers only two other southern émigrés for comparison. Frank's girlfriend, Vicki Arcenault, is a callow and provincial Texan who harbors no particular ties to her past. The former southerner who maintains such allegiances is Fincher Barksdale, a doctor from Tennessee who proposes that his plan for building an air-conditioned mink ranch in Memphis could constitute what he calls a "high-water mark for the New South" (69). Frank expresses a particular disdain for Barksdale, whom he describes as "the kind of southerner who will only address you through a web of deep and antic southernness, and who assumes everybody in earshot knows all about his parents and history and wants to hear an update on them at every opportunity" (S, 68). Bored by Barksdale's absorption with the South, Frank lampoons him with an acute satire of the stereotypical southern expatriate: "He is the perfect southerner-in-exile, a slew-footed mainstreet change jingler in awful clothes—a breed known only *outside* the south. At Vandy he was the tallish, bookish Memphian meant for a wider world—brushcut, droopy suntans, white bucks, campaign belt and a baggy long-sleeved Oxford shirt, hands stuffed in his pockets, arrogantly bored yet supremely satisfied and accustomed to the view from his eyrie. (Essentially the very way he is now.)" (S, 69). One might expect Ford to provide a glimmer of rebuke to the shallow material culture of the urban Northeast, to hold up some kind of essential alternative to commercial America. He does not. Not only is southern fraternalism entirely absent here, it is ridiculed. Regional consciousness and networks of family connections are reduced to the level of petty narcissism in an iconoclastic vision of the southern expatriate and his community. There is no coterie of expatriates in league against the creeping homogeneity around them in New Jersey. In contrast, these fellow southerners seem, like Frank, amenable to their new surroundings—Barksdale's mink ranch scheme being the closest thing to an echo of Quentin Compson's anguished link to home. The region is left behind, and so are regional issues. The past is indeed past, and there are no elegies here.

Independence Day carries these issues of place and the past a step further. The setting of the second novel continues postmodern as Frank and his son embark on a trip through a commercial landscape of almost unbelievable crassness. They pass through the Vince Lombardi Rest Area in New Jersey, which "is a little red-brick Colonial Williamsburg-looking pavilion" filled with "Roy Rogers burgers, Giants novelty items, joke condoms" and "families walking around semi-catatonically eating."[10] The Basketball Hall of Fame they visit ("which looks less like a time-honored place of legend and enshrinement than a high-tech dental clinic") offers "basketball-history-in-a-nutshell" via its "Action Theatre" and replicas of Doctor Naismith's signature and the original peach basket

10. Ford, *Independence Day*, 178. Subsequent references to this text are cited parenthetically within the essay as *ID*.

(*ID*, 264, 266). Pheasant Meadow makes another appearance, but it has "already visibly gone to seed" in the intervening years, now "abutting a strip of pastel medical arts plazas and a half-built Chi-Chi's," reduced in five years from a new development to "the architecture of lost promise" (*ID*, 141). It is indeed a decadent landscape, poorly versed in tradition yet fluent in the commercial vernacular.

Frank's notion of community in this sequel has changed to reflect his increasingly fragmented surroundings. His former praise of the generic has been augmented with a pronounced sense of relativism. Now he thinks of communities not as "continuous" but as "isolated, contingent groups trying to improve on the illusion of permanence, which they fully accept as an illusion" (*ID*, 386). He notes that "we want to *feel* our community as a fixed, continuous entity . . . as being anchored in the rock of permanence; but we know it's not, that in fact beneath the surface (or rankly all over the surface) it's anything but. We and it are anchored to contingency like a bottle on a wave, seeking a quiet eddy" (*ID*, 439). Here is confirmation of a postsouthern identity, for Frank not only denies the stability of communities (so vital to regionalism), he also implicates their constituents in a sort of wide-ranging scheme of self-delusion. There are no bedrock absolutes for Frank, only contingency. If in *The Sportswriter* he was willing to grant a small measure of legitimacy to a toe-tapping Terre Haute or wide-eyed Bismark, he seems at this later phase to deny any measure of authenticity to community *esprit*.

Frank has chosen a new vocation that suits both his environs and his evolving conception of community. He has left sportswriting and—in a career move of commercial proportions not seen in literature since Rabbit Angstrom assumed the mantle of Fred Springer's Toyota dealership—is pursuing another livelihood: he is now a real-estate agent, or, as he prefers to be called, a "Residential Specialist" (*ID*, 91). Frank thinks of real estate as the "ideal occupation" because it allows him "the satisfaction of reinvesting" in his community and thus "establishing a greater sense of connectedness" with it (*ID*, 111, 27). His duties as a Residential Specialist include "lifting sagging spirits, opening fresh, unexpected choices, and offering much-needed assistance toward life's betterment"—altruistic enterprises that accord with his "plan to do for others while looking after Number One" (*ID*, 47, 112).

If Ford intends for his sportswriter novels to be ironic commentaries on place, he could not have made a better choice for his protagonist's later career. In the role of Residential Specialist, his southern expatriate fuses a dialectic between place and late capitalism. The role allows Frank to maintain, in a radically altered fashion, the fabled southern attachment to place while yet embracing the commercial aesthetic—he becomes a commodity southerner. For what is real estate, after all, but the reification of place, the packaging of locale? If place holds no more value than the consumer goods it provides, and if community is hardly more than an illusion, Frank's decision to buy and sell these entities is logical. His approach to place is one that nearly all the southern modernists would reject—it does not privilege local culture and participates fully in the homogenizing process they dreaded—yet it is distinctly of its era. With his foray into real estate, Frank completes the trajectory begun by Ford's rejection of the traditional southern setting after *A Piece of My Heart*; his method of "establishing . . . connectedness" with his community might serve as epitaph for modernist modes of following the same impulse.

The transformation is not without its elements of pathos. Frank's final comment on southern identity emerges during a chance meeting with another former southerner, the stepbrother he has not seen for over two decades. Irv Ornstein is the son of Frank's mother's second husband, a sibling from the non-nuclear family that evolved after the death of the elder Bascombe. Irv is the closest approximation of the dissociated southerner of Renascence tradition that Ford offers in his sportswriter novels. Unlike Fincher Barksdale, he is a sympathetic character who seeks to recover a vital tradition beyond the narcissism of self-indulgence. He tells Frank that he feels "detached from his own personal history" and finds himself obsessed with the lack of "continuity" in his life (*ID*, 388, 390). He clings to the validity of family connections and attempts to draw Frank into a coherent framework with the past as its basis: " 'I was remembering . . . that you and I were around Jake's house together while our parents were married. I was right there when your mother died. We knew each other pretty well. And now twenty-five years of absence go by and we bump into each other up here in the middle of the north woods. And I realized . . . that you're my only link to that time. I'm not going to get all worked up over it, but you're as close to family as anyone there is for me. And we don't even know each other' " (*ID*, 387).

But Irv finds little solace in Frank, who is ambivalent about their shared history and can offer no better explanation for the family's dispersal than the observation that "life's screwy" (*ID*, 387). When Irv shows him a faded picture of "four humans in a stately family pose, two parents, two adolescent boys, standing out on some front porch steps," Frank does not recognize the family as his own—can in fact only think, "Who are these? Where are they? When?" (*ID*, 391). It is a shocking moment, and an illuminating one: clear evidence of Frank's severance from a southern past, from family connection, from an identity rooted in personal history. The "quickening torque of heart pain" he feels is "unexceptional," a reluctant nod to a "long-gone past" captured in a photograph he is quick to return to its owner (*ID*, 391). The snapshot Irv preserves in laminated, blurred, and decaying form is for Frank a memento of an anterior world so long gone as to be unreal, ephemeral. The past is no longer even past, but something further removed in time and place from the setting of this postmodern "family" reunion.

The poignancy of this episode indicates that Ford is not simply an iconoclast, or that he considers the present an ideal alternative to the past. Further, it is doubtful that he intends to praise the mass culture of the novels, and in fact his rendering of Frank's philosophy of consumption is tinged with irony in several passages, most notably in the protagonist's ode to rental cars and his praise of real estate. Yet Ford never uses Frank as the object of satire in the manner of Sinclair Lewis's Babbitt, and he certainly does not approach him with an authorial stance at all similar to those of his southern predecessors. Rather, like Bobbie Ann Mason and others of the so-called "Dirty Realists," he presents cultural shifts that would have elicited authorial commentary from earlier writers without following the familiar path of indicating that the present is a lapse from a better past. In southern modernist terms, such a narrative strategy would be deemed suspect, if not corrupt, in its failure to defend the community of tradition, in the very nonchalance with which it accepts the changes wrought by (post)modernity. But as the stark contrast in my epigraphs demonstrates, Ford inherited a South so different from that of Renascence figures like Lytle that the distinction between a realist and an iconoclast has become nearly indistinguishable. Ford is writing southern fiction at another crossing of the ways, perhaps, but with a realist's eye—not with the goal of adhering to a mythologized region that no longer exists for the contemporary writer. To do otherwise, Ford's career illustrates, would be to become docent to Renascence concerns that have no more authenticity in his own experience than the "bad stereotypes" of Frank's fiction.

In this indifference to the past lies Ford's importance to contemporary southern fiction. He declines to maintain any of the modernist concerns still engaged, in however attenuated a fashion, by fellow southern realists like Larry Brown and Dorothy Allison. As Frank's encounter with Irv demonstrates emphatically, there is no South in Ford's mature work to compare with the South depicted on the cover of that first novel—it has been abandoned. We may rightly ask, then, how southern is a fiction that chronicles the death of region without lament? As answer, I conclude with Ford's recollection of his hometown, Jackson, Mississippi, from his essay "An Urge for Going." His description of Jackson in the 1950s undermines our broad conception of the region in the primarily rural, agrarian, and regenerative terms that Ford has rejected—a definition with which we have perhaps grown too comfortable. Ford writes: "Place, that old thorny-bush in our mind's back yard, is supposed to be important to us Southerners. It's supposed to hold us. But where I grew up was a bland, unadhesive place—Jackson, Mississippi—a city in love with the suburban Zeitgeist the way Mill was in love with utility, a city whose inert character I could never much get interested in."[11]

11. Richard Ford, "An Urge for Going: Why I Don't Live Where I Used to Live," *Harper's* 284 (February 1992): 61.

Placing the Postsouthern "International City": Atlanta in Tom Wolfe's *A Man in Full*

Martyn Bone

Tom Wolfe's ambitious debut novel, *The Bonfire of the Vanities* (1987), was heralded for its "brilliant evocation of New York's class, racial and political structure in the 1980s." When news emerged in 1998 that Wolfe's long-awaited follow-up would similarly analyze the social forces at work in Atlanta, and that the U.S. hardback first-edition print-run would amount to 1.2 million copies, there was a sense that this was more than a merely literary phenomenon. *A Man in Full* became a cultural and economic event—nowhere more so than in Atlanta itself. Optimistic boosters hoped *A Man in Full* might promote "cultural tourism" in the way that Margaret Mitchell's *Gone With the Wind* did sixty years before, and as John Berendt's *Midnight in the Garden of Good and Evil* had done recently in nearby Savannah.[1]

However, many leading civic figures worried that Wolfe's novel would damage Atlanta's self-promoted image as an "international" and

1. Quote from *Publishers Weekly* on the back cover of Tom Wolfe, *The Bonfire of the Vanities* (1987; London: Picador, 1990); Maria Saporta, "ACVB [Atlanta Convention and Visitors Bureau] to Welcome Author of New Controversial Book," *Atlanta Journal-Constitution*, 27 October 1998, B3.

"world-class" city. For if *A Man in Full* brought fictional focus and cultural capital to Atlanta like no novel since *Gone With the Wind*, it also prompted more skeptical discussion of the city. As sociologist John Shelton Reed sagely observed, "all this coverage [of *A Man in Full* in the *Atlanta Journal-Constitution*] could only remind readers how long it has been since the last bestseller about this pushy, acquisitive New South city—which raises the question of why Atlanta produces or even attracts so few good writers, which raises the question of what 'world-class' really means."[2]

Before the book's publication in November 1998, there was particular concern in Atlanta regarding rumors that Wolfe paid close attention to real-estate development. Commentators in the *Journal-Constitution* speculated as to which of the prominent local developers provided the model for the novel's mooted central protagonist. Among those most often mentioned, John Portman commented that "I'm sure his [Wolfe's] characters are composites," while Charlie Ackerman admitted that "[w]e've kidded about who's in the book at parties." However, other developers were more obviously perturbed: Portman's great rival Tom Cousins "refused to comment, remember[ing] how Wolfe skewered New York bond traders in *The Bonfire of the Vanities*," and clearly fearing that Atlanta real-estate developers would suffer a similar fate.[3]

Cousins's concerns were not unfounded: Wolfe does use his man at the center, Charlie Croker, to emphasize the role of land speculation and real-estate development in metropolitan Atlanta. In this essay, I consider how *A Man in Full* critically represents the capitalist production of place in the so-called "international city." I draw upon social and spatial theorists such as Fredric Jameson and Manuel Castells to elucidate *A Man in Full*'s interrogation of Atlanta's "international" image: an image largely defined by the boosters, according to the city's burgeoning role within a (finance) capitalist world-system. I also refer to studies by geographer David Harvey and—with specific reference to Atlanta—anthropologist Charles Rutheiser to explicate the novel's representation of the local "politics of place" resulting from the speculative development and division of Atlanta's social geography.[4]

2. John Shelton Reed, Review of *A Man in Full*, *Southern Cultures* 5, no. 2 (Summer 1999), 93.

3. Don O'Briant, "A Wolfe at Our Door? Writer's Friends Say Atlanta Will Emerge Unscathed from New Novel About Race and Real Estate," *Atlanta Journal-Constitution*, 24 September 1998, D1.

4. Charles Rutheiser, *Imagineering Atlanta: The Politics of Place in the City of Dreams* (New York: Verso, 1996).

However, I also want to suggest that *A Man in Full*'s critical cartography of Atlanta reconfigures the canonical, literary-critical map of "the South," with its oft-cited "sense of place." Reed rightly suggests that contemporary Atlanta's economic claim to "world-class" status is weakened without the cultural capital provided by Atlanta-based fiction. Yet we might also ask whether Atlanta's *historical* role as a "New South" capitalist city has anything to do with its *ongoing* nonrepresentation in southern literature. The ideological influence of Agrarianism upon literary-critical canon-building warrants brief consideration here. William Gleason has recently emphasized that the contributors to the original Agrarian manifesto, *I'll Take My Stand* (1930), were reacting against the "frenzied materialism" underlying "the Atlanta Spirit"—a civic-corporate initiative established by city boosters in the 1920s. In 1958, that most unreconstructed Agrarian, Donald Davidson, explicitly stated the Fugitive-Agrarians' opposition to businessmen who were less interested in art than in "the value of real estate in Atlanta."[5]

If we subsequently consider that the invention of "southern literature" proceeded largely under the aegis of the Agrarians and their followers, it seems unsurprising that the *locus classicus* of New South capitalism has been conspicuously absent from the canonical *literary* landscape. The city is, at best, marginal to a literary-critical "South" that situates either Eudora Welty's Mississippi River Country or William Faulkner's Yoknapatawpha as its *rural* ground zero. Even Scarlett O'Hara's Peachtree Street has been excluded from such maps; of the bleak inner-city 1930s Atlanta wandered by young, doomed Blackie Pride in Donald Windham's *The Dog Star* (1950), there has been barely a trace. Since 1930, then, there has been a distinct narrative divergence. On one side, there is the (neo-) Agrarian representation of the southern "sense of place" as anti-urban, anti-industrial and (however implicitly) anti-Atlanta. On the other side, there is the city boosters' simultaneous—and often similarly performative—promotion of Atlanta as a "New South" city, a "national city," and "the world's next great city."[6]

5. William Gleason, *The Leisure Ethic: Work and Play in American Literature, 1840–1940* (Stanford: Stanford University Press, 1999), 309–10; Donald Davidson, *Southern Writers in the Modern World* (Athens: University of Georgia Press, 1958), 1.

6. Beyond the familiar emphasis on the antebellum romance of Tara, *Gone With the Wind* is a pro–New South, pro-Atlanta novel. See Donald Windham's afterword to a new edition of *The Dog Star* (1950; rprt., Athens: Hill Street Press, 1998) for his remarks on the cool reception that "the city that had loved *Gone With the Wind*" (226) afforded his depiction of working-class, inner-city Atlanta. In 1961, the Atlanta Chamber of Commerce out-

However, as southern social geographies, and Atlanta in particular, continued to change during the 1970s and 1980s, some writers and critics recognized the repercussions for southern literature. In 1989, Stephen Flinn Young invoked and extended Lewis P. Simpson's neologism "postsouthern" to posit that postsouthern art was specifically concerned to reconsider the old shibboleth, "sense of place." Young wondered whether "we may have even become prisoners of our own fascination" with the sense of place, "for when change overtakes us and place, even the place we call the South, is not the place it used to be, anxiety strikes." Less than a year later, Julius Rowan Raper offered a skeptical "postmodern view" as to why "the extraordinary sense of place . . . is a mainstay still of Modern Southern Fiction—but, less and less, of modern Southern life." Raper cited "the skylines of Atlanta" as evidence that "we are becoming the Postmodern South." Perhaps most pointedly of all, in 1986 Walker Percy wrote that he had "notice[d] a certain tentativeness in young Southern fiction writers—as if they still had one foot in Faulkner country, in O'Connor country, but over there just beyond the interstate loom the gleaming high-rises of Atlanta." Percy hoped that the contemporary southern novelist would "not try to become a neo-Agrarian" in order to evade the daunting challenge of depicting this corporate cityscape.[7]

Though his father was a Richmond-based gentleman farmer and agronomist who wrote for *The Southern Planter*, Tom Wolfe rejects any such neo-Agrarian attitude in *A Man in Full*. Indeed, with characteristic hubris, Wolfe commented that "[t]here should be 25 or 50 novels about Atlanta by now. What are these novelists doing?"[8] *A Man in Full* not only focuses on contemporary Atlanta, it reveals that—for all that Davidson would despair—real-estate development and multinational capital dominate the production of place in the *post*southern "international city."

---

lined its vision of Atlanta as a "national city" according to its ability to exert "a powerful economic force far beyond its normal regional functions." See Rutheiser, *Imagineering Atlanta*, 49. The slogan "The World's Next Great City" was officially adopted by Mayor Sam Massell in 1971.

7. Stephen Flinn Young, "Post-Southernism: The Southern Sensibility in Postmodern Sculpture," *Southern Quarterly* 28, no. 1 (Fall 1989): 41; Julius Rowan Raper, "Inventing Modern Southern Fiction: A Postmodern View," *Southern Literary Journal* 22, no. 2 (Spring 1990): 9, 17; Walker Percy, "Novel Writing in an Apocalyptic Time" (1986), in *Signposts in a Strange Land*, ed. Patrick Samway (London: Bellew, 1991), 166–67.

8. Quoted in Don O'Briant, " 'Full' Visit: Lots of Dining, No Whining," *Atlanta Journal-Constitution*, 20 November 1998, G6.

I want to begin my analysis of Wolfe's novel by considering an important scene in which Charlie Croker observes Atlanta from his private plane. The flight path of the Gulfstream Five (G-5) charts how, as Rutheiser has observed, "the cutting edge of [land] speculation has shifted" away from Downtown and Midtown into "the outer tier of metropolitan counties," where "edge cities" now rise.[9] But more interestingly, this panoramic set-piece also suggests how Charlie's *visual sense* of Atlanta is inextricable from his status as a capitalist developer.

When Charlie first looks down from the window of the G-5, he consciously focuses upon the towers of Downtown, Midtown, and Buckhead because these (phallic) structures emphasize his exclusive status as one of the powerful (male) producers of Atlanta's corporate cityscape:[10]

> Charlie knew them [the skyscrapers] all by sight. He knew them not by the names of their architects—what were architects but neurotic and "artistic" hired help?—but by the names of their developers. There was John Portman's seventy-story glass cylinder, the Westin Peachtree Plaza, flashing in the sun. (Portman was smart; he was his own architect.) There was Tom Cousins's twin-towered 191 Peachtree. . . . There was Charlie's own Phoenix Center; and, over there, his MossCo Tower; and over there, his TransEx Palladium. . . . Many was the time that the view from up here in the G-5, looking down upon the towers and the trees, had filled him with an inexpressible joy. *I did that! That's my handiwork! I'm one of the giants who built this city!*[11]

Fredric Jameson has posited that, under the postmodern cultural logic of late capitalism, "aesthetic production today has become integrated into commodity production generally" and that, "[o]f all the [postmodern] arts, architecture is the closest constitutively to the economic, with which, in the form of commissions and land values, it has a virtually un-

9. Rutheiser, *Imagineering Atlanta*, 77. The term *edge city* was popularized by journalist Joel Garreau; see his chapter on Atlanta in *Edge City: Life on the New Frontier* (New York: Anchor, 1991), 139–78.

10. All of the main protagonists in *A Man in Full*, barring Charlie's ex-wife, Martha, are male. Hence, ways of seeing Atlanta in the novel are expressed through what the feminist geographer Gillian Rose has termed "the masculine gaze." In this essay, I emphasize that this masculine gaze is much more powerful—indeed, proprietorial—when augmented by economic power. See Gillian Rose, *Feminism and Geography: The Limits of Geographical Knowledge* (Cambridge, U.K.: Polity Press, 1993), ch. 5.

11. Tom Wolfe, *A Man in Full* (London: Jonathan Cape, 1998), 63. All further page references will be cited parenthetically in the text.

mediated relationship." Such an argument seems substantiated by Charlie's dismissive view of the architect and his celebration of the capitalist developer. From Charlie's perspective, the architect is no longer an artist at all, but merely commissioned "help"; Atlanta's towers are evacuated of any aesthetic or auratic quality by the developer's fetishizing gaze. Indeed, the architectural artwork has been superseded by monumental mixed-use developments (MXDs) attributed entirely to the developers themselves, "the Creators of Greater Atlanta" (69). Tellingly, Charlie admires the man whom Jameson has deemed the doyen of postmodern hyperspace, John Portman—"a businessman as well as an architect and a millionaire developer, an artist who is at one and the same time a capitalist in his own right"—precisely because Atlanta's preeminent developer is also "his own architect."[12]

However, when Charlie "look[s] away from the buildings and out over the ocean of trees," he is forced to recognize that Atlanta is populated by *people*, and that these people do not reside in the corporate "islands" of Downtown and Midtown. Rather, "most of them" (63) live beneath the trees—obscured from Charlie's omniscient gaze. And yet, if Charlie cannot *see* the suburbs of Greater Atlanta, he can *mentally* map them. This is because Charlie was involved in their development; he rapturously recalls "[h]ow fabulous the building booms had been" in "those subdivided hills and downs and glades" (63–64). As the semantic fusion of "subdivision" and "hills" subtly suggests, Nature has been penetrated by—co-opted to—the radical reconstruction of Atlanta's residential real estate.

Charlie is well aware that "most of them [the residents of Greater Atlanta] are white," whereas "[f]ewer than 400,000 people lived within the Atlanta city limits, and almost three-quarters of them were black" (63). However, the developer clinically constructs his vision of Atlanta according to property values. It is thus hardly surprising that, while Charlie concentrates his omniscient gaze upon Downtown's corporate towers or mentally maps the suburban landscape of Greater Atlanta, he never focuses his (mind's) eye upon the unprofitable, profoundly racialized inner city.

Charlie's gaze only shifts away from the suburban treetops when the plane turns and he sees Perimeter Center, "the nucleus around which an

---

12. Fredric Jameson, *Postmodernism, or, The Cultural Logic of Late Capitalism* (London: Verso, 1991), 4–5, 44. Portman coauthored the tellingly titled *The Architect as Developer* (1976).

entire edge city . . . had grown" (64). Charlie's attention is engaged by Perimeter Center because he has begun to build his own edge city in Cherokee County, north of Atlanta. The project got underway when Charlie tried to purchase 150 acres of rural real estate, only to discover that speculators had already bought up south Cherokee, transforming the "trees and pastures" into "investor land." As Charlie's ex-wife, Martha, explains, this is "land that's too valuable to be devoted to farming or timber but not yet ready for developing. So investors buy it for a song, like Charlie thought he was going to, and then they just sit on it, waiting for the time when they can sell it for a big price for development" (511). Because land values have been inflated by such speculation, Charlie found that 150 acres would "cost approximately $4 million" (595).

Wolfe here suggests the extent to which agricultural production in traditional, rural north Georgia has been replaced by finance-capitalist land speculation in contemporary metropolitan Atlanta. In his contribution to *I'll Take My Stand*, Andrew Lytle attacked what he saw as an "effort to urbanize the farm . . . to convince the farmer that it is time, not space, which has value." Lytle optimistically hoped this "industrial" scheme would fail. However, in *A Man in Full*, speculation in the (sub)urban expansion of Atlanta into previously rural areas has resulted in what Lytle called the "abstract" social relationship of capitalist "absentee-landlordism." The economic abstraction of Cherokee's former farmland is compounded by the fact that *finance*-capitalist property speculation is divorced from any mode of production, agricultural or otherwise; it is solely "oriented towards the expectation of future value," what David Harvey calls "future profits from the use of the land." In other words, and *pace* Lytle, rural space *has* been (de)valued by time—the future time of finance capitalist profits from "investor land."[13]

Viewing this scene in relation to a familiar southern literary landscape, and citing Walker Percy once again, one can say that large-scale land speculation and development have moved beyond the "gleaming high-rises of Atlanta" itself and out into "O'Connor country." In Flannery O'Connor's short story "The Artificial Nigger" (1955), the central character, Mr. Head, defines a pastoral sense of place in his all-white home county in terms of its difference from black, urban Atlanta. At the

---

13. Andrew Lytle, "The Hind Tit," in Twelve Southerners, *I'll Take My Stand* (1930; rprt., Baton Rouge: Louisiana State University Press, 1977), 211, 243; Harvey quoted in Fredric Jameson, "The Brick and the Balloon: Architecture, Idealism, and Land Speculation," *New Left Review* 228 (March/April 1998): 43.

end of the story, after a day-long encounter with the Atlantan enemy, Head and his grandson gratefully return to the rural, racial refuge that is home. But in 1990s Georgia, the geographical boundary between Atlanta and the outlying counties of O'Connor country has been blurred by real-estate speculation. Indeed, Charlie finally acquires the required acreage for his Concourse project by *co-opting* the white southern racism of Head's spiritual descendants. In unlikely cahoots with Ku Klux Klan member Darwell Scruggs (and populist black politician Andre Fleet), Charlie simulates a KKK rally and a subsequent civil rights march "protesting racism and de facto segregation in this old rural county that's practically all white" (511). This pseudo-event makes "the national news on television for a couple of nights" (510) and serves to devalue the investor land, enabling Charlie to buy it up at a knockdown price. If Wolfe's plot device seems improbable, we might usefully see it as an example of postsouthern parody—albeit with serious implications for the traditional southern "sense of place." The familiar rural racism of O'Connor's Head is played out in desultory, stylized fashion by the latecomer Scruggs; even then, the Klan's stand for white racial (and spatial) purity has been exploited by a capitalist developer. Here is an irony that Scruggs does not appear to understand, and that Head would have hated: if racial integration does not destroy rural Georgia's all-white enclaves, Atlanta real-estate development will. For not only Cherokee but also Paulding and Forsyth Counties are *becoming* metropolitan Atlanta.[14]

Yet Charlie receives comeuppance for his shady dealings in rural real estate. Having since completed the construction of Croker Concourse, the developer's original speculations in Atlanta's spatial "futures" market have proven awry anyway: "A few years down the line somebody would make a fortune off what he had put together . . . but for now—*too far* north, *too far* from the old city, Atlanta itself" (65). Suddenly, the sight of his failing edge city reminds Charlie that his major creditors, PlannersBanc, are threatening to repossess all of his Atlanta properties—including the Concourse itself. The developer's gaze no longer seems so imperious: "Did he dare open his eyes and look down? He didn't want to, but he couldn't help himself. Just as he feared, the G-5 was in the perfect spot for an aerial view of Croker Concourse. There it was . . . a pre-

14. Land speculation on the rural, northern fringe of metropolitan Atlanta in the 1990s was such that one developer secured options on one-fifth of the land in Paulding County. Development included "the construction of high-priced luxury housing" in "the longtime Klan stronghold" of Forsyth County. See Rutheiser, *Imagineering Atlanta*, 77.

posterously lonely island sticking up out of that ocean of trees. Croker's folly!" (64–65). Charlie's proprietorial perspective on metropolitan Atlanta has been rendered so precarious by the prospect of bankruptcy and repossession that he is glad when the G-5 finally heads south to an old place—the neo-antebellum sanctuary of his plantation, Turpmtime (to which I will turn later in this essay).

Jameson has posited that "in the realm of the spatial, there does seem to exist something like an equivalent of finance capital, indeed a phenomenon intimately related to it, and that is land speculation."[15] I have tried to show how the speculative shenanigans over investor land on the northern edge of metropolitan Atlanta exhibit this equivalence. I now want to focus on Charlie's dealings with PlannersBanc, for here we find a further, deeper relation between (global) finance capitalism and (local) land speculation.

PlannersBanc is the Atlanta-based institution that supplied the loans that funded Croker Concourse. In total, PlannersBanc loaned $515 million (42) to Croker Global at a time when "big loans were spoken of as 'sales'" (44). In the "palmy days" when those loan "sales" were arranged, the bank provided a forty-ninth-floor room with a view that, much like the G-5, indulged Charlie's proprietorial gaze: "beyond the glass window walls, always exquisitely curtained against glare, all of Atlanta . . . was laid out before him. *(It's all yours, Charlie)*" (46). However, the debt-ridden developer is no longer invited to the lavish, vertiginous confines of the executive floor. Charlie's descending status within PlannersBanc's customer hierarchy is symbolically enacted when the bank's Real Estate Asset Management Department conducts its emergency meeting with the developer in a "cunningly seedy and unpleasant" (36) room on only the thirty-ninth floor. At the start of this meeting, PlannersBanc's senior loan officer, Raymond Peepgass, observes of Charlie that "[t]he fool seemed to think he was still one of those real estate developers who own the city of Atlanta" (35). The emergency meeting is designed to disabuse Charlie of this possessive attitude toward the city. Most explicitly, the Real Estate Asset Management team demands that Charlie sell some of his properties in order to start paying back the loans. But the bank also announces its dissatisfaction—and asserts its own superiority within the visual economy of Atlanta's corporate power structure—by obscuring Charlie's previously privileged, proprietorial view of

15. Jameson, "The Brick and the Balloon," 26.

the city from PlannersBanc Tower: "he should have been able to look out through the plate-glass wall and seen much of Midtown Atlanta . . . But he couldn't. . . . It was the glare. He and his contingent had been seated so that they had to look straight into it" (36).

When the recalcitrant Charlie continues to default on the loans, PlannersBanc ups the pressure by focusing its own proprietorial gaze upon Croker Concourse itself. Tricked into watching a fake promotional video for his edge city, Charlie is subjected to PlannersBanc's panoptical, (re)-possessive view of his underoccupied MXD: "Now the camera lingered lovingly on the tower itself . . . Looking through the window on this side you could see through the window wall on the far side . . . floor after floor after floor . . . because there were no tenants in them" (594). By this point, Charlie is deeply depressed by the commercial failure of the Concourse project and the prospect of repossession and bankruptcy. When the lawyer Roger White visits the developer's office on the thirty-ninth floor of Croker Concourse and comments upon the "[s]pectacular view!" (553), Charlie responds in an uncharacteristically reflective manner: "If you look at Atlanta real estate long enough, you'll notice there was a time, not all that long ago, when folks didn't care about views one way or the other. Views came cheap as the air and a lot cheaper than dirt. Then . . . folks discovered views, and that gave everybody one more thing to get competitive about" (553–54).

Charlie's despondency here reveals that PlannersBanc's merciless financial pressure has finally destroyed his own possessive gaze. But his mournful musings also help us to understand another dimension to the capitalist production of place in Atlanta. This process has gone beyond the financial valuation of land ("dirt," in Charlie's down-home rubric) as real estate; beyond the Marxist problem of ground rent; and even beyond the material construction of MXDs. In what might be seen as a variation on Guy Debord's famous declaration that even the image has become a reified commodity in "the society of the spectacle," Charlie suggests that optical experience of the city has been infiltrated by the ideology of land speculation—that the *visual sense* of place itself has narrowed into "spectacular views" of "Atlanta real estate."[16] This is a telling critique coming from a man who, moving and working within the cityscape of corporate Atlanta, has internalized the speculative spatial economy of "spectacular views" as his own existential-visual sense of place. If, as Roger observes,

16. Guy Debord, *The Society of the Spectacle* (1967; rprt., New York: Zone Books, 1995).

Charlie waxes like "the Old Philosopher" (554), it is because he not only stands to lose the property and capital he has accrued through land speculation; he also stands to lose his very way of seeing the city, even his way of being-in-the-world.

Situated amidst the prime corporate real estate of Atlanta, PlannersBanc Tower's *symbolic capital* serves as a material, spatial sign of Planners-Banc's immense resources of *finance capital*.[17] However, there is one moment in *A Man in Full* when PlannersBanc Tower seems peculiarly *im*material. This is when, during a meeting of the Real Estate Asset Management Department, Ray Peepgass finds himself looking "[t]hrough the glass inner wall of [an] office": "he could look through other glass walls, into other offices, in toward the very core of the forty-ninth floor. And everywhere he looked, he could see the eerie luminous rectangles of computer screens, and across those screens blipped the two hundred to three hundred *billion* dollars that moved through PlannersBanc every day" (238). PlannersBanc's window walls effect an optical illusion: the erasure of the forty-ninth floor's local, material geography. The divisions between the various offices appear to have vanished. In this moment, Ray—despite working at the bank for years—loses any familiar physical or visual sense of place.

I would suggest that Ray's dislocation arises because the glass walls of PlannersBanc Tower express, in barely mediated architectural form, what Jameson calls "the fundamental source of all abstraction," the money form—more particularly, the bank's dealings in massive amounts of international yet placeless finance capital. Looking at the figures on the screens, Ray tries to comprehend the bank's daily billion-dollar dealings in material, spatial terms—"*mov[ing] through* PlannersBanc every day." The problem is that, as Jameson has observed, finance capital "separates from the 'concrete context' of its productive geography," becoming a "second degree" abstraction of the money form, which "always was abstract in the first and basic sense." So, unlike capital abstracted to only the first degree, the *finance* capital "seen" by Ray is not represented by any *material* sign, such as gold or paper money. Nor does it "move through" any physical location ("concrete context") in PlannersBanc—

17. "Symbolic capital" is Pierre Bourdieu's term. See David Harvey, *The Condition of Postmodernity* (Cambridge, U.K.: Blackwell, 1989), 77–78, on how symbolic capital, as "the collection of luxury goods attesting the taste and distinction of the owner," is actually transformed "money capital."

except as *numerical* signs on the computer screens (if a computer screen "can properly be regarded as a place").[18]

In this scene, then, PlannersBanc Tower seems to have melted into air. At the very least, the building appears to have attained a "second sense" of placelessness that approximates the "second degree" abstraction of finance capital itself: the (albeit illusory) dematerialization of the forty-ninth floor's office space is compounded by the placelessness of figures on the screens. All told, Ray's momentarily defamiliarized view of the forty-ninth floor enables him to perceive that PlannersBanc is less a visible, physical locus (PlannersBanc *Tower* in Midtown Atlanta) than a node within the immaterial, transnational matrix of technologically mediated finance-capital exchange. To employ Manuel Castells's distinction, the forty-ninth floor is less a "space of places" than a "space of flows" within the "global network of capital flows."[19]

This brings us to the issue of Atlanta's status as an "international city." PlannersBanc's evident role in what Castells calls the "internationalization of the process by which capital circulates" seems to bear out the boosters' rhetorical claims that Atlanta is an "international city." Indeed, the bank has semiotically shed its provincial "Old South" image—changing its name from the Southern Planters Bank and Trust Company—in order to perform a more suitably *post*southern, "international" identity. Adopting the compound fashion of "NationsBank, SunTrust, BellSouth" and others, "PlannersBanc" is intended "to show how cosmopolitan, how international, how global [the bank] had become" (37–38). However, such a definition of "international(ization)" is entirely economic, tied to the "international financial markets themselves, increasingly working in their own sphere according to a logic distinct from that of any national economy"—and distinct from *Atlanta's* local economy or social geography. In 1936, Allen Tate attacked a form of "finance capitalism . . . top heavy with a crazy jig-saw network of exchange value"; Tate was dismayed by the disorienting effect that this "remote" system had upon individual lives. Yet Tate could hardly have imagined PlannersBanc Tower's abstract "space of flows"—the apotheosis of

18. Jameson, "The Brick and the Balloon," 25 (see also p. 44 on the "abstract dimension or materialist sublimation of finance capital" in postmodern glass towers); Fredric Jameson, "Culture and Finance Capital," in *The Cultural Turn* (London: Verso, 1998), 142; David Harvey, *Justice, Nature, and the Geography of Difference* (Oxford: Blackwell, 1996), 246.

19. Jameson, "Culture and Finance Capital," 142; Manuel Castells, *The Informational City* (Oxford: Blackwell, 1989), 348, 311.

placelessness in an "international city" increasingly defined by global finance/capital exchange.[20]

However, it is vital to qualify that, however "placeless" the finance capital in which PlannersBanc deals, such abstract economic power *does* impress itself upon Atlanta's material geography. I have already cited the monumental case of PlannersBanc's own Midtown tower, which Castells might explain as an example of "the increasing tension between places and flows." In *The Informational City* (1989), Castells emphasizes that even though the *organization* of finance-capital exchange is placeless, *control* of finance-capital exchange is place-specific. Even if, as Castells suggests, Atlanta still seems regional by comparison with New York, the city's growing role in the centralized control of multinational finance capital is revealed in "Manhattanized" towers like PlannersBanc.[21] PlannersBanc Tower, then, is not simply symbolic capital *signifying* finance capital; it locates the *control* of finance capital. Certain areas of Atlanta, at least—Downtown, Midtown, and Buckhead—have thrived upon the dialectic between local, material place and multinational, abstract capital flows.

One can make further connections between global finance capital and local land speculation, between the abstract "space of flows" and the material "space of places," in *A Man in Full*, for PlannersBanc's involvement in billion-dollar exchanges of capital empowers the bank's own role in the production of Atlanta's corporate space *beyond* its Midtown tower. The most notable example of PlannersBanc's investment in Atlanta is, of course, Croker Concourse. Indeed, it is international capital speculation that makes PlannersBanc a *more* significant force in the Atlanta real-estate market than Charlie Croker. Whereas the rebranding of the "Southern Planters Bank and Trust Company" legitimately referred to the bank's dealings in global capital, "Croker Global" is an egotistical, entirely performative misnomer: as the Real Estate Asset Management Department meeting reveals, Charlie has no overseas operations (51).[22] Despite Croker Global's synergic expansion into wholesale food produc-

20. Castells, *The Informational City,* 310, 339; Allen Tate, "Notes on Liberty and Property," in *Who Owns America,* ed. Herbert Agar and Allen Tate (1936; rprt., Freeport: Books for Libraries Press, 1970), 84.

21. Castells, *The Informational City,* 171, 169–70, 346. See Rutheiser, *Imagineering Atlanta,* 125, on Atlanta's "Manhattanization."

22. Rather aptly, PlannersBanc's "international" investments are not geographically located, but Ray Peepgass's stewardship of a $4.1-billion loan package for Finnish government bonds (p. 161) hints at the extent and value of such investments.

tion, the corporation's capital resources are measly compared to those of the bank. PlannersBanc accrued multimillion-dollar debts through its disastrous dealings with Charlie and other developers—and yet the bank's resources are such that it is able to write off those debts, even as it prepares to seize Croker Global's various properties. Ultimately, it is this "international" economic power that enables PlannersBanc to exert its omniscient, possessive gaze upon Charlie and his edge city.

Discussing the "postmodern cartographies" produced by leftist cultural critics in recent years, Brian Jarvis has observed that "[Fredric] Jameson and [David] Harvey often appear mesmerized by the awesome incorporative power of late capitalism." Jarvis further notes that "Jameson's views of landscape often seem to come from *within* the centres of luxury and affluence" (the most famous example being Jameson's view from within Portman's Bonaventure Hotel in Los Angeles). From what we have seen of *A Man in Full* so far, it might seem that similar criticisms could be leveled at Tom Wolfe's literary map of postsouthern, "international" Atlanta. The breathless litanies of Downtown and Midtown MXDs ("There was John Portman's seventy-story glass cylinder," and so on) might suggest that *Wolfe* is "mesmerized" by the large-scale capitalist development of Atlanta. We might wonder whether the "spectacular views" of the city "from *within* the centres of luxury and affluence" (PlannersBanc Tower and Croker Concourse) merely reproduce, in omniscient narrative form, the possessive visual economy of a capitalist real-estate developer—or, as John Shelton Reed worried, an Atlanta booster.[23]

However, *A Man in Full* not only observes and represents Atlanta from within postmodern capitalist hyperspaces; as Reed noted, *A Man in Full* also reveals the "largely unknown parts of the city." Citing Michel de Certeau, one might say that Wolfe shows how the spectacle of the "panorama-city" from Croker Concourse or PlannersBanc Tower is the land speculator's own "optical artifact . . . a projection that is the way of keeping aloof." As we have seen, Wolfe critiques the reifying visual ideology of capitalist land speculation via Charlie's remarks on the "spectacu-

---

23. Brian Jarvis, *Postmodern Cartographies: The Geographical Imagination in Contemporary American Culture* (London: Pluto, 1998), 46, 48; Reed, Review of *A Man in Full*, 95–96. Reed observed that "Wolfe's bravura depiction" of Atlanta "gives it almost mythic power. We see it both from the air (aboard Charlie's private Gulfstream 5) and from the ground." Reed concluded his review by wondering how the boosters would try to co-opt Wolfe's "vividly realized" view of Atlanta.

lar views" of Atlanta real estate. However, the novel also features those whom de Certeau calls "ordinary practitioners of the city [who] live 'down below,' below the thresholds at which visibility begins." Mapping MXDs from the G-5, Charlie may not have seen "An-other Atlanta(s)," but they are visible in *A Man in Full*.[24]

The socio-spatial chasm between those "above" and those "down below" is evident in a brief encounter between PlannersBanc's chief executive, Arthur Lomprey, and an immigrant market-stall operator in Underground Atlanta, the Downtown commercial complex. Despite PlannersBanc's speculative influence on the "international" image and material development of Atlanta, its senior employee is detached from the everyday lives of most citizens. We witness Lomprey only within a particularly exclusive version of what V. S. Naipaul has called "the bubble in which the white professional people of Atlanta lived: the house, the air-conditioned car, the office . . . the luncheon club."[25] In Lomprey's case, the rarified loci are the Piedmont Driving Club, the High Museum, and his forty-ninth-floor office at PlannersBanc Tower. This office affords a panoramic view "north toward Buckhead, east toward Decatur, and south toward Downtown and, assuming you wanted to, the vague expanse of the lower half of the city" (606). There is here a subtle implication that Lomprey's speculative gaze is much like Charlie's: it glazes over the poor, black Southside, which is decidedly not prime development land.

Lomprey is, then, in unfamiliar surroundings when he purchases "a fake Patek Philippe watch from a Senegalese street vendor out in front of Underground Atlanta with $65 of his own money" (236). Lomprey buys the watch to acknowledge a particularly effective performance by the Real Estate Asset Management Department's "workout artiste," Harry Zale, who (literally) seized a $30,000 Patek Phillippe watch from one of the bank's intransigent debtors. However, Lomprey's jest achieves its effect not just by celebrating Harry's chutzpah; it also plays upon the incongruous image of PlannersBanc's chief executive undertaking a petty financial transaction with an immigrant market-stall operator. Put another way, the joke evokes the socioeconomic chasm between Planners-

---

24. Reed, review of *A Man in Full*, 96. Michel de Certeau, *The Practice of Everyday Life* (Berkeley: University of California Press, 1984), 93. "An-other Atlanta(s)" was the title of a 1975 project organized by historians Tim Crimmins and Dana White that "focused on developing a 'usable urban history' of both the city's infrastructure and key locales and neighborhoods." See Rutheiser, *Imagineering Atlanta*, 56–57.

25. V. S. Naipaul, *A Turn in the South* (London: Penguin, 1989), 29.

Banc's position in the global finance-capitalist space of flows, and the local immigrant-operated space of places that is Underground Atlanta.

There are two extended set-pieces in *A Man in Full* that more thoroughly depict other, (under)ground-level Atlantas. The first of these is Roger White's limousine tour from Buckhead to Vine City with Mayor Wes Jordan; the second is Conrad Hensley's experience as a fugitive among the immigrant population of "Chambodia."

Roger White's tour emerges out of a conference in City Hall with Mayor Jordan, during which the two men discuss the rumor that Georgia Tech's star running-back, Fareek Fanon, has raped Elizabeth Armholster, the daughter of the "chairman of Armaxco Chemical and about as influential a businessman as existed in Atlanta" (4). Wes identifies the larger social issues surrounding the impending scandal: "Okay, not to belabor the obvious, there are two Atlantas, one black and the other white . . . You see all the towers in Downtown and Midtown—that's all white money, even though the city is 70 percent black, perhaps 75 percent black by now." However, black Atlantans are fully aware of the city's socio-spatial inequality—an awareness that, Wes suggests, arises from their own *visual sense* of place: "Our brothers and sisters in this city are not blind. . . . They see" (183).

The usually loquacious mayor admits to Roger that "[i]t's hard to put it [Atlanta's unequal geography] into words. . . . It's going to be a whole lot easier if I *show* you" (183). Interestingly, *A Man in Full* here echoes a similar scene in Anne Rivers Siddons's *Peachtree Road* (1988). In Siddons's Atlanta-based novel, the (white) mayor-elect Ben Cameron tells the (white) narrator Gibby Bondurant that "I'd rather show you"; the two men then proceed on a chauffeur-driven limousine tour from Buckhead to a poor, black South Atlanta neighborhood. Because *A Man in Full*'s mayoral tour exhibits an intertextual relation to *Peachtree Road*'s earlier, equivalent journey (set in 1961), it is possible to map the "historical continuities" of racial segregation and geographical uneven development that yet survive within the "international city."[26]

Mayor Jordan first has the chauffeur, Dexter Johnson, drive by the expensive Buckhead properties of Croker and Armholster. These houses are hidden on private, tree-lined roads away from the general public's

---

26. Anne Rivers Siddons, *Peachtree Road* (1988; rprt., New York: HarperPaperbacks, 1998), 533. See Rutheiser, *Imagineering Atlanta,* 5, on "historical continuities" in Atlanta's uneven development.

gaze, yet their "sheer homage to conspicuous consumption" (190) attests to their owners' financial and social status. The mayor then directs the limousine through Atlanta's decentered business districts. Here, the narrative offers another awe-inspiring perspective on the material geography of multinational capital: a "canyon" of skyscrapers "streaming past on either side of Peachtree [Street], which was *the* place to have a tower" (195). However, Wes adds a commentary that *sees through* (rather than *from within*) this mesmerizing spectacle—a commentary that furthers the novel's critique of how the "national" and "international city" has been defined. The mayor incredulously observes that "[a]ll these towers were supposed to show you that Atlanta wasn't just a regional center, it was a national center." Wes points out International Boulevard, CNN Center, the Georgia World Congress Center, and International Plaza—the latter a monument to "Atlanta's greatest international coup: the 1996 Olympics"—as evidence of the boosters' attempts "to make Atlanta a *world* center, the way Rome, Paris and London have been world centers in the past, and the way New York is today" (195). Yet Wes tempers this skeptical view of "international" Atlanta's performative signification. He recognizes that the "business interests" *have* succeeded in transforming (this part of) Atlanta into a "*national* center"—according to their own *economic* criteria. The mayor also ventures that the boosters may yet make the globalization rhetoric an (economic) reality: "They may just pull it off, turn this town into *the world center*. . . . They know how to generate money" (197).

However, the tour subsequently takes a turn that directly indicts both Atlanta's putative *global* status and its *local* politics of place. The limousine suddenly leaves behind "all the glossy pomposity of the center of the world" (197) when it enters the black neighborhood of Vine City. Roger's gaze shifts abruptly from the "world center" that is "the business interests' dream" (195) to witness a local poverty much like that which Siddons's Bondurant saw in 1961: "Three vacant lots in a row . . . overgrown with weeds and saplings . . . Through the weeds on one side of the house he could see a pool of collected water, out of which protruded . . . *junk* . . . of every sort" (198). Like Bondurant before him, it has taken a mayoral tour to enable Roger to visually and mentally map the contrast between "the top" and "the bottom" (202) of Atlanta: "Roger looked round about the Bluff . . . in his mind's eye he could see Armholster's Venetian palazzo and Croker's pile" (204).[27]

27. In *Peachtree Road*, Gibby Bondurant offers a strikingly similar description of the poor, black neighborhoods he encounters during *his* mayoral tour: "Most of the houses had long since lost their paint and some had lost their windowpanes. . . . Occasional vacant lots choked with the brown skeletons of kudzu vines" (Siddons, 536). Gibby also contrasts the

There are, though, qualifications that should be made regarding this powerful depiction of Atlanta's historical-geographical uneven development. To do so, it is useful to return to the start of the tour and Mayor Jordan's disquisition on how commercial cartographies of Atlanta reproduce racialized ways of seeing (or *not* seeing) the city: "Did you happen to see any of those 'guides to Atlanta' they published for the Olympics? . . . The maps—the *maps!*—were all bobtailed—cut off at the bottom—so no white tourist would even *think* about wandering down into South Atlanta." Because such texts guided the white tourist's gaze toward what Rutheiser has termed the "ornamental nodes" of the Olympian "stage set [created] for visitors and viewers," the black majority population of Atlanta were, as Wes notes, made "invisible" to "the rest of the world" (185).[28] Indeed, the supposedly objective, omniscient views of the city offered in such tourist guides approximate nothing so much as the selective, speculative gaze of Charlie or Lomprey—perspectives that, as we have seen, ignore "the vague expanse of the lower half of the city."

A Man in Full's mayoral tour can be seen as Wolfe's attempt to rectify or *re-place* the Olympian maps' ideological bias. The journey from Buckhead through Peachtree Street to Vine City appears to be a more authentic, even mimetic (narrative) cartography of the so-called "international city." However, it is important to recognize that the reader still experiences Atlanta from a particular, ideological point of view. Mayor Jordan's mapping, and lawyer White's reading, of the city emerge from a middle-class perspective. The two men themselves grew up in Vine City but have joined the black middle-class flight to the West End (199); Roger is so estranged from his old neighborhood that he does not even recognize much of it (an effort not helped, it must be said, by English Avenue's dilapidated state). There are echoes here of James Baldwin's observations on the black middle-class's post-1960s "limbo" from an increasingly ghettoized inner-city Atlanta.[29] It is true that the two men enter a black neighborhood omitted from the Olympic maps, and that Wes wants to show Roger the contrast between the Buckhead background of Elizabeth Armholster and the ghetto youth of Fareek Fanon. Yet the mayor and the lawyer *do* seem to be "sightseeing" (183) in Vine City. Much like the Olympic books, Mayor Jordan acts as a "guide to Atlanta"—albeit an

---

poverty-stricken black tenants of Pumphouse Hill—which Mayor Cameron has just told him that the Bondurant family owns—with his mother's privileged life in Buckhead (p. 543).

28. Rutheiser, *Imagineering Atlanta*, 6.

29. James Baldwin, *Evidence of Things Not Seen* (London: Michael Joseph, 1985), 26.

other Atlanta—directing Roger's tourist gaze. Ultimately, like Mayor Cameron and Gibby Bondurant before them, Wes and Roger can go home again (in their case, to the West End rather than Peachtree Road).

Moreover, if the reader experiences the tour through Roger's eyes (and "mind's eye"), there is also a certain overlap between Wolfe's status as omniscient narrator and Wes's position as Roger's (our) guide. Wolfe perhaps slyly acknowledges this equivalence by having the mayor state that "I'm just trying to construct a narrative, you might say, and I'm just hoping it'll unfold naturally" (193). The sense that Wes's tourist gaze/ narrative overlaps with the omniscient author's is confirmed by the knowledge that, while researching the novel, Wolfe drove through English Avenue with former city-planning director Leon Eplan. The implication here is not that Wolfe is a white, bourgeois author and should therefore be disqualified from writing about black South Atlanta. Such a claim would be a simpleminded echo of Quentin Compson's undialectical claim to "southern" authenticity, which here becomes: "You can't understand black South Atlanta. You would have to be born there." Nonetheless, Toni Morrison had a point when she observed that: "You have *Gone with the Wind*. . . . Then you have this Tom Wolfe book. And that's Atlanta. Boom. Over. . . . And I thought, 'No, no, no.' No one is talking about Atlanta from the point of view of these people who know it—not the political way, not the way the marketers knew it, but on the streets, in the houses, in the schools." We should simply recognize that, for all the power of Wolfe's map of "the lay of the land" (187) between Buckhead and Vine City, we do not experience Atlanta "from the point of view" of those "on the streets, in the houses" of the black Southside. For such a perspective, one has to turn to another recent Atlanta novel (edited by Morrison): Toni Cade Bambara's *Those Bones Are Not My Child* (1999).[30]

Conrad Hensley, the white former Croker Global warehouse laborer *cum* fugitive, arrives in Atlanta via a space of flows rather different from that which facilitates the immaterial movements of multinational capital. Conrad's journey from Oakland via Portland to Atlanta involves a sophisticated transportation network that more usually assists the passage of (often illegal) immigrants into and across the United States. Upon ar-

---

30. O'Briant, "A Wolfe at Our Door?" D1; Michael Kreyling, *Inventing Southern Literature* (Jackson: University Press of Mississippi, 1998), 6; Valerie Boyd, "Toni Morrison Brings Friend's 'Bones' to Print," *Atlanta Journal-Constitution*, 17 October 1999, L1.

riving at Hartsfield International Airport, Conrad is met by his contact, Lum Loc, and taken to Chamblee, located in the northeast of metropolitan Atlanta. Chamblee, Doraville, and Clarkston, where around ten thousand Vietnamese, Cambodian, Laotian, and Hmong refugees settled during the 1980s, comprise a district that offers an alternative vision of Atlanta as an "international city"—defined by its multicultural population, not by the globalization of finance-capital flows.

Walking in Chamblee for the first time, Conrad is astonished to discover a commercial strip of small shops operated by Southeast Asian immigrants. Conrad eventually comes to "ASIAN SQUARE" which, as a modest but apparently popular public space, contrasts with the simulated cosmopolitanism of Downtown's International Plaza (519). Indeed, as Rutheiser notes, on account of the burgeoning immigrant population "the stretch of Buford Highway near the cities of Doraville and Chamblee became known as 'Atlanta's *Real* International Boulevard.' "[31] Chamblee's residents themselves celebrate their origins by unofficially renaming the town "Chambodia" (515).

However, for all that Chambodia allows these immigrants to maintain a place-specific sense of identity and community, and for all the international origins of the heterogeneous populace, the district is distinctly segregated from the "international city." Conrad is struck by how the built landscape of immigrant-owned businesses around Buford Highway is "another world" (519). Wes Jordan ostensibly "belabor[ed] the obvious" by referring to "two Atlantas"; in fact, the mayor's bipolar map "rendered invisible" outlying areas like Chamblee and Doraville that have complicated the "polar shades of American-born black and white."[32] Yet, by a grim irony, the new arrivals themselves, isolated on the northeast edge of the metropolis, are forced to map Atlanta in similarly binary terms. As Lum Loc notes: "This side, America. Other side, Chambodia" (518).

Chambodians' status as second-class citizens is especially evident in their experience of police surveillance, which severely restricts their ability to achieve a mobile, *social* sense of place in Atlanta. As an escaped convict, Conrad is circumspect about walking around Chamblee, even though he has acquired a false driver's license and birth certificate. Nonetheless, he is better off than the illegal Vietnamese immigrants he lives with, who cannot alter their appearance. Because of police surveillance,

31. Rutheiser, *Imagineering Atlanta,* 89.
32. Ibid., 88.

most new arrivals are told that they "[c]annot always walk around doing nothing in Chambodia" until Lum Loc "give[s] them IDs and they get work" (518). Consequently, many immigrants' everyday lives are literally confined to the private rooms of rented accommodation. We witness an example of this from Conrad's point of view: "The tiny living room was now packed with people, with Vietnamese—must be fifteen or sixteen of them at least . . . The place was ripe with the smell of too many human bodies in a small space" (515). The contrast between this restrictive, all-too-physical sense of place and the abstract space of PlannersBanc Tower could hardly be more stark.

Eventually, Conrad himself comes under police scrutiny during an excursion into Chamblee. There are few pedestrians—not only because the immigrants are careful not to be caught on the sidewalks, but also because the built landscape around Buford Highway epitomizes Atlanta's status as an "autopolis." Hence, Conrad is conspicuous *despite* his respectable appearance and white skin, and sure enough, he is soon pulled over by a police patrol car and asked where he is heading. Chambodia may be beyond or below the elevated world view of a Croker or a Lomprey, but the locals *are* subjected to the gaze of state authority. In this instance, de Certeau's "pedestrian speech acts"—the belief that "the long poem of walking manipulates spatial organizations, no matter how panoptic they may be"—seems like little more than a postmodern fantasy.[33]

Finally though, Chambodians' unequal status within Atlanta is best exemplified by the labor market. Vietnamese immigrants invariably have to take "work on the assembly line" at the "[v]ery big chicken plant in Knowlton" (517). It is Brother, the eccentric poor white who rents Conrad a room in a decrepit antique shop in "Old Chamblee," who explains the "place" that Southeast Asian immigrants occupy in the local job market, and how such labor relations have redefined Chamblee's demography: "It's 'at chicken plant in Knowlton. Won't no white man work there and no black man, either, these days. So they wants the Orientals, but they don't want 'em living in Knowlton, so they park 'em in Chamblee and Doraville" (626). Knowlton and Chamblee, then, are not merely peripheral parts of metropolitan Atlanta; they are also buckled onto "the Broiler Belt" of chicken-processing factories, the "latest industry of toil

---

33. Ibid., 82 (Rutheiser takes the term *autopolis* from H. L. Preston's *Automobile Age Atlanta: The Making of a Southern Metropolis* [Athens: University of Georgia Press, 1979]); de Certeau, *The Practice of Everyday Life*, 98, 101.

to reign in the South."[34] Wolfe here provides *A Man in Full*'s most sober-ing example of how, out on the less-glamorous edges of the postsouthern metropolis, beyond finance-sector employment in the space of flows, tra-ditionally "southern" manual labor is still being performed. The only his-torical change is that the workers are not southern-born blacks but the newest and most truly international residents of the so-called "interna-tional city."

A Man in Full does focus upon one older southern place that appears to have little or no connection to the "international city": Charlie Croker's plantation, Turpmtime. Charlie has convinced himself that he is the patri-arch of Turpmtime through some "natural" selection of southern man-hood: "this was the South. You had to be man enough to *deserve* a quail plantation" (9). In fact, the developer became "Cap'm Charlie"—as he enjoys being called by Turpmtime's black employees—by purchasing twenty-nine thousand acres of South Georgia real estate. Aboard the G-5 during the flight from his failing edge city to the sanctuary of Turpmtime, Charlie rhapsodizes over the aerial view of South Georgia's fecund land-scape. However, there is a telling limit to Charlie's dream of arcady. This limit is first evident when he looks out over a "breathtaking" peach or-chard, "gorgeous beyond belief," only to conclude his meditations by "[w]onder[ing] who owns it?" (75). Shortly afterward, Charlie follows the eyes of his financial adviser, Wizmer Stroock, to a house "amid a swath of orchards"; upon focusing his gaze, the developer muses that it "[m]ust cost a fortune to keep up a place like that" (77). So it is that Charlie views South Georgia plantation country in much the mode that he mapped Atlanta's MXDs from the G-5—through the capitalist gaze of a real-estate developer. Despite Charlie's rhetoric, Turpmtime and its environs remain less "real life" (80) than real estate.

Charlie embellishes the plantation's arcadian image by contrasting it with the postsouthern metropolis: "When he was here at Turpmtime, he liked to shed Atlanta, even in his voice. He liked to feel earthy, Down Home, elemental; which is to say, he was no longer merely a real estate developer, he was . . . a man" (5). No matter that, according to Allen Tate, we "cannot pretend to be landed gentlemen two days of the week

34. See Harvey, *Justice, Nature, and the Geography of Difference*, 335. On the har-rowing experiences of the broiler-chicken industry's underpaid and largely nonwhite work force, see also Jennifer Smith, "Workers Demand 'Poultry Justice,'" *Creative Loafing*, 15 April 2000, 27. (*Creative Loafing* is a weekly free newspaper published in Atlanta.)

if we are middle-class capitalists the five others," Charlie's weekends as the "master of Turpmtime" (276), *not* his weekdays as a developer in Atlanta, make him feel like a man in full. However, this urban/down-home dualism is disingenuous; the plantation's economic base is firmly rooted in Atlanta real estate. In various interviews at the time of *A Man in Full*'s publication, Wolfe explained how the genesis of the novel, and its location in Atlanta (rather than New York), derived from the moment when "[s]ome friends invited me to see a couple of plantations down in Georgia in 1989." Wolfe discovered that "[t]he plantations were owned largely by real-estate developers." It seems certain—though it is never explicitly stated in the novel—that Charlie, the son of poor whites from Baker County, bought Turpmtime on the back of his success as "one of the Creators of Greater Atlanta." What is more, the plantation is far from self-sufficient: the capital that maintains its antebellum image can also be traced back to land speculation in Atlanta. At the emergency meeting in PlannersBanc Tower, Charlie claims that Turpmtime is an "experimental farm" and "the main testin' ground for our food division" (52–53). In fact, the meretricious upkeep of Turpmtime is written off to Croker Global's food division (74)—which the developer bought in 1987 on the basis of his success in the "booming" Atlanta real-estate market (72).[35]

This seems to be a particularly postsouthern irony: for Charlie to act like the "master of Turpmtime," the plantation requires capital accrued during Cap'm Charlie's "real life" as a real-estate developer. Yet for all its subsidized, neo-antebellum artifice, Turpmtime does have a subtle *use-value* that repays its debt to the Atlanta real-estate arm of Croker Global. Charlie utilizes the plantation's simulated Old Southernness to woo potential corporate tenants (or "pigeons") to Croker Concourse and his other Atlanta MXDs: "Turpmtime might not be, strictly speaking, an experimental farm, but it had paid for itself many times over in terms of bagged pigeons, a point he didn't know quite how to get across to those small-brained niche-focused motherfuckers at PlannersBanc" (278).

Croker's relationship with Turpmtime's black work force appears to be that of a rather ludicrous latecomer playing out a part-time postsouthern pastiche of what Richard H. King has termed the "Southern family

35. Allen Tate, "What Is a Traditional Society?" in *Essays of Four Decades* (Chicago: Swallow Press, 1968), 548; Harry Ritchie, "Tom Wolfe in Full," *Waterstone's Magazine* 15 (Autumn 1998): 4. One of the developer "friends" who showed Wolfe around Georgia plantations was C. Mackenzie Taylor. Taylor cofounded the Perimeter Center edge city that so engages Charlie's omniscient gaze.

romance." However, "the Turpmtime Niggers" perform a crucial role in the seduction of Charlie's real-estate clients: they provide an authentic sheen of slavelike labor to the plantation's simulated Old South. Charlie casts the profoundly racist "Turpmtime Spell"—a calculated version of what King calls the old "Southern conception of itself" as master and slave knowing "their place"[36]—upon his prospective MXD tenants: "he knew that the magic of Turpmtime depended on thrusting his guests back into a manly world where people still lived close to the earth, a luxurious bygone world in which there were masters and servants and *everybody knew his place*. He didn't have to say who Uncle Bud was. He merely had to say his name in a certain way, and one and all would realize that he was some sort of faithful old retainer, probably black" (277; my italics). If it is shocking that "Cap'm Charlie" requires his black employees to perform a minstrel-like image of antebellum slave labor (albeit for a cash wage), it is perhaps even stranger that these "real *country*" (55) people effectively work in the field of Atlanta real-estate development.

Yet there remains one final turn to the case of labor relations at Turpmtime—a turn that leads not only to Atlanta, but also to California. Swayed by his romantic, proprietorial vision of southern land—and, to some degree, his paternalistic sense of responsibility to the black employees—Charlie refuses to sell Turpmtime. Instead, he resolves to lay off 15 percent of the national work force in Croker Global's food division. At this point, Charlie's peroration (during the emergency meeting at PlannersBanc) on "how Croker Global was today one of the biggest employers of unskilled black labor in that part of Georgia" (55) takes on dramatic irony. For among those whom Charlie lays off are the similarly "unskilled" (and not only black) laborers at a frozen/foods warehouse in Oakland—including, of course, one Conrad Hensley. Ultimately, Charlie's desire to maintain his paternalistic, simulated, Old South sense of place at Turpmtime has an all-too-"real" impact on the lives of workers elsewhere in the Croker Global corporation.

In his famous essay "The Search for Southern Identity," C. Vann Woodward contrasted a generally American "quality of abstraction," a "superiority to place, to locality, to environment" with what he—following his friend, the lapsed Agrarian Robert Penn Warren—saw as the South's

---

36. Richard H. King, *A Southern Renaissance: The Cultural Awakening of the American South, 1930–1955* (New York: Oxford University Press, 1980), 21. On the southern family romance, see especially ch. 2.

"fear of abstraction." Woodward went on to cite the South's concrete focus on "place, locality, and community," as evidenced in the work and "experience of Eudora Welty of Mississippi."[37] Yet neither Welty nor Warren ever confronted the degree of abstraction we find in *A Man in Full*. In Wolfe's postsouthern Atlanta, we witness a profoundly abstract sense of placelessness that derives from (to update Allen Tate) a top-heavy focus on *international* finance capitalism. Yet *A Man in Full* also emphasizes an apparent paradox of such abstract, placeless finance capital: its power to create (and creatively destroy) the concrete geography of metropolitan Atlanta through the construction of monumental MXDs.

Welty seems to have seen "real estate people" as at least partly responsible for the destruction of the South, and her fiction mostly returns to an era when a more familiar sense of place remained intact.[38] By contrast, Wolfe focuses on contemporary Atlanta to show how land speculation and real-estate development have produced a locus unlike any of those earlier places we have called "southern." The rural landscape to the north of postsouthern Atlanta—O'Connor country—has been transformed into "investor land." Meanwhile, Charlie Croker uses his South Georgia plantation, an elaborate simulation of the antebellum South, to market Atlanta MXD office space to unsuspecting "pigeons." All told, *A Man in Full* seems to suggest that there is no residual or unmediated "South" that has escaped the effects of speculative capitalist development.

However, such a reading would be to elide the end of the novel, evocatively and, I think, accurately described by Norman Mailer as "a mess, a *tidy* mess." Having been converted to Stoicism by his recently hired personal home-care assistant—none other than Conrad Hensley—Charlie Croker decides to surrender all his "worldly goods" to his creditors (722). There then follows a brief epilogue in which, as Mailer incredulously observes, "Charlie is not even present." Only in "a short paragraph" narrated by Mayor Jordan do we learn that Charlie has become a Stoic evangelist back home in Baker County and on "into the Florida Panhandle and southern Alabama" (732).[39]

37. C. Vann Woodward, "The Search for Southern Identity," in *The Burden of Southern History* (Enlarged ed.; Baton Rouge: Louisiana State University Press, 1968), 22–23.

38. "Growing Up in the Deep South: A Conversation with Eudora Welty, Shelby Foote, and Louis D. Rubin, Jr.," in *The American South: Portrait of a Culture*, ed. Louis D. Rubin Jr. (Lexington: Voice of America Forum Series, 1979), 80.

39. Norman Mailer, "A Man Half Full," *New York Review of Books*, 17 December 1998, 20.

Whatever the manifest problems with *A Man in Full*'s denouement, there are aspects that are particularly germane to my focus on the post-southern sense of place(lessness). I would argue that Wolfe resorts to a peculiar kind of "spatial fix" in the epilogue. This term is usually understood to refer to "the absorption of excess capital and labor in geographical expansion . . . the production of new spaces within which capitalist production can proceed."[40] *A Man in Full*'s spatial fix involves the fictional production of (or vague reference to) places—Baker County, the Florida Panhandle, and southern Alabama—that enable the text to escape the problem of capitalist spatial production in metropolitan Atlanta. Finally, Wolfe *does* appear to have been trapped *within* his own image of the "awesome incorporative power of late capitalism" to create, destroy, and unevenly develop a place. Having so thoroughly delineated the depressing limits imposed on everyday life in "other" Atlantas (Vine City and Chambodia), Wolfe seems to have resorted to an escapist anticlimax in which Charlie simply surrenders his properties to PlannersBanc and other creditors before disappearing down home into rural South Georgia. After seven hundred pages suggesting that there is no southern "sense of place" unaffected by land speculation or real-estate development, the epilogue vaguely invokes a residual, rural "South" that—unlike Atlanta, the investor land of North Georgia, or the plantations to the South—somehow remains outside the spatial realm of capital.

Charlie's conversion to Stoicism is bound up in *A Man in Full*'s troublesome ending. Wolfe does offer hints that we should be suspicious of the reborn Stoic's evangelical motives: Mayor Jordan mentions Charlie's ability to "talk . . . the bills out of your wallet" and his "syndication deal with Fox Broadcasting" (732). Ultimately, however, Wolfe seems seriously to propose classical Stoicism as a moral counterpoint to the materialism of contemporary capitalist society. Like the Stoic philosopher Epictetus, Charlie comes to see being-in-the-world per se as a hindrance to "freedom." Such a yearning for transcendence evacuates the novel's earlier emphasis on *social* being mediated by and between processes local *and* global, abstract *and* material. It is telling that, upon resolving to proselytize the Stoic creed, Charlie (like Conrad) leaves Atlanta: the practical value of his new faith is therefore never tested *within* the capitalist metropolis. By depositing the reborn Stoic back in Baker County, well away from his earlier Atlanta-based economic tribulations, Wolfe finally (if fuzzily) privileges the rural South as one "worldly" locus that is freer

40. Harvey, *The Condition of Postmodernity*, 183.

than the postsouthern "international city." This is not to imply that, in reality, there is nowhere like Baker County, no (rural) place that has resisted large-scale land speculation. My point is that *A Man in Full*'s all-too-"tidy" epilogue allows Wolfe to abandon postsouthern Atlanta and the complex issues of place, race, and (finance) capital that he explored so effectively earlier in the novel.

Outsiders with Inside Information: The Vietnamese in the Fiction of the Contemporary American South

Maureen Ryan

Miss Giau, the thirty-four-year-old, pitiably unmarried narrator of "Snow," one of the fifteen stories in Robert Olen Butler's Pulitzer Prize-winning 1993 collection, *A Good Scent from a Strange Mountain,* is a waitress at a Chinese restaurant in Lake Charles, Louisiana. Dozing during a slow Christmas Eve at the Plantation Hunan, Miss Giau dreams of her first Christmas Eve in America, when she fell asleep in another restaurant in St. Louis, Missouri, and woke to her first snowfall. "I had no idea things could change like that," Miss Giau tells the grandfatherly Jewish customer who has caught her sleeping. "I was terrified."[1]

Change, loss, dislocation; these are the realities of their new lives for the Vietnamese—refugees from the American war in Vietnam who have found their way to the American South—who populate *A Good Scent from a Strange Mountain* and a handful of other imaginative works that present the stories of the South's newest citizens. The lives of these characters—uprooted from a society and a culture that are older; more de-

---

1. Robert Olen Butler, *A Good Scent from a Strange Mountain* (New York: Penguin, 1992), 131. Subsequent references to this work will be given parenthetically in the text.

fined by family, community, and place; more ghost-haunted than Yoknapatawpha County ever was—are a commentary on and a challenge to the changing contemporary South.

The Plantation Hunan, Miss Giau observes, really was once a plantation house. And, she surmises, "this plantation house must feel like a refugee. It is full of foreign smells, ginger and Chinese pepper and fried shells for wonton, and there's a motel on one side and a gas station on the other, not like the life the house once knew, though there are very large oak trees surrounding it, trees that must have been here when this was still a plantation" (126). Like Miss Giau, like the ancestral home in Faulkner's "A Rose for Emily," "lifting its stubborn and coquettish decay above the cotton wagons and the gasoline pumps," the Plantation Hunan is a refugee—dispossessed, stuck in a place where it does not belong.[2] And in a place where the old truths no longer apply. Miss Giau is not alone in Lake Charles; she lives with her mother, and there are other Vietnamese there as well. "But," she observes, "we are not a community. We are all too sad, perhaps, or too tired. But maybe not. Maybe that's just me saying that. Maybe the others are real Americans already" (126–27). Sad, exhausted, or successfully assimilated, the Vietnamese refugees in contemporary southern literature both reflect and belie the stereotypes about their own culture, and in doing so, complicate the traditional verities about the South and southern literature.

Today, a generation after the Vietnam War, a war that changed American society fundamentally and forever and displaced a million and a half Vietnamese, the absurdities and mistakes of America's long misadventure in Southeast Asia are well known: inflated body counts; the official disinformation in military briefings known as the Five O'clock Follies; napalm—the list is lengthy. And on this list perhaps no practice or policy so clearly demonstrates the peculiarly American combination of naïveté and arrogance that characterized our presence in Vietnam as the misguided strategic hamlet program. Designed by American military advisors and implemented in 1962, the strategic hamlet program was a plan to isolate rural villagers in newly constructed compounds—sometimes called sunrise villages—that would protect them from infiltration by the Viet Cong and from the firepower of the Americans, while allowing the Americans to separate friend from foe. Though shoddy construction, concentration-camp conditions, and easy penetration by the Viet Cong doomed the stra-

---

2. William Faulkner, "A Rose for Emily," in *The Faulkner Reader: Selections from the Works of William Faulkner* (New York: Random House, 1954), 489.

tegic hamlet program, its failure was guaranteed for reasons more fundamental and more profound. Ignorant about Vietnamese culture, American
military strategists failed to comprehend the deep connections to family,
the past, and place that are the essential values of the Vietnamese. "To
the Vietnamese," Frances FitzGerald notes in *Fire in the Lake*, her early,
important study of "the Vietnamese and the Americans in Vietnam,"
"the land itself was the sacred, constant element." Whereas Americans
are, according to myth, forward-looking and optimistic, writes FitzGerald, "the traditional Vietnamese were directed towards the past, both by
the small tradition of the family and the great tradition of the state." The
loyalties of the Vietnamese are to family, village, and state, and Vietnamese removed from their ancestral lands "were without a social identity."
Forcibly removed from her family's home, "inside the safe circumference
of [a] strategic hamlet," the grandmother of Mai Nguyen, the protagonist
of Lan Cao's 1997 novel *Monkey Bridge,* dies amidst "the unmoored
lives of villagers who had once anchored themselves by the roots of the
earth."[3]

The centrality of place, family, and the past in the lives of the traditional Vietnamese almost eerily parallels the similar obsessions of southerners in countless imaginative and critical texts about the South and
southern culture. At least since the publication in 1930 of the Agrarian
manifesto *I'll Take My Stand,* southern commentators have espoused the
commonly accepted characteristics of literature and other imaginative
texts about the South. Subsequently, influential critics like Louis D.
Rubin Jr. and Lewis P. Simpson, among others, articulated the deep-
seated, "changeless" values of southern life and southern letters: "a sense
of place; a special conception of time that would take account of the past
and the timeless; and an interest and aptitude for narrative that includes
a vigorous oral tradition as well as formal narration in stories and novels." The southerners who introduce into their contemporary fiction the
transplanted culture of Vietnamese refugees understand that native
southerners and the recently arrived Vietnamese share an appreciation
for family, place, and past. In *Prisoners,* his 1998 novel about a Vietnam-
veteran archeologist, a runaway half-American, half-Vietnamese teenager, and a Civil War prisoner-of-war camp, Wayne Karlin explores the
literal and psychological ghosts that haunt his past- and place-obsessed

3. Frances FitzGerald, *Fire in the Lake: The Vietnamese and the Americans in Vietnam*
(New York: Vintage Books, 1972), 11, 15, 13; Lan Cao, *Monkey Bridge* (New York: Viking, 1997), 246.

characters. As Russell Hallam, an African American Vietnam veteran and the descendant of an extended family that has lived for generations in the Tidewater area of southern Maryland, notes, "Time touched him back. It wasn't a matter of searching it out. It was simply there, the weight of an internal presence. It was something the Vietnamese would probably understand: their ancestry and history were felt as points of reference, of lookout, in a person's soul."[4]

Yet Russell Hallam and Cleanth Brooks, in their failure to question or problematize the traditional myths of southern culture, are the exceptions among contemporary authors, critics, and characters of southern fiction. Far more common are challenges to the long-standing legend of the South as a conservative, ghost-ridden culture still grappling with defeat in a war now almost 150 years in the past. Contemporary commentators on southern society and culture recognize that the South today is more urban than rural, more progressive than backward-looking, more secular than religious, more middle class than either aristocratic or impoverished, more like the rest of the country than uniquely tragic. Richard Gray, Michael Kreyling, and others have demonstrated convincingly the extent to which even the notion of "the South" is a construction of self-appointed conservators of a narrow myth. Some contemporary critics and historians of the South emphasize that southern literature and life have always been more complex than the myth allows: "Southern writing," C. Hugh Holman notes, "certainly shared a number of distinctly regional characteristics, but its variety and diversity are even more important. And when we concentrate on the similarities, we run the risk of stripping from it much of its vitality." Others underscore recent changes in the South that inevitably influence southern letters; James Justus, for instance, argues insistently for a new day in southern literature:

> If traditionalists, in defining the particular slant of modern Southern fiction, insist upon the dominance of the organic community, . . . its accrued wisdom and handed-down superstitions, its tolerance for reiterated stories from the family archives, then the great period known as the Southern Renascence has passed. The Civil War in its fiction is finally over. The backward glance from a twentieth-century war that now compels Southern storytellers to reevaluate their region is Vietnam.
>
> Contemporary Southern fiction is frankly engaged with contemporary social problems, especially race relations and the struggle of the poor and

---

4. Cleanth Brooks, "Southern Literature: The Past, History, and the Timeless," in *Southern Literature in Transition: Heritage and Promise,* ed. Philip Castille and William Osborne (Memphis: Memphis State University Press, 1983), 5; Wayne Karlin, *Prisoners* (Willimantic, Conn.: Curbstone Press, 1998), 64.

marginal working class to wrest some meaning out of their lives beyond survival itself. Its familiar space for the italicizing of the problems tends to be a mobile home, not a ruined mansion. It is a fiction of social dislocation, dealing often with the fragmentation of family following divorce, with the psychologically wounded seeking healing rituals to overcome familial incoherence.

Contemporary southern authors recognize that the modern South is a rapidly changing and complex place. Bobbie Ann Mason creates a contemporary western Kentucky where "the small country churches . . . are dying, as people move to town or simply lose interest in the church." Lucille Odom, in Josephine Humphreys's *Rich in Love,* notices that new housing developments are always named as "memorials to what had been bulldozed into oblivion."[5]

Yet even the critics who challenge the old stereotypes about southern literature acknowledge that much contemporary southern writing is, in Richard Gray's words, "amphibious, attached partly to the old structures of perceptions and partly to the new." Noting that in the lifetime of contemporary southern writers, the South "has changed more than it had in all its previous history," John Lowe asserts that it is inevitable that "most of today's southern narratives . . . aspire to mirror a culture in the throes of dynamic and dramatic change." And yet, he allows, "somehow southern writers . . . see some kind of constant, enduring presence in southern settings. Place, despite dramatic changes, still casts the same old spell in many ways." Novelist and poet Jack Butler complicates it a bit: "we have roots, yes, but we have become like those plants that send rootlets out into the air: a sense of *places,* not a sense of place."[6]

Forty-odd years ago, Eudora Welty noted evocatively that "location is the ground conductor of all the currents of emotion and belief and moral conviction that charge out from the story in its course." Contemporary critical theorists, such as Francesco Loriggio, have recognized that space, as "the dimension of power and resistance," is, in a postmodern world,

5. Holman, C. Hugh. "No More Monoliths, Please: Continuities in the Multi-Souths," in *Southern Literature in Transition,* xv; James H. Justus, "Foreword," in *Southern Writers at Century's End,* ed. Jeffery J. Folks and James A. Perkins (Lexington: University Press of Kentucky, 1997), xii; Bobbie Ann Mason, "The Retreat," in *Shiloh and Other Stories* (New York: Harper and Row, 1982), 134; Josephine Humphries, *Rich in Love* (New York: Penguin Books, 1987), 6.

6. Richard Gray, *Writing the South: Ideas of an American Region* (Cambridge: Cambridge University Press, 1986), 231; John Lowe, "Introduction," in *The Future of Southern Letters,* ed. Jefferson Humphries and John Lowe (New York: Oxford University Press, 1996), 6, 8; Jack Butler, "Still Southern After All These Years," ibid., 36.

a more viable paradigm than the more familiar time. "Today," Edward Soja writes, "it may be . . . the 'making of geography' more than the 'making of history' that provides the most revealing tactical and theoretical world. This is the insistent premise and promise of postmodern geographies." Francesco Loriggio anchors the recent reevaluation of literary regionalism in the predominance of space and place in a constantly changing world. "Greater global unity" and the call for a new world order parallel disintegration and fragmentation, Loriggio writes, and these in turn compel "the reconsideration of space as an analytical category." Similarly, contemporary cultural critics have recognized that a "mood of questioning, of writing between cultures, of being both outsider and insider, is exemplary in cultural criticism. So too is movement into the past to explain the present." Cultural criticism, notes David Jordan in his examination of "ways in which social communities are marginalized by discourse that suppresses the representation of difference," has enlivened regionalism as a viable approach to the study of contemporary society and literature.[7]

In contemporary southern fiction, the significance of space and the traditional southern hegemony of place are at once underscored and problematized by the insertion into the paradigm of the displaced Vietnamese, whose own renegotiation of traditional Vietnamese values in a new culture complicates further the already challenged myth of the South. Struggling, like the unnamed narrator of Robert Olen Butler's "Relic," to find, in America, "the place where I belong" (142), Vietnamese characters in contemporary fiction set in the South offer both a challenge to and a reinforcement of traditional southern perceptions of place, history, and family. Emmett Wheeler, the veteran-protagonist of Wayne Karlin's *Lost Armies* (1988), returns from war and postwar wandering to the marshes of southern Maryland that have been his family's home for generations. Seeing his home county through the eyes of its Vietnamese refugees (to whom he teaches English at the local community college), Wheeler "realize[s] how strange the country was to him," but Xuan, his

7. Eudora Welty, "Place in Fiction," in *The Eye of the Story: Selected Essays and Reviews* (New York: Vintage Books, 1979), 128; Francesco Loriggio, "Regionalism and Theory," in *Regionalism Reconsidered: New Approaches to the Field*, ed. David Jordan (New York: Garland Publishing, 1994), 3–4; Edward W. Soja, *Postmodern Geographies: The Reassertion of Space in Critical Social Theory* (London: Verso, 1989), 1; Marianna Torgovnick, "Introduction," in *Eloquent Obsessions: Writing Cultural Criticism*, ed. Marianna Torgovnick (Durham: Duke University Press, 1994), 2; David Jordan, "Introduction," in *Regionalism Reconsidered*, xv.

refugee girlfriend, recognizes that he loves the place, "not only as it is, but because its time is in you. . . . I never thought of Americans as having that kind of connection to land, a place." Xuan understandably thinks of Wheeler as an American rather than a southerner. For these Vietnamese characters, the journey and the adjustment are from Vietnam to America, and they could as easily be in Iowa or Pennsylvania as in Louisiana, Virginia, or Texas. Much as the average American is insensitive to the differences among the Vietnamese—whether they are Catholic or Buddhist, or from the North or the South of Vietnam, for example—the Vietnamese perception of the new world to which they must become acculturated is that it is, simply, America.[8]

For some, America is the stereotypical dream of immigrants always: the golden land of opportunity. Like most of the adult Vietnamese refugees in the U.S., *Boat People*'s Hai Truong has left her parents behind, but "her mother had told her that she would grow fat in America. In America, there was so much rice that men came to your house and filled baskets with it. There were chickens that grew big in a week, and they cost only a little piece of money." And indeed, in Lan Cao's *Monkey Bridge* and Karlin's *Lost Armies*, middle-aged Vietnamese women grow fat in America, not on rice but on a diet of "frosted cupcakes and Hostess Twinkies."[9] For Hai Truong, one of the boat people—the uneducated, rural Vietnamese who fled to America in the second wave of emigration from Vietnam in 1978—the promise of the brave new world is more than having enough to eat. For Robert Olen Butler's more educated and sophisticated characters, those who supported the Republic of Vietnam, worked for and with the Americans during the war, and arrived in the U.S. by plane or ship after the fall of Saigon in 1975, America promises a reprise of the business success that they had enjoyed in prewar Vietnam. The proud owner of John Lennon's right shoe, the narrator of "Relic," has made "much money" in his "new country":

> It is a gift I have, and America is a land of opportunity. I started in paper lanterns and firecrackers . . . at the time of Tet, our Vietnam New Year celebration, when the refugees wanted to think of home . . . and later I opened a restaurant and then a parlor with many video games. . . . the young men love these games, fighting alien spaceships and wizards and kung-fu villains with much greater skill than their fathers fought the com-

8. Wayne Karlin, *Lost Armies* (New York: Henry Holt and Company, 1988), 22, 79.

9. Mary Gardner, *Boat People* (New York: W. W. Norton, 1995), 13; Cao, *Monkey Bridge*, 62.

munists. And now I am doing other things, bigger things, mostly in the shrimp industry. In ten years people from Vietnam will be the only shrimp fishermen in the Gulf of Mexico. I do not need an oracle bone to tell you this for sure. And when this is so, I will be making even more money. (139)

Emmett Wheeler, the alienated protagonist of *Lost Armies,* takes "a proprietary, vicarious pride" in the local Vietnamese shopkeepers' success in America: the new Buick and VCR, the granddaughter's academic prizes. "But he found it a strange sort of pride, strange to see these people come, inevitable as justice in a fairy tale, to take over dreams he no longer had."[10]

If America signifies baskets of rice and a chance to get rich for some of these characters, it promises a more complex adjustment for the more ruminative refugees. Mai Nguyen, the teenaged protagonist of *Monkey Bridge,* wants America to mean the freedom to start over: "It was the Vietnamese version of the American dream; a new spin, the Vietnam spin, to the old immigrant faith in the future. Not only could we become anything we wanted to be in America, we could change what we had once been in Vietnam." Lan Cao's novel, the first by a Vietnamese refugee to America and the only text considered in this essay written by a Vietnamese, is set in Little Saigon in Arlington, Virginia, in 1979, four years after Mai and her mother have fled the North Vietnamese takeover of Saigon. Younger, more successfully assimilated into American culture than her mother (who is, like Hai Truong in Mary Gardner's *Boat People,* a haunted middle-aged Vietnamese woman), Mai is in fact caught between two worlds: the transplanted ancestral community of her mother and the other refugees, with their "foreigners' ragged edges," and the promise of another escape, to college, to an unencumbered adulthood in America, "a country in love with itself, beckoning us to feel the same."[11]

Gabrielle Tran, the narrator of Robert Olen Butler's "The American Couple," likes America because "there is always some improvisation, something new, and when things get strained, you don't fall back on tradition but you make up something new" (158). Gabrielle loves American television: the romance of old Hollywood movies, with their inevitable happy endings; the cheerful game shows; the soap operas whose "daily disasters" make her appreciate "this wonderful lightness before my eyes

10. Karlin, *Lost Armies,* 3.
11. Cao, *Monkey Bridge,* 40–41, 146, 31.

in America" (157). Yet Gabrielle's husband, Vinh, a businessman and former officer of the Army of the Republic of Vietnam, a "man who'd been through a war and survived," a man "who'd made his way in a strange land," rejects "the light and lively and less filling and soft as a cloud and reach out and touch someone culture that America had to offer" (213). Like other Butler protagonists—former soldiers, successful businessmen—Vinh, as Gabrielle comes to understand, is a man who once felt something important—"rage, fear, the urge to violence, just causes, life and death"; he thus disdains the "feel-good . . . empty-headed culture around him" (230, 233).

For many of these Vietnamese characters, the myth of America as a place of opportunity and new beginnings belies the burden of ancestry, past, and place that accompanies them from Vietnam. The successful Lake Charles businessman who narrates Butler's "The Trip Back" is proud that he is "a good American now. . . . I found that I myself was no longer comfortable with the old ways. Like the extended family. Like other things, too. The Vietnamese indirectness, for instance. The superstition. . . . [I]t was not an unpleasant thought that I had finally left Vietnam behind" (36). But when he drives from the Houston airport with his wife's grandfather, newly arrived from Vietnam, the narrator comes to understand that it is he—not the old man who cannot recall his granddaughter—whose loss is profound. While the grandfather, Mr. Chinh, remembers his past and his life in Vietnam, the narrator, who has jettisoned his past for success in a new country, comes to fear that "deep down I am built on a much smaller scale than the surface of my mind aspires to. . . . I'd lost a whole country and I didn't give it a thought" (42).

The narrator of "Ghost Story," a former employee of the American Embassy in Saigon, tells willing listeners on his bus ride to Biloxi a true Vietnamese ghost story, the tale of a Vietnamese Army major who is saved from the Viet Cong but later eaten by the ghost of a beautiful dead girl named Linh. The narrator knows that his audience will not believe this story, that they may not even listen to it, since he is merely a "shabby Oriental man" who can be boring (as he is to his daughter's American husband), but, he insists, several years later, at the fall of Saigon, he too was spared death by Miss Linh. And how does the narrator, as he tells his story to "strangers from this alien land" of America, know that the major's story of the succubus is true? Because "Ghost Story" ends as he, with Miss Linh's help, was whisked away in the ambassador's car to safety in America, he "looked out the window and saw Miss Linh's tongue slip from her mouth and lick her lips, as if she had just eaten me up. And indeed she has" (111, 123). For some of these refugees, living in America is a kind of annihilation.

Lost Armies' Xuan even more forcibly rejects the American dream, and adds her resentment of the American arrogance that propelled so many Vietnamese to a foreign land: "You Americans have the freedom to invent your own lives—it gives you the illusion you can invent other people's lives also. Invent and then grow tired of your inventions. You came to kill us and to love us, all to prove some idea you had about yourselves. But we were nothing to you. Only your dreams, your shadows, your whores." Whether liberated or destroyed by their relocation to America, these characters are new Americans with a fresh, often critical perspective on their adopted country. They are, in Lan Cao's words, "outsiders with inside information." If these Vietnamese characters themselves demonstrate no conception of living in a culturally unique region of the United States, the authors who place them in Virginia, Maryland, Louisiana, and Texas do; their novels and stories offer an exploration and critique of the self-conscious myth of the South as burdened by past and place in much the same way that the Vietnamese are.[12]

Frightened and feeling buried by the St. Louis snow, Miss Giau thinks that she will feel better "if I could just go to a warm climate, just like home. So I came down to New Orleans, with my mother . . . and then we came over to Lake Charles. And it is something like Vietnam here. The rice fields and heat and the way the storms come in. But it makes no difference" (134). What Miss Giau cannot understand is that it *does* make a difference. For her, the challenge is to make a new life in a foreign land; there is no reason for her to appreciate that the peculiar characteristics of the South to which she has emigrated—again—offer an intriguing parallel to her own ethnicity. Today, more than a million Vietnamese and Amerasian refugees or native-born Americans of Vietnamese descent live in the United States, and while a third of them reside in California, nearly 160,000 have congregated in the southern region of the country. The attraction of Vietnamese refugees to Louisiana, Texas, and Florida is not coincidental.

The opening shot of Louis Malle's 1985 film *Alamo Bay* shows a young Vietnamese man walking along a rural, sunlit road. Only when a car pulls up to give the man a lift (and, when the stern female driver sees that the smiling hitchhiker is Vietnamese, pointedly pulls away) do we see that the rural road borders a South Texas field, not a Vietnam rice

12. Karlin, *Lost Armies,* 129; Cao, *Monkey Bridge,* 41, 212.

paddy. Thieu (called Ted for the past decade in Lake Charles), the narrator of Butler's "Crickets," confirms that "the flat bayou land of Louisiana, where there are rice paddies and where the water and the land are in the most delicate balance with each other [is] very much like the Mekong Delta, where I grew up" (60). The Vietnamese characters living in the South—Malle's and Gardner's shrimpers; Butler's and Lan Cao's small-business owners; Karlin's twice-relocated Tidewater "boat folks . . . who weren't adjusting to urban life"[13] in Arlington, Virginia—migrate to the Deep South because it looks and feels like home. But if the heat, the proximity to water, and the flat green horizon are the visible similarities between the country that borders the South China Sea and the region of the United States that abuts the Gulf of Mexico and the Atlantic Ocean, they are not the most interesting parallels that these authors explore. Allen Tate's famous "backward glance," the South's fascination with a lost war and a romantic antebellum past, is for Vietnamese refugees a visceral connection back to Vietnam, to familial lands and the very real spirits of honored ancestors. The forty-one-year-old narrator of Butler's "Mr. Green" has learned from her grandfather in Vietnam that "the souls of our ancestors need love and attention and devotion," that "given these things, they will share in our lives and they will bless us. . . . But if we neglect the souls of our ancestors, they will become lost and lonely and will wander around in the kingdom of the dead no better off than a warrior killed by his enemy and left unburied in a rice paddy to be eaten by black birds of prey" (18). And now, though she insists that she does "not believe in the worship of my ancestors, especially in the form of a parrot," she tends to Mr. Green, her grandfather's beloved parrot, who, she knows, holds "the spirit of my grandfather and all his knowledge" (20). But since the narrator learns from her grandfather that only a son, not a daughter, can worship his ancestors, her destruction of the old, ailing parrot at the end of the story is both an act of mercy and a sly protest against her grandfather's rejection of her.

In *Monkey Bridge*, Mai Nguyen wonders, throughout the four years since she and her mother fled Vietnam for Arlington, Virginia—where they settle because it is near their new country's capital and therefore, Mai's mother believes, the safest place in America—why her grandfather had failed to meet them, as arranged, for the trip to the United States. Not until late in the novel does Mai learn the tragic truth of her mother's life and the secret that her grandfather was a Viet Cong sympathizer.

13. Karlin, *Lost Armies*, 18.

Until then, Mai accepts the quite-plausible scenario that her grandfather simply could not bear to leave his home: "The constancy of the ancestral land and the village burial ground . . . these were things that mattered to him. My grandfather would not be easily convinced of the need to cross the ocean's depths for the purpose of starting a more convenient and modern life." And Mai's mother knows, when her mother dies in the strategic hamlet, that "I would have to find a way back there, back to the graves of my ancestors, back to the sacred land. . . . She would have to die where she was born, and I would have to construct this circle for her, a beginning and an end that converged toward and occupied one single, concentrated space."[14]

Lang Nguyen, the successful young doctor in Mary Gardner's *Boat People,* eschews in Galveston, Texas, the ancestral rituals that are his birthright, but when his mother dies back in Vietnam, he (like Mr. Chinh's son-in-law in "The Trip Back") regrets his rejection of his traditional past: " 'I never built the altar. I never welcomed my ancestors at Tet. I never gave them what they had a right to demand. I put my feet on the face of my homeland. I forgot my own people.' " Caught up in veneration of its own tragic past, the traditional South offers a welcoming space for Vietnamese reverence for family and place—even if, as Linh, Hai Truong's daughter, understands when she asks her ancestors to bring her mother safely home from the hospital, "their spirits would have to come a long way from Vietnam to do it." *Lost Armies'* Emmett Wheeler, a southerner who lives on land that has been in his family since the seventeenth century, recognizes that the influx of Vietnamese into his lifelong home is "an odd haunting . . . Asian ghosts that had followed him to the altars of his ancestors."[15]

And yet, as countless commentators tell us, the old myth of the South was an artificial construction, and one that is undermined even further by the realities of the so-called New South. Growing, changing, the South, as Edward L. Ayers asserts, "is continually coming into being, continually being remade, continually struggling with its pasts."[16] Emmett Wheeler's affection for his Vietnamese neighbors and his alienation from his home county make him relatively sanguine about the "odd

14. Cao, *Monkey Bridge,* 159, 248.

15. Gardner, *Boat People,* 202, 25; Karlin, *Lost Armies,* 3.

16. Edward L. Ayers, "What We Talk About When We Talk About the South," in *All Over the Map: Rethinking American Regions,* ed. Edward L. Ayers et al. (Baltimore: Johns Hopkins University Press, 1996), 82.

haunting" of his ancestral place; but for many native southerners, the insertion of the Vietnamese into the fabric of their daily lives evokes and echoes not reassurance that the newcomers revere history and the ancestral space too, but fear of the Other and the resulting racial tensions that have also characterized southern life and letters.

With the arrival of the hard-working Vietnamese in Port Alamo, Texas, the setting of Malle's *Alamo Bay,* the competition to make a living by shrimping and crabbing has increased dramatically. The bank has just repossessed Shang Pierce's boat when the Vietnam veteran and shrimper angrily orders the local Vietnamese priest to keep his people "out of my family's fishing grounds." Shang's claim of ancestral space is more a desperate response to immediate economic pressures than a proud Texan's commitment to family and tradition. And, significantly, Shang's working-class life is threatened, but not by other Texans, or even by Mexicans, whom the native shrimpers have obviously accommodated. It is fear of the Other that Shang articulates: the odd, new foreigners who work hard, "work cheaper than Americans," and don't follow the rules. As the town grocer/city councilman complains, "the federal government abandoned these people here in our town without educating them on how we do things." Joining forces with the Ku Klux Klan, whose local organizer asserts that the coming of the Vietnamese to Port Alamo is a Catholic and Communist plot, Shang and his frightened fellow native shrimpers run the Vietnamese out of Galveston Bay—though only temporarily, since the end of the 1985 movie tells us (confirming the prediction of Butler's John Lennon fan) that "today, more than 15,000 Vietnamese live and work on the Gulf Coast of Texas."[17]

Throughout these texts, the unadulterated redneck southern racism typically directed in southern literature against African Americans is transposed to the Vietnamese. In a startling example of racial profiling, *Boat People*'s doctor, Lang, is stopped for speeding by a policeman who is happy to write a ticket for a "gook doctor" whom he resents: " 'you come to our country and we put you through school, feed you, give you a good life you'd never have in that Vit-nahm. . . . Buy your cars . . . send our good money back to all your gook family in that Vit-nahm." "All those damn names," complains Russell Hallam's white cousin Alex, the county sheriff, a Vietnam veteran, and a character in both *Lost Armies* and *Prisoners*; "Phuong and Huong and Nguyen and Pham Dam and

17. *Alamo Bay,* dir. Louis Malle, 99 min., TriStar Pictures, 1985.

Phuc Duc and Duct Tape and Fuck a Duck. . . . I get with those people and suddenly I'm sounding like a redneck jarhead again."[18]

Alex Hallam's recognition of his own racism illustrates a self-consciousness about race and the identifications between African Americans and the Vietnamese that is developed throughout these texts. In Robert Olen Butler's "Love," the narrator, another proud Vietnamese businessman, feels both blessed and cursed by marriage to a beautiful woman. As a spy for the Americans at Homestead Air Force Base, in Vietnam the jealous husband could vanquish his wife's many suitors by summoning upon them an air strike by the unwitting Americans. For a dozen years in Gretna, Louisiana, he has not had to worry about his wife's attractiveness because "it seems as if somehow the men of Vietnam have lost their nerve in America . . . these men are beaten down" (77). But now, when a competitor appears, "in a foreign country, behind enemy lines, as it were," the vulnerable husband must find other means to discourage the man. "You can't live around New Orleans without hearing about voodoo," he reports, and promptly sets off for the French Quarter to consult an expert. Eschewing the "phony" voodoo shops on Bourbon Street, the narrator makes his way to the black neighborhood, where he acquires some black magic from an elderly African American "low-down papa" named Dr. Joseph. "I have learned the lessons of history and I felt a kinship with these people," the narrator observes about the black people in the Quarter (81).

The lessons of history teach the kinship between the Vietnamese and African Americans in *Boat People* as well, in which the Vietnamese refugees live together with American blacks in a public-housing project in Galveston, Texas. Since her mother died there, Azelita Simpson, a black school aide, volunteers at the hospital where Lang Nguyen practices. " 'She was very close to her mother,' " nurse Shirley explains to Lang, who observes that "the black people were like the Vietnamese in this regard" (30). Wilson, Azelita's new African American boyfriend and a Vietnam vet, at first dislikes the Vietnamese who live near Azelita and whose children she works with at the school, but the motherly black woman responds to the small, silent children: " 'I like those little Viet kids,' " she says. " 'They got their own kind of slavery to grow out of.' " Gardner develops the theme of shared slavery: when one of the Vietnamese children identifies Azelita's house as "the nigger house," Trang, the Amerasian teenager who is searching for her American father, admonis-

---

18. Gardner, *Boat People*, 90; Karlin, *Lost Armies*, 16–17.

hes him: " 'Why you talking? . . . Americans just call you little gook shit. Black people came here by boat too. Just like us. . . . They talk funny because they have to keep their mouths shut for so long. Otherwise they get killed by the people who own them.' " At the novel's sentimental ending, Wilson assures Trang, that, no, he is not her father, but that her father doesn't matter: " 'What matters is who *you* are. . . . We boat people, we all special. . . . We worked so hard and hurt so much, we gonna get every single thing we got coming to us.' "[19]

Trang inhabits a unique racial identity and, along with other Amerasian characters, therefore offers a special challenge for the South and the American southerners among whom she lives. No one knows how many children were fathered by American servicemen in Vietnam, though estimates range upward to two hundred thousand.[20] Beginning in 1987, with the Amerasian Homecoming Act, some thirty thousand Amerasian children were airlifted to the United States. In Vietnam, these mixed-blood Vietnamese, born during the years of the Vietnam War, are called *bui doi,* or "the dust of life." Considered by many Vietnamese to be not truly Vietnamese and thus doubly victimized by racism, many Amerasians were nonetheless exploited by would-be Vietnamese relatives who claimed kinship in order to escape Vietnam. Most Amerasians arrived in the United States in their late teens; many, abandoned by the erstwhile relatives and not reunited with their American fathers, live a difficult, often peripatetic life in the homeland of their fathers. As Louise Hallam, Alex's wife and a social worker in *Prisoners,* explains about Kiet, the self-described "half-a-dink, half-a-splib mutant" runaway, " 'in Vietnam, kids like her were despised until people found out that American features could get entry visas. . . . Then they were called golden children. Only a lot of them were abandoned when they got here.' " Trang is not alone in Galveston, but she might as well be. Sent to America five years earlier with her aunt and uncle, she is mistreated by her aunt, who resents Trang's survival of the dangerous boat trip from Vietnam that has killed her oldest son. Lang Nguyen, jogging along the Galveston beach, drags Trang back from a suicide attempt in the waves of the Gulf. " 'Is that west?' " she asks him. " 'I wanted to go back.' "[21]

Kiet, the tough Amerasian teen in *Prisoners,* is on the run from an

19. Gardner, *Boat People,* 30, 166, 254, 272.

20. Paul James Rutledge, *The Vietnamese Experience in America* (Bloomington: Indiana University Press, 1992), 133.

21. Karlin, *Prisoners,* 14, 123, 80.

abusive foster father, her third, and she has been rejected before. When Minh, a local Vietnamese, will not take her in—" 'We're all dust in this country, little sister. But I can't afford the trouble' "—Kiet heads to nearby Washington, D.C., and the Vietnam Veterans Memorial, searching, like Trang, for her American father. Kiet is angry, confrontational—an "off-brand grrrl ghost. . . . Viet Cong With an Attitude.' " She applauds the "VC homies" on the streets of "the enemy capital" who sell "t-shirts saying *tough shit yeah we're here now*" and "hot dogs and egg rolls and copper Washington Monuments and Sno-Globes (turn them over and shake them and napalm falls on a thatched roof village)."[22]

Amerasians present a particular challenge for the assimilating culture; ethnically as much American as Asian, they straddle two worlds and belong to neither. As Fran, the Amerasian narrator of Butler's "Letters from My Father," recognizes about "the children of the dust. . . . At one look we were Vietnamese and at another look we were American and after that you couldn't get your eyes to stay still when they turned to us, they kept seeing first one thing and then another" (66). Fran lives in Louisiana now, where she reads the hundreds of passionate letters that her American father sent years before to authorities trying to get Fran and her mother out of Vietnam and wonders how her distant, silent father could be the man who wrote those letters. As the story ends, Fran waits for him to find her reading the letters, "and I will ask him to talk to me like in these letters, like when he was so angry with some stranger that he knew what to say" (72).

It is significant that it is Vietnam vets, those fathers and could-be fathers of the *bui doi* (Malle's Shang Pierce, Gardner's Wilson), who demonstrate most blatantly the resentment and fear of the refugees that reverberate throughout these texts; for, as Lan Cao and veteran-author Wayne Karlin understand, the attitudes of Americans toward the Vietnamese are very much entangled with Americans' feelings about the war (and the veterans of the war) that made so many Vietnamese a part of American life. "We were," Mai Nguyen recognizes, "a ragtag accumulation of unwanted, an awkward reminder of a war the whole country was trying to forget."[23]

In *Vietnam and the Southern Imagination*, Owen W. Gilman Jr., accepting "the resonance of history in the South as an enabling factor for writers of that region," asserts that southern writers have responded to

22. Ibid., 52, 93, 11, 91–92.
23. Cao, *Monkey Bridge*, 15.

the Vietnam War uniquely because of the consciousness of loss and defeat that has characterized southern literature since the Civil War. "When the Southern writer surveys the Vietnam War and its impact, he or she sees the South," Gilman argues. At the Vietnam Veterans Memorial on the Mall in Washington, Karlin's Kiet gravitates to a bamboo cage with a sign that announces that "AMERICANS ARE STILL HELD CAPTIVE BY ASIA: POW'S NEVER HAVE A NICE DAY." The cage is the makeshift home of a veteran, an amputee who challenges Kiet: " 'You don't remember nothing, do you? . . . Got on the boat, got off the boat. Got welcomed with open arms. Meanwhile, me, I never got back. I'm missing. I never had a parade. . . . The thing was I was afraid to come back. . . . Better to stay missing. People'd treat me just like I was a gook. . . . Me, you, same-same, right?' " Karlin emphasizes the parallels between America's obsession with its lost war—and the consecration of a sacred place dedicated to its memory—and the Vietnamese refugees' reverence for their own losses: " 'Since when Americans build altars for wandering souls, come here, talk to 'em, leave offerings? . . . Just like the altars over there where they died.' " Even veterans who embrace rather than resent the Vietnamese recognize that they are aliens together. The Mekong Grocery in Lan Cao's Little Saigon is a haven for local Vietnam veterans. Mrs. Bay, Mai's mother's friend who works at the grocery, senses "a continuing connection with the American soldiers who visited the store, for the simple reason that a common base, she believed, existed to connect us exiles, on one point, to these lost men, on another point on the American triangle." In the Mekong Grocery, the veteran "would bring his little piece of a big history with him, and even though it was not the same as ours, we were in fact parts of a shared experience."[24]

When James Justus writes that "the backward glance from a twentieth-century war that now compels Southern storytellers to reevaluate their region is Vietnam," he is not thinking of the thousands of Vietnamese whose own personal histories and cultural values offer both a corollary and a challenge to the contemporary South; he writes more metaphorically of the complex legacy of the Vietnam War that reverberates throughout American society. Similarly, Michael Kreyling's assertion that "when the central historical referent for southern identity is no longer the Civil War but Vietnam, radical change can be felt in the foundations of southern society and literature" means to awaken us to the realities of a new South, a

24. Owen W. Gilman Jr., *Vietnam and the Southern Imagination* (Jackson: University Press of Mississippi, 1992), 6, 21; Karlin, *Prisoners*, 97–99; Cao, *Monkey Bridge*, 209.

South no longer defined by the loss of a southern war. But these critics are right to recognize the Vietnam War as the watershed event of late-twentieth-century America. And these authors of fiction set in the contemporary South—native southerners and transplanted northerners; women and men; Americans, a Frenchman, and one new Vietnamese-American voice—have recognized that the lives and stories of Vietnamese refugees yanked from their homes and thrust, as the residue of that transforming war, into American soil offer fertile material for an exploration of that southern story of what Edward Ayers calls "unresolved identity, unsettled and restless, unsure and defensive." Spiritually connected to place and family, these characters are torn from both; they have come to a new land that offers its own traditional reverence for past and place, but it is a veneration that their very presence compromises and complicates. "It is . . . becoming clear," Francesco Loriggio writes, "that independence does not abolish contact with . . . colonizing countries: the interested parties remain conjoined by the past, by what *has* happened between them. . . . Cultural hybridism is more and more the normal condition of communities, individuals, literatures." Twenty-five years after America's longest war, and its only military defeat, the United States and Vietnam are inextricably linked by their shared tragedy. The presence of more than a million Vietnamese refugees in the U.S. is a daily reminder of this shared past; the thousands of Vietnamese in the South live in a society at once "conjoined [with them] by the past," and further adjoined by their shared interest *in* the past.[25]

In his 1995 book *Natives and Newcomers: Ethnic Southerners and Southern Ethnics,* southern historian George Brown Tindall asserts that "one new frontier for southern historians is the role of the ethnic diversity in the region—more than just that represented by black and white."[26] Contemporary authors of southern fiction have been working the fields of this new frontier of cultural hybridism for more than a dozen years.

25. Justus, "Foreword,"' xii; Michael Kreyling, *Inventing Southern Literature* (Jackson: University Press of Mississippi, 1998), 121–22; Ayers, "What We Talk About," 81; Loriggio, "Regionalism and Theory," 4, 16.

26. George Brown Tindall, *Natives and Newcomers: Ethnic Southerners and Southern Ethnics* (Athens: University of Georgia Press, 1995), 51.

Postmodern Southern Vacation: Vacation Advertising, Globalization, and Southern Regionalism

Amy J. Elias

On January 5, 1999, the evening news programs in Birmingham, Alabama, reported that the upcoming Martin Luther King Jr. Day might be marred by civic unrest. The Knights of the Ku Klux Klan had spent the 1998 King holiday inciting riots in Memphis, Tennessee, and this year they were apparently planning to focus on downtown Birmingham. Newscasters such as the urbane African American female anchor from Channel 13, Malena Cunningham, featured clips of Birmingham's five-term African American mayor, Richard Arrington, saying gracefully and with a hint of condescension that constitutionally the Klan had the right of public protest but that Birmingham's best strategy would be to pay them no mind. The Klan was coming to Birmingham, Alabama. From *Indiana*.

Thirty years earlier, when Martin Luther King Jr. himself was the one labeled an outside agitator by Birmingham's white segregationists, this scenario would have been unimaginable. The cultural geography of the U.S. has changed, and since the 1980s southern identities and agendas seem to be changing even more rapidly. As scholars such as Fred Hobson, Robert C. McMath Jr., Howard L. Preston, John Shelton Reed, Peter

Applebome, and others have noted in recent years, some southern "insiders" have become in odd ways "outsiders," and vice versa.[1] Moreover, while some outsiders are rejected or at least media-managed because they represent what the postmodern South publicly wants to dissociate itself from, other kinds of outsiders are being solicited as southern residents and tourists.

With its ongoing move from an agrarian to a service-based and white-collar economy, the South is now a high-growth and stable area of the nation. It is also a place where Americans want to live and visit. In 1998 the U.S. South was the destination of 40 percent of *all* vacation travel in the United States.[2] But why do these travelers come to the South now, when they didn't come before? (Is Disney World the only reason?) What is it that they are promised by vacation-travel advertising featuring southern destinations? Who are being defined as insiders and outsiders in southern vacation advertising, and—more important—how do these definitions *re*define southern regionalism within a postmodern market economy? I would like to look at southern vacation advertising in *Southern Living* magazine to posit some specific points of inquiry in relation to these questions and to argue that vacation advertising for southern travel destinations may be a unique and revealing index to how postmodern market economies are reconstructing southern geographic and literary regionalism.

Southern Living originated in a homes column in *Progressive Farmer*—a magazine owned by the Progressive Farmer Company, started in North

1. Fred Hobson, *The Southern Writer in the Postmodern World* (Athens: University of Georgia Press, 1991); Robert C. McMath Jr., "Variations on a Theme by Henry Grady: Technology, Modernization, and Social Change" in *The Future South: A Historical Perspective for the Twenty-First Century*, ed. Joe P. Dunn and Howard L. Preston (Urbana: University of Illinois Press, 1991), 81–99; Howard L. Preston, "Will Dixie Disappear? Cultural Contours of a Region in Transition" in ibid., 188–216; John Shelton Reed, *One South: An Ethnic Approach to Regional Culture* (Baton Rouge: Louisiana State University Press, 1982); Peter Applebome, *Dixie Rising: How the South Is Shaping American Values, Politics, and Culture* (New York: Random House, 1996).

I would like to thank Suzanne Jones for organizing the 1998 Modern Language Association session "South to a New Place" in San Francisco, which generated the ideas here; the editors and staff at *Southern Living* for generously granting me interviews; and the state and city travel bureaus and corporations for generous permissions to reprint these ads.

2. According to a former chair of the Southeast Travel Association. All quotes cited from Southern Progress personnel and *Southern Living* editorial staff were obtained in on-site interviews with the author at Southern Progress Corporation in 1998.

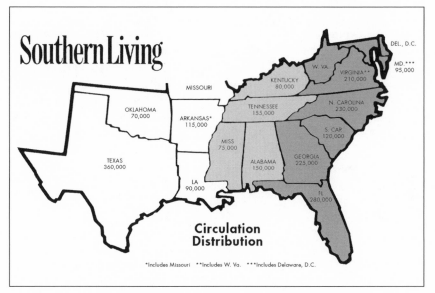

Fig. 1. Circulation distribution of *Southern Living* magazine, 1998. *From Southern Living's* 1999 rate card. *Copyright © Southern Living, Inc. Reprinted with permission.*

Carolina by an ex-Confederate colonel named Leonidas L. Polk. The Progressive Farmer Company became Southern Progress Corporation in 1980, and Southern Progress Corporation was bought out by Time, Inc. (now Time Warner) in 1985 for $480 million. Southern Progress Corporation is the parent company of *Southern Living*, first issued in 1966. With a readership of more than 12 million people, *Southern Living* has been called one of the most successful magazines in the country. According to its ABC statement, in 1998 the magazine enjoyed a paid circulation of more than 2.4 million copies, with individual subscriptions accounting for more than 2.2 million copies, or 92 percent of the total. *Southern Living* is mainly distributed in seventeen states of the Census South, though special editions such as the Vacation Issue are placed on newsstands outside this area (see fig. 1). A geographic analysis of total paid circulation shows that *Southern Living* is sold principally in the southern regions of the U.S.; it has only limited circulation in five major geographic areas of the U.S. including the Pacific and Northeast regions.[3]

Marketing the magazine in these limited areas has proven a successful strategy. The magazine's sales statistics underscore the success of *South-*

3. Within the four U.S. regions where *Southern Living* is sold, the South Atlantic region—including Florida, Georgia, South Carolina, North Carolina, West Virginia, Virginia, Maryland, and Delaware and shown in dark gray in figure 1—accounts for nearly half of the magazine's circulation (44.9 percent). The East South Central region—including Kentucky, Tennessee, Alabama, and Mississippi, and shown in light gray in figure 1—surprisingly accounts for only 18 percent of the magazine's circulation, but when population numbers are figured in, this region has the highest index number for subscriptions per population density. These statistics about *Southern Living* are printed in *Magazine Publisher's Statement for 6 months ended June 30, 1998, Southern Living* (Audit Bureau of Circulations, 1998); *Southern Living 1999 Rate Card*, Rate Card no. 38 (*Southern Living*, Inc., 1999); *Southern Progress Corporation*, a brochure provided by Southern Progress Corporation in Birmingham, Alabama; and information provided by *Southern Living*'s Circulation Department, "*Southern Living* Demographic Analysis, 1998 Fall MRI." The best discussion of *Southern Living*'s formative history can be found in *Life at Southern Living: A Sort of Memoir* by John Logue and Gary McCalla (Baton Rouge: Louisiana State University Press, 2000). Other important earlier discussions include Sam G. Riley's *Magazines of the American South* (New York: Greenwood Press, 1986), 239–44; James Flynn's "Upscale Graciousness: A Thematic Approach to *Southern Living*," *Studies in Popular Culture* 8, No. 2 (1985): 1–6; Peirce Lewis's "The Making of Vernacular Taste: The Case of *Sunset* and *Southern Living*," in *The Vernacular Garden*, ed. John Dixon Hunt and Joachim Wolschke-Bulmahn (Washington, D.C.: Dumbarton Oaks Research Library and Collection, 1993), 107–36; and Diane Roberts, "Living Southern in *Southern Living*," in *Dixie Debates: Perspectives on Southern Cultures*, ed. Richard H. King and Helen Taylor (New York: New York University Press, 1996), 85–98.

ern Living's editorial policies and analysis of its target audience. According to one senior-level spokesperson at Southern Progress Corporation, *Southern Living* "is a magazine that is written for the South, or written for Southerners, by Southerners, about Southern things." Other commentators have remarked in print about this specialized focus for the magazine, but what intrigued me was the obvious question of how one defined "southerner" in the first place. When quizzed on this point, a travel editor for *Southern Living* noted, "I don't think we look at it as you have to be born in the South to be a Southerner."

This definition struck me as central to the issue of southern regionalism. Redefining "southerner" in this way—as someone who wasn't necessarily born in the South—must lead to utterly new definitions of southern identity. If heritage and place are no longer the index of southern identity, what is? The South in *Southern Living* doesn't look much like the Faulknerian swamps of sweat, lust, and family honor that I spent my graduate education reading about. Nor is it much like the Delta farmland or the rural cattle and timber country I've seen over the years when traveling through Alabama, Mississippi, Arkansas, and Louisiana to visit family. The *Southern Living* South is a stylized magazine country with an almost adolescent narcissism—consumed with itself, checking itself out in the mirror, practicing its walk, yet also filled with a defensive confidence about who it is. It looks in fact a lot like a Northeast mall with hydrangeas and sweet gum trees. Pottery Barn, only southern-style.

Style is the operative word here. It is in fact this stylization in the magazine that substitutes for heritage as an index of southern identity. To *Southern Living,* a southerner is not someone linked to the South necessarily by family history, residence, or employment. Rather, a southerner is someone who participates in a southern "lifestyle." "I think it's important," an executive at Southern Progress said to me, "that you understand the basic essence of *Southern Living*. And that is, it is a 'lifestyle' publication. . . . We reflect the lifestyle, in our editorial product, of the Southerner. What they like." This lifestyle is a very different kind of southern cultural life than that referenced by C. Vann Woodward, Louis D. Rubin, and other scholars of the U.S. South. Although in one study John Shelton Reed has argued that southerners are a kind of ethnic group that struggles for mainstream acceptance but stops short of mainstream assimilation, in another context he notes, "If I am right about how Southern identification works these days, to become Southerners outsiders don't have to change their grandfathers. They don't even have to de-nounce them. . . . All they have to do is talk and act like Southerners."[4]

In other words, southern regional identity is fast being redefined as postmodern simulation, which Jean Baudrillard defined some time ago as an image, created by the media and the market, without a referent. Contextualizing southern identity within a postmodern frame radically affects how agency is attributed to the act of identity construction. When lives become "lifestyles," citizens are potentially entering a hall of mirrors created by profit-driven media venues.

According to a Southern Progress executive, travel advertising is the number-one revenue category for the magazine. "We [*Southern Living* magazine] are indeed the *authority,* if you will, on travel in the Southern marketplace," he said. This is a significant claim, given the magazine's superior sales record: to be the authority on travel in the South and also to be read by more than 12 million readers is a significant advantage to promoting certain locations in specific ways.[5]

Southern Living promotes vacation travel in the South in at least four significant ways. First, there is the travel advertising, which takes the form of classified ads or larger, glossier stand-alone ads for specific travel locations or resorts. Second, there is advertising by states' travel bureaus, often taking the form of multipage spreads and sometimes including classifieds. A *Southern Living* editor informed me that these first two kinds of vacation advertising are composed (and paid for) by the state featured in the ad.[6] The third kind of travel promotion takes the form of feature

4. Reed argued the first thesis in *Southerners: The Social Psychology of Sectionalism* (Chapel Hill: University of North Carolina Press, 1983); the second quote is from Reed's *My Tears Spoiled My Aim, and Other Reflections on Southern Culture* (Columbia: University of Missouri Press, 1993), 51. Reed briefly discusses *Southern Living* in *One South,* 119–26.

5. In fact, *Southern Living* runs its own travel service, where readers can buy featured travel packages or arrange their own vacation itineraries. This travel service is linked to travel advertising: in each issue, *Southern Living* puts together vacation travel packages featuring destinations showcased in its larger paid advertisement spreads. The magazine uses this as a hook for potential advertisers: if they buy a big advertising spread, they can be featured as a special destination package in the travel service. McCalla writes in *Life at Southern Living,* "We would never have survived those first years without the advertising of the Southern travel industry" (46).

6. However, for the larger travel states such as Florida or Louisiana, *Southern Living* writers assist in writing copy for special multipage spreads. This copy is meant to break up the ad visually and also give promotional editorial content to the section; the copy is referred to by *Southern Living* as an "advatorial."

stories by *Southern Living* writers on specific travel destinations in the South. This kind of travel promotion includes longer, more detailed feature articles on specific travel destinations. An editor for *Southern Living* informed me that all personnel at the magazine, from editors to assistants, suggest and help to select the subjects of these feature articles. (The staff is bombarded with press releases and invitations from resorts hoping to land a positive review and free publicity in the magazine, but the magazine prefers to evaluate sites anonymously.) The editor explicitly stated that *Southern Living* considers these features not advertising but "a service to our readers." A fourth kind of travel promotion is the *Southern Living Summer Vacation* special-issue magazine, which is published once a year, is devoted exclusively to travel in the South, and contains each of the other three kinds of travel promotion (see fig. 2).

As Diane Roberts, Peirce Lewis, and James Flynn have noted, the southern lifestyle in *Southern Living* is a worry-free zone that reflects identifiable market choices based on an upper-middle-class consumer model: what food one eats, how one decorates one's home, one's choice of garden products. This applies to vacation advertising and promotion in the magazine as well. Editorials and advertising for southern vacation destinations must conform to one rule in *Southern Living*: they must show a positive image of the South. "Our first editor . . . referred to *Southern Living* when we started this magazine in '66 as really the 'good news guys,' " said one Southern Progress executive. "We try to reflect the positive aspects of the South."[7] In vacation advertising, this often means showcasing the South as a vacation playland—clean, safe, echoing with if not history then at least tradition, suffused with grace and down-home charm.

On the one hand, this perspective is one that the editorial staff at *Southern Living* seems genuinely to believe in; when talking to editors and executives at Southern Progress Corporation, I sensed a sincere love of this region and an old-fashioned belief in the American Dream that *Southern Living* is meant to represent.[8] On the other hand and less hap-

7. Peirce Lewis writes that *Southern Living* is "relentlessly domestic and relentlessly optimistic" and "fiercely and self-consciously regional" ("The Making of Vernacular Taste," 118). Logue and McCalla are very clear about these aims and note early fights with *Progressive Farmer* editor Clarence Poe and with Alexander Nunn over prosegregation copy (*Life at Southern Living*, 39), and McCalla wrote in an early mission statement for the magazine, "These stories will not deal with civic problems, socio-economic issues, or politics" (ibid., 142).

8. This is reflected in the comments of one executive, who noted that while *Southern*

Fig. 2. Cover, *Southern Living Presents Summer Vacations*, 1998.
Copyright © Southern Living, Inc. Reprinted with permission.

pily, this kind of editorial agenda turns all of history into romance: in this South, there is no Civil War anguish, only Civil War memorials; no features of the Stars and Bars (except as decoration on the walls of coffeehouses); no sharecropper poverty, only picturesque landscape; no slavery or racial strife, only quaint bed-and-breakfast plantations with golf courses and four-star accommodations. In this sense, the magazine participates strongly in the phenomenon of commodification and simulation identified for some time by Jean-François Lyotard, David Harvey, Fredric Jameson, and others as the condition of postmodernity.[9]

Southern Living's strong focus on southern themes and heritage highlights aspects of southern place that appeal to consumer desire. This is not necessarily a bad thing: many of the features in the magazine are beautifully photographed and help to promote the economic development of the region. Yet it is important to consider how its enormous circulation, combined with its editorial policy of presenting the positive aspects of the south and its strong editorial focus on vacation destinations, allows Southern Living to create a market-driven definition of authentic southern place. Because it is sold principally in the South, Southern Living's positive message about life in the South seems largely to be preaching to the choir, geared to those who already live in this region.

Yet when one looks at vacation advertising in the magazine, the audience—and the picture of the South that is sold to that audience—become more complex. Although the magazine is written "by Southerners, for Southerners," the editors acknowledge that travel editorials do focus on locations that might appeal to nonsoutherners—those who are going South for 40 percent of all the vacations in the U.S. Marketing the South as a vacation site requires acknowledgment of this split readership. And this can lead to new constructions of southern regionalism in the national imagination.

It can lead, first, to a reshaping of geographical boundaries for the South itself. Since to Southern Living, being a southerner is about lifestyle—not so much about where one lives but about how one lives—the

Living is addressed "really [to] the more affluent Southerner," yet "there are a lot of people that are younger that are coming along that aspire to have better, nicer things. Usually it's the process of you just have to put in your time and pay your dues and when you get to that point where you're making a little more money you do those things. That's I guess the life process."

9. See Preston, "Will Dixie Disappear?" for a discussion of southern cultural differences that might still be seen as defining the area in nonmedia-mediated ways.

magazine occasionally reports on vacation destinations that fall outside of what most people might consider "The South"—Colorado, for example, or locations within the "Sunbelt" such as San Antonio, Texas; Mexico; and the Caribbean Islands.

For example, the ad shown in figure 3 advertises Puerto Rico as a *Southern Living* vacation site. The ad copy and pictures emphasize two aspects of this vacation locale: first, that it is in the Caribbean; and second, that vacationers have complete control over their lifestyle choices in this place. In this ad, the emphasis on lifestyle (*how* rather than *where* one lives) constructs a libidinal language about place: in this island paradise, vacationers register not the majesty of Mother Earth or their own southern heritage but the fact that "eating is a function of desire." This is postmodern Puerto Rico, packaged for the American tourist and redesigned as a part of the New South; and as pictured, it is a place perfectly in keeping with *Southern Living*'s editorial policy of positivity: "We're going to tell you about those spas, we're going to tell you about those warm summer nights standing on the beach in the Keys watching the sun set."[10] This ad links the South to the Caribbean or even to coastal South America, admittedly something that has been done before by writers in the literary community. (There is the famous claim by Gabriel García Márquez, for example, that William Faulkner should be seen as a Latin American writer because the magical realism of his work has more in common with Latin American writing than it does with writing from other regions of the U.S.) In this vacation ad, however, the co-option is in the opposite direction: given the market for the magazine, the Caribbean is being redesignated as southern space rather than vice versa.[11]

This co-option, combined with the obsession about time in the ad, recalls Raymond Williams's observation in *The Politics of Modernism* that the nineteenth-century middle class's obsession with time coincided with its redefinition of space as colonial space. In this ad, Puerto Rico as a vacation location is pictured as a place implicitly supporting colonial politics. The small print in the bottom right of the ad oddly says, "Discover

10. Southern Progress executive, in an interview with the author.

11. One editor for *Southern Living* noted that in terms of southern place, "We do stray from time to time. We have always considered the Caribbean and Mexico not part of the South but an extension of where our Southern people do vacation. . . . We try to not overemphasize those places. For instance, we will do an editorial on Bermuda, but that will not be the first story in the magazine. Something definitely Southern will be the first story in the magazine. Something we do on Bermuda will fall further into the pages in that particular issue and we won't at the same time do something on the Caribbean and Mexico."

Fig. 3. Advertisement for Puerto Rico, published in *Southern Living Presents Summer Vacations*, 1998.

the Continent of Puerto Rico." One of the things to discover, it appears, is the complete absence of native Spanish-speaking Puerto Ricans. Indeed, one of the attractions of this vacation locale is that "everyone understands what I'm saying." Vacation travelers are positioned as a new, English-speaking colonial elite, traveling to "discover" new "continents" and to occupy the new and—from the perspective of the colonizers— virgin lands. What is accomplished through the use of the first-person voice in the ad copy (the "I") is also an advertising version of Jean-François Lyotard's "acinema," which Janine Marchessault has called "spectatorial reflexivity—the desire for the spectator to be an active participant, the paradox of distance, [and] the shattering of disembodied vision" that have been "realized by the processes of spectatorship under global capital."[12] In this postmodern space, the southern I/eye looks through the lens of global capital and not only blocks out the view of the native Other with its own reflection; it also becomes part of the thing viewed, an active participant in the romance of place that is being constructed. The ad nicely illustrates how the vacation advertising "for Southerners, about Southern things" in *Southern Living* is redefining both what is inside the southern boundary and also who counts as important within those new southern borders. What is also interesting is that this ad was made up not by the magazine but by the Puerto Rico Tourism Company.

Second, marketing the South as a vacation site to a split readership can also lead to a reconstruction of southern regionalism as a new kind of postmodern hyperreality, one where regional characteristics are logos to be put on T-shirts and bumper stickers rather than something rooted in the real habits, manners, customs, and history of a geographic location. The Disney-effect of postmodern media that turns every place into a historyless shopping mall has of course been discussed by Jean Baudrillard, Fredric Jameson, Clifford Geertz, Tony Bennett, and others for some time. And it is only fair to note that cultural tourism also has had real economic benefits for southern cities such as Savannah and Charleston. The vacation advertising in *Southern Living* may, however, point to a less advantageous, more subliminal construction of southern regionalism by business interests. The issue may not be whether the South *has* a regional distinctiveness; as James C. Cobb has pointed out, there are many debates about that question that posit a "great mass of Americans

12. Janine Marchessault, "Spectatorship in Cyberspace: The Global Embrace," in *Theory Rules: Art as Theory/Theory and Art*, ed. Jody Berland et al. (Toronto: University of Toronto Press, 1996), 224–25.

who apparently could care less whether the South has retained its unique-ness." Rather, the issue may be one concerning the control of the *representation* of southern identity—who controls representation of regional characteristics, for what audiences, and with what objectives.[13]

One ad for the Hyatt Regency at Hilton Head Island illustrates how difficult it is to sort out these questions in relation to vacation advertising's constructions of southern regional identity.[14] The full-page *Southern Living* ad, copyrighted in 1995, is composed of a posed scene: at the center of the ad, an African American man in his twenties or thirties and outfitted in retro golf attire stands leaning comfortably on his golf club. It is a beautiful summer day; the man stares out from the ad, looking affably at the reader. Behind him is the ocean and a waving palm tree; he stands on a manicured, ocean-front green, the red flag for the hole waving from the cup to his right. The colors in the ad are vibrant: the golf-course grass is vivid-green beneath the man's feet; the outfit he wears (complete with 1930s knickers, round and tasseled golf hat, and plaid vest) is ablaze in reds and yellows; the ocean and sky backdrop behind the golf green is awash in blue. A small caption tag near the man's head informs us that this is Hyatt Door Captain Charlie Ferguson. Above Mr. Ferguson's head is another caption, in large type. It reads, "They are a coastal people who greet you with clubs, taunt you with traps, and confront you with hazards. But first, they'll hold the door open for you." Beneath the picture of the man, at the bottom of the ad, is a strip of copy, where we find out from the small print that Mr. Ferguson, as a Hyatt employee, "will take your bags, assist you with check-in, and give you the names of the best golf pros on the island. *All with a hospitality the South is known for*" (emphasis mine).

On the one hand, this ad might be seen as empowering its subject in a number of ways. First, it shows a black man on a southern island-resort golf course in expensive, if goofy, golf attire; the implication is that at Hilton Head, the golf course—notoriously associated in the U.S. with exclusive, "whites-only" country clubs—is open to everyone, even black door captains of the hotel itself. Charlie Ferguson is in fact a real person

13. See, for example, Michael Shnayerson's discussion of the effects of tourism on Charleston's economy in "Southern Revival," *Condé Nast Traveler* 32 (August 1997): 94–101, 126–27; James C. Cobb, "Tomorrow Seems Like Yesterday: The South's Future in the Nation and the World," in *The Future South,* ed. Dunn and Preston, 229.

14. Hyatt Inc. holds the copyright to this ad and denied me permission to reprint it in this article because the chain was in litigation. A Hyatt representative did note that Hyatt was no longer running this particular advertisement.

and, last time I checked, was indeed employed as a door captain at Hyatt Regency Hilton Head; this ad thus might be seen as complimenting a real worker on real performance excellence. In this kind of reading, this is a charming ad that shows how far the South has come in terms of class and race politics.

I admit, however, that I have trouble reading the ad this way. It's hard to explain the visual impact of this ad, but it hits you like a truck when you first see it. Every single person to whom I've shown the ad has recognized its potential for racial offense. To me, this ad illustrates how simulations of Old-South racial stereotypes can be problematically encoded in contemporary vacation advertising for southern locations. The ad seems aggressively to encode racist images of the black man as savage, as coastal cannibal, and as lawn jockey. (Charlie's pose as well as his outfit are significant in this regard; his outfit mimics even in its colors the "lawn jockey" attire, and he could as easily be holding a lantern or a bridle as a golf club in his posed position). The ad copy seems to construct a subliminal association between Ivory Coast and U.S. southern coast, for if this is a southern location, then the copy seems to position Charlie as a newly civilized antebellum slave, formerly one of the coastal people who allegedly would taunt and greet explorers. The ad's "humor" depends upon the jarring juxtaposition of the "civilized" space of the golf course to the "savage" space of the ocean coastline; the implication is that the coastal vacation locale advertised can "tame" this savage and reconstruct his cultural citizenship safely within a market-defined cultural site. In this kind of reading, the ad seems to disempower Charlie in a number of ways: giving his name in the familiar as "Charlie" rather than "Charles" or "Mr. Ferguson"; coordinating him with objects in the landscape (both he and the flag are wearing red) as well as putting him in a costume as artificial as (and reversing the racial references of) minstrel attire; and constructing him as someone whose off-hours identity is still determined by his worker's role. For even though he is presumably off duty in this ad, he seems not the person one will *play* on the links, but rather the person who can direct hotel residents to other real, professional players. (Many people to whom I've shown the ad in fact see Charlie at first as a caddy—that "lawn jockey" pose elicits associations with holding things for others—and only secondarily ask why a door captain would be serving as caddy on the links.) It may be significant as well that there are three golf courses affiliated with the Hyatt Regency Hilton Head, and at the time of this writing, greens fees ranged from $85 per game to $55 per game (after one o'clock in the afternoon); hotel employees were given a "slight discount" if they played late in the day.[15] I was not able to determine how much Hyatt Regency pays its door captains or to find out Mr. Ferguson's own financial state; however, the greens fees do seem a bit steep for a service employee to handle on a regular basis, even with a "slight discount." In addition, the real situation at Hilton Head is not one where African Americans are faring well: the *New York Times* reported in 1994 that Hilton Head Island, which once had an all-black population, now overwhelmingly serves white, wealthy, largely *northern* vacationers, and that the remaining native African American islanders work in low-paying jobs in the corporate hotels and restaurants.[16]

A second kind of reading of this ad, then, might posit that the ad recuperates Old-South anxieties about race and diffuses them for a white readership through the reconstruction of a new southern corporate regionalism. Showing Mr. Ferguson in a "lawn jockey" pose and emphasizing not only his service but also his "savage" background that has been tamed by work, the ad seems intentionally constructed to encode subliminal references to Old South plantation-slave economies in order to sell the values of that former time. This ad cost Hyatt a lot of money: *Southern Living* charges about $94,000 for a full-page, four-color ad like this one.[17] All throughout *Southern Living,* readers see ads for hotel chains and resorts that play on southernness as a selling point; advertisers seem acutely aware of their southern audience and often take pains to portray themselves as at one with southern "lifestyle," values, and history. Certainly, a hotel conglomerate like Hyatt that is willing to spend nearly $100,000 on a one-page advertisement would work hard to gear its ad to this market demographic. So the questions logically follow: who is the target audience for this ad? What picture of the South is really being shown here? Is it a true picture? If Hilton Head is a southern destination with a largely northern clientele, for whom is this seemingly coded regional identity being constructed? And by whom?

Another ad that raises these questions is one for Radisson, shown in figure 4. This ad shows concièrge Roberto Vivas talking to two young children, and the italicized caption reads, "By the end of their vacation,

15. Information obtained from phone conversation with employees at Hyatt Regency Hilton Head, 20 May 1999.

16. For example, see Peter Applebome's discussion of Hilton Head and African Americans in "Tourism Enriches an Island Resort, But Hilton Head Blacks Feel Left Out," *New York Times* (Late New York Edition) (2 September 1994), A18.

17. Advertising rate based on 1998 figures in "Southern Living 1999 Rate Card."

Fig. 4. Advertisement for Radisson Hotels, published in *Southern Living* (April 1998). *Reprinted with permission of Radisson Hotels.*

these kids will think 'concierge' is French for 'uncle.' " Again, one might read this ad two ways. On the one hand, the ad seems to praise actual Radisson workers for their outstanding contributions and performance. Roberto Vivas was a real concièrge at Radisson; a company representative said that this ad is in fact a favorite of the corporation president's and that the president has distributed it, as a poster, to Radisson workers in different departments. In fact, the president of the corporation gave the ad an award: one Radisson worker noted, "If we have employees that go *way* above what they need to do, they'll actually get a framed, signed letter from the president of the company, a handwritten personal letter from him, and he sends that to the actual employee—actually, overnight. It's kind of neat."[18] When I asked if this letter was considered a reward to excellent Radisson workers, this employee noted, "I don't know if it would be actually a reward. I would probably say that it's maybe a recognition of what they do. . . . From what I understand, that's just the way he [Mr. Vivas] *is.*" In other words, it was this employee's understanding that workers featured in these Radisson ads were being recognized for their outstanding work performance, and it was high compensation not only to be featured in the ad but also to be recognized by the company president for one's outstanding service.

However, when I tried to talk with Mr. Vivas, I was told first that he worked not in Florida but in a Radisson in San Francisco, and when I telephoned there, I found out that he is no longer a Radisson employee but in fact has moved on to work for another hotel chain. Because the ad in which he is featured, however, is so popular, it continues to run in *Southern Living, Outside* magazine, and elsewhere. Also of interest to me was how Mr. Vivas was selected for this ad in the first place. When I talked with the Radisson corporate office, I was told that rather than selecting workers who have excellent performance records, "there are photographers who go to different hotels and the ones that turn out the best are the ones that are featured." In other words, selection had nothing to do with worker performance; it had to do with the subject's photogenic potential, picture quality, and timing.

This information can lead one, I think, to a different reading of this advertisement, particularly in terms of how it is constructing identity and place in a southern magazine. Mr. Vivas might have been selected for this ad because he is handsome and because the photographer caught him at

18. All quotes are from telephone interviews conducted with Radisson employees on 20 May 1999.

a particularly photogenic moment. The ad copy was written later and has nothing to do with the actual scene we are witnessing. In this ad copy, the Latino male is linked to house management for wealthy patrons, a role granted to Latino and South American immigrants in western and southern states but also a role with unique subliminal associations for southerners: *uncle* is a term associated with the old plantation-house slave. Although this scene could be taking place anywhere in the world, the ad specifically states that what we are witnessing is a scene in Orlando, Florida, at 5:33 P.M., in the South associated with Juan Ponce de León. (In fact, as noted above, it wasn't taking place there at all, but in San Francisco.) Orlando has associations for some white U.S. consumers with illegal immigration by Spanish-speaking people, and this ad (probably unintentionally but also fortuitously) defuses anxiety about improper citizenship by including in the scene a surveillance camera (pointing directly at the top of Roberto Vivas's head) and Mr. Vivas's own identification tag, clipped prominently to his shirt pocket. The hotel chain's slogan—"The difference is genuine"—begins to take on multiple semiotic implications. It ostensibly refers to the difference in quality of service offered by Radisson hotels, but it also seems, unwittingly or not, to embed a reference to racial difference as well. Roberto's is the difference that is genuine here, for the ad copy states that he and other staffers are "people who are helpful and courteous not because it's their job. But because it's their *nature*" (emphasis mine). This is obviously intended to be praise for the patience and professionalism of Radisson workers, but I would argue that the linkage of "human nature" to "service work" figured in the body of the Latin American male in these ads contributes not only to an infantilization of all workers but also to a specific construction of the Latino male as service worker. What is emphasized in these ads is not employees' training or even their commitment to organizational goals, but rather their innate "natural" proclivities to patience and service. What is particularly striking is how this ad copy seems to undercut the rewards rationale of Radisson corporate management, which sends letters to employees congratulating them on their superior job performance, not their "natures." A different kind of reading of this ad, then, could posit that this man was chosen not for his job performance but for his photogenic face, to target a specific market demographic, and to promote a specific corporate image; that as a low-paid service worker, he was probably not monetarily compensated for his appearance in an ad that would make Radisson countless dollars in profit and for which the corporation would normally have to pay a professional model at least a standard modeling fee; and he is featured in this ad as a "natural" servant rather than as a motivated corporate employee in order to sell a panacea to white racial anxiety concerning Latino people in the southern U.S. Even if this is an overstated case, one is prompted at least to ask what values are being sold here and how they are being linked to place when these ads appear in a magazine for southeastern readers.

However, it isn't only multinational hotel chains that make up ads that arguably tie appeals to Old and New South racial anxieties to southern regions or audiences. In the pages of *Southern Living,* vacation advertising by specific states also embeds these kinds of appeals. For example, one ad by the San Antonio Convention and Visitors Bureau appeared in *Southern Living* in 1998 (see fig. 5), and the ad copy also links race, culture, and place in a provocative way. The ad is a full-page, multicolor advertisement showing a picture of a central-city river canal and small stone footbridge crossing it; going down the canal on the water, away from the reader, is a flat boat in which about fifteen (white) tourists sit and listen to a (white male) tour guide as they drift past the city's shopping district. On the sidewalks along the canal, other shoppers (all heterosexual couples holding hands) walk. To the right of the picture is a column of ad copy: "It's a stream of pure, undiluted love. Where laughter and colors splash together with joyful abandon. Come aboard. Get caught up in the ebb and flow. For this river which gave us life, gives us life. And it will take you on a voyage deep into our city's very soul. You'll find it in the dizzying whirl of a folklórico dancer. The cool, chiseled stone of ancient Spanish missions. And the shy smile of a child with cinnamon skin, chocolate eyes. All in all, it's a sparkling, effervescent concoction. Of cultures. Flavors. Centuries past and present."

The first thing that seems odd about this ad is its subject: in a magazine that is written "for Southerners, by Southerners, about Southern things," what is San Antonio? Texas may be included in the Confederate South, but San Antonio is traditionally seen as a western, not a southern, city. But the ad's language would appeal to a Bible-Belt audience: what is emphasized in New Testament language are the "city's soul," the Spanish missions, and the river site that can provide a kind of salvation: "For this river which gave us life, gives us life." (What is conveniently not noted, of course, is that the river is actually severely depleted by agriculture and the water that tourists float on may be pumped from artesian wells specifically to provide atmosphere for the city.) And, as in the other ads discussed above, in this ad the local population is figured as innocent, dark, and exotic children: what visitors encounter is "the shy smile of a child

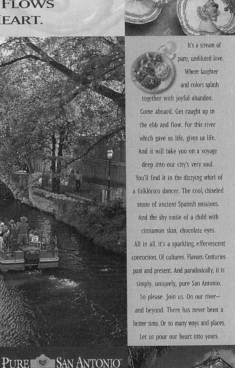

Fig. 5. Advertisement for San Antonio placed by the San Antonio Convention and Visitors Bureau and published in *Southern Living Presents Summer Vacations*, 1998. *Reprinted with permission of San Antonio Convention and Visitors Bureau.*

with cinnamon skin, chocolate eyes." The business community's linked images of Christian Promised Land *and* exotic colonial state where natives—figured as innocent brown children—provide atmosphere and love to visiting white people demands analysis and gives an unsettling connotation to the banner motto of the ad: "Pure San Antonio."

Likewise, ads by Oklahoma state and city travel bureaus and chambers of commerce were part of an ad campaign running in multiple issues of *Southern Living* (see fig. 6). The slogan the state chose was "Oklahoma Native America," with a banner motto stating "America In Its Native State." Ostensibly, the state seems proudly to refer to its large Native American population and the presence of many tribal capitals within its borders, and to showcase Native American cultures as its main tourist attraction. A number of the ads use language specifically meant to evoke a Native American way of life or cultural value, such as one ad (not shown) that states, "The Earth is your companion / in this secret place, / this Native State." Other ads on the page by Oklahoma City, Tulsa, and Woodward travel and tourism centers are less poetic and more directly addressed to specific visitor sites.

However, what's interesting about all of the ads in Oklahoma's campaign is that they never show Native American people. In the ads shown here, for instance, we see a forest populated not with Indians but with suburban hill cabins; an ad for Oklahoma City whose attraction is its historical identification with white settler land rushes ("In 1889, it was the free land" that brought in visitors); an ad for Woodward that references Custer and features an armed white calvary officer in nineteenth-century dress; and an ad for the Convention and Visitors Bureau where history takes the form of children's crafts in a postmodern style. Ironically, what starts to emerge from these ads is a sense that what the state is subconsciously advertising is its historical association with Indian *removal,* for Oklahoma is of course the state to which Native American tribes from the Southeast were forcibly removed, on genocidal trails of tears, in the nineteenth century. A tourist slogan ostensibly lauding Oklahoma's multicultural heritage seems unintentionally to encode pride in "ethnic cleansing" of Southeast Indian tribes in a magazine sold exclusively in the Southeast. "America In Its Native State" begins to signify not Native America, but "native" American Manifest Destiny.

What is encouraging is a change emerging in the travel advertising in *Southern Living.* In the magazine's August 2001 issue, six advertising pages (by credit-card companies, department stores, paint manufacturers, and pharmaceutical companies) featured African Americans promi-

Fig. 6. Page of advertisements placed by the Oklahoma State Travel Bureau, Oklahoma City, the Tulsa Convention and Visitors Bureau, and Woodward, and published in *Southern Living Presents Summer Vacations*, 1998. *Reprinted with permission of the Oklahoma State Travel Bureau, the Oklahoma City Chamber of Commerce, the Tulsa Convention and Visitors Bureau, and the City of Woodward, Oklahoma.*

nently and positively. There were four feature editorials by the magazine itself that also included African American southerners, and three of these were for southern travel destinations: one a feature in the "Travel in the South" section for Chattanooga's Coolidge Park that included a full-page color picture of black and white kids playing happily in the city fountains; another in the same section touting the shopping at Epcot and in its three-picture spread featuring both a man in a wheelchair and an African American girl decked out in Mickey ears; and a full-page color ad for Nashville's art museum that features an African American woman who seems to be a docent guiding three children (two white, one black) through the exhibits. It seems that the magazine is tuning its ear to the increasing diversity of the southern market, and it may be that multinational companies in the South are beginning to understand that Dixie can be marketed to more than one population demographic.

Travel advertising complicates construction of place because by definition it hides its own rhetorical strategies. By definition, advertising aims to blend fact with fiction, fact with desire, and to merge both in the consumer's mind. At Southern Progress Corporation, one travel editor noted, "It has been much to our chagrin [at *Southern Living* that] there are a lot of readers who don't . . . differentiate between an advertisement and our editorial content." The construction of place in vacation advertisements seems to have as much impact on consumers' ideas of place as does anything else. The representations of southern vacation sites participate in a complex construction of a simulated, fantasy South, and—if Deleuze and Guattari were right, that fantasy is both an extension of and an intervention in the multiple relations of power and desire—we need to pay more attention to how this fantasy South, the postmodern South of simulation and desire, is being constructed. Rather than speaking abstractly about "postmodern simulation," can we analyze in what ways communities are taking charge of this representation? I think we can, but only in the context of the relation between economic globalization and constructions of regional identity.

For the past ten years or so, there has been emerging a critical conversation about globalization—the process whereby capitalism spreads throughout the world to create markets irrespective of national boundaries or politics through the growth of transnational corporations (TNCs). In the context of this conversation, there is an ongoing debate about the relation between the global and the local that applies to this new construction of southern regionalism. On the one hand, theorists of postmodernism such as David Harvey, Noam Chomsky, Fredric Jameson, and Robert Young have argued that there is no counter to tentacled capitalist expansion, no possibility for local resistance or self-definition in the face of a globalized capitalism that can always shift its grounds of production and always has available a ready labor pool and consumer market. In contrast, others have argued that the very processes by which markets expand globally allows for the creation of small, local alliances and new definitions of local identities. Diversifying markets create multiple local communities, thereby creating a possible alternative to the globalization that in fact produced them. For Jean-François Lyotard, these were the *petits recits* that could oppose multinational postmodernity; for Benedict Anderson, they are the "imagined communities." If as Masao Miyoshi notes, "consumerism offers a powerful allurement for homogenization," one must also recognize that it offers a powerful allurement for diversification as well.[19]

My point here is not to enter the globalization debate but to note that the South has entered it, and that the question of southern regional identity will not be divorced from discussions of consumerism in the future. When one examines how the South is marketed as a region for specific consumer purposes, one immediately sees an opposition created between local and global consumer interests. Because it is *about* southern place construction, vacation advertising for southern destinations can potentially provide concrete illustrations of regional place construction in a global marketplace. In many ways, the ads I've discussed may be concrete examples of what one might call a "multinational media regionalism." As noted earlier, although *Southern Living* sets its own editorial agenda, its advertising is constructed by outsiders, namely the hotel chains or resorts wishing to advertise in the magazine. Advertisers provide all the materials and the "creative" (the copy) for the ad and purchase space for it in the magazine. Identifying the aims of these ads is problematical at best, though I would argue that some of these ads seem to encode images of Old and New South racial anxieties and defuse/diffuse them through the construction of a safe site of cultural consumption.

But understanding how the ads are received by the public is even more

19. See Jean-François Lyotard, *The Postmodern Condition: A Report on Knowledge,* trans. Geoff Bennington and Brian Massumi (Minneapolis: University of Minnesota Press, 1984); Masao Miyoshi, " 'Globalization,' Culture, and the University," in *The Cultures of Globalization,* ed Fredric Jameson and Masao Miyoshi (Durham: Duke University Press, 1998), 259.

difficult. *Southern Living* editors claim that the magazine is written "by Southerners, for Southerners," but the magazine in actuality has multiple audiences and readerships. First, there is the audience outside the South, particularly people in the Northeast who might read the magazine to learn about southern vacation destinations. Second, there are multiple audiences in the South itself. *Southern Living* acknowledges that these days the South does not offer a unified, homogeneous readership. Indeed, Southern Progress publishes split runs of the magazine, different monthly versions of *Southern Living* targeting specific regional vacation markets. While the core articles of each issue appear in all copies of the magazine, travel editorials and advertising that appear in an issue for North Carolina will be different from those in an issue of *Southern Living* appearing in Texas. This corporate practice of running split-run editions of the magazine with nonoverlapping regional travel advertising may, oddly enough, signal a developing sense of imagined communities birthed through separating the South into ever-more-discrete, localized destinations based on the diversification of consumer desires.

In addition, although we can analyze postmodern southern regionalism as "multinational media regionalism," we might also need to recognize how southerners themselves are selling and thereby constructing regional identity in this commercial way. For example, a powerful organization emerging in the Southeast is the Southeast Tourism Society, a membership organization that consists of travel-related personnel in ten southeastern states. According to a former chairperson, the primary role of the society is to function as a networking organization for travel personnel. The society runs an annual, week-long Marketing College at North Georgia State Community College, where society members and others can train with travel professionals. In addition, this former chairperson noted, "the Society has a very strong lobbying effort. We work with the states and also at the national level. If there's major legislation that is pending that impacts the travel industry . . . we get very involved in that." The Southeast Tourism Society is thus a hybrid in terms of regional interests: a business collective representing some of the most powerful corporations in the Southeast, and a regional representative supposedly taking its cues from its regional southern constituency. Interestingly enough, the founder of the Southeast Tourism Society was a former editor of *Southern Living* magazine.

It is also important to note that John Logue and Gary McCalla argue that *Southern Living*'s travel and features reporting tries to balance pro-development with preservationist perspectives. They note that the magazine won the (now discontinued) DATO Award in 1969 and 1971 for its travel editorials, and that "the magazine was cited by DATO for its editorial support of the Bankhead National Forest wilderness proposal in Alabama, for its support of the preservation of the Big Thicket in East Texas, for helping save seven endangered historic homes in Lexington, Kentucky, for speaking out against the pollution of Sanibel-Captiva Islands in Florida, for the magazine's salute to San Antonio for the protection of its scenic downtown river, and for its salute to Kentucky for the protection of its Land Between the Lakes." The questions of who is defining southern regionalism and according to what criteria becomes urgent but muddy. As Larry Lohmann has argued, "different actors contend with and influence what is loosely called 'globalization,'" and constructive and engaged understanding of the power struggles of these actors depends upon how they themselves interpret these struggles and also "on where they are placed, and where they place themselves, in what is an increasingly broad intercultural landscape or field of action."[20]

What an organization such as the Southeast Tourism Society may face, to some extent, is what Lohmann has called in a different context the "globalizers' dilemma": the need to "find their way through the blizzard of consequences which blows back at them from each local area as a result of this attempt to reduce unique spaces to locations on national or global grids."[21] Is southern regionalism something that is defined by the "intercultural micropolitics" of those living in the South, or is it something now being defined by "global macropolitics" from outside its borders? How might business interests affect representations, and hence actualizations, of southern place and cultures? How is the South's own history of race being commodified? And perhaps the most disturbing question, is regional identity being created by multinational outsiders now marketing southerners to themselves as lifestyle *products* as well as lifestyle producers? Are southerners, in other words, now products rather than consumers in the global market?

*   *   *

20. Logue and McCalla, *Life at Southern Living,* 157; Larry Lohmann, "The Globalizers' Dilemma: Contention and Resistance in Intercultural Space," in *Globalization and the South,* ed. Caroline Thomas and Peter Wilkin (New York: St. Martin's, 1997), 213. See also Benita J. Howell's article "Weighing the Risks and Rewards of Involvement in Cultural Conservation and Heritage Tourism," *Human Organization* 53 (1994): 150–59, for a different perspective on cultural tourism.

21. Lohmann, "The Globalizers' Dilemma," 215.

As a brief coda, I might add that for those of us trained in literary analysis as well as cultural analysis, yet another question arises from the observations above: what might be the connections between the postmodern southern regionalism constructed by vacation advertising and contemporary southern literary regionalism?

Literary scholars in the past used to argue that there *was* such a thing as a distinctive Southern Literature. And certain critics still argue this. But how would one reconcile Donald R. Noble's definition of a southern writer as someone who spent his childhood in the South with *Southern Living*'s attitude that one need not be born in the South to be a southerner? How can one reconcile John Crowe Ransom's distinction between southern life (seen as agrarian, fundamentalist, and traditional) and mainstream American life (seen as centralized, urban, and materialistic) with the picture of southern life in *Southern Living*, which takes pains to associate southern life with American upper-middle-class, urban materialism?

Oddly, in fact, popular culture and the travel industry seem intent upon constructing and marketing southern regional identity at precisely the moment when noteworthy southern writers themselves frequently express frustration, perplexity, or even disgust at the notion of a unique southern literature. Writers as different as Walker Percy, Alice Walker, Roy Blount, Lee Smith, and Padgett Powell have presented the post–World War II South as more like the rest of the country than as a separate territory with a unique sensibility. Barry Hannah is on record as grumbling, "You can't *imagine* how often I get asked about how Faulkner influenced me and why there's so many good Southern writers and all that shit."[22] Fred Hobson has observed that contemporary writers such as Bobbie Ann Mason, Barry Hannah, Harry Crews, and Lee Smith seem comparatively devoid of influence from past southern literary giants, immerse their characters in a world of mass culture, and seldom attempt to write the "big novel" in the manner of Faulkner and Wolfe. Bobbie Ann Mason has in fact been discussed at least as much in the company of Raymond Carver, Amy Hempel, and Jay McInerney as in that of Walker Percy and Vicki Covington, while Cormac McCarthy and Richard Ford "pass" as non-southern writers.

For all this, though, *Southern Living* seems intent upon emphasizing the distinct character of southern writing. The magazine regularly fea-

22. Doris Betts, "Many Souths and Broadening Scale: A Changing Southern Literature," in *The Future South,* ed. Dunn and Preston, 171.

tures a column called "Books About the South"; it runs features on popular southern writers such as Anne Rice; and it runs a monthly column called "Southern Journal," often written by recognized southern fiction writers such as Lewis Nordan, author of *Wolf Whistle*. (Mark Childress also wrote for *Southern Living* at one point.) On the one hand, we can applaud the magazine's inclusion of southern literature as part of its lifestyle concerns. On the other hand, we may need to inquire about how literary prestige is used here to legitimize this postmodern vision of the South, and how in turn that Reconstructed South is affecting the literature it produces.

I would argue that these days fiction and media do collaborate in constructing a contemporary myth of the South, but they do so in very different ways and to radically different ends. After all, it was Walker Percy—in 1978—who had the presence of mind to note that the South was turning into an "agribusiness-sports-vacation-show biz" culture.[23] The difference is that in contemporary literature, the fractured culture of the South is not reintegrated under a comforting set of lifestyle characteristics. In other words, contemporary southern literature does indeed show the South as fractured, diversified, and increasingly homogenized under capitalist market influences. But unlike *Southern Living* magazine and southern vacation advertising, it tends *not* to turn back to capitalism to fix the problem. In *Southern Living,* the potentially upsetting, fractured state of the postmodern South is reintegrated and safely redefined through the very capitalism that caused the problem: the South is redefined as the predictable landscape of Pottery Barn and J. Peterman, which can spin a new, cozy narrative about southern "lifestyle" as southern life itself becomes, perhaps, extinct. As McCalla himself wrote in a mission statement for the magazine in its fourth year of publication, *SL* would place major emphasis on travel to make the South "the playground of eastern America."[24]

Sometimes in *Southern Living,* the connection between *vacation* regionalism and *literary* regionalism seems explicit, as in figure 7, where ads for both bump up against one another on the pages of the magazine.

23. Walker Percy, "Random Thoughts on Southern Literature, Southern Politics, and the American Future," *Georgia Review* 32 (1978), 505. My reading of contemporary, "postmodern" southern fiction differs significantly from the condemnation of "K-Mart realism" by John W. Aldridge in his denunciatory *Talents and Technicians: Literary Chic and the New Assembly-Line Fiction* (New York: Charles Scribner's Sons, 1992).

24. Logue and McCalla, *Life at Southern Living,* 140.

Miserable Mealybugs

If you should find what looks like specks of cotton on your houseplants or garden shrubs, take a closer look. That "cotton" is a sign of mealybugs—little insects that will deform or even kill plants if not checked.

Mealybugs are much like the common pest scales, except mealybugs have soft bodies covered with white, waxy filaments. Although the filaments look like cotton, they will rub off and smear between your fingers.

Unlike scales, mealybugs are free to crawl about plants, albeit slowly. Their bodies are oval and ⅛ to ⅓ inch long. One species, the long-tailed mealybug, has four tail-like filaments that extend from its abdomen, each as long as its body.

Mealybugs may be easily overlooked because they prefer to live in the hidden, tighter areas of a plant. Your first clues to their presence are the sight of "cotton" or the damage caused by their feeding. As these pests suck sap from leaves and stems, plants react by turning yellow in the feeding spot, or by growing in a distorted manner so leaves become rumpled and misshapen. If mealybugs have a chance to overrun the plant, there is no growth at all, just yellowing and sure decline.

One of the easiest ways to control a small number of mealybugs is to simply remove them and their cottony egg masses by hand. However, you have to keep watching for hatchlings that still remain on the plant. You can use a swab dipped in mineral oil or alcohol to clean up the pests.

You can also control them by spraying the plant thoroughly with insecticidal soap. Be sure the soap solution runs down into the buds and leaf-stem joints where the pests congregate. ◇

Fig. 7. Page from *Southern Living* (August 1998). Copyright © *Southern Living, Inc. Reprinted with permission.*

Here, an ad for a (of course, audio) collection of short memoirs by southern writers sits atop a vacation ad for the state of Georgia; bordering both is a *Southern Living* editorial on gardening. Taken together, the three seem equalized as fenceposts for the postmodern southern "lifestyle"—all equally based on the availability of surplus capital and leisure time. We need to keep asking, I think, if this is the kind of regionalism the South will, or should, be known for in the future. And in this day and age, when people seem increasingly willing to fight and die for regional identity, we need to keep examining what exactly that identity is and who really is producing it in our time.

PART III　**Making Global Connections**

Italy and the United States: The Politics and Poetics of the "Southern Problem"

Michael Kreyling

Both nations were invented in the 1860s. One was proclaimed on March 17, 1861; the other began a doomed civil war for its autonomy on April 12, 1861. The architect of Italian unification, Count Camillo Cavour, did not live to see the national reality; he died a few months after the proclamation. The martyr to American union, Abraham Lincoln, died before the image in his rhetoric became a political reality. As a means to unification, one victorious North dissolved monasteries without anticipating negative effects on employment and social services for the poor. The other victorious North abolished slave labor in the defeated states without adequately anticipating the effect on employment and social services for the freedmen. In the southern regions of one new nation, the primary organization of land for agricultural use was a large holding, usually owned by one family, and rented to peasants: *latifundia*. In the southern regions of the other nation, the primary organization of land for agricultural use was a large holding, usually owned by one family, and worked by slave labor: plantations. Southerners in one new nation tended to view their civilization as distinct within the new nation, "an ancient and glorious nation in its own right." Southerners in the other new nation tended to view their civilization as distinct within the nation as a whole, "ancient" by New World standards and "glorious" by virtue of its traditions. Because of its rural nature, one South was prone to diseases such as malaria and malnutrition, and to the ills of underdevelopment such as illiteracy.[1] To the present day, most of the states of the other modern nation that rank at or near the bottom in health care, education, and social services were states of the failed southern rebellion. As late as the 1950s, the southern region of one nation languished with one-half the per-capita income of its sister regions. In 1936, the president of the other nation declared the South to be his nation's "No. 1 economic problem." In the U.S., conservative southern traditionalists are sometimes metaphorically called "Bourbons"; in Italy, the South actually had been a separate Bourbon kingdom.

In the respective histories of the two nations for the past century and a half, the most stubborn knot in the straight line toward national unity has been given the name "South," and the literature produced by and about these Souths is perennially coaxed to surrender an explanation of the problem. From historical novels written in the age of national unification or reconstruction to ethnographic accounts of visits to a South bypassed by an established nation, the literary histories of both nations exhibit similar evolutions. The parallels are more than coincidental. "South" becomes a "new place" not only by adding new geography and social reality to a pre-existing national map. "South" is also the name of the resistance to new narratives of cultural identity, resembling what James Clifford, in his study of modern literature and anthropology, has termed "ethnographic allegory": "Twentieth-century identities no longer presuppose continuous cultures or traditions. Everywhere individuals and groups improvise local performances from (re)collected pasts, drawing on foreign media, symbols, and languages."[2] The term *South,* especially when embedded in the discourse suggested by the ubiquitous phrase "The *Problem* of the South," signifies the knot of contradiction generated by nostalgia for "continuous cultures and traditions" in collision with the modern West's investment in progressive history, as limned in the successful histories of nations. "South" is not simply a problem in history but also a problem in promulgating a single nationalistic narra-

1. Dennis Mack Smith, "The Southern Problem," in *The Making of Modern Italy, 1776–1870* (New York: Harper Torchbook, 1968), 364; Martin Clark, *Modern Italy: 1871–1982* (London and New York: Longman, 1984), 36.

2. James Clifford, *The Predicament of Culture* (Cambridge: Harvard University Press, 1988), 14.

tive, and a comparative study of Italian and U.S. representations of "the South" illustrates a shared process of emergence from history to narrative, map to episteme.

In *Confederates in the Attic: Dispatches from the Unfinished Civil War* (1998), Tony Horwitz interviews several actual and virtual southerners in the U.S. as they re-enact a southern identity that is no longer continuous with their lived lives. Horwitz keys his investigations with a short memoir of his great-grandfather, a post-Appomattox Jewish immigrant who found one aspect of his new American history worthy of interest, if not veneration: the rebellious and defeated South. Horwitz's great-grandfather's adopted memories become the great-grandson's "Confederates in the attic," the problem of a "South" originating as lived experience but evolving into performative self.[3] If Horwitz presents a South lost in postmodern reenactments of itself, he nevertheless suggests a new temperament for southern cultural study: the study of improvisatory, migrant, perhaps even virtual Souths, appropriated as narratives by individuals and ad hoc groups more or less in the fix of diaspora. The historical South that fought a civil war for secession from the United States from 1861 to 1865 may serve as the vessel for the performative memories of diasporic "southerners" who, like Horwitz's great-grandfather, have no claim to continuous historical or cultural memory. This "new place" for the South in virtual memory rather than exclusively in corroborated history suggests the possibility of similar historical coincidences and dynamics in other national literatures.

American literary scholarship is not new to such comparative, nationalistic study. Latin American writers of fiction, with Vargas Llosa and García Márquez in the lead, have for decades laid claim to the influence of William Faulkner and the U.S. South of doomed imperial designs, guilt, defeat at arms, and oppression. Parallels in Italian and U.S. literature and history suggest strong possibilities for further comparative study of the evolving "place" of the South in national discourse. Some of the parallels imply that in "early" phases of national-cultural construction (that is, in times of national trauma when governments' attentions are explicitly aimed at nationalizing regions), familiar (i.e., Lukacs-ian) versions of the historical novel lend themselves to cultural work. With the passage of time and the accumulation of what James Clifford calls "modernity's inescapable momentum,"[4] the calculus of history and literature, event and

3. Tony Horwitz, *Confederates in the Attic: Dispatches from the Unfinished Civil War* (New York: Pantheon, 1998), 3–5, 389.

4. Clifford, *The Predicament of Culture*, 5.

text, becomes problematic. Adapting Clifford's model of the literary critic/writer as ethnographer in the latter half of this essay, I argue that parallels between Italian and U.S. representations of our southern problem(s) trigger similar politics and poetics. In what appears to be a late or "posthistorical" phase of southern identity, the cultural work of "South" is not so much nationalization as it is relief from the ennui of accomplished modernity. In this latter cultural environment, "South" seems to take on a complex of meanings far more intricate than those it carries in its historical-policy, or "early," incarnation. Bringing the laggard region up to national speed seems, to several constituencies, less desirable, less feasible, less possible. Northern or metropolitan intellectuals—such as, in the Italian case, Antonio Gramsci or Carlo Levi—seek to reformulate "the Southern Problem" within boundaries of reassessed politics and poetics. In the U.S., a similar complication might explain the cultural constructions of the South by Agrarian aesthetic-conservatives as well as progressive aesthetic-liberals (most notably James Agee and Walker Evans). My essay, then, is organized on an implicit historical time-line that runs quite plainly from early, through middle, to late.

Risorgimento and Reconstruction novels stand on a pedestal of cultural myth that is older, in both cases, than the nations eventually established in history. Students of southern literature in the U.S. are familiar with the regional typology that Thomas Jefferson enunciated in his letter to Chastellux in 1785:

In the North they are	*In the South they are*
cool	fiery
sober	voluptuary
laborious	indolent
persevering	unsteady
independent	independent
jealous of their own liberties and just to those of others	zealous for their own liberties, but trampling on those of others
interested	generous
chicaning	candid
superstitious and hypocritical in their religion	without attachments or pretensions to any religion but that of the heart[5]

5. Thomas Jefferson. "Letter to Chastellux, 1785," quoted in John Richard Alden, *The First South* (Baton Rouge: Louisiana State University Press, 1961), 17–18.

Jefferson made regional differences in climate generative of differences in human and social character. By proposing a graduated dichotomy, Jefferson also supplied the basic infrastructure for a narrative system: specifically, the encounter romance in which characters from one category (or region) clash with those from the other. In antebellum history, the encounter plot informs John Pendleton Kennedy's foundational novel in the plantation tradition, *Swallow Barn* (1832). During Reconstruction, the encounter plot evolved into the reconciliation plot, which heals the national dichotomy with marriage and the promise of offspring who reconcile opposing traits. Both sides used the romance of reconciliation to protect cultural memory: New Englander John Willliam De Forest romanced Unionist sympathies in *Miss Ravenel's Conversion from Secession to Loyalty* (1867), and diehard separatist Thomas Dixon took the opposite view (but the same narrative form) in *The Clansman* (1905). If the demographic situation was ripe for intersectional marriages, the literary situation was overripe for romances of reconciliation. William R. Taylor's *Cavalier and Yankee* (1961) is an early exploration of cultural propaganda by means of such regional stereotyping. Recent articles by Karen A. Keely and Jane Turner Censer suggest that cultural-studies methodologies have provided new ways of exploring the nexus of historical events and narrative structure.[6]

At virtually the same moment in the middle of the nineteenth century, Italy was undergoing a similar nationalization ("Risorgimento") of sectional differences along a north/south axis. The idea of nationhood came administratively, philosophically, and militarily from Camillo Cavour's Piedmont (North) and was resisted by the Bourbon Kingdom of the Two Sicilies—the South, also called informally *il mezzogiorno*. Both nations faced the challenge of creating one nation out of pockets of identity resistant to amalgamation. Like their counterparts in the U.S., Italian novelists used the historical novel with graftings of romance to negotiate the nationalizing process.

Pivotal works in the history of Italian literature had prepared the public for recognition of the intersectional romance. Alessandro Manzoni, like Kennedy in the U.S. antebellum period, reaps credit for anticipating the national purpose in Italian literature with *I Promessi Sposi* (1827),

---

6. Karen A. Keely, "Marriage Plots and National Reunion: The Trope of Romantic Reconciliation in Postbellum Literature," *Mississippi Quarterly* 51, No. 4 (Fall 1998): 621–48; Jane Turner Censer, "Reimagining the North-South Reunion: Southern Women Novelists and the Intersectional Romance, 1876–1900," *Southern Cultures* 5, No. 2 (Summer 1999): 64–91.

whose pair of lovers, Renzo and Lucia, are as universally known in Italy as Rhett and Scarlett are in the U.S.[7] Manzoni's classic strives, through the romantic plot of separated lovers overcoming dangers before finally embracing, to claim an essential Italian national character. Manzoni's lovers Renzo and Lucia are lovers across borders who endure political complications to the consummation of their love, an allegory of national striving. Generations of Italian readers know that once the lovers are united, national unity is part of the promise of their union.

Military action enriches literary material for the crucial unification novels of the latter half of the nineteenth century in both national settings. Works by Italian authors such as the Catanian Giovanni Verga, *Mastro-Don Gesualdo* (1888), and the Neapolitan Federico De Roberto, *I Vicere* (1894), deploy romance to plot new distributions of material, class, and cultural power in a nation in the process of becoming unified.

Verga follows the transfer of such power (via marriage) from the nobility, brought low by the "revolutions" leading up to nationhood, to an emerging bourgeoisie who make money and social position out of the wreckage of the aristocratic order. Verga's plot would be familiar to readers of U.S. Reconstruction novels: the marriage of a woman from a higher class and social order to a man from the lower who, despite his low status, possesses the energy and ambition to accumulate what the upper classes are losing. Gesualdo Motta is an international member of a class of U.S. southern characters represented by Ellen Glasgow's Nicholas Burr in *The Man of the People* (1900) and Faulkner's Flem Snopes in *The Hamlet* (1940). The plots of these novels follow money from the gentry to the underclass, raising the latter and turning the status quo topsy-turvy. Like Glasgow and Faulkner, Verga sees both fulfillment and failure for his upstart.

Echoing Flem Snopes, who marries the princess of Frenchman's Bend, Eula Varner, Gesualdo marries Isabella Trao, the daughter of the local grandee. Their successful and fruitful marriage should, on the allegorical level, predict the successful unification of competing interests in the political creation of Italy. Verga, however, is a pessimist. Gesualdo Motta's marriage to Isabella Trao is neither happy nor fruitful. Gesualdo is not as satanic as Flem Snopes; rather, he is confused by the rapid pace of his acquisition of land and money. The pre-Risorgimento caste system that had, like the caste system in the antebellum South, insured harmony

---

7. Spencer M. DiScala, *Italy: From Revolution to Republic* (2nd ed.; Boulder, Colo.: Westview Press, 1998), 49.

among social classes gave way to a bourgeois individualism that eventually threw a controlled market open to ungoverned forces. Faulkner used the Snopes clan to revel in the crass indignity of perpetual economic accumulation, penny by penny. Verga's novel diagnoses a similarly devalued social system. As Gesualdo continues to accumulate wealth, his chances for personal and family happiness disintegrate, for there is no tradition in which he can enjoy his gains. Like a recurring admonition, the peasant woman he *should* have married reappears in the text, each time a more faded hint of a prelapsarian happiness rooted literally and allegorically in the original Motta farm. As Gesualdo goes down in misery yet up in material wealth, he escapes into memories of a former happiness on the land—an Agrarian nostalgic dream. Verga's aristocratic characters have no such redeeming virtue.[8]

Federico De Roberto uses a similar plot to follow generations of the titled Uzeda family through the upheavals of revolution and republic in Sicily. *I Vicere* (1894) bears a strong formal resemblance to the U.S. Reconstruction romance. The Uzeda family parallels the often-represented southern plantation family. The Uzedas see their identity in terms of land held over generations, not in terms of their own work on the land, and in terms of inherited ("natural") social authority over the lower classes who do the work. One Uzeda son, Eugenio, becomes so obsessed with genealogy, and the social control it represents, that he goes mad, like the addled Jarman Posey in Allen Tate's *The Fathers* (1938), who likewise loses touch with reality by concentrating too much on his family's past. Another Uzeda son, Raimondo, bears a strong resemblance to Margaret Mitchell's Ashley Wilkes, the male inheritor of family and regional traditions who proves weak-blooded in times of upheaval. Raimondo's son, Consalvo, is a scoundrel-hero similar to Scarlett O'Hara. Both prosper in the new age, but the methods they use for survival mark them as predators who lack sufficient moral vision to know or care whom they hurt on their way to survival.

I Vicere begins with dynastic transfer: the matriarch of the house of Uzeda chooses the third son, Raimondo, for the patrimony. Raimondo appears to be the best defender of the family name and social position. He might also play a part in the reconciliation romance through his announced marriage to Matilde, daughter of a nobleman who had sup-

---

8. Giovanni Verga, *Mastro-Don Gesualdo* (Milan: Biblioteca Universale Rizzoli, 1987). An English translation by D. H. Lawrence (1925) is available (London: Daedalus, 1984).

ported the "rivoluzione del Quarantotto" ("the revolution of '48") and had subsequently suffered exile to Malta.[9] Yet, in the turbulent times from 1848 to 1861, Raimondo proves shallow. He confesses contempt for his benighted South and moves with his wife to cosmopolitan Florence as the Garabaldini sweep through Palermo.

Raimondo's son, Consalvo Uzeda, grows up during the "reconstruction" of Sicily, the "South" of *I Vicere*. During Consalvo's youth and early manhood, such progressive innovations as public works, paper money, and central banking come to his formerly feudal homeland. Consalvo, sensing like Scarlett O'Hara that there is money to be made in the wreck of a civilization, becomes mayor of his town. But his motives prove self-serving. He dresses municipal firefighters in new, flashy uniforms but does not improve service. Adhering to the policy that "image is everything," Consalvo runs the municipality into debt, then escapes to Rome as a deputy to the national assembly before the bills are due.

I Vicere is clearly not a bullish recommendation for reconstruction. De Roberto foresees a plethora of conditions undermining unification. His aristocrats prove adept at missing the point of nationhood altogether. Raimondo Uzeda, like Ashley Wilkes and Faulkner's Mr. Compson, wilts when the new order calls upon him. Consalvo, his son, disappears into the ranks of smooth profiteers—Scarlett without the charm.

Perhaps the most famous Italian novel on the reconstruction theme, Sicilian Giuseppe di Lampedusa's *Il Gattopardo* (1958; English translation as *The Leopard*, 1960),[10] takes a long, dreamy look back on the transition from traditional community to modern nation from the perspective of a well-established modern age. Di Lampedusa uses a simplified North/South schema. As the novel opens in May 1860, the Bourbon South is about to be replaced by a northern mechanism: the nation of Italy. Prince Fabrizio Salina, whose ancestors go back to the Byzantines, seeks refuge in Donnafugata, one of his several *latifundia*, or plantations, where he can still maintain the image of the feudal pyramid with himself at the apex. At Donnafugata, as on the southern plantation, history disappears and idyll prevails. The Prince's peasants (to his face) treat him

9. Federico De Roberto, *I Vicere* (Milan: Garzanti, 1993), 101.

10. Giuseppe Di Lampedusa, *The Leopard*, trans. Archibald Colquon (New York: Time Reading Program, 1966). The original was published in Italian in 1958 by Feltrinelli; first English-language publication, in Colquon's translation, in U.S. and U.K. 1960, by William Collins Sons, Ltd. and Pantheon Books. Further references are included parenthetically in the text.

with the kind of deference shown by traditional slaves to the master of the plantation; the Prince in turn shows them *noblesse*. But, like all idylls, this one cannot last. History forces its way back into the Prince's world in the person of Don Calogera Sedara—like Verga's Gesualdo Motta or Faulkner's Flem Snopes, one of the new men spawned by changes in the social and economic order.

The marriage of the Prince's son Tancredi to Angelina Sedara marks the beginning of the end, because the Sedara family, in spite of Angelina's personal beauty, represents the "ignorant vulgarity" of the unrefined underclass (130). The recession of the old aristocratic order results in a social and economic vacuum (or opportunity), and the Snopeses/Sedaras are inducted into a new order that exposes the ruthlessness of acquisition that years of aristocratic myth have burnished almost to a blinding sheen. Prince Fabrizio Salina himself succumbs to the inevitability of the new order when he declines nomination to the newly created office of senator—a nobleman with genealogical ties to Byzantium would only be dishonored by such a public title. He suggests Don Calogera Sedara instead. Di Lampedusa is quite clear on the Prince's motivation: the old aristocrat possesses too much inflexible pride in the old order, is too identified with/ in the Past. W. J. Cash, whose *The Mind of the South* (1941) is still cited as authoritative on such issues, sketched the U.S. version of this character type under the title "the savage ideal."[11]

The Leopard concludes in the early years of the twentieth century; the remnants of the Salina family are threadbare, and the Catholic authorities cart away their private religious relics to the trash heap. An older prelate, Father Pirrone, extols noblesse oblige and explains the hierarchical social order, like a true Old South cavalier, by invoking natural aristocracy (199–200). But that was 1861. The priest who comes to confiscate the survivors' religious charms "was not a Sicilian, not even a Southerner or a Roman, and many years before had tried to leaven with Northern activity the inert and heavy dough of the South's spiritual life in general and the clergy's in particular" (278).

Spiritual or economic, the life of the South is represented as resistant to "improvement" by the North. Reconstruction novels written during the Italian unification period, like those of Verga and De Roberto, tend to characterize the process of nationalization in a romance plot. Those like *The Leopard*, written in reminiscence of that period, hew to a similar plot structure but wrap nationalistic propaganda in a nostalgic, even re-

11. W. J. Cash, *The Mind of the South* (New York: Knopf, 1941). See Book One, chapter 3 for Cash's concept of "the savage ideal."

gretful, batting. The regions produce two different, and opposed, types of character and society. Amalgamation, touted as a plank in unification political programs, is in practice elusive or impossible. The peasants of *il mezzogiorno*, like the peasants of the U.S. South, are too miserably educated and too inured to centuries of feudal hierarchy to learn what their saviors from the North have to teach.

Antonio Gramsci, who knew "the Southern Problem" by virtue of being born and bred a Sardinian, could repeat the litany from his prison cell:

> It is well known what kind of ideology has been disseminated on a vast scale by bourgeois propagandists among the masses in the North: that the South is the ball and chain that is holding back the social development of Italy; that Southerners are biologically inferior beings, semi-barbarians or complete barbarians by natural destiny; that if the South is backward, the fault does not lie with the capitalist system or any other historical cause, but with Nature, which made Southerners lazy, inept, criminal and barbaric—only tempering this cruel fate with the purely individual explosion of a few great geniuses, who stand like solitary palm trees in an arid, barren desert.[12]

Gramsci wrote this in 1926, shortly before he was incarcerated by Mussolini. It could have been written by U.S. southerners of a range of political persuasions, the Vanderbilt Agrarians, or the Chapel Hill Progressives. Mencken's imagery in "The Sahara of the Bozart" (1917) uncannily echoes Gramsci's own "barren desert." The convergence of imagery, and the emergence of the South from historical discourse into ideology brings the Souths of the U.S. and Italy into even closer coincidence in the twentieth century.

The passage from history to ideology in both Italy and the U.S. can be traced in the deployment of the South in the formulation of political policy. With the dismissive phrase "it is well known," Gramsci implies that the ideological signifier "South" can be manipulated by anyone and for a range of purposes, not necessarily progressive. One such example of ideological manipulation occurs in Norman Douglas's *South Wind* (1920).[13] Set in a thinly disguised Capri, the island in the Bay of Naples

12. Antonio Gramsci, "Some Aspects of the Southern Question" (1926), in *Pre-Prison Writings*, ed. Richard Bellamy, trans. Virginia Cox (Cambridge: Cambridge University Press, 1994), 316–17.

13. Norman Douglas, *South Wind* (1920; New York: Modern Library, 1925). Further references will be included parenthetically in the text.

where Douglas lived a relatively open homosexual life, *South Wind* resembles its near-contemporary in Faulkner's early work *Mosquitoes* (1927). The same blurb could apply to both novels: as the south wind blows and the characters in both novels mostly just talk, their talk, in the "semi-barbaric" medium of the southern ideological climate, ranges freely over subject matters ruled out of order in northern, or official, discourse—desire, sex, taboo.

Early in *South Wind*, Douglas distinguishes between the English (northern) clergyman Mr. Heard, Anglican bishop of the African region of Tampopo, and the sophisticated southern Catholic priest, Don Francesco: "Worldly-wise, indolent, good-natured and, like most Southerners, a thorough-going pagan, Don Francesco was deservedly popular as ecclesiastic. Women adored him; he adored women. He passed for an unrivaled preacher; his golden eloquence made converts everywhere, greatly to the annoyance of the pyrrhic, the parish priest, who was doubtless sounder on the Trinity but a shocking bad orator and altogether deficient in humanity" (23). Douglas, deploying Gramsci's formula, depicts an ideological as well as a travelogue South where the undermining of official religion is as natural as the tides. Don Francesco's southernized character traits—indolence rather than industry, sensuality rather than moral strictness, style rather than doctrinal or intellectual rigor, warmth of humanity over analytical intellect—redistribute the authority of orthodox religion from doctrine to taste. In other words, in the figure of Don Francesco, desire cohabits with religion, and southernness as an inflection makes that mixture of pure and impure topics possible.

Another southerner in *South Wind*, Count Caloveglia, presents his own theories on what makes a southerner superior and distinct:

> "But as for other Northern men, the enlightened ones—I cannot help thinking that they will come to their senses again one of these days. Oh yes! They will recover their sanity. They will perceive under what artificial and cramping conditions, under what false standards, they have been living; they will realize the advantages of a climate where nature meets you half-way. I know little of England but the United States are pretty familiar to me; the two climates, I imagine, cannot be very dissimilar. That a man should wear himself to the bone in the acquisition of material gain is not pretty. But what else can he do in lands adapted only for wolves and bears?" (101–2)

Climate is at the foundation of all difference; the farther North one goes the more acquisitive and greedy, the farther South the more gracious and humane. The Count brushes up Thomas Jefferson's first draft.

Both Jefferson in the eighteenth century and Douglas in the twentieth plot culture on climate. Douglas, though, with a nation to critique rather than to build, loads the South with more positive traits. In this shift, we sense the move of history to narrative. This repositioning is perhaps clearer in *South Wind* in the words of another exile, the Scotsman Keith. In the character of Keith, Douglas utilizes the trope of the exotic, and with the exotic the outlines of James Clifford's ethnographic allegory appear: " 'Perhaps this capacity of the Southern scenery to bear a mortal interpretation accounts for the anthropomorphic deities of classical days. I often think it does. Even we moderns are unaccountably moved by its varying facets which act sometimes as an aphrodisiac, and sometimes by their very perfection, their discouraging spell, their innocent beauty, suggest the hopelessness of all human endeavour' " (224). The southern place, Keith goes on to say, is not simply natural. Rather, the South is a supernatural place where human ideas and moods are changed into religion. The North cannot be supernatural; it is always a place of spiritual exile. One's travel to the South becomes an allegory of character and cultural transfiguration: " 'They [the native people of Nepenthe-Capri-the South] do what you cannot so effectually do in the North; they humanize it, identifying its various aspects with their own moods, its features with their own traditions' " (224). Refuge in the "South," then, is refuge in what Clifford categorizes as the "exotic," an aesthetic and cultural artifact used "as a primary court of appeal against the rational, the beautiful, the normal of the West."[14] I contend here that, as nationalistic urgency wanes, South emerges as a cultural topos. Jettisoning its function as a denominator of place and condition, South—under the flag of "the exotic"—functions as the rejection of modernity. A new narrative supplants or revises the reconciliation romance narrative—the narrative of internal exile.

Historical circumstances—the continuing resistance of South to the economic progress of North—proved an ambivalent trigger mechanism for the function of South as exotic release. But, if the Souths in both national cases continue to be perceived and represented as backward and resistant to change and progress, there is a rear-guard contingent of northern intellectuals and aesthetes whose texts reveal a surreptitious interest in keeping the South "barbaric," a kind of internal rebuke to the triumphant state. Gramsci, from his ideological position as a Communist, clearly saw the bourgeois political interests to be protected by pre-

14. Clifford, *The Predicament of Culture*, 127.

venting a coalition of southern peasants and northern proletariat; he agitated to make both classes aware of the divide-and-conquer strategy. In his early writings, he only saw "the Southern Problem" in terms of politics, not in more fine-grained terms of cultural narrative. To a certain intelligentsia in both U.S. and Italian Norths, keeping the South primitive was a vital, if unacknowledged, interest. Clifford's study of modern enthnographers suggests one reason: the hunger in modernist consciousness for appropriating the Other as an antidote to its (our) own *anomie*. The professional ethnographers whom Clifford studies *needed* the Nuer or the Bororo, or exhibitions of their artifacts in metropolitan museums, as escape routes from the dead-end of bourgeois subjectivity. For other "ethnographers," however, the South functioned as an internal Other. Two texts, almost contemporary, illustrate this crossover of usages: James Agee and Walker Evans's *Let Us Now Praise Famous Men* (1941) and Carlo Levi's *Cristo si è Fermato a Eboli* (*Christ Stopped at Eboli*), published in 1945.[15]

Both books record the exile of urban intellectuals to their respective Souths. Agee was sent by *Fortune,* one of the publications in Henry Luce's magazine empire, in July 1936 to discover what was making the South the "nation's number one economic problem." Levi, a Socialist painter and writer from Turin who became a small stone in the Fascist shoe, was sent into internal exile in Basilicata, a remote and mountainous region south and inland of Naples, on the grounds that he harbored ideas harmful to Mussolini's state apparatus. He was shuttled from village to village lest the locals learn too much about the outside world from which he came. Levi's year of exile was 1935 to 1936, one year before Antonio Gramsci (considered a more lethal threat to the state) died in prison after ten years of a twenty-year sentence. Levi's written record of his exile was not published for ten years. The story of Agee, a writer, and Walker Evans, a photographer, is more widely known to U.S. readers. Evans, a documentary photographer with the Farm Security Administration, would produce in images what Agee would explain with the written word. Their site of "internal exile" was Hale County, Alabama, a fair U.S. equivalent to Basilicata.

To James Agee, even though he was born in Tennessee, the natives of the sharecropping, rural South were as exotic as undiscovered tribes in the Amazon rain forest. Every moment he spends with the Woods or

15. Ibid., 53, 193; James Agee and Walker Evans, *Let Us Now Praise Famous Men* (1941; rprt., New York: Ballantine, 1966), hereafter cited parenthetically in the text.

Gudger or Ricketts families is an encounter of ethnographer and primitive tribe, the initiating scene in the "ethnographic allegory," as Clifford might very well read it: "Moreover, all really simple and naive people incline strongly toward exact symmetries, and have some sort of instinctive dislike that any one thing shall touch any other save what it rests on" (141). Because, as he amply shows in his text, he sensed his own life as a maelstrom of sexual, political, aesthetic, and class anxieties, Agee-the-modern projects his desire for order on the poor. He strove for the exact symmetry and simple rest he imagined in Alabama primitives. Since the South is the reduced condition in which the "really simple and naive" do in fact exist, the South then is open for ideological and psychological appropriation by those who cannot generate simplicity on their own.

As he professes to try to understand their lives as "light, casual, totally *actual*" (203), Agee also clearly attempts to justify himself as the consumer of their lives' work. His supercharged prose appropriates their lives as an exhibit of folk objects—suitable for collection and museum display—and Evans's images seal the transaction. One of Agee's descriptions of a sharecropper shack is particularly implicated in his role as aesthetic consumer and curator. After minutely inventorying the things arrayed about the interior, Agee takes to meta-commentary: "It is my belief that such houses as these approximate, or at times by chance achieve, an extraordinary 'beauty.' In part because this is ordinarily neglected or even misrepresented in favor of their shortcomings as shelters; and in part because their esthetic success seems to me even more important than their functional failure; and finally out of the uncontrollable effort to be faithful to my personal predilections, I have neglected function in favor of esthetics" (181). At frequent junctures in *Let Us Now Praise Famous Men,* Agee invokes a modern pantheon of holy madmen—Blake, Celine, Kafka, and others—as if seeking identification with the visionary company of wretched, alienated moderns. He diagnoses his malady from theirs: he shares with them the modern problem of living a derivative life. All of his consciousness is secondhand and potentially otherwise. A particular scene metamorphoses in his vision from "rembrandt" to photograph, missing the original altogether (367).

This internal conflict is not lost on Agee; like Kafka, he is a connoisseur of his own suffering, guilt, and the psychic mechanisms that perpetuate them. In fact, retelling the story of his guilt functions as his attempt to exorcise it:

If I were going to use these lives of yours for "Art," if I were going to dab at them here, cut them short here, make some trifling improvement over here, in order to make you worthy of The Saturday Review of Literature, I would just now for instance be very careful of Anticlimax which, you must understand, is just not quite nice. It happens in life of course, over and over again, in fact there is no such thing as a lack of it, but Art, as all of you would understand, if you had had my advantages, has nothing to do with Life, or no more to do with it than is thoroughly convenient at a given time. (333)

Agee uses his exile first to exoticize the South, then to position himself within the Other in such a way as to feast on his guilt for not knowing or caring enough as a member of the class consuming it. A self-proclaimed Communist (often without the upper-case C), Agee found himself working for arch-capitalist Henry Luce, who owned *Fortune*. Clearly, as writer-employee, Agee suffered severe internal contradictions that the elemental life he imagined for the rural southern poor offset.

Levi creates the same prehistorical existence for the rural southern people to whom he was dispatched by a paranoid Fascist government. The title of Levi's memoir, as translated into English—*Christ Stopped at Eboli*—can be misleading. A more effective translation might be "Christ Never Got as Far as Eboli." Levi wished to signal with his title that Eboli, like the rural Alabama of Agee's memoir, had not yet entered History:

> Many years have gone by [Levi's opening chapter begins], years of war and of what men call History. Buffeted here and there at random I have not been able to return to my peasants as I promised when I left them, and I do not know when, if ever, I can keep my promise. But closed in one room, in a world apart, I am glad to travel in my memory to that other world, hedged in by custom and sorrow, cut off from History and the State, eternally patient, to that land without comfort or solace, where the peasant lives out his motionless civilization on barren ground in remote poverty, and in the presence of death.[16]

Like Agee, the modern Levi, far from the comforts of Turin in the North, loses his sense of time after a few days in the South. He becomes convinced that he has passed beyond or beneath history by living with a people who have themselves (like Agee's "primitives") been bypassed by modern life. To Levi, "magic" explains both the South's history and its metaphysics. Giulia, his first housekeeper, Levi ultimately decides, is a

16. Carlo Levi, *Christ Stopped at Eboli,* trans. Frances Renaye (New York: Time Reading Program, 1982), 1. Originally published by Einaudi as *Cristo si è Fermato a Eboli* in 1945. Subsequent references to this work will be given parenthetically in the text.

witch; nothing else can explain her power over him and the village. And Levi, who continued to paint while in exile, observes a young malarial boy mimic his gestures with cobbled-together materials, believing that a "painting" will appear like magic (217–18).

Also like Agee, instead of trying to interrogate the history that has marginalized the people he encounters in exile, Levi prefers to turn them into aesthetic objects by painting their portraits, their things, their landscapes. Evans's photographic images of the sharecroppers and their houses reified the special "beauty" that Agee reserved for the poor and labeled "classicism" (181–82). To his cosmopolitan eye, Agee confessed, usage of the word *classicism* obscured the real deprivation of means and materials that permitted only shacks, nothing like a house. And he was candid about the appropriation of those substandard dwellings as aesthetic objects: "To those who own and create it this 'beauty' is, however, irrelevant and undiscernible. It is best discernible to those who by economic advantages of training have only a shameful and thief's right to it: and it might be said that they have any 'rights' whatever only in proportion as they recognize the ugliness and disgrace implicit in their privilege of perception" (182). Evans's photographs, Agee's verbal fugues, Levi's portraits and memoir turn the southerners into commodities in an economy of aesthetic perception, a voyeurism—action was the (failed) response of an earlier time.

Levi himself blocks peasant action. Late in his exile, he is called to attend a man with a ruptured appendix. Levi had made, and reveled in, something of a reputation as a shaman by practicing rudimentary (but modern) medicine in the countryside. His jailers, fearful of this reputation, banned him from giving such aid. In the case of the man suffering the ruptured appendix, Levi notes, his aid would have done no good: the man was too far gone and Levi himself had no instruments or skill for the required surgery. Still, his peasants considered him a Dr. Schweitzer, and when news of the man's agonizing death reached the village, the peasants mobilized to revolt:

> Revolt was in the air. The peasants' deep sense of justice had been outraged and, gentle, passive, and resigned as they were, impervious to political reasoning and party slogans, they felt stirring in them the old spirit of the brigands. These downtrodden folk have always been given to wilful and ephemeral explosions. . . . That day, if I had wished, I might have put myself at the head of several hundred brigands and have either laid siege to the village or fled to the wilds. For a moment I was sorely tempted, but

in 1936 the time was not yet ripe. Instead, after considerable effort, I man-
aged to calm the peasants. (234–35)

Realistically, the peasants were probably better off not taking up arms
against the better-equipped and more numerous police. Ideologically,
however, it is also fitting that Levi prevented them from claiming agency
in history. The modern, enmeshed in the role of ethnographer, confesses
an interest in keeping the primitive in his/her place. If the aesthetic construct should speak, hail the "thief" in the act of making away with its
image, then the voyeur would be self-accused.

Agee has no solution to the material problem of the South either. Even
though he identifies himself "by sympathy and conviction a Communist," *Let Us Now Praise Famous Men* carries no call to action, no program (225). Agee might rail against other intellectuals who voice
ineffectual concern for the economic problems of the southern sharecropper, but he does not venture his own (even partial) solution. Levi, a Socialist, is less aloof. His call to action, however, preserves the South as a
kind of aesthetic enclave. Rejecting solely Fascist, Communist, and "even
Liberal" forms of government as wrong for the South, and for Italy, Levi
proposes a kind of mythic preserve for the rural South, a privileged historical and social status exempt from change and eerily like that proposed by the Twelve Southerners who contributed to *I'll Take My Stand*
(1930) (259). Those Agrarians were avowed conservatives, even proud
reactionaries, yet Levi's conclusion sounds, in part, like theirs:

> The State can only be a group of autonomies, an organic federation. The
> unit or cell through which the peasants can take part in the complex life
> of the nation must be the autonomous or self-governing rural community.
> This is the only form of government which can solve in our time the three
> interdependent aspects of the problem of the South; which can allow the
> co-existence of two different civilizations, without one lording it over the
> other or weighing the other down; which can furnish a good chance for
> escape from poverty; and which, finally, by the abolition of the powers and
> functions of the landowners and the local middle class, can assure the
> peasants a life of their own, for the benefit of all. (259–60)

Levi and Agee needed "the co-existence of two different civilizations,"
I would argue, not for political reasons having to do with the functions
and relative powers of classes and parties, but for psychological reasons
having to do with their respective senses of displacement as modern intellectuals faced with the economic rendering of their work and the lurking

sense of obligation and guilt they felt face-to-face with the conditions of "the wretched of the earth."[17] Borrowing that phrase from Fanon, I also suggest his concept of the co-opted bourgeois intellectual who is torn between identification with the victim and the pleasures of class favor. It was clear to Fanon—and, borrowing his clarity, arrestingly clear to us— that in both Italy and the U.S. the historical urgency of region gave way, over time, to its deployment in a network of cultural politics. This politics negotiates both more and less than the actual South. The absurd formulation "more and less" attempts to capture the reciprocal cultural politics of center and margin played out in the encounter of modern visitor and "South." "More" signifies the concrete thingness of object and relationship, figure and ground in the primitive; "less" the modern yet comparatively empty world of the modern.

The South functions in the earlier stage of nation-making as a tractable set of material circumstances which, by means of implementation of a political program, can be made to change from something unlike the self or center to another version of that center. Later, when it is clear that the problem of the South is its intractable Otherness, the problem rather than the solution becomes vital, and a different model—that of the ethnographer as critic—enshrines the South's changelessness. For it is that mythic changelessness that relieves the modern of the burden of history.

17. Frantz Fanon, *The Wretched of the Earth*, trans. Constance Farrington (New York: Grove, 1963).

North, South, East, West: Constructing Region in Southern and East German Literature

Christine Gerhardt

The emergence of a new regionalism that operates in the field of tension between a marked global dimension and an emphasis on decentered perspectives opens up challenging new vistas for the study of southern literature. Yet even though it is widely accepted that "area studies (national and regional) are usually done best . . . in a cross-cultural and comparative perspective," transatlantic comparisons have so far won surprisingly little attention. In this essay, I demonstrate how the study of regional literature from the American South can profit from a simultaneous discussion of East German texts. Specifically, I analyze how the characteristics of southern literature can acquire sharper contours through a reading that brings America's north-south antagonism into a cross-cultural dialogue with Germany's east-west dichotomy. This perspective highlights unexpected thematic parallels between the southern and East German literary traditions while at the same time underscoring how regional identifications can assume vastly different implications in specific cultural and political contexts.[1]

1. Thomas J. Schlereth, "Regional Culture Studies and American Culture Studies," in *Sense of Place: American Regional Cultures*, ed. Barbara Allan and Thomas J. Schlereth

For a transnational reading of southern literature, East German fiction—though commonly not regarded as regional—is well suited because southern literature and East German literature share a remarkable number of characteristics, particularly with regard to their parallel attempts to define, respectively, the American South and the German East as a distinct alternative to what was and still is perceived as the dominant culture (i.e., the American North and West Germany). The American South and the German East also share histories of regional secession and reunification, loss and defeat, inviting comparative analyses of the ways in which both regional literatures have tried to make sense of these formative crises. Furthermore, such a comparison sheds new light on Germany's currently most pressing regional conflict—the conflict between East and West German cultures. The intensity with which East Germans still disassociate themselves from the dominant German culture has even led to debates about an East German ethnic identity,[2] dramatically underscoring how central is the east-west dichotomy in Germany's regional landscape.

By defining East German literature as regional here, I do not mean to belittle East German fiction as small-scale, local-color literature, nor do I want to negate the forty-year existence of the GDR as a politically and economically independent state. Although regions have conventionally been defined as small parts of a nation, recent works in the field of regional studies have started to challenge all-too-rigid notions of the concept. Michael Steiner and Clarence Mondale, for instance, point out that whereas "in popular usage, a region is often thought to be of a certain scale, smaller than the nation and larger than the locality," cultural critics have "blurred conventional understanding of what size an area must be to be called a region." Particularly, the ways in which regional identifications persist across and beyond national borders, as in the Andes or in the former Yugoslavia, have led scholars to reconsider the applicability of the concept to increasingly unconventional regional constellations.[3]

(Lexington: University Press of Kentucky, 1990), 168. For an analysis of the ways in which such a comparative approach can be made productive in the classroom, see Christine Gerhardt, "Exploring Unexpected Regions: Teaching Southern Literature from an (East) German Perspective," *Profession 1999* (New York: MLA, 1999), 68–78.

2. Marc Howard, "Die Ethnisierung der Ostdeutschen," *Freitag: Die Ost-West Wochenzeitung,* 16 October 1998, 12.

3. Michael Steiner and Clarence Mondale, "Introduction," in *Region and Regionalism in the United States: A Source Book for the Humanities and Social Sciences,* ed. Michael Steiner and Clarence Mondale, Garland Reference Library of Social Science, no. 204 (New York: Garland, 1988), xiv; Ricardo J. Kaliman, "Unseen Systems: Avant-Garde Indigenism in the Central Andes," in *Regionalism Reconsidered: New Approaches to the Field,* ed.

Placing myself in the context of the current redefinitions of region, I regard the former GDR not as a mere subgroup of Germany, as some conservative historians would have it, but as a very distinct culture whose literature in particular speaks of a strong sense of an East German cultural identity. The case of the GDR shows, then, that not only a smaller or larger section of a country but a country itself can constitute a region—as a socially, politically, and culturally unified territory that displays not only a sense of pride and belonging but also a sense of its distinctness from the larger West German master culture.

This essay pairs six southern and East German short stories to show how region can function as a productive category of cross-cultural comparison, focusing on certain recurrent themes that dominate the construction of regional spaces in both literatures. As a starting point, Thomas Nelson Page's "Polly: A Christmas Recollection" (1887) and Willi Bredel's "Petra Harms" (1950) work particularly well, since they represent two ideals that have long dominated the cultural imagination in their respective regions—the myth of the aristocratic Old South and the myth of the socialist, egalitarian GDR. Even though published more than seventy years apart, they can still serve as a productive basis for a textual comparison, since both are closely linked to a key moment in the process of constructing a distinct (southern or East German) regional identity: "Polly" exemplifies the vastly popular plantation fiction of the 1880s, which after the Civil War, Reconstruction and its aftermath turned into a major field of romanticizing the Old South; "Petra Harms" belongs to the so-called East German *Aufbauliteratur,* a body of texts specific to the 1950s that addressed the practical and ideological challenges of building a socialist society in the first years of the GDR.

"Polly" is one of the lesser-known texts that Thomas Nelson Page included in his first collection of stories about the plantation South, *In Ole Virginia* (1887). Characteristically, the protagonists have to face challenges that threaten to upset the intricate social order of their idyllic world. Polly, a high-spirited southern belle who grew up on her uncle's plantation, has fallen in love with Bob, son of a poor farmer. Faced with her uncle's harsh disapproval, Polly secretly elopes to marry her sweetheart. In the end, however, Bob—who happens to be a distant relative—turns out to be a perfect gentleman, and the young couple is allowed to move back to the old plantation. As family harmony is reestablished, the

David Jordan (New York: Garland, 1994), 159–84; Petar Ramadanovic, "Language and Crime in Yugoslavia: Milorad Pavic's *Dictionary of the Khasars,*" ibid., 185–95.

inherent nobility of the southern aristocracy is once more reinscribed into the cultural memory of the entire nation.

The region that is constructed in this story is firmly linked to several core character types of the Old South. The paternalistic plantation-owner, a passionate and warm-hearted patriarch, dominates the scene: "Presently the Colonel came in, bluff, warm, and hearty. He ordered dinner from the front gate as he dismounted, and juleps from the middle of the walk, greeted Bob with a cheeriness which that gentleman in vain tried to imitate, and was plumped down in his great split-bottomed chair, wiping his red head with his still redder bandana handkerchief, and abusing the weather, the crops, the newspapers, and his overseer before Bob could get breath to make a single remark."[4] Even though the text subtly undercuts the old planter's position as a model of masculine nobility and unlimited powers, the other players in this well-known social drama reaffirm his symbolic status as they stick to the inferior roles assigned to them. The slaves, in particular, appear to be entirely unfit for a life independent of their "Marse." Following a staple pattern of the southern plantation myth, the lazy, permanently drunk, but utterly loyal slaves in "Polly" are the mainstay of the white elite—a typical yet highly ironic constellation that points to the inherent fragility of the southern economic and ideological system. Polly, too, plays her role to perfection: as charming, innocent southern belle, "dressed all in soft white, and with cheeks reflecting the faint tints of the sunset clouds" (211) and "surpass[ing] in loveliness the rose-buds that lay on her bosom" (216), she is the supreme symbol of southern stability and order. Yet when she runs off with her lower-class neighbor, she momentarily destabilizes the system, since her action is implicitly directed against the oppressive gender structures that mar southern Arcadia as much as its virulent racism does. The profoundly oppressive character of the plantation ideology remains visible even as the story culminates in an uncritical celebration of the old order. When the colonel consents to Polly's and Bob's marriage, he mockingly mentions that he is about to sell his niece, reformulating the occasional threat with which he used to address his slaves: " 'Damme if I don't sell you! Or if I can't sell you, I'll give you away—that is, if he'll come over and live with us' " (239). Such casual references to women and slaves as mere commodities in the region's political economy undermine

---

4. Thomas Nelson Page, "Polly: A Christmas Recollection," in *In Ole Virginia; or, "Marse Chan" and Other Stories* (New York: Scribner, 1890), 214. Subsequent references to this work will be given parenthetically in the text.

the idealizing rhetoric of this entirely uncritical recollection of the Old South.

At first sight, Bredel's story, which stands in the tradition of the proletarian, revolutionary writing of the Weimar Republic, seems to have little in common with Page's unspectacular romance about the southern aristocracy. In the East German text, a young female office worker, who is part of a nationwide effort to rebuild a small town after a natural catastrophe in the first year of the GDR, wants to work as a bricklayer. Challenging herself as much as her co-workers, she succeeds against all odds, becomes the leader of the bricklayers' brigade, and is eventually awarded a gold medal. Clearly, professional relationships rather than rigid social hierarchies structure Bredel's text. Instead of the private, family-centered southern community in "Polly," there is a socialist collective from which biological families are altogether absent, and the story culminates not in marriage and family reunion but in a political mass meeting: "Out of the loud cheering and applause a song emerges, and Petra knows that her collective started it."[5] The social and political ideals formulated in "Petra Harms"—solidarity, gender equality and a socialist work ethic in the interest of the common good—are also diametrically opposed to the norms and values of Page's Old South.

If one considers the prominence of stereotypical characters in "Polly," however, it becomes apparent that in Bredel's text, too, an ideal cultural space is invented via the perfectly orchestrated interaction of certain core characters who follow their prescribed roles. Even though their social position is tied not primarily to their class, race, and gender identity but to their role in the socialist production process, the characters in "Petra Harms" are hardly more individualized than their transcultural literary equivalents. One of the key figures is, for instance, the bricklayer Emil Kuntz, a prototypical member of the working class that assumes social, political, and cultural leadership in the East German system. His prominent position is structurally comparable to that of the southern planter. Their different social and political notions notwithstanding, Kuntz surveys the development of the younger generation much like the fatherly colonel, and just like the southern aristocrat, he is surrounded by a host of minor players—in this case, workers and peasants, students and journalists, local officials and politicians—who stabilize the system by fulfilling their assigned roles.

5. Willi Bredel, "Petra Harms," in *Frauen in der DDR: Zwanzig Erzählungen*, ed. Lutz-W. Wolff (München: Deutscher Taschenbuch, 1986), 25 (my trans.). Subsequent references to this work will be given parenthetically in the text. All translations are mine.

Curiously, Bredel's text also centers on an ideal female protagonist who personifies the region's social norms and values. Petra Harms envisions a life as an activist, building a better world designed for the common people: "Here in Bruchstedt she wanted to learn and to work, which she enjoyed and which best served the overall objective. She thought it wonderful to build with her own hands a home for people in which they would feel at ease" (20). However, Petra and Polly represent conflicting ideals of femininity. Unlike the beautiful, chaste belle who after a brief moment of rebellion willingly succumbs to male interests, the heroine of "Petra Harms" is a politically conscious activist to whom romance does not even occur and who is unwilling to have her professional options limited on the basis of gender: "He wanted to be a socialist, she asked, and explained to him right then what he was in her eyes: nothing but a senile, a thoroughly senile reactionary. This male arrogance was downright ridiculous. . . . And on top of it, to call her 'Miss'! It was unbelievable" (18–19). Yet even though the ideal southern belle and the hard-working heroine of an allegedly genderless socialist society occupy opposing positions on the scale of women's social roles, Page and Bredel apparently place the conflict over controversial standards of femininity at the heart of their regional self-definitions.

Both stories' sole reliance on characters who wholeheartedly support their political system also brings to the fore that the ideological makeup of the socialist, egalitarian GDR—just like that of the patriarchal, essentially feudal, and rigidly hierarchical Old South—leaves no room for dissenting voices. Specifically, the characters' repeated, passionate identification with communal living and working conditions in Bredel's text suggests that in the socialist framework, an overt interest in privately owned property would amount to treason. Ironically, the sheer force of the argument hints at a rather strong undercurrent of resistance against collectivism.

In what appears to be a stark contrast to Page, Bredel clearly uses art as a political instrument. Yet it is precisely the rather explicit argument of the East German text that throws into relief crucial parallels with the American story. First, "Petra Harms" focuses directly on the modes of socialist production. The story provides details about the skill of a bricklayer and also illustrates the principles of the so-called socialist competition, which is spurred not by higher wages but by a personal identification with socialist ideals. Combining high productivity with superior moral standards, Petra is a model socialist personality who realizes that boosting the national economy is necessary for the survival of the socialist vision. Even though Page constructs the plantation South as entirely private and familial space and excludes from his vision the harsh realities of slavery, the region's cultural self-definition is equally based on a particular (and highly controversial) economic system. Second, Bredel's heavily politicized rhetoric is obviously directed against West Germany, most evidently at the end of the story when party officials interpret the successful reconstruction of the town as a symbol of the moral superiority of East Germans: "The minister points out to the news reporters that this act of solidarity was unprecedented in the history of our people. Nothing showed more clearly than this achievement our intellectual and moral development" (23). Read in the context of the American story, this implicit critique throws light on the way in which "Polly" too was written against the dominant (northern) culture, even though it avoids direct references to it and displays a naïve and seemingly apolitical rhetoric. Third, the rebuilding of an East German small town, symbolically related to the (re)-construction of a distinct East German culture, underscores that in "Polly" literature also serves as a means to reconstruct a fragile regional identity in the midst of a collective cultural crisis. Clearly, Page, like Bredel, uses literature for political purposes even though his propaganda operates in more subtle and indirect ways. In a structurally similar fashion, both stories formulate entirely uncritical regional utopias from which the dire consequences of the respective mechanisms of oppressions are excluded.

Two other short stories, Charles Chesnutt's "The Passing of Grandison" (1899) and Stefan Heym's "Mein Richard" (1976), also invent the Old South and the GDR as distinct regional spaces, yet they do so from a radically different perspective. Highly skeptical of the political systems they are concerned with, they provide critical answers to the worlds of regional pride, harmony, and resourcefulness evoked by Page and Bredel. Interestingly, Chesnutt and Heym both explore the issue of escape from a region as a geographically and ideologically limiting space, thus enabling a comparative discussion of the ways in which culturally specific repressions and restrictions are represented in southern and East German fiction.

In Chesnutt's "The Passing of Grandison," the son of a southern planter tries to secretly free one of his father's slaves in order to win the respect of his future wife, a typical southern belle. The slave Grandison, however, ignores the numerous chances "Marse Dick" provides for him to escape; even after having been left with abolitionists in Canada, he walks back to his Kentucky plantation. The old planter celebrates his return excessively, only to find that a few weeks later Grandison actually does escape, this time joined by his entire family. Thus, what appeared to be a model slave who utterly identifies with his position turns out to be a highly complex, subversive figure who successfully hides his keen political awareness behind an inscrutable mask of subservience and fidelity.

Obviously, this story "is the ultimate parody of plantation fiction's favorite ploys—the tested young lover, the generous master, the faithful retainer."[6] Complete with all the major characters and plot elements that also structure Page's "Polly," Chesnutt's text works with the popular pattern that for decades dominated the region's cultural memory. What so profoundly unsettles the traditional narrative formula is the issue of escape—a concept that implies that someone manages to break free from a space he or she is otherwise forced to stay in, thus defining a cultural territory as circumscribed by rigid boundaries that certain groups of people are not allowed to cross.

In "The Passing of Grandison," the motif of escape is a key narrative element. Set in Kentucky in the 1850s, most local planters have followed the public trial of a northern "slave-stealer," and the fear of losing more of their valuable property via the Underground Railroad has started to dominate their daily lives: "[These rascally abolitionists are] becoming altogether too active for our comfort, and entirely too many ungrateful niggers are running away. I hope the conviction of that fellow yesterday may discourage the rest of the breed."[7] When young Dick Owens, who paradoxically interprets the slave-stealers' deed as a supreme act of chivalry and uses it as a model for his own courtship, proposes to travel north with a slave, his father, too, immediately refers to the prospect of escape: " 'I don't think it safe to take Tom up North,' he declared, with promptness and decision. 'He's a good enough boy, but too smart to trust among those low-down abolitionists. I strongly suspect him of having learned to read, though I can't imagine how' " (177). Acutely aware of their precarious situation, the regional elite is forced to distrust even its "good boys" and to suspect treachery at all times; since the most deadly mechanisms of control cannot prevent slaves from attempting to flee, the white southern self is honeycombed by pervasive fear and a growing sense of insecurity.

6. Lucinda H. MacKethan, "Plantation Fiction, 1865–1900," in *The History of Southern Literature*, ed. Louis D. Rubin Jr. et al. (Baton Rouge: Louisiana State University Press, 1985), 218.

7. Charles W. Chesnutt, "The Passing of Grandison," in *The Wife of His Youth and Other Stories of the Color Line* (Ann Arbor: University of Michigan Press, 1968), 176. Subsequent references to this work will be given parenthetically in the text.

This profound feeling of insecurity generates all the more pompous declarations of regional superiority and pride. In the case of the old colonel, for instance, the prospect of losing the slave who will accompany Dick triggers extensive references to the supposedly ideal design of the southern system: " 'I want to warn you, though, Grandison,' continued the colonel impressively, 'against these cussed abolitionists, who try to entice servants from their comfortable homes and their indulgent masters, from the blue skies, the green fields, and the warm sunlight of their southern home, and send them away off to Canada, a dreary country . . . where, when runaway niggers get sick and can't work, they are turned out to starve and die, unloved and uncared for' " (180). For a moment, even Grandison joins the argument: " ' 'Deed, suh, I would n' low non er dem cussed, low-down abolitioners ter come nigh me, suh. I'd—I'd—would I be 'lowed ter hit 'em, suh?' " (180). Yet the later developments of the plot, particularly Grandison's unexpected escape, unveil the utter falseness of the myth of white southern benevolence and of the "faithful slave" who desires the protection that this supposed benevolence grants him. Even the most tightly woven argument of the plantation as family institution cannot induce a slave to choose bondage—except as a rhetorical tool to outwit his owners.

The repeated outbursts of southern pride, provoked by the impending threat of large-scale escapes, also expose a curious obsession with "those cussed abolitionists." As Chesnutt's story so aptly shows, the region's self-image is inextricably linked to an ideological competition with the North. The colonel urges his son to "keep [his] eyes and ears open to find out what the rascally abolitionists are saying and doing" (176), and he is so concerned about the northern strategy to use stories of runaway slaves for their political purposes that he suggests an interview with his "abolitionist-proof" slave in order to undermine this propagandistic scheme: " 'I really think,' the colonel observed to one of his friends, 'that Dick ought to have the nigger interviewed by the Boston papers, so that they may see how contented and happy our darkeys really are' " (189). Not only does the colonel misinterpret Grandison's actions, his remarks also betray a keen awareness of the other side's ideological power. The antebellum South emerges as a region that has long lost control over its own destiny: in the face of massive threats, the ruling class, blinded by its own pretensions, maintains its impotent rhetoric of regional pride.

Heym's story "Mein Richard" also deals with a paradoxical escape from a rigidly fenced-in space, in a way that intersects on several levels with Chesnutt's ironical view of the Old South. The text addresses the controversial topic of East Germans illegally leaving their country via the Berlin Wall: seventeen-year-old Richard and his friend have crossed the so-called antifascist bulwark fourteen times—through a window of Richard's home right next to the wall. Yet all they ever did in that other Germany so utterly different from their own was to go to the movies, after which they always promptly returned from their clandestine excursions. However, when the East German secret police find out about these precarious acts of transgression, the boys are put on trial and sentenced to prison. Only at the very end of the story does the boys' lawyer comment on the strange irony of the situation, addressing the district attorney: "If I were you, comrade, I would have awarded the two boys a gold medal. . . . Because they have, as it is now known to the court, demonstrated their utter loyalty towards our Republic fourteen times in a row."[8]

Set in a time when the GDR, after a period of more relaxed domestic politics in the early 1970s, returned to Stalinist methods of repression, "Mein Richard" sheds a critical light on the region so fervently praised in affirmative texts such as Bredel's "Petra Harms." In part, Heym's commentary is so effective because it employs the literary conventions of socialist realism. The text is dominated by faithful party members and representatives of the working class, as for instance Richard's mother, "an old comrade and the widow of an old comrade who always stood in a position of responsibility" (331), who mechanically refers to the dominant ideology as she tries to comprehend the situation. Also, the story addresses aspects of the ideological education of East Germans; specifically, it provides insight into the prominent role that official social activism played in people's everyday lives:"Monday had been the meeting of the Democratic Women's Union, Tuesday the union leaders' meeting, discussion of the collective contract for the plant; . . . Wednesday was the German-Soviet Friendship meeting" (333). These structural elements, which are reminiscent of Bredel's text, suggest that East German literature, too, is characterized by certain stock characters, places, and even (sub-)plots that set this region apart from the West German master culture—much like regional literature from the American South.

Yet just as Chesnutt's text works with but critically undermines the conventions of southern plantation fiction, Heym employs elements of socialist realism to tell an entirely different story. Again, the issue of es-

---

8. Stefan Heym, "Mein Richard," in *Gesammelte Erzählungen* (München: Goldmann, 1990), 348 (my trans.). Subsequent references to this work will be given parenthetically in the text. All translations are mine.

cape is what disrupts the dominant narrative pattern. Reminiscent of the planters in "The Passing of Grandison," official representatives of the East German working class are obsessed with the problem and highly aware of the personal and larger political consequences of any successful attempt to cross the border: "As an old comrade I knew how comrades reacted to repeated violations of the passport law on the part of the son of a comrade" (342). Always on the alert in the face of this omnipresent danger, East Germany is saturated with a fundamental insecurity: "One has to have an eye on one's children nowadays; they have learned to say one thing and to think another" (331). Here, too, the mere suspicion that anyone might transgress the rigidly defined regional boundaries activates excessive references to the official political rationale.

In a striking parallel to what happens in Chesnutt's story, the East German political elite refers to socialism's supreme interest in the well-being of its inhabitants and stresses that the laws of the working-class state need to be respected: "The lawyer read something about the antifascist bulwark as a bulwark in the struggle against imperialism, and how our youth in their vast majority show through their words and actions that they understand its significance quite well and appreciate it—unlike the two culprits" (343). Considerable energy is expended to interpret the severe limitations in people's local mobility as a safety measure that protects the region from what lies beyond it. Yet the official rhetoric also unveils that there is a homology between the white southern fear of northern print media in Chesnutt's text and the extent to which East German political decisions are determined by an obsession with West German propaganda machinery. In "Mein Richard," the worst of regional nightmares has already come true—a West German journalist has interviewed the "escaped" boys, causing a fit of anger back east: "They even went so far as to boast about their deeds to representatives of the West German press, thus ridiculing the laws and institutions of our republic and providing grist for the imperialist propaganda mills" (343–44). Regardless of the fact that the two boys never planned to actually run away and that they told the journalist nothing but their harmless story, the representatives of the East German order are so caught up in the need to defend the boundaries of their region that they confuse the boys' naïve curiosity with treason. Reminiscent of the planters in "The Passing of Grandison" who hail the slave's return without suspecting the intricate design of his plan, the German officials also misread the true content of the protagonists' actions. In each case, a paradoxical pattern of escape and return undermines the myth of the region as utopian space whose boundaries protect its inhabitants from the hostile outside world—be it northern American or West German capitalism.

The particular circumstances of return, however, also distinguish Heym's critical reflection on East Germany's geographical and political restraints from Chesnutt's story about the slaveholding South. The fact that curiosity and a spirit of adventure are interpreted as serious offense accentuates the spatial limitations of the region and the narrowness of its ideology alike; yet that the boys always returned to stay indicates that life in the GDR cannot be compared to slavery—not even structurally. Even though both systems severely circumscribed people's human rights, a simple equation of American slavery with Stalinist repression would erase the specificities of both systems. This difference is inscribed in the texts themselves: whereas Chesnutt clearly denounces the practice of slavery that shaped the South's regional identity, Heym's text, though no less critical, addresses specific problems of East Germany without necessarily dismissing the entire regional economic and cultural system.

Eudora Welty's "No Place for You, My Love" and Gabriele Eckart's "Feldberg and Back" provide yet another perspective on this particular cross-cultural dialogue. As they view the American South and the German East through the eyes of regional outsiders who fail to establish a lasting relationship to the place they visit, they bring to the fore an issue that shapes the invention of regional spaces in all six texts discussed here—the strained relationship between a geographically, socially, and politically distinct region and the dominant culture that lies beyond it. Americanists working in the field of regional studies have long observed that "regional groups perceive themselves by making reference to how they perceive other groups and how they imagine *other* groups perceive them,"[9] which is precisely what happens in these two texts. Here, the patterns of cross-regional (mis)understanding that evolve between the inhabitants of a region and outsiders who represent the respective dominant culture challenge widespread stereotypes regarding region and regionalism in the U.S. and Germany. Read against the stories by Page and Bredel as well as those by Chesnutt and Heym, these texts demonstrate that the difficulties to communicate across regional boundaries are a key force in the regional imagination of the American South and the German East.

In "No Place for You, My Love," two northern visitors are hopelessly displaced in New Orleans in the late 1970s. Together, they decide to

9. Schlereth, "Regional Culture Studies," 173–74.

travel to the southern tip of the region, to "south of South."[10] But even
though both are longing for a more intimate relationship, they fail to relate to each other; in the end, the woman realizes only that "had she
waked in time from a deep sleep, she would have told him her story"
(480). What makes this story interesting in a regionalist framework is
that this utter inability to love is strongly linked to the ways in which
place is perceived in this story. The northerners' uneasiness in this strange
southern neighborhood and the estrangement between them powerfully
reinforce each other: "They were strangers to each other, both fairly well
strangers to the place" (465). Throughout the story, each silently speculates about the other's possible spouse. They hardly talk. When they finally dance with each other, they do so like "Spanish dancers wearing
masks" (478). The same preconceived expectations that keep them from
relating to each other preclude the possibility of communication with the
foreign region. Suffering from hordes of mosquitoes and the "*degrading
heat*" (467), both are unwilling or unable to shed their northern arrogance and keep comparing the Louisiana wilderness to their hometowns:
" 'It's never like this in Syracuse,' he said. 'Or in Toledo, either' " (471–
72). They may be well equipped with their fast car and a new map, but
the landscape they are rushing through offers no familiar signs to hold
on to. Their sense of place remains vague and dreamlike: "It was a
strange land, amphibious—and whether water-covered or grown with
jungle or robbed entirely of water and trees, as now, it had the same loneliness. He regarded the great sweep—like steppes, like moors, like deserts
(all of which was imaginary to him); but more than it was like any like-
ness, it was South" (479). Unable to read southern nature's unfamiliar
signs, they remain strangely illiterate. Later, on a ferry that is jammed
with local natives, their silence turns them into outsiders even amidst a
cheering crowd: "They were having such a good time. They all knew each
other. Beer was passed around in cans, bets were being loudly settled and
new bets made, about local and special subjects on which they all doted.
. . . everybody said something—everybody else" (469). When the two return as nameless strangers, the inability to communicate with another region becomes a metaphor for human isolation. Marjorie Pryse has argued
that regionalist stories "often provide readers with examples of cross-
cultural interaction that will not work; it is as if regionalist writers want

---

10. Eudora Welty, "No Place for You, My Love," in *The Collected Stories of Eudora
Welty* (New York: Harcourt, 1980), 480. Subsequent references to this work will be given
parenthetically in the text.

to make sure their readers can recognize the need for empathy by illustrating what happens when it is not present."[11] Welty's story functions precisely along these lines, facing readers with the challenge to relate to an other and with the difficulties of reading across cultural boundaries.

Eckart's "Feldberg and Back" similarly tells a story about the problems of transregional communication and can be read as an East German response to Welty's exploration of this particular theme. Here too a curious outsider enters a cultural region that is both strange and oddly familiar to him, and here too an erotic relationship fails. Armin, a West German visiting the GDR, meets Cornelia from East Berlin. The two spend the day together and are strongly attracted to each other, yet when Armin has to leave, Cornelia decides to terminate the relationship by giving him a fake address.

As in Welty's story, the region emerges as a place of difference that resists immediate "understanding," a cultural space that poses considerable communicational difficulties for those who approach it from a position of power. A successful physician who has traveled around the world, Armin is caught in his romantic notions about the authentic and "pure" East, looking for a new adventure: " 'Well,' said Armin, 'isn't this a bit of paradise? One doesn't have to go hiking across Malaysia with a backpack.' "[12] His insights remain limited because, like the two northern visitors in "No Place for You, My Love," he depends on the cultural difference for his own sense of identity. The conversation with the young woman from the East proves to be particularly difficult because they speak different languages:

> "That's how I became a Berlin resident," he concluded.
> "Cornelia corrected him: "*West* Berlin resident."
> He laughed, said something that included the word *Wall.*
> She corrected him: "*national border.*" (84)

Faced with such unexpected communicational barriers, the West German repeatedly pulls back and tries to evade such difficult issues: " 'Let's drop the subject,' the man said accomodatingly, 'otherwise we'll never get to the lake' " (85).

Yet Eckart's vision differs from Welty's in significant ways. Unlike the

---

11. Marjorie Pryse, "Reading Regionalism and the 'Difference' It Makes," in *Regional Reconsidered,* ed. Jordan, 56.

12. Gabriele Eckart, "Feldberg and Back," in *Hitchhiking: Twelve German Tales,* trans. Wayne Kvam (Lincoln: University of Nebraska Press, 1992), 88. Subsequent references to this work will be given parenthetically in the text.

two northerners in Welty's story, Cornelia and Armin do engage in a complicated and rather painful, but nonetheless productive cross-regional dialogue—with each other as well as with the eastern landscape. Compared to the utter inability of the two northerners to relate to one another in "No Place for You, My Love," Armin and Cornelia truly engage with each other as representatives of opposing regions, explore their mutual stereotypes and manage to address some of their contradictory political views. For instance, when Armin questions her identification with the socialist world view ("Isn't that too easy?" [89]), the seemingly narrow-minded East German proves to be rather critical of the GDR and exposes Armin's political naïveté by telling him about her negative experiences with the system: " 'If you've expressed your opinion three times without results, the fourth time you forget about it,' she said. 'And then how much of yourself have you got left? Just don't make trouble, always be careful who you are saying something to. Do you think that's good, too?' " (86). For a brief moment, the text demonstrates the possibilities of dialogue across vast cultural and political differences, between two people precariously caught between two antagonistic regions. Reminiscent of what happens in Welty's story, the communication between the protagonists is paralleled by the ways in which they relate to the landscape they are visiting. Armin and Cornelia spend the day getting to know a part of East Germany and its people: "When they had gone, Cornelia said: 'But we already knew that.' He smiled. 'It's nice the way one gets information here' " (85). Yet whereas the two northerners in "No Place for You, My Love" lose their way in the New Orleans swamps— "crawling hides you could not penetrate with bullets or quite believe, grins that had come down from the primeval mud" (468)—the East and West German enjoy a pleasant hike, eat wild berries, and swim in a lake—an almost total immersion of the stranger in the other region's environment that suggests nourishment and harmony. Led by their common curiosity, they make surprising discoveries:

> Then a surprising view opened to them.
> Beyond the lake a sandy slope. The sun, having made its way through the cloud cover, turned it the color of ocher.
> Reddish roofs in the background.
> The man turned toward her. "Do you see?"
> He seemed cheerful and relaxed, his face was almost handsome. She regretted her suspicion. (87)

Formulated at a time when the official political developments indicated that both German countries might enter a phase of open dialogue and cooperation, Eckart's story suggests that some Germans have developed strategies that allow them to tap communicative resources even under exceedingly difficult circumstances. Read against this vision, the utter silence in "No Place for You, My Love" appears to be all the more appalling since almost a century after the escalation of regional conflicts in the Civil War, North and South seem to be more estranged from each other than ever.

Eckart, however, does not create a myth of mutual understanding across the Berlin Wall. In "Feldberg and Back," the cross-regional dialogue fails mainly because of the severe structural constraints connected to the isolationist self-definition of the East German region. Right at the beginning of the story, Cornelia seems unwilling to let go of her ideological bias and uses official East German rhetoric to protect herself from questions that undermine her identity: "I just took an examination in civics. When you see a West license, you think: enemy of the working class" (81). During her increasingly open talk with Armin, she remains hesitant: "And if he happened to be a journalist and her wailing showed up next week in the *Spiegel*?" (94). Here, Eckart takes up what seems to be one of the recurrent motifs in southern as well as East German regional fiction, the persistent fear of the dominant culture's political press. In the end, Cornelia returns to familiar patterns of binary thinking and refrains from trying to establish a lasting relationship with Armin: "What was she getting herself into? With a *man from West Berlin*" (92). Read against Welty's "No Place for You, My Love," Eckart's story aptly illustrates the pitfalls of constructing a cultural region as a closed system that does not allow for cross-regional communication. In the case of East Germany, regional identifications that can satisfy the human longing for a familiar place and a stable community have been dominated by limiting and outright oppressive impulses—so much so that an otherwise dynamic line of difference is turned into a rigid means of enclosure.

On the most general level, such a transnational juxtaposition of southern and East German texts shows that the concepts of region and regionalism can function as a productive model for constructing cultural identities in vastly different social, political, and economic contexts. Interestingly, the American South with its characteristic intersections of regionalism, sectionalism and nationalism, the particular historical transformations of regional consciousness, and its intricate network of race, class, and gender hierarchies emerges as a remarkably well-suited reference point for the analysis of regional identity formations in other cultures. For Germany, such a comparison draws attention to the multicultural and especially multiregional character of its national landscape, an aspect that has only recently started to receive critical attention. With regard to the specific structural parallels between southern and East German regional literatures, the comparison discloses that both regions draw definitional certainty from their perception by the respective dominant culture—a shared preoccupation that manifests itself in a number of common plot patterns and topoi. Apart from a distinctly textual interest, such regional commonalities can also add an important "marginal" perspective to the dynamics of the transatlantic dialogue, particularly in a time when the U.S. and Germany are faced with a new quality of American-European relationships in an increasingly globalized world.

"Of the Same Blood as This America and Its History": William Faulkner and Spanish American Literature

Deborah Cohn

Faulkner's influence on Spanish American writers has been a topic of great critical interest for the past sixty years. In 1997, in honor of the centennial of Faulkner's birth, Gabriel García Márquez wrote that:

> Ever since I first read Faulkner in my twenties . . . he has seemed to me to be a writer from the Caribbean. This became more apparent when I tried to describe settings and characters from Macondo, and I had to make a great effort to keep them from resembling those of Faulkner. . . . A few years went by before I discovered the key to the problem; the Caribbean is poorly delineated. It is not a geographical area around the sea, but, rather, a more vast and complex region, with a homogeneous cultural composition which extends from northern Brazil to the U.S. South. Including, of course, Yoknapatawpha County. Within this realistic conception, not only Faulkner, but the majority of the novelists from the U.S. South, are writers possessed by the demons of the Caribbean. But it was Faulkner who showed me how to decipher them.[1]

1. Gabriel García Márquez, "William Faulkner 1897/1997," in *A Faulkner 100: The Centennial Exhibition. With a Contribution by Gabriel García Márquez,* ed. Thomas M. Verich (University, Miss.: University of Mississippi Library Special Collections, 1997), n.p.

This is, of course, an echo of his famous declaration in 1968 that "Yok-napatawpha County has banks on the Caribbean Sea; so in some way Faulkner is a writer from the Caribbean, in some way he's a Latin American writer."[2]

From the early 1930s to the present, authors such as Jorge Luis Borges, José Donoso, Carlos Fuentes, Gabriel García Márquez, Lino Novás Calvo, Juan Carlos Onetti, Juan Rulfo, Mario Vargas Llosa, and many others have claimed to find in the southerner a model who helped them to forge a style that they could consider their own. The fact that the Spanish American authors seemed to find in the South a region whose difficult past and present reminded them of their own—in Borges's words, Faulkner's world was "of the same blood as this America and its history"—further facilitated his making inroads into Spanish American fiction. The whys, wherefores, and hows of Faulkner's legacy are the subject of the following discussion. I will not attempt to exhaust all of the different means and instances of his influence, for these have been very well documented by numerous scholars over the years. Rather, I will identify general trends in the rewritings of his works between 1950 and the mid-1970s, with the hope of delineating his role in the development of the Spanish American "new narrative" and the Boom. I will conclude by showing how he has continued to influence younger generations of writers in a different manner with an analysis of his presence in the works of contemporary Puerto Rican writer Rosario Ferré. Several questions that I will address are: which of Faulkner's works were most influential? why? and were there any specific aspects of these works that Spanish American authors found particularly compelling? The answers to these questions, I believe, suggest that Faulkner's influence was critical precisely because it inspired the Spanish American authors not just to rework his templates but to make them their own, expressing through them some of their deepest concerns about their own nations' future.[3]

This essay was first published in *Do the Americas Have a Common Literary History?* ed. Barbara Buchenau and Annette Paatz (Frankfurt: Peter Lang, 2002). Brief sections of this essay also appeared in *History and Memory in the Two Souths: Recent Southern and Spanish American Fiction* (Nashville: Vanderbilt University Press, 1999), and are reprinted with the permission of the publisher.

2. Gabriel García Márquez and Mario Vargas Llosa, *La novela en América Latina: Diálogo* (Lima: Carlos Millá Batres/Universidad Nacional de Ingeniería, 1968), 52–53. This and all further translations from this work are mine.

3. For a discussion of this topic, see Cohn, *History and Memory in the Two Souths*, ch. 1.

As an aside, it should be noted that although the subject of Faulkner's influence has traditionally been the domain of Latin Americanists, recently it seems not just to have crossed the disciplinary boundary line between literature departments but to have become a central question for Faulknerians as well: an entire recent double issue of the *Faulkner Journal,* one of the field's most prestigious journals, was dedicated to the subject of "The Latin American Faulkner."[4] Prominent critics such as Philip Weinstein and Richard H. King are exploring the question of influence within a postcolonial context. And the quotation from García Márquez that opens this essay was the final piece in the centennial exhibition of one hundred items of Faulkneriana sponsored by the University of Mississippi in 1997. Billed as "an admirer of Faulkner, and a writer who is indelibly associated with the number one hundred," García Márquez was invited by the exhibition's organizer to contribute because he was "the one contemporary writer I thought a magisterial match for Faulkner, and the one writer I most wanted to contribute to our catalogue."[5] These trends offer, in my view, much hope for a fruitful interdisciplinary dialogue.

Interest in Faulkner initially evolved in tandem with the transformation of Spanish American literature occasioned largely by the dissemination of Euro-American modernism. The circulation of modernist works (most notably those of James Joyce, Franz Kafka, Marcel Proust, and Virginia Woolf, in addition to Faulkner, of course) began in Spanish America in the 1930s, mainly through translations (French as well as Spanish) and criticism appearing in the Argentine journal *Sur.*[6] Techniques such as narrative perspectivism, a lack of authorial direction, interiorized narration, the rejection of linear time and chronological order, and long, fluid sentences that disregarded grammatical conventions were widely adopted as they offered welcome alternatives to the constraints

4. *Faulkner Journal* 11, Nos. 1–2 (Fall 1995/Spring 1996).

5. Philip Weinstein, "Can't Matter/Must Matter: Setting up the Loom in Faulknerian and Postcolonial Fiction," in *Look Away! Comparatist Approaches to U.S. Southern Literature,* ed. Jon Smith and Deborah Cohn (Durham: Duke University Press, forthcoming); Richard H. King, "Faulkner and Latin America: Escaping the South" (paper presented at the British Association of American Studies Conference, University of Birmingham, April 1997); Thomas Verich, ed., *A Faulkner 100,* n.p.

6. For information on the publication and reception of Faulkner's works in Spanish America, consult Arnold Chapman, *The Spanish American Reception of United States Fiction: 1920–1940,* University of California Publications in Modern Philology 77 (Berkeley: University of California Press, 1966); and Fayen, *In Search of the Latin American Faulkner.*

of the realist and regionalist narration that dominated Spanish American literature in the first half of this century. We find them, moreover, to be the foundations of the marvelous real, baroque, and fantastic discourses whose foregrounding of difference permitted the expression of amplified and otherly conceptions of reality, thus rendering them narrative correlatives to ongoing efforts to establish national and regional identities. At the same time, these literary transformations formed part of the broader contemporary process of what José Donoso described as the "internationalization" of Spanish American culture, which went hand in hand with the development of a sense of a continental consciousness. Lois Parkinson Zamora characterizes the 1930s through 1960s as giving rise to "an unprecedented literary conversation," in which writers read and responded to one another's works, "emphasiz[ing] the communal nature of their literary project . . . self-consciously engaging, and in some sense also creating, a reality shared by the many countries and cultures of their region." During these years, authors such as Fuentes and García Márquez openly declared that they wrote as Latin Americans, rather than, in Donoso's words, writing for their "parishes."[7] The cultural effervescence of this period, which was even greater following the Cuban Revolution of 1959, was evident on the literary scene in the dramatic increase in literary production, much broader distribution of new works to a non–Spanish American and non-Spanish-readership, and the aforementioned renovation of technique and style, the so-called "Boom" in which Spanish American literature entered and became a full participant in the international "mainstream."

What concerns me most within the context of this general movement toward developing a collective identity and a discourse through which this could be expressed is the question of why it is that, of all the modernists, the Spanish Americans gravitated toward Faulkner so overwhelmingly, and why he—and virtually he alone—continues to be the object of homage and tributes. I have argued elsewhere that Spanish American authors saw in the South, its defeat in war and resulting sense of regional difference and marginalization, its experience of poverty, underdevelopment, and neocolonization by the North, as well as its difficult race relations, a set of experiences akin to their own nations' struggles to break the yoke of colonialism and dependency, and to break out of the "back-

---

7. José Donoso, *The Boom in Spanish American Literature: A Personal History*, trans. Gregory Kolovakos (New York: Columbia University Press, 1977), 9–10, 11; Zamora, *Writing the Apocalypse*, 20–21.

ward" position to which they had been relegated.[8] That is, in addition to the appeal of his stylistic and technical experimentation, Faulkner described a world that resembled their vision of Spanish America. Time and again, they claimed both the southerner and his homeland as their own. As Fuentes, who has often acknowledged his debt to Faulkner, once told an American audience, Sinclair Lewis "is yours, and as such, interesting and important to us. William Faulkner is both yours and ours, and as such, essential to us. For in him we see what has always lived with us and rarely with you: the haunting face of defeat."[9] Thus the Spanish Americans, many of whom further saw the rejection of realism as the cornerstone of their efforts to break free of their dependence on cultural models inherited from Spain, were drawn to Faulkner's unique symbiosis of content and a nonrealist style as a model for representing their own realities and, ultimately, a point of departure for forging their own identities.[10]

8. See Deborah Cohn, " 'He Was One of Us': The Reception of William Faulkner and the U.S. South by Latin American Authors," *Comparative Literature Studies* 34, No. 2 (1997): 149–69; and Cohn, *History and Memory in the Two Souths.*

9. Carlos Fuentes, "Central and Eccentric Writing," in *Lives on the Line: The Testimony of Contemporary Latin American Authors,* ed. Doris Meyer (Berkeley: University of California Press, 1988), 111–25.

10. Rulfo once remarked that the literary models most popular during his school years represented the "worst of Spanish literature": "Pereda, the Generation of '98 . . . I knew that was the backwardness of Spanish American literature: the fact that we were absorbing a literature that was foreign to our character and disposition." Quoted in Luis Harss and Barbara Dohmann, *Into the Mainstream: Conversations with Latin American Writers* (New York: Harper & Row, 1967), 272. Chilean novelist Jorge Edwards rejects most of the Spanish tradition, including even the later and more innovative movements, for their inability to express his reality: "After the great writers of the seventeenth-century, there was no prose writing of [Faulkner's] particular poetical force in the Spanish language. There were writers like Gabriel Miró, Azorín, Ramón del Valle Inclán, that tried to be poetical through elegance. . . . The problem was that the writing of Ramón del Valle Inclán sounded anachronistic to us, strange to our own world, a sort of cardboard prose." Jorge Edwards, "Yoknapatawpha in Santiago de Chile," in *Faulkner: International Perspectives. Faulkner and Yoknapatawpha, 1982,* ed. Doreen Fowler and Ann Abadie (Jackson: University Press of Mississippi, 1984), 64. And, finally, Donoso offers a similar critique: "In the Spanish novel that teachers liked to offer us as an example and, to a certain degree, as something we also might call 'our own'—in Azorín, Miró, Baroja, Pérez de Ayala—we discovered stagnancy and poverty when we compared them to their contemporaries in other languages. . . . [T]oday's Spanish American novel was from the very beginning a *metizaje* . . . a disregarding of Hispanic-American tradition . . . and draws itself almost totally from other literary sources, because . . . our orphaned sensibility let itself be infected by the North Americans, the French, the English, and the Italians, all of whom seemed to us more 'ours,' much more 'our own' than a Gallegos or a Güiraldes, for example, or a Baroja" (Donos, *The Boom,* 13–14).

For whereas modernism, like realism, was also a discourse whose origins lay outside of Spanish America and that was also learned from foreign models, it nevertheless represented a choice, and it was seized on precisely because its flexibility allowed for further experimentation and was suited to a different way of understanding and experiencing reality. As García Márquez commented, "The 'Faulknerian' method is very effective for describing Latin American reality. Unconsciously, that was what we discovered in Faulkner. That is, we saw this reality and wanted to narrate it, and we knew that the method of the Europeans didn't work, nor did the traditional Spanish method; and suddenly we found the Faulknerian method extremely apt for describing this reality."[11] But just what made the "Faulknerian method" so cognate with Spanish American reality? And what were the specific techniques, motifs, themes, and works that were most influential on the new narrative and Boom? These are the questions that I will now try to address.

The first item that I would like to examine is a fairly localized device that appears in several of Faulkner's works and that seems to have appealed to the Spanish Americans: the use of narrators with a limited mental capacity, such as Vardaman Bundren of *As I Lay Dying* and Benjy Compson of *The Sound and the Fury*. A young child unable to comprehend the death of his mother, Vardaman believes that she is a fish because she, like the fish that he catches the day that she dies, is dead; that is, he associates the two on the basis of the quality that they share and looks for his mother to reappear in rivers and ponds. The severely retarded Benjy is similarly incapable of grasping abstractions and anything other than what he experiences through his senses. Critics have commented on how this grants his version of his family's history a certain amount of objectivity: as he can only perceive *what* is happening without understanding *why,* his section is relatively free of cognition, interpretation, and judgment. Also, because he cannot place the events in his life in any order, time has no real meaning for him: he lives in a continual present in which he does not remember people or events but rather sees or experiences them each time anew. As this type of perspective deploys many of mod-

---

11. García Márquez and Vargas Llosa, *La novela en América Latina*, 52–53. Given García Márquez's many homages to modern European writers, and his insistence that the Virginia Woolf of *Mrs. Dalloway* as well as Faulkner had provided him with "a method and a manner to go with it," the European method to which he refers should be understood as realism rather than modernism. Quoted in Harss and Dohmann, *Into the Mainstream,* 322.

ernism's signature qualities—both thematic and stylistic—several authors experimented with it in their earlier works, using it to describe without analyzing a rather bleak set of social circumstances. Examples may be found in Rulfo's story "Macario" and in García Márquez's "Nabo: The Black Man Who Made the Angels Wait," as well as in the sections attributed to the young boy in the latter's *Leaf Storm*. The latter novel additionally uses this perspective as a filter for describing Macondo's historical and social collapse in a manner similar to Benjy's transcription of his family's and region's decline.

More important, however, on the whole, is Faulkner's representation of community, which lies at the heart of his works and constitutes a central part of his legacy to Spanish American literature. His depictions of community may be approached synchronically, as in the relationship of the individual to his or her society (e.g., insider or outsider, adherent to or alienated from the social codes), or diachronically, as in the community's relationship to its past and present. I would argue, in fact, that Spanish American writers have been drawn much more to the sagas of the Compsons, Sartorises, and Sutpens, than, say, to the Snopes trilogy, precisely because the former's depiction of dynasties and societies that continue to live by the codes of the Old South, becoming isolated and stagnant, trapped in a past that history—and modernity—have left behind, resonated with their own experiences.[12] On this front, Faulkner's

12. García Márquez observes that "Macondo is the past, and, well, since I had to give this past streets and houses, temperature and people, I gave it the image of this hot, dusty, finished, ruined town, with wood houses with zinc roofs, which look very similar to those in the southern U.S.; a town which looks very similar to Faulkner's towns, because it was constructed by the United Fruit Company" (García Márquez and Vargas Llosa, *La novela en América Latina,* 54). Vargas Llosa describes the aftermath of the United Fruit Company's presence in Colombia in markedly similar terms: "When García Márquez was born, almost none of this was left: paradise and hell alike belonged to the past, the present reality was a limbo made of misery, heat, and routine. However, this extinct reality was still alive in the memory and imagination of the people . . . and it was their best weapon for fighting the abandon and emptiness of the present reality. For want of anything better, Aracataca—like so many American towns—lived off of memories, myths, solitude, and nostalgia." Mario Vargas Llosa, "García Márquez: de Aracataca a Macondo," in *Nueve asedios a García Márquez* (3rd ed.; Santiago, Chile: Editorial Universitaria, 1972), 128; translation to mine. Jorge Edwards writes that, following the War of the Pacific and Chile's civil war in 1891, within buildings "that had represented the nitrate splendor of the nineties, a sort of créole 'belle époque' . . . there were impoverished families, and in the rear dormitories . . . old people that remembered and told stories about that lost splendor and about the terrible civil strife." He further claims that his generation grew up "between memories of a brilliant and glorious past, in contrast with a decayed present, a present whose main quality

style is inseparable from his subject matter, for his portraits of historical stagnation drew on the stylistic and thematic aspects of modernism's exploration of alternatives to linear time. For example, his desire to condense "everything into one sentence—not only the present but the whole past on which it depends and which keeps overtaking the present" resulted in the long and baroque sentences that lead the reader through great distances in time and space.[13]

This ubiquitous theme of collective historical paralysis also plays out at the level of the individual in some of Faulkner's most memorable characters, who spend their lives at an emotional impasse that is often reified in the houses into which they lock themselves, shutting out the world and its changes. Spanish American authors found models for their own works in Miss Emily Grierson of "A Rose for Emily," a "tradition, a duty, and . . . a sort of hereditary obligation upon the town," who spends over forty years shut up in her decaying house sleeping with the body of the lover whom she killed to prevent him from leaving her, refusing to acknowledge the passage of time both within her house and in the town. There is also Gail Hightower of *Light in August,* who lives in a house that no one enters for twenty-five years, thinking only of his grandfather's death in the Civil War "as though the seed which his grandfather had transmitted to him had been on the horse too that night and had been killed too and time had stopped there and then for the seed and nothing had happened in time since, not even him." And, of course, there is Quentin Compson of *Absalom, Absalom!,* who lives in "the deep South dead since 1865 and peopled with garrulous outraged baffled ghosts . . . who was still too young to deserve yet to be a ghost, but nevertheless having to be one for all that, since he was born and bred in the deep South," and who listens to Rosa Coldfield, "one of the ghosts which had refused to lie still even longer than most had, telling him about old ghost-times."[14]

Spanish American authors found this image of people who are unable to extricate themselves from a personal past that is in some way bound up with their region's history—people for whom the past is that door through which Quentin Compson simply cannot "pass"—and who func-

---

was stagnation, frustration, poverty, underdevelopment" (Edwards, "Yoknapatapha in Santiago de Chile," 69).

13. Quoted in Malcolm Cowley, *The Faulkner-Cowley File: Letters & Memories, 1944–62* (New York: Viking Press, 1966), 115.

14. "A Rose for Emily," in *The Portable Faulkner,* ed. Malcolm Cowley (New York: Viking Press, 1946), 489; *Light in August* (1932; rprt., New York: Vintage Books, 1987), 69; *Absalom, Absalom!* (1936; rprt., New York: Vintage Books, 1972), 9.

tion as objective correlatives of a society in decline, to be ideally suited to representing the unresolved conflicts that overshadowed the present in their homelands. Thus we find numerous examples of this character type in works from the 1950s through the 1970s. In *Pedro Páramo,* for example, Rulfo's characters submerge themselves in memories of a long-gone past in order to thwart the pain entailed by the passage of time: Susana San Juan immerses herself in erotic memories of her dead husband; Dolores Preciado evokes memories of a prelapsarian Comala; and Pedro Páramo dedicates his life to regaining Susana and avenging his father's death, and additionally succeeds in denying Comala both a present and a future. The title character of Fuentes's *The Death of Artemio Cruz* presents the obverse of this scenario: he is simply unable to cope with the past, and at each stage of his life he wipes the slate clean, excising all memories that would remind him of his primal expulsion from family and love, a practice that condemns him to repeat all of the errors of the past. His grandmother, in contrast, spends thirty-five years immersed in her memories, sealed off in a chamber that no news of historical change penetrates: "She did not want to know more, but only to remember the old times. And within these four walls, she lost track of everything, except the essentials: her widowhood, the past." García Márquez of course offers us quite a few similar characters as well: there is Adelaida of *Leaf Storm,* who closes off the room where an ungrateful guest had lived, essentially reifying his memory, and who—like Macondo as a whole—has decided to stop living and simply await the Judgment Day; there is also Rebeca of *One Hundred Years of Solitude,* who "closed the doors of her house and buried herself alive" after the death of her husband and, oblivious to and forgotten by the outside world, continues to use the outmoded dress and currency of the previous century. Finally, in Juan Carlos Onetti's "The Purloined Bride," Moncha Insaurralde, unaware that her fianceé has died, awaits his return wandering around town in her wedding gown, a "ghost . . . always dressed with the smell and appearance of eternity."[15] Faulkner and the Spanish American authors alike used this paralysis to reflect at the level of the microcosm the predicament of regions suspended in limbo, clinging to a way of life now irremediably lost to war or the advent of modernity, and unable to enter the present.

15. Carlos Fuentes, *The Death of Artemio Cruz,* trans. Alfred MacAdam (New York: Noonday Press, 1991), 286; Gabriel García Márquez, *Cien años de soledad* (Barcelona: Bruguera, 1967), 164; Juan Carlos Onetti, "La novia robada," in *Tan triste como ella* (Barcelona: Seix Barral, 1984), 300–301. These and all further translations from the latter two works are mine.

In addition to this character type, the themes and structure of several specific works seem to have had a lasting impression on the generation of writers that was instrumental in consolidating modernism's place in Spanish American fiction. It is to these works—"A Rose for Emily," *As I Lay Dying,* and *Absalom, Absalom!*—that I now turn, for the manner in which they were read and rewritten sheds light on additional commonalities between Faulkner's world and that of the Spanish Americans. "A Rose for Emily," one of Faulkner's best-known short stories, is set in a town caught between the old and the new; it is paradoxically forced to adhere to the antebellum past by a woman who is at once representative of the old order and an outsider who defies the town's codes and ignores its efforts at modernization. Told in the first-person-plural from the perspective of the people of Jefferson, the narrative voice complements and underscores the depiction of Miss Emily's alienation, for the collective voice articulates shared norms and visits judgment on Emily for failing to conform, while her own perspective is granted no outlet.[16] Here, as in the Spanish American works, this device also functions as a means of social criticism by implicating communal values in the protagonist's fate. As the first-person-plural is an extremely uncommon narrative perspective in Western literature, its use in a number of works by avowed Faulkner fans—in conjunction with the symbiotic relationship between structure and content—directly points toward "A Rose for Emily" as a prototype. One example of such modeling is to be found in Vargas Llosa's *The Cubs,* which alternates between two narrative voices, a first-person-plural and a focalized third-person perspective, both of which reflect the middle-class values to which the novel's alienated protagonist is denied access. Jean O'Bryan-Knight has shown how in Faulkner and Vargas Llosa this narrative strategy illustrates how marginalized individuals are rejected when they are perceived to have committed "sexual transgressions that threaten the [group's] identity," whether this is predicated on the myth of the Old South (bound up in the image of the southern woman) or on *machismo*. Additionally, from start to finish, the community's codes are shown to be responsible in both cases for the individuals' suffering and ostracism, as well, ultimately, as the very deviations for which they are condemned.[17]

Fuentes made similar use of a collective narrator—albeit with an inter-

16. Jean O'Bryan-Knight discusses the use of this narrative voice extensively in "From Spinster to Eunuch" (see especially 335–45).

17. Ibid., 341, 342.

esting twist—in *The Death of Artemio Cruz*. The narration of the magnate's life and death is fragmented into the three grammatical persons (all of which refer to Cruz) and the three temporal divisions: the first-person "I," narrated in the present tense, centers on the protagonist's dying moments; the third-person sections revisit significant events in his past; and the second-person sections use the future tense to confront him with people, facts, and memories that he denies throughout his life. The latter sections are often interpreted as the voice of Cruz's conscience, but they may also speak for a collectivity that is determined to hold him accountable for his actions. As Fuentes once remarked, "A Rose for Emily" "is narrated by a 'we.' In fact, I think that all of Faulkner's novels are narrated by a collective voice. So for me the '*tú*' was totally important as a recognition of the other, as a stylistic means of recognizing the other. It is not just Artemio Cruz's double who speaks to him; it is perhaps the Mexican people—the collective voice—that speaks to Artemio Cruz saying '*tú, tú, tú.*'" And Onetti incorporates both the image of a woman living by time and a community's wayside as well as the communal narrator in "The Purloined Bride." The story begins with a deliberate nod to Faulkner's story: Moncha's tale, he writes, "had already been written and . . . lived by another Moncha in the South liberated and destroyed by the Yankees." Like Emily, Moncha shuts herself up in her house imagining an impossible wedding day, as oblivious to the modernization transforming Santa María as Miss Emily was before her. The first-person plural narrator here likewise conveys the opinions and judgment of the townspeople, as well as implicating them in Moncha's condition: they, too, insist on "denying time, on . . . believing in Santa María's static existence," and on fomenting her illusions in order to protect themselves from having to face a scandal. Hence the doctor's identification of the cause of Moncha's death as "Santa María, all of you, I myself."[18]

If forced to choose, though, I would have to say that, of all Faulkner's works, I believe that *As I Lay Dying* and *Absalom, Absalom!* have had the most profound and lasting impact on Spanish American fiction. *As I Lay Dying,* which narrates the death of the Bundren family matriarch from the perspectives of her family and neighbors, provided the basic

18. Fuentes, "Diálogo con Carlos Fuentes," in *Simposio Carlos Fuentes*, ed. Isaac Jack Levy and Juan Loveluck (Columbia: University of South Carolina Press, 1978), 225 (translation mine); Onetti, "La novia robada," 283, 299, 306. Josefina Ludmer identifies many other links between "A Rose for Emily" and "La novia robada" in "Onetti: 'La novia (carta) robada (a Faulkner),'" *Hispanamérica* 9 (1975): 3–19.

paradigm for a genre of novels in which multiple perspectives centering around a dying or dead figure offer a kaleidoscopic view of her and his life, family, and the social order.[19] María Luisa Bombal's *The Shrouded Woman*, Rulfo's *Pedro Páramo*, García Márquez's *Leaf Storm* and *The Autumn of the Patriarch*, and Fuentes's *The Death of Artemio Cruz* all trace some of their roots back to Faulkner's novel. While *The Shrouded Woman* follows *As I Lay Dying* in circumscribing its focus within the sphere of the experience of a woman and her family, the scope of the other novels was amplified through amalgamation with the panoramic historical vision of *Absalom,* generating a polyphonic novel of the dead in which the central figure's life recapitulates the history of an entire nation or region. Rulfo's novel refracts Mexican history from the 1880s through the 1930s through the life and death of the patriarch and the town that he destroyed. Both García Márquez and Fuentes, in turn, use the deathbed narration in conjunction with one of modernism's most powerful innovations for subverting linear narrative time, the novel-in-a-day tradition initiated by Joyce with *Ulysses* and Woolf in *Mrs. Dalloway* (and used four times over by Faulkner himself in *The Sound and the Fury*), to telescope national history into the narrative frame of a single calendar day: *Leaf Storm* condenses forty years of Colombian history, from the wars of the late nineteenth century through the prosperity and decline ushered in by the banana company and on up until 1928 into a mere half-hour; *The Autumn of the Patriarch* spans within a twenty-four-hour frame the history of Spanish America from the Conquest through the twentieth century, as well as the life and death of the dictator who was considered immortal and whose reign was thought to be eternal; and Artemio Cruz, whose tale begins and ends on the day of his death, and his family likewise constitute a microcosm of Mexican history since the first stirrings for independence through the 1960s. These deathbed and posthumously narrated novels thus served to depict the changing of ways occasioned by war, modernization, and the paralyzing legacy of authoritarian, patriarchal social structures.

The reworking of *As I Lay Dying* in conjunction with the epic scope of *Absalom* is indicative of the pervasiveness of the latter novel in modern Spanish American literature and, especially, of its vision of history and

19. While *As I Lay Dying* was the immediate precursor to and model for these novels, this paradigm actually has a largely unacknowledged precursor in Latin American fiction: it forms the basis of Brazilian writer Machado de Assis's *Memórias póstumas de Bras Cubas,* published in 1881. I thank Djelal Kadir for bringing this to my attention.

fiction. To this day, authors such as Fuentes and García Márquez invoke it as one of their favorite works. The novel's appeal is due in large measure to the fact that most of the thematic, stylistic, and structural elements that were admired in Faulkner appear together here, complementing one another. *Absalom* deploys many modernist techniques to recreate the past, most notably narrative perspectivism (the novel is told by four separate narrators whose versions of events are irreconcilable and, in the end, unreconciled) and the refutation of linear time and chronological order; it also draws on a nonlinear strategy of delaying the disclosure of critical information. Additionally, one finds in *Absalom* the thematic nucleus of many of the new narrative's most canonical novels: first, a patriarch (or, in some cases, family) who is both founder and emblem of the prevailing order, whose authority is coextensive with the implementation of its codes, whose relationship to the members of the community determines their position within it, and whose death parallels the end of the historical era; and, second, a historical backdrop of civil war, cycles of boom and bust, and the changing of orders. *Absalom* narrates the rise of Thomas Sutpen from poor white to rich plantation owner, identifying the practices and prejudices upon which he builds his empire and showing how they ultimately lead to his downfall; as numerous critics have observed, his trajectory spans the greater part of the heyday and decline of the plantation system, recapitulating the history of the Old South. Sutpen's ascent begins with the foundational crime of original accumulation, the mythic creation "out of the soundless Nothing . . . [of] the Sutpen's Hundred, the *Be Sutpen's Hundred* like the oldtime *Be Light.*"[20] The partition of the land and the financial transaction whereby he essentially purchases an appropriate wife usher in a new order grounded in economic values. He dies without a legitimate male heir to inherit the world he has built, signaling the end of the plantocracy, albeit not of the racist and classist assumptions upon which it was predicated.

This template for the relationship between the founding patriarch or family and the macrocosm of national history is rather closely followed in several Spanish American novels. In Rulfo's *Pedro Páramo,* for example, the cacique similarly ushers in a new order in which money is the only value: he negates all previous financial agreements, rewrites the law, redraws property boundaries in order to take over all of the town's land, and essentially buys himself a wife even as he buys his way out of honoring a debt. Historically, Pedro Páramo's centralization of landownership

20. Faulkner, *Absalom,* 8–9.

dates to the years of Porfirio Díaz's regime, which was notorious for facilitating the expansion of large estates, and his downfall takes place in the years following the Mexican Revolution but is not a product of its reforms. His trajectory clearly allegorizes the failure of the Revolution to bring about change and the dire state that is *caciquismo*'s legacy, both of which hinder Mexican's entrance into modernity. Fuentes's *The Death of Artemio Cruz* draws on the same paradigm to cover the first one hundred and fifty years of Mexican independence. The fate of Cruz's paternal grandparents is that of the conservatives in the nineteenth century: his grandfather fought with Santa Anna and died alongside the emperor Maximilian, "the end of a life of chance and spins of the wheel of fortune, like that of the nation itself," whereas his grandmother, born in 1810, the year of the first uprising for independence, experiences firsthand all of the century's subsequent upheavals, including the loss of her land to the liberals' reforms and, later, to new landowners under Díaz. Cruz himself incarnates "the new world rising out of the civil war": he is the self-made man who erases the past and sets out to map the nation's future. His actions, of course, set the stage for the postrevolutionary period: he, too, purchases a wife and, with her, her family's properties, and subsequently usurps the lands of neighboring small landowners, heralding the failure of land reform and the corruption of the new bourgeoisie. Finally, the founding of Macondo in *One Hundred Years of Solitude* entails the transformation of a virgin world "that was so new that many things still did not have names" into parcels of land owned by man. Although the initial result is a semi-utopian order where all of the houses have equal access to water and the sun, the town and Buendía family's subsequent development encapsulates that of Colombia and Spanish America as a whole, from the development of a creole aristocracy to the nineteenth-century civil wars through the U.S. imperialism that starts Macondo along the final path to ruin.[21]

21. Fuentes, *Artemio Cruz*, 293, 44; García Márquez, *Cien años*, 9. *Absalom*'s problematization of historiographical discourse, perspectivism, withholding of critical information, and setting against a backdrop of revolution and historical change also figure prominently in Vargas Llosa's *The Real Life of Alejandro Mayta*, which unfortunately falls outside of the temporal scope of this study. For further discussion of this topic, see Deborah Cohn, "The Case of the Fabricated Facts: Invented Information and the Problems of Reconstructing the Past in William Faulkner's *Absalom, Absalom!* and Mario Vargas Llosa's *Historia de Mayta*," *The Comparatist* 21 (May 1997): 25–48. The paradigm discussed here—the patriarchal system as a microcosm of the social order and an index of national destiny, the rise and fall of the patriarch himself, the consequences of his denial of paternity, and the use of multiple perspectives to challenge the truth of the dominant order—is also

In addition to the preceding paradigms, stylistic and thematic parallels with *Absalom* abound in the modern Spanish American novel. George Handley, for example, has shown that Alejo Carpentier reworked a number of these and related motifs and themes from *Absalom* in *Explosion in the Cathedral,* his exploration of regional identity and self-identity within the context of revolution (the novel explicitly addresses the French Revolution but was published three years after the Cuban Revolution): the incestuous menage à trois; questions about the origins, nature, and fate of plantation society; the relationship of the plantocracy to the French Revolution and Haiti; and the matter of U.S. imperialism in the Caribbean.[22]

All of the aforementioned novels conclude with the death of the patriarch or family through whom national history is allegorized. In some cases, this signals the downfall of the way of life with which they were coextensive and opens up the possibility of change for the collectivity: the death of Artemio Cruz in 1959, the year of the Cuban Revolution, signals the end of the postrevolutionary period in Mexico and looks hopefully toward the beginning of a new order inspired by Cuba; in *The Autumn of the Patriarch,* in turn, the dictator's death awoke the city from "its lethargy of centuries," announcing "the good news that the uncountable time of eternity had come to an end."[23] In other cases, however, it serves to underscore the permanent damage wrought by the previous

---

the foundation of Isabel Allende's *The House of the Spirits.* Rather than Faulkner, however, it is *One Hundred Years of Solitude* that served as Allende's model. Consult the following works for discussions of this subject: Robert Antoni, "Parody or Piracy: The Relationship of *The House of the Spirits* to *One Hundred Years of Solitude,*" *Latin American Literary Review* 16, No. 32 (July–December 1988): 16–28; and Mario Rodríguez Fernández, "García Márquez/Isabel Allende: Relación textual," in *Los libros tienen sus propios espíritus,* ed. Marcelo Coddou (Xalapa, México: Universidad Veracruzana, 1986), 79–82. I have not, in fact, ever seen any references to Faulkner's influence on Allende, nor has Allende discussed him as a model. Allende clearly saw herself as writing within and against a Spanish American tradition, which indicates the degree to which Faulkner had been assimiliated within this tradition.

22. I am grateful to Dr. Handley for sharing portions of his book *Family Portraits in Black and White* with me prior to its publication. Also, as Efraín Kristal has discussed, *Absalom* served Vargas Llosa as a model for his study of Peruvian society in the multilayered conversations of *Conversation in the Cathedral,* in which Santiago Zavala, like Henry Sutpen, repudiates his birthright and, with it, the successful father whose corruption is emblematic of that of his social world. Efraín Kristal, *Temptation of the Word: The Novels of Mario Vargas Llosa* (Nashville: Vanderbilt University Press, 1998), 58–59.

23. Gabriel García Márquez, *The Autumn of the Patriarch,* trans. Gregory Rabassa (New York: HarperPerennial, 1976), 1, 269.

power structure, a much bleaker forecast for the potential for change: the Comala of Rulfo's novel and the Macondo of both *Leaf Storm* and *One Hundred Years of Solitude*, for example, are paralyzed, condemned to extinction by their leaders and the social and political orders that they implemented. Whether the endings promise new beginnings or not, though, they are, in one way or another, pronouncements on the future by authors who were deeply influenced by contemporary debates over the nature and fate of Spanish America.

Faulkner's works thus served as a point of departure that allowed Spanish American authors to explore their own interests and history. It is, however, important to recognize that his influence has not been monolithic, nor has it been circumscribed to the period that has been my focus to this point. Although most contemporary authors confess to having been influenced by Faulkner, his specific role has changed significantly over time. He has meant different things to authors such as García Márquez and Vargas Llosa, who encountered him in the early stages of their careers (and of the new narrative in general) and who have had occasion to revisit him over the course of decades. Consider, for example, the difference among García Márquez's *Leaf Storm*, published in 1955, *One Hundred Years of Solitude* (1967), *The Autumn of the Patriarch* (1975), and *Chronicle of a Death Foretold* (1981), or among Vargas Llosa's 1967 *The Cubs, Conversation in the Cathedral* (1969), *The War of the End of the World* (1981), and *The Real Life of Alejandro Mayta* (1984). Additionally, Faulkner's impact was quite different on younger authors such as Alfredo Bryce Echenique, Rosario Ferré, and Ricardo Piglia, who began to write in the 1970s and 1980s, by which time modernist stylistics had become commonplace, the norm rather than the exception. In these writers, Faulkner's influence can be identified less at the level of style than in the presence of specific themes, motifs, and images adopted from his works. Thus I would like to conclude with an overview of his presence in one of these authors, Rosario Ferré. The similarities between previous rewritings of Faulknerian themes and images and her appropriation thereof demonstrate the continuity of the southerner's appeal even as they reflect a sensibility that seeks to revise history and society from the perspective of women and blacks and to challenge the "truths" of the "white" patriarchy.

Starting with her 1976 collection, *Papeles de Pandora*, Ferré depicts a segment of Puerto Rican society that bears a strong resemblance to Faulkner's Yoknapatawpha County, with elements of the Sutpens, Sartorises, and, especially, Snopeses. The parallels are evident implicitly in her description of the agenda that she set for herself when writing her first story, "The Youngest Doll": "I thought it best to select a historical anecdote, perhaps something related to how our Puerto Rican bourgeois culture changed from an agrarian one based on sugar cane and ruled by a rural oligarchy to an urban or industrial one ruled by a new professional class, an anecdote that would convey how this change brought about a shift in values at the turn of the century—the abandonment of the land and the replacement of a patriarchal code of behavior, based on exploitation but also on certain ethical principles and on Christian charity, with a new utilitarian code that came to us from the U.S."[24] In Faulkner and Ferré alike, then, a postbellum plantocracy is displaced by factories and replaced by an upwardly mobile, materialistic bourgeoisie. Also, the standard of femininity to which her female characters are expected to conform is strikingly akin to that of the southern belle: they are to be pure and demure, they are used to acquire or preserve a family's honor and social status, and they are subject to rigid, unchanging roles authorized by an authoritarian patriarchal system.

Faulknerian images play a small, decorative role in the story "A Poisoned Tale." Here, Don Lorenzo, the patriarch, is one of those "ruined landowners who still dream[ed] of the past as of a paradise lost"; he madly defends his own Cult of the Lost Cause, literally reenacting throughout his life the U.S.'s 1898 invasion of the island, which had precipitated the downfall of the creole aristocracy. The image of Don Lorenzo "enthusiastically re-enact[ing] the battle scene as he strode vigorously through the halls and parlors . . . thinking of those heroic ancestors who had gloriously died for their homeland" while treading termite-ridden floors whose holes revealed the chicken coop that he kept in the cellar invites comparison with Gail Hightower of *Light in August,* who spends his life reliving his grandfather's death in the Civil War, and with the grandfather himself, who was killed not in battle but while stealing chickens from a henhouse—bitter truths about the decline of a class and region.[25]

But it is in Ferré's 1986 *Maldito amor,* and particularly in her significantly modified translation of the novel as *Sweet Diamond Dust,* that we find the most heavy-handed borrowing from *Absalom, Absalom!* at the

24. Rosario Ferré, "The Writer's Kitchen," in *Lives on the Line,* ed. Meyer, 217.

25. Rosario Ferré, "A Poisoned Tale," in *Short Stories by Latin American Women: The Magic and the Real,* ed. Celia Correas de Zapata, trans. Rosario Ferré and Diana Vélez (Houston: Arte Público Press, 1990), 69, 65.

level of motif, historical backdrop, and structure. *Maldito amor* and *Sweet Diamond Dust* exhibit a number of superficial parallels with Faulkner's novel: the family houses around which the novels revolve are built by French architects; the characters who are ultimately revealed to have "black blood"—e.g., Eulalia Bon and Julio Font—are initially described as being of Spanish origin; the presence of characters named Eulalia; and the marriage of Ellen Sutpen, like that of Nicolás De la Valle, is arranged as a financial transaction in exchange for services rendered. More important, however, like *Absalom, Absalom!*, *Maldito amor* and *Sweet Diamond Dust* condense a significant period in a region's history—in this case, Puerto Rico's twentieth-century racial and political tensions and the decline of the creole plantation industries—into the saga of a house divided. As in *Absalom,* the story of the patriarch's rise and fall and the rebuilding of his heritage to deny the "black blood" in his family is presented from several contradictory points of view. Also, in both cases, each of the narrators explains the unresolved events in terms of a single cause: Sutpen's fall is attributed to God, Fate, and Fortune, incest and miscengenation, whereas Ubaldino De la Valle's raison d'être is explained variously by the changing of orders precipitated by the arrival of the U.S., the quest to resolve Puerto Rico's political status in a manner that would also bring reform to the island's poorest inhabitants, and the racism that erases all evidence of miscegenation from the family tree. In Ferré's novel, however, the final truth, which Faulkner had left to the reader to construct from the various discrepant versions of events, is clearly to be found in those perspectives which are furthest—in terms of both textual space and content—from those offered by the rich "white" male creoles and the power structure that they represent.[26] The novel closes with Gloria, Ubaldino's daughter-in-law (who is variously described and thereby marginalized as a mulatta, a crazy woman, and the town whore), burning down the house on the island's last independent sugar plantation, the house that was a microcosm of the system and its racial and political dynamics—an obvious parallel with the actions of Clytie, Sutpen's daughter by a slave, who at the end of *Absalom* sets the

---

26. It is, of course, no accident that Don Hermenegildo, whose voice frames *Sweet Diamond Dust* and who is writing a novel about the town of Guamaní's great *independentista* senator (and having to falsify and invent numerous data as he proceeds), is a lawyer: like the epic hero that he is trying to create for his community to rally around, Hermenegildo both represents and embodies the written code that was implemented by his class (and gender).

fire that destroys herself, Sutpen's son and only possible heir, and his mansion.

I am, however, even more interested in Ferré's reworking of the twinned issues of incest and miscegenation that are at the heart of *Absalom*. (It must be noted that this is only apparent in *Sweet Diamond Dust*, to which she has added the mestizo genealogy of Gloria's son.) In Faulkner's novel, a love triangle develops between Sutpen's legitimate children, Henry and Judith, and their half-brother, Charles Bon, whom Sutpen had disowned when he realized his mother had "black blood" in her family. Unaware of these family ties, Judith becomes engaged to Bon; Henry, half in love with Bon himself, rationalizes the relationship when he learns of the incest involved but is simply unable to reconcile himself to the possibility of miscegenation, and he kills Bon to prevent the marriage. In *Sweet Diamond Dust*, two divergent explanations are offered of Gloria's son's paternity. The only living son of the patriarch tries to discredit his sister-in-law by accusing her of having had relations with his father, brother, and himself, and characterizes her offspring, the product of these incestuous relations, as a "monster . . . be it reptile, fish, or fowl." In contrast, Ubaldino's wife says that the child was the product of relations that Gloria had had as a prostitute with northerners and Puerto Ricans, foreigners and islanders, the rich and the poor. As in Faulkner's novel, the primal taboo of incest is swept away and revealed to be a smoke screen behind which an even more explosive motive for murder lurks. However, where both the fact and issue of incest had horrified the patriarch's son, Ubaldino's wife takes great pride in the fact that Nicolasito is "the child of all. In [Gloria's] body . . . both races, both languages, English and Spanish, grew into one soul."[27] The would-be accusation of miscengenation is thus defused by the explicit positing of the mestizo child as a source of renewal and the true direction of Puerto Rico's future.

Faulkner's Clytie, "who in the very pigmentation of her flesh represented that debacle which had brought Judith and me [Miss Rosa] to what we were and which had made of her (Clytie) that which she declined to be just as she had declined to be that from which its purpose had been to emancipate her, as though presiding aloof upon the new, she deliberately remained to represent to us the threatful portent of the old," was a living refutation of racial categories and, as such, a bridge between the past and future.[28] By destroying the family mansion, she, like Gloria

27. Rosario Ferré, *Sweet Diamond Dust and Other Stories*, trans. Rosario Ferré (New York: Penguin, 1988), 49, 76.

28. Faulkner, *Absalom*, 156–57.

after her, casts off the past. However, where both Clytie and Henry Sutpen perish in the blaze and thereby forfeit the future as well, the readers of Ferré's novel never learn definitively the fate of the scion of the De la Valle family. We are simply left to hope that he does survive to preside over the new order heralded by the patriarch's death.

Long after Faulkner was hailed for his stylistic innovations, then, it is this image of an insular society trapped by the burden of its history, its longstanding racial and class tensions, and the struggle between official and unofficial stories and genealogies that has become his most outstanding legacy to modern Spanish American fiction. Fuentes's assertion that "maybe Latin America begins south of the Mason-Dixon line, the South is in a way Latin American, as is Faulkner" speaks directly to the commonalities of experience that drew the Spanish Americans to Faulkner and his world.[29] Fuentes and his contemporaries found in Faulkner and his South a set of concerns with which they could identify. Yoknapatawpha County does not just share a border with Spanish America, it shares a history as well.

29. Carlos Fuentes, "Carlos Fuentes: An Interview," by John King, in *On Modern Latin American Fiction*, ed. John King (New York: Noonday Press, 1987), 139.

The South and Britain: Celtic Cultural Connections

Helen Taylor

In the final decades of the twentieth century, saturation advertising and films with a southern theme reinforced British fascination for the American South. There is a strong affection between the South and Britain, in terms of both sociohistorical roots and ties, and of cultural and mythic connections. In terms of demographic influence, it is not a specifically *English* connection, of the kind that exists in New England and other northern states that saw a great deal of English immigration. The earliest census in 1790 (albeit disputed by some historians) established that the European majority in the southern states were *Celts* rather than English—Scottish, Irish, Scots-Irish, Welsh, and Cornish—and by the time of the Civil War the South's white population was over three-quarters Celtic. From the late seventeenth century to the American Revolution, the southern backcountry was flooded with one of those groups, the Scotch-Irish, and it is said that their heritage and style are the characteristics most associated with white southerners over the last two centuries: herding rather than tilling, leisurely, musical, tall-taletelling, violent, clannish, family-centered, fiercely Protestant, with a strong sense of honor.[1] In-

1. See Grady McWhiney, *Cracker Culture: Celtic Ways in the Old South* (Tuscaloosa: University of Alabama Press, 1988); E. R. R. Green, ed., *Essays in Scotch-Irish History*

deed, the term most used, usually pejoratively, to describe poor white southern frontiersmen from the mid-1700s is the Scottish term for a noisy, boasting fellow—a "cracker."

The white cracker has acquired a new spin in recent years. The neo-Confederate, white supremacist League of the South[2] was set up to defend the notion of the true South as Celtic, thus by definition white; other Souths (notably African American) thus become illegitimate and inferior. The League's central text, written by board member Grady McWhiney, is *Cracker Culture,* which argues, as Diane Roberts puts it, "Celtic culture rolls down uninterrupted through two millennia from Queen Boudicca in her chariot to Cale Yarborough in his stock car." Arguing euphemistically for "heritage not hate," among other things, the League has declared a wish to return to British spelling, seeing the American *Webster's* dictionary as an example of "cultural ethnic cleansing." The Celtic card is being played belligerently against what is perceived as a politically correct celebration of multicultural southern diversity. Leftist Celtic organizations such as the Scottish Nationalist Party and Plaid Cymru are embraced for their nationalist separatism, which is (mis)interpreted as conservative supremacism. In the case of Scots nationalism, the movies *Rob Roy* and *Braveheart* are highly recommended; the latter is the film the League Website recommended that all "Southrons" (Walter Scott's pejorative term) should see—a recommendation also endorsed strongly by the Ku Klux Klan and the John Birch Society. And the League of the South is not the only white supremacist group to have resorted to Celtic mythology. The twentieth-century rededication of the Ku Klux Klan was inspired by D. W. Griffiths's *The Birth of a Nation* (1915), the film version of Thomas Dixon's novel *The Clansman* (1905). In Dixon's novel, cross-burning is used by the Klan after the old practice in the Scottish highlands for calling clans together. In 1915, on Stone Mountain, Atlanta, the Second Wave of the Klan revived the Scottish practice and burned a cross during Thanksgiving weekend; thus the pernicious practice always associated with Klan intimidation was born. The Celtic cross has become a potent symbol of a rash of "patriot movement" groups in the United States, such as Christian Identity, the North American Liberation Association, and the Neo-Nazis.[3]

(London: Routledge and Kegan Paul, 1969); and Andrew Hook, *From Goosecreek to Gandercleugh: Studies in Scottish-American Literary and Cultural History* (East Linton, Scotland: Tuckwell Press, 1999).

2. Originally known as the Southern League, its name was changed after complaints from a baseball team with the identical name.

3. Diane Roberts, "Ghosts of the Gallant South," *The Guardian,* 22 July 1996, 14, 15; Kirsty Scott, "The Fatal Attraction: The Disturbing Phenomenon of America's Violent Rac-

*   *   *

Of all Celtic influences on the American South (apart from a general recognition of the supreme importance of Scottish and Irish music), one
name, that of Walter Scott, is the most cited. Plantation houses and humble street names alike testify to the enthusiasm that Victorian southerners
had for reading his work; his novels still sit proudly on southern book-
shelves. Scott's historical novels inspired a tradition of cavalier romances
by writers such as William Alexander Carruthers, in tomes called *The
Cavaliers of Virginia* (1834) and *The Knights of the Golden Horseshoe*
(1841). The renowned ex-slave Frederick Douglass, when choosing his
own name rather than that of a slave master, settled on Douglass after a
character in Scott's *The Lady of the Lake,* ironically because a northern
abolitionist suggested it. It is common to blame Scott for much of the romanticism and feudal aspirations established firmly within the nineteenth-
century South and still continuing into the present century. Mark Twain
famously attacked "Sir Walter Scott with his enchantments" for checking
progress in the South and for the South's embrace of "dreams and phan-
toms . . . decayed and swinish forms of religion . . . sillinesses and empti-
nesses, sham grandeurs, sham gauds, and sham chivalries of a brainless
and worthless long-vanished society." To him, Scott's "jejune romanticism of an absurd past that is dead" was largely responsible for the Civil
War itself.[4]

The Cavalier Myth, in which the Old South was created by an aristocracy of English Cavaliers fleeing Cromwell, is blamed for many of the
South's most persistent and damaging myths about itself. W. J. Cash, in the
most famous deconstruction of this myth, saw Scott as central to the ideology of the medieval southern gentleman, living in a world "wholly dominated by ideals of honor and chivalry and *noblesse.*" He argued that Scott
"was bodily taken over by the South and incorporated into the Southern
people's vision of themselves," and that his books inspired southerners
to see themselves as "the chivalry."[5] Even in twentieth-century southern
historiography, Scott's influence is recognized. The South is described as
the region most enthusiastically supportive of the American Military-

ists and Their Bond with Scotland," *The Herald,* 6 August 1997, 12; Robert O. Stephens,
The Family Saga in the South: Generations and Destinies (Baton Rouge: Louisiana State
University Press, 1995), 145.

   4. Mark Twain, *Life on the Mississippi* (1883; New York: Harper, 1904), 347.

   5. W. J. Cash, *The Mind of the South* (New York: Alfred A. Knopf, 1941), ix, 67, 68.
Also see William R. Taylor, *Cavalier and Yankee: The Old South and American National
Character* (New York: Harper and Row, 1961).

Industrial Complex, especially since World War II. Militancy and martial behavior have long been dominant in the South (partly because of engagement with Indian uprisings and slaves): "Many southerners, weaned on the novels of Sir Walter Scott, were obsessed with a sense of honor."[6] And, alert to the resonances of this cavalier myth, Brown-Forman Beverages Worldwide, which owns Jack Daniel's, has a "Tennessee Squire Program" that makes loyal Jack Daniel's drinkers "squires" who co-own plots of land in Lynchburg. The company will cheerfully acknowledge the playful spuriousness of this "program" (they boast that the late Frank Sinatra was a squire, who circled his helicopter over his designated plot—though there is no legal entitlement), but it illustrates how saturated the contemporary South still is in its feudal mythology.

Many British cultural influences on, and dialogues with, the South have partly made it what it is. British speech patterns, dialects, and pronunciations have endured there, with southerners retaining many words and pronunciations common in seventeenth- to nineteenth-century Britain. Critic Cleanth Brooks argued for more than fifty years that southerners speak an older, purer form of "King's English" than most English-speakers, and that there are clear links between southern English and the English of southwest Britain; other sociolinguists have published lists of southern words that demonstrate the persistence of terms from Chaucer and Shakespeare.[7] Despite Jefferson's Anglophobia, there has been less effort in the South than in the North to break the colonial connection. The Yankee tradition in the Jacksonian era to Americanize the language and literature, along with tariffs and economic rivalry, have no counterpart in the South. Northern cities, with strong immigrant voices in the urban culture, have no counterpart in the South. Fawning over the British monarchy has persisted longer in southern states. English influence, widely recognized in New England and the earliest English colonies, endures in the South through the names of English former plantations and colonies, now states, as well as cities and towns: Virginia (for Elizabeth I), Carolina (Charles I), Georgia (George II), the James River (James I),

6. Alvin R. Sunseri, "Military and Economy," in *The Encyclopedia of Southern Culture*, ed. Charles Reagan Wilson and William Ferris (Chapel Hill: University of North Carolina Press, 1989), 731.

7. See James B. McMillan and Michael B. Montgomery, eds., *The Annotated Bibliography of Southern American English* (2nd ed.; Tuscaloosa: University of Alabama Press, 1986).

Birmingham, Norfolk, Richmond, Raleigh, and so on. British folk music is acknowledged as a major source for the "country" element in "country and western" music. While it is well known that European Gothic inspired both prominent state capitols and also major plantation houses, it is less recorded that southern Episcopalian church architecture was often modeled on English parish churches. British literature, too, was very important to the planter and politician in antebellum culture. Victorian figures such as Arnold, Carlyle, Mill, Tennyson, Browning, and Darwin were read avidly; Carlyle reciprocated this admiration with his enthusiastic espousal of the Confederate cause, while Browning's robustly optimistic Christian work inspired the establishment of hundreds of Browning Societies throughout the South. In New Orleans, as Anglo-Southerners tried to capture and control the Creole-French tradition, the nineteenth-century Mardi Gras "krewes" (itself a term invented to sound like archaic English) invoked Milton's *Comus* and *Paradise Lost* and Spenser's *Faerie Queene* in order to accumulate cultural capital.[8] English Victorian attitudes about sexuality echoed southerners' own patriarchally repressed views: the white Madonna southern belle on her pedestal owes much to the "Angel in the House" of Coventry Patmore and Tennyson's *Idylls of the King.*

Many parallels exist between colonial attitudes toward the colonized, as described and defended in Victorian discourses, and the South's defense of the Peculiar Institution of slavery. Of course, conservative and progressive politicians alike pointed fingers at Britain to make points for and against chattel and wage slavery, and the institution of slavery bound together British and southern trade and other relationships throughout the eighteenth and nineteenth centuries. The abolition debate on both sides of the Atlantic shared ideas, champions, and documents; proslavery southern writers like James Henry Hammond felt obliged, after the abolition of slavery in Britain, to defend themselves against their own countrymen and those English abolitionists who began to stir up northern opposition to the Peculiar Institution. In the years and months leading up to Secession, there was strong support at all levels of British society for the Confederate cause. And in 1845, years before the Civil War began, former slaves Frederick Douglass and Harriet Jacobs traveled to England (Douglass first to Ireland). While there, he promoted his *Narrative of the Life of Frederick Douglass, an American Slave,* while she worked as

---

8. Joseph Roach, *Cities of the Dead: Circum-Atlantic Performance* (New York: Columbia University Press, 1996), 258.

nursemaid to a child whose mother had just died; he found ready support for his abolition cause, and she (whose *Incidents in the Life of a Slave Girl* was to appear over a dozen years later) would later work in the antislavery reading room above the North Star offices in Rochester and try unsuccessfully to find a British publisher for her own slave narrative.

Indeed, a literary relationship has been one of the most enduring links and exchanges between Europe and the South. Apart from the towering Celtic figure of Scott, there are many mutual literary influences and admirers. In autobiographies by southern writers from Richard Wright to Maya Angelou, frequent reference is made to the young writer's introduction to European, especially English, literature, and of its hold over the southerner's imagination. In an exhibition of Mississippi fiction printed in England, mounted in 1992 at the University of Mississippi, Americans were referred to as "literary step-children of 'the Brits,' and no greater source of inspiration exists for American authors than the 500-year-long tradition of English English literature." The catalog reflects on the fact that southern writers still see theirs as a lesser literature, while English letters are the real McCoy. Ellen Gilchrist, writing in the catalog of her love for the English Faber and Faber editions of her fiction, notes wryly, "I was raised to think I was an Englishwoman who only happened to be living in the Mississippi delta because my family were colonists"; indeed, on the dust jacket of her first British collection, the 1982 Faber *In the Land of Dreamy Dreams,* she describes herself as "an Englishwoman and a Scot." Richard Ford offers a telling anecdote about English cultural imperialism; renting a converted barn from an Englishman, he found himself avoiding meeting his landlord on rent-collection days: "Probably, he imagined, I was ducking my rent. But I was only ducking him—his choice of words—my own hold on literature being, then as now, somewhat fragile."[9]

The affection felt by white southerners for Europeans, and especially for the British, is well reciprocated. The closeness of ties is manifest in genealogical, cultural, and political terms, not to mention a shared heritage and guilt about the slave trade and slavery itself. The South appears in British culture through a number of stereotypes: there is the Simple South of comical accents and mountain people or small-town folk asleep on front

9. Glenn Horowitz, "Foreword," in Thomas M. Verich, *English Magnolias: An Exhibition of Mississippi Fiction Printed in England* (Oxford: University of Mississippi, 1992), n.p., 27.

porches; the romantic antebellum South of courtly beaux and beauteous belles; and, most familiar in recent years, the violent or gothic South of evil stirrings behind the magnolia in moonlight, usually some terrible racial or sexual sin or secret. Since in recent decades the South has acquired a less conservative and separatist reputation within the United States, international attention has focused less on its violent past and more on its cultural production and tourism possibilities. This does not mean that whenever another Death Row prisoner's case is highlighted or an abortion clinic is firebombed the South's murky history and characteristics are forgotten; it does mean that these no longer obscure its heterogeneous cultural forms and achievements.

You do not have to look far to see how British culture is infused with reminders and traces of those many cultures. For a start, there is the omnipresence of southern music, on disc, radio, TV, film, in church service, and over supermarket loudspeakers. Popular, too, are American Civil War weekends, the Southern Skirmish Association re-enacting battles, a Minstrel Spectacular (reviving in the 1990s the much-discredited "Black and White Minstrel Show" of the 1950s and early '60s), and *Gone With the Wind*–themed weddings. There are restaurants and bars called The Big Easy, Old Orleans, and The Jefferson Experience; New Orleans jazz groups, Cajun and zydeco bands, and gospel and country singers. On BBC as well as independent TV and radio, popular series focus on country, jazz, and soul.[10] Most of all, there is no decline in enthusiastic homage paid to The King, Elvis.

In the last years of the twentieth century, a fascination with all things southern grew and grew. Supermarkets sold Cajun dishes, bourbons with reassuring names like Old Forester, Old Times, and Southern Comfort, and "dairy cocktails" in flavors "Louisiana Peach," "Mississippi Mud," and "Wild Jack Chaser." Secondhand bookshops and libraries boasted novels by prolific writers Frank Yerby and Frances Parkinson Keyes, as well as crime and gothic bestsellers by John Grisham and James Lee Burke. The romance section of large stores is crammed with titles like *Riverboat Seduction, Moon over Black Bayou,* and *Southern Passions,*

10. Two excellent examples at random, in the summer of 1998, were a Channel 4 four-part series, *Naked in Nashville* (Oxford Television Company), that produced a CD of the series's music as well as a glossy brochure, *Naked in Nashville: Selling and the Soul of Country Music* (London: Broadcasting Support Services, 1998); and BBC Radio 3's four-part documentary on the British jazz revival, featuring Humphrey Lyttleton, *Take Me Back to New Orleans.*

while there is a new taste for movie adaptations of southern writings, from *Steel Magnolias* (1989) to *Midnight in the Garden of Good and Evil* (1998).

In recent years, scholars have become fascinated by the idea of circulating and dynamic, rather than fixed, cultures. "Authenticity" and "origins" are seen as political inventions, thus politically loaded. A search for roots has been transformed into a tracing of routes, while cultures are now seen as intersections of meanings. American culture has become a "superculture," detached from roots, being adapted, absorbed, and mediated through the processes of globalization and transnational communities (especially via the airwaves, the Internet, and tourism). Cultural imperialism is being replaced by postimperial notions of a global mass-mediated culture that takes particular local forms, adopted, assimilated, and appropriated in various ways.[11] Nelson Mandela listened to Motown in jail; a Serbo-Croat family sang "Deep River" to tourist Maya Angelou when she entered their store; Elvis Presley loved to watch British Monty Python programs on TV; at the 1996 summit meeting between Presidents Yeltsin of Russia and Clinton of the U.S., a Finnish professor sang Presley songs translated into Latin.

So how can Europeans and Americans alike consider the paradox of a region that is both steeped in a singular social and especially racial history, developed from its own particular cultural roots, and that is also a hybrid, performative mixture of European, African, and Protestant American routes? Is there a single southern culture, or, as Richard Gray suggests, "a rich, pluralistic, sometimes warring and at other times embracing series of influences and energies: not so much southern culture, really, as southern cultures"? Are there not also multiple responses to, and interpretations of, that culture(s) in a wide variety of readerships, audiences, spectators, and tourists? These questions have intrigued many southern commentators, and thus one of the most exciting challenges we face is the documentation of the ways southern culture has circulated through different continents. One notable example of such circulation is the Celtic revivification of the South's best-known text, *Gone With the*

---

11. See Paul Gilroy, *The Black Atlantic: Modernity and Double Consciousness* (London: Verso, 1993); Edward Said, *Culture and Imperialism* (London: Chatto and Windus, 1993); David Ellwood et al., *Questions of Cultural Exchange: The NIAS Statement on the European Reception of American Mass Culture*, Working Paper No. 13 (Odense, Denmark: Odense University, 1994). See also a timely set of articles in *American Quarterly 50* (September 1998).

Wind. This novel-made-film, in all its manifestations—book, film, video, soundtrack, memorabilia, sequel, plagiarized novel, fictional reworking, biographical and critical study, not to mention countless advertisements, spoof posters, songs, heritage plates, pop-up books, themed restaurants, and colloquial expressions—has reached a vast worldwide market. Margaret Mitchell's novel, *Gone With the Wind* (1936), a long and loving backward glance at the traumatic American Civil War and the devastation of the South, sealed in celluloid immortality through its highly successful 1939 David Selznick film version, is instantly recognized, much cited and quoted, and has come to be associated in the international mind with American southernness, indeed with nineteenth- and twentieth-century America itself.[12]

The novel belongs to a long tradition of southern plantation fiction and white apologist historiography. It focuses on the South's most dramatic historic period, Secession, followed by the 1861–65 "War Between the States" (Civil War), the bloody demise of plantation culture and the slave economy, and the violent chaos of Reconstruction. Although this period had been fictionalized by other southern writers, Mitchell was

---

12. Richard Gray, "Afterword," in *Dixie Debates: Perspectives on Southern Cultures,* ed. Richard H. King and Helen Taylor (London: Pluto Press, 1996), 220; Margaret Mitchell, *Gone With the Wind* (New York: MacMillan, 1936). For a summary of the history of reception and the phenomenon of *Gone With the Wind,* see Richard Harwell, ed., *"Gone with the Wind" as Book and Film* (Columbia: University of South Carolina Press, 1983); and Helen Taylor, *Scarlett's Women: "Gone With the Wind" and Its Female Fans* (New Brunswick, N.J.: Rutgers University Press, 1989). Books, articles, and vast Web sites detail a plethora of cultural reference, artifacts, and ephemera: memorabilia collections, Scarlett pop-up book, porcelain figurine and music box, Civil War Society costume ball, Scarlett O'Hara impersonator, and so on. See Herb Bridges, *"Frankly, My Dear . . .": "Gone With the Wind" Memorabilia* (Macon, Ga.: Mercer University Press, 1986). The film, repremièred seven times in Atlanta, shows somewhere daily across the globe and is frequently broadcast on television. The videotape—reissued in a newly colorized print in 1989—is a constant bestseller, and any publication or film relating to the work is guaranteed good sales. And since the book and film anniversaries in 1986 and 1989, the sons of David O. Selznick compiled a TV film, *The Making of "Gone With the Wind,"* using unseen footage of screen tests, edited-out scenes, interviews with the cast, and so on. The scholar Darden Asbury Pyron published his authoritative comprehensive biography, *Southern Daughter: The Life of Margaret Mitchell* (New York: Oxford University Press, 1991), a book designed to expand the field of serious scholarship on the writer and her work. In 1995, Mitchell fans were excited by the discovery of a cache of letters, photos, and two unpublished manuscripts of juvenilia. *Lost Laysen* is a 107-page romance novella set in the South Pacific and was swiftly published (ed. Debra Freer; New York: Scribner, 1996); "Lady Godiva," described enthusiastically on the Margaret Mitchell Website, will undoubtedly follow into print.

unique in focusing on such a complex sweep of history from the perspective, and through the experiences, of a young white woman who begins by expressing boredom at the thought of war, then lives through extreme reversals of fortune and wealth, loses parents, husbands, a child, and many friends, yet survives to rebuild her plantation home, way of life, and self-esteem.

Gone With the Wind has sealed in popular imagination a fascinated nostalgia for the glamorous southern plantation house and an ordered hierarchical society in which slaves are "family," and there is a mystical bond between the landowner and the rich soil that those slaves work for him. It has spoken eloquently—albeit from an élite perspective—of the grand themes (war, love, death, conflicts of race, class, gender, and generation) that have crossed continents and cultures. For women reader-viewers, Scarlett O'Hara has provided a rich source of imaginative play and has stood for a quality of female strength, power, and bloody-mindedness that is rare in twentieth-century fiction and film. Characters (Scarlett, Mammy, Rhett), iconic sayings ("Tomorrow is another day,"), and dramatic moments (Atlanta burning and "birthin' babies"), in film as well as novel, acquired international significance for *GWTW* enthusiasts and inspired a tradition of writing and film-making that keeps the work alive, in both its imitations and detractions. Even when, in recent years, African American writing and film from *The Color Purple* to *The Wind Done Gone* have embarrassed *GWTW* fans into a recognition of its historical distortions and the southern belle and her beau are now the subject of TV soap opera and literary parody, the original retains its popular mystique.

From its first publication and the film that followed the novel faithfully, there are many—not least black and white southerners anxious for their region to be represented as modern and progressive—who have wished this work would fade away and occupy a minor role in the representational history of the American South, to be overtaken by versions of the American Civil War of greater verisimilitude and relevance for a multicultural American society. During the decades since the Civil Rights Movement, and especially in a racially sensitive postcolonial world climate, this glorification of a lost world of slavery and socioeconomic exploitation has seemed anachronistic and racially provocative. However, the publicity machine for *Gone With the Wind* ignores such political sensitivities, invoking its character as a work that is "timeless," "legendary," and "immortal." And whereas there is some truth in the claim that *Gone With the Wind* (known familiarly as *GWTW*) appeals enormously to very different nations and cultures, it is important to remember that the legend and longevity of this work have been carefully nurtured by the many groups and individuals—publishers, literary estate, film and television companies, porcelain figurine-makers and so on—who have profited handsomely from the work's "universal" success.

Sharing in this bonanza, European audiences and financial interests have allowed *GWTW* to "endure." Published in the pre–World War II Depression 1930s, this epic work addressed issues close to European hearts: economic and social upheavals, the inevitability of an imminent catastrophic war. As the world recovered from war and holocaust in the 1940s and 1950s, it was a costume drama and heroic story for drab, utilitarian days. In the final three decades of the century, it became a feminist or "Me-Generation" text, as well as a *fin-de-siècle* wallow in nostalgia for days of certainty, continuity, and order. There are still fascinating histories to relate about the popular significance of, and relationships with this work in, say, Finland, Germany, or the Netherlands. For example, after many years of local people's failed attempts to create a Margaret Mitchell Museum in Atlanta, the project succeeded only with the enthusiastic injection of capital support from the German company Daimler Benz AG.

Margaret Mitchell was unusual among 1930s southern novelists in gesturing strongly to Catholic European cultures. Scarlett O'Hara is the daughter of an Irish father, Gerald, and a French mother, Ellen Robillard. Mitchell was very conscious of her own Irish maternal ancestry, and throughout the novel she drew on a romantic Celtic mythology to explain the O'Haras' passionate love for family ties and the land itself. The very name of the plantation, Tara, has that mythic weight that both Gerald and Scarlett draw on to justify the white South's defense of its property— houses as well as slaves. Meanwhile, Ellen's Frenchness is that element of refinement and elegance that made rough farmer Gerald marry her, but it also signifies the deep passion that she suppresses (for lost love, her French cousin Philippe) but which emerges in her willful daughter Scarlett. Scarlett O'Hara, the hybrid product of these two characters and cultures, bridles against the orthodox manners and mores of conventional American southern society, invoking and expressing her Irishness and Frenchness in various ways, from working on the land she loves to keep Tara within the family, to appreciating the fancy bonnet Rhett brings her from Paris.

Mitchell's reference to these European cultures within her own work undoubtedly appealed to European readers and audiences. When other writers turned their attention to the ur-text, either as inspiration or model, they recognized that the ethnic mix within *GWTW* was one of its most appealing features, so they followed suit. During the 1980s, two sequels to the original novel were commissioned; one was published and made into a television series. A French writer, Régine Deforges, was taken to court on a *GWTW*-plagiarism charge, while Julian Green, a distinguished American southerner who had lived most of his life in France, published a trilogy closely following Margaret Mitchell's subject matter.[13] None of these works broke the mold of the original. All played their part in keeping it alive. The Celtic theme was used to a more politically reactionary effect than in Mitchell's and Selznick's work, and the French perspectives cast little new transatlantic light on the old story. The real effect of European engagement with *GWTW* was that European (mainly British) writers and actors, and Europe-based companies (publishing, film, TV, and publicity) financed and profited from new versions of the work to ensure the longevity of the *Gone With the Wind* story well into the twenty-first century.

The Mitchell Literary Estate's commissioning of a sequel to Margaret Mitchell's novel in the 1980s played the most significant part in ensuring new life for the work. After long deliberation, and rumored bids from writers as disparate as lesbian American novelist Rita Mae Brown and British romance queen Barbara Cartland, the Mitchell Estate hired as near a clone of Margaret Mitchell as could be found: Alexandra Ripley, southern author of such historical sagas as *On Leaving Charleston* (1981) and *New Orleans Legacy* (1987). The sequel was promised in 1989 or 1990, to coincide with the film's fiftieth anniversary, around which much media publicity was anticipated. The eventual publication, in 1991, was said to be late because Ripley's first draft was refused by the Estate; she claimed difficulties with an editor. It hardly mattered, since the suspense only aroused further interest in the book.

Scarlett: The Sequel to Margaret Mitchell's "Gone With the Wind"[14] ends by reuniting Scarlett and Rhett, but only after a long series of picaresque adventures involving trips to Charleston, Savannah, Atlanta, and

13. Régine Deforges, *La Bicyclette Bleue* (Paris: Ramsay, 1981), translated by Ros Schwartz as *The Blue Bicycle* (London: W. H. Allen, 1985); Julian Green, *The Distant Lands* (London: Marion Boyars, 1990).

14. Alexandra Ripley, *Scarlett: The Sequel to Margaret Mitchell's "Gone With the Wind"* (New York: Warner, 1991).

finally—for much of the book—Ireland. Scarlett hands over the management of Tara to sister Suellen and with her considerable wealth goes off to get Rhett back, as we knew she must. Rhett, who (as Mitchell made him promise) returned to Charleston, is living with his mother and working as an upmarket camellia grower and fertilizer salesman. After some skirmishing, and a passionate roll on the beach after near-drowning (an encounter that fortuitously impregnates our heroine), Rhett rejects her and marries a dull schoolteacher, who later conveniently dies in childbirth. Scarlett secures the major shareholding in Tara, then turns her back on the South and, inspired by Irish relatives she met in Savannah, sails to her father's birthplace, County Meath, influenced by Gerald O'Hara's memories and love of the Irish soil. Her destination is Adamstown, home of her hundred-year-old grandmother Katie Scarlett, and nearby Tara, that mythic place which gave its name to Scarlett's family plantation. Buying a huge, decaying estate called Ballyhara, Scarlett becomes known as The O'Hara, the most significant landowner and citizen in the area. Taking on a series of curiously feudal roles and responsibilities, she exercises power with benevolent tyranny.

Her extended family are all active members of the Fenian Brotherhood, and for a while—until she begins to hunt and socialize with the Anglos—she finances their activities. An Irish witch delivers her of a daughter, Cat, by cesarean section on Halloween night. The O'Hara clan is idealistic and eminently superstitious, and their revolutionary fervor is finally condemned as pathological and murderous—especially when they try to turn on the newly reunited Scarlett and Rhett, in the final chapter huddled together with their daughter fearing for their lives. As one would expect, this implausible saga has a neat, conservative happy ending, the nuclear family reconstituted with Cat, substitute for the dead daughter Bonnie Blue.

Scarlett appeared in September 1991 in eighteen languages, including Japanese and Chinese, and in forty countries simultaneously. It became the fastest-selling book in publishing history, with 5.5 million copies sold worldwide in its first two months. By 1993, it had sold over 20 million copies worldwide. On 4 October 1991, the *New York Times* ran a full-page advertisement from Warner Books boasting of its success as the "record-breaker for biggest first day sales," and "the overnight national bestseller," quoting booksellers across the land on the lines of people waiting to buy, the "epidemic of Scarlett fever," the mobbing of one store from opening bell to closing time, and so on. The William Morris Agency director of foreign rights described it bombastically as the most successful publication of all time.

Ripley's contract, almost certainly influenced by Mitchell's devout Catholic heirs, proscribed any interracial sex scenes, steamy sex, and homosexuality; Ripley was glad to comply. Indeed, she went further; assuming a mildly politically correct persona, she agreed that racial problems might have been a prickly issue. "I couldn't lie about what things were like in the Nineteenth Century . . . so I just tiptoed around it," she told her *Newsday* interviewer.[15] "Things" were of course the contest over the freed slaves' rights in the Reconstruction South, followed by the "Redemption" of white power. Her white characters would have brutally ensured the restoration of land and wealth, denying freedmen and women access to land, property, the vote, and education through physical intimidation and political chicanery. Ripley acknowledged to her interviewer: "I'm sure there was also a lot of long-suppressed anger [among former slaves], but I didn't bother with that. It's not my story . . . I'm not a sociologist. I'm a novelist." Her narrative decisions, then, included killing off Mammy early on, removing Prissy to another place, and giving the extremely docile ex-slaves minor, insignificant roles. Slave dialect is almost completely absent, as is any discussion of racial issues. The only two black characters given any profile are Scarlett's maid in the South, Pansy (a little in-joke, given the name that Mitchell originally chose for Scarlett herself), and a caricature of "Queen of Sheba," a rich Charleston whorehouse madam and indispensable ladies' seamstress. Most significant of all, halfway through the action Ripley removes Scarlett to Ireland, where she retraces her roots and reestablishes her plantation home in the Anglo-Irish estate Ballyhara. The political struggle on which she focuses is that between the Anglo-Irish and the Irish nationalists in the shape of the Fenian Brotherhood. "[M]ercifully," she said, "everybody is white, so I don't run into that minefield." The defiant tone of the writer's comments can leave readers in little doubt as to her political commitment and racial allegiance.

The book jacket of Ripley's novel, pledged to follow Mitchell's trajectory, claims to "seamlessly pick up the narrative, bringing us back to Tara and the people we remember so well." *Scarlett* takes its eponymous heroine through a series of picaresque adventures during which she gains control of Tara, establishes her own Tara in the land of her family's origins,

15. Aileen Jacobson, "An Author Tiptoes Through the Times," *Newsday*, 25 September 1991, 61.

and regains the loving arms of Rhett Butler. In terms of the focus on the importance of dynasty and land to Irish southerners, and of love as well as independence in women's lives, she continues Mitchell's 1930s preoccupations, the products of Mitchell's family, race, and class. Both novels construct a mythic southern dynasty derived from an idealized version of Irishness—one steeped in hedonism, cunning, family loyalty, and passion, contrasted with the pallid refinement and genteel style of the Anglo-Saxon and French South. Ripley enacts Mitchell's revenge or retribution fantasy, continuing Scarlett's career as a shrewd capitalist ("I am the O'Hara of Ballyhara," she cries),[16] but also making her symbolically restore the rights, dignity and honor of the defeated and brokenhearted South. In case this smacked too uncomfortably of the white South's "Redemption" of its powers after Reconstruction, it all takes place many thousands of miles away.

But Ripley's novel has an interesting contemporary spin. It appeared in 1991, three years after the first publication of a key historical study of Celtic southernness written by a respected if controversial southern scholar. Grady McWhiney's *Cracker Culture,* which has become the Bible of the extreme right-wing League of the South, could well have provided some of the historical inspiration and backbone for the novel. Ripley claimed to have read widely in scholarly materials; given the critical attention that McWhiney received at the time *Scarlett* was being written, and the similarity of their interests, it is unlikely she was ignorant of the book and/or its central argument. McWhiney focuses on Celtic (Irish, Scottish, Welsh, and Cornish) immigration to and cultural assimilation into the South from the seventeenth century to the Civil War. In a polemical prologue, Forrest McDonald argues that, over the centuries, conditions in the English Uplands, Wales, Scotland, and Ireland became unsympathetic to Celtic "traditional ways" and that by migrating to the American South such ways could be preserved and flourish: "[I]n a manner of speaking, their entire history had prepared them to be Southerners."[17]

McWhiney himself claims that the English/Celtic cultural conflict within the British Isles shaped the entire history of the U.S., notably exporting there a sectionalism that "exploded into the War for Southern Independence." English northerners and Celtic southerners are predict-

16. Ripley, *Scarlett,* 556.
17. McWhiney, *Cracker Culture,* liii.

able types: Yankees are commercial, disciplined, hardworking, and WASPishly uptight, whereas southerners (like their Celtic ancestors) are fond of idleness, sensual, good at conversation and leisure pursuits—in short, a lot more fun than the English and Anglo-Yankees. This thesis sees the "leisurely Celtic lifestyle" as central to "Cracker culture," a lifestyle shared by poor and wealthy southerners alike. Shared at least by male whites: McWhiney notes without irony that they "much preferred to enjoy life while their animals, their women, or their slaves made a living for them." He documents the way northerners and Europeans described southerners in the terms often ascribed to premodern British Celts (and, indeed, as McWhiney astonishingly does not acknowledge, to blacks): superstitious, degenerate, licentious, uncontrolled, violent, savage, and barbaric. The antebellum South, in this account, was created and developed by white Celts, then suffered from the cultural imperialism of a North dominated by English peoples and values that were forced onto the South and its Celtic people. The Civil War was the re-run of a former struggle between the English and Celtic cultures, and white crackers (like their Celtic ancestors) "would fight, even if beforehand they knew that their cause was lost."[18]

McWhiney's book has been seen as part of a backlash against postmodern historians and cultural critics who argue that one can no longer speak of a separate "North" and "South," and that "the South" is a largely politically motivated construct of right-wing ideologues who are still fighting a virtual Civil War. It is also seen as a defensive response to liberal academics' championing of African American sociopolitical history and their arguments about the "Africanization" and multicultural nature of southern culture itself. McWhiney's subtext is pretty clear: the South's Celtic settlement, rather than any other, was the central determining factor in its separate development and unique culture. The "cracker," rather than being a buffoon loafer in the region's history, should be seen as its most authentic character type; the Celtic heritage of

18. McWhiney, *Cracker Culture*, 7, 144, 41, 217. This is not the appropriate context for lengthy discussions of McWhiney's thesis. Authoritative countertexts to *Cracker Culture* would, however, include Ted Ownby, *Black and White Cultural Interaction in the Antebellum South* (Oxford: University Press of Mississippi, 1993); William D. Piersen, *Black Legacy: America's Hidden Heritage* (Amherst: University of Massachusetts Press, 1993); Walter Benn Michaels, *Our America: Nativism, Modernism, and Pluralism* (Durham: Duke University Press, 1995); and Minrose C. Gwin, *Black and White Women of the Old South: The Peculiar Sisterhood in American Literature* (Knoxville: University of Tennessee Press, 1985).

the American South therefore becomes its myth of origin. The Civil War is the last stand-off between Celtic man and his longstanding English oppressor.

*   *   *

Whether or not Ripley read McWhiney's reactionary book that has been challenged by most other southern historians and cultural critics, she adhered to its ideological line fairly closely and produced a romantically charged fictional version of the thesis. In many ways, the novel attempts to legitimize those Celtic southern myths of origin and centrality (a very white version that excludes other ethnic groups, especially African Americans) and also to confirm white southerners' sense of themselves as semi-aristocratic descendants of Irish kings. Indeed, the first half of the novel may be read as setting up the competing national cultures within the South in order to establish a kind of authenticity within Ireland itself, near the historic site of Tara, where Scarlett settles and establishes a new dynastic line with daughter Katie (Cat). After burying Melanie and Mammy, Scarlett socializes with Rhett's (very English) Charleston-based mother, Eleanor Butler, and tries unsuccessfully to fit into demure Anglo ways, later moving on to Savannah and her maternal grandfather, the French Pierre Robillard, who demonstrates the rigid *froideur* of the French, from which she flees. Finally, triumphantly, Scarlett discovers her paternal heritage by going to meet a bunch of Irish cousins living in genteel poverty in Savannah, providing an occasional base for another cousin, the priest and Fenian gunrunner Colum, who persuades her to return to her father's native land.

Irishness, in Savannah and later in County Meath, constitutes the "bit of rough" that Scarlett has always craved: physical ease and sensuality, simple pleasures like music and dance, and a chaotic and friendly intergenerational family life. For the white southerner who wishes to validate an authentic vernacular southern style that has no associations with the region's slave history, a celebration of folk culture to the tune of "Peg in a LowBack'd Car" or "The Wearing of the Green" must have seemed a shrewd alternative. And Gerald O'Hara's choice of the name "Tara" for the plantation he won at poker invites a mythic reworking of Celticness, returning Scarlett to her father's homeland, which is essentially a female space ("'to anyone with a drop of Irish blood in them the land they live on is like their mother,'" as Gerald reminds her).[19] It is there that she is converted to the Fenian cause, persuaded of the parallels between her

19. Mitchell, *Gone With the Wind*, 38.

own desire to restore Tara to "rightful" hands after the imperialist ravages of the Union army and the desire of Irish nationalists to throw off the tyranny of English Home Rule and get back Ireland for its "own" people. Colum tells his wide-eyed cousin: "Remember your South, with the boots of the conqueror upon her, and think of Ireland, her beauty and her life's blood in the murdering hands of the enemy. . . . Do you but think of it now, Scarlett, when your Tara was being taken from you. You battled for it. . . . With all your heart, all your wit, all your might. Were lies needed, you could lie, deceptions, you could deceive, murder, you could kill. So it is with us who battle for Ireland."[20]

Thus Ripley draws on the two very disparate histories to link together the two main parts of Scarlett's story and to elevate her heroine's individual quest into an epic one. By taking Scarlett back to the real Tara, and the real rather than yearned-for birthplace of her father, Gerald, Ripley animates a whole mythic space that gives the land and the plantation Tara their suggestive resonance in the original work and ensures a receptive readership from the many Irish Americans, especially perhaps those in the South. Furthermore, this schematic parallelism allows Ripley to tap into a mass international readership that is assumed to be able to absorb facile historical lessons and accept a simple colonialist model of power relations.

During the 1990s, the "Troubles" in Northern Ireland were at their height and were the subject of serious peace talks only in the latter part of the decade; no Irish or British citizen could be in any doubt of the complexity of the situation within the Province, and only the most naïve or blinkered ever saw the conflicts in terms of a one-dimensional imperialist model of Englishness oppressing Irishness. To an American, and especially a Catholic Irish American reader, this simplistic model has often been invoked—especially for Noraid fund-raising for Sinn Fein during a period of violent and often random attacks on both the military and civilians within Northern Ireland and the British mainland. *Scarlett* follows a well-worn trail in drawing deeply from the well of sentimentality and passion that both Celtic and non-Celtic Americans feel for that country. Despite the long history of fierce anti-Catholicism within American mainstream politics, it has been virtually obligatory for modern U.S. presidential contenders, beginning with John F. Kennedy, through Ronald Reagan, Bill Clinton, and Newt Gingrich, to establish their leadership credentials by tracing some Irish family roots. For these politicians, as for

20. Ripley, *Scarlett*, 565.

the vast majority of readers, Ireland is so steeped in mythic properties, such a site of desire and longing, that the unpleasant realities of social and ethnic conflicts, not to mention the political fray, may disappear in a cloud of Celtic twilight and leprechaun-leaping superstition. It is also arguable that Ripley's implied international reader had even hazier notions about nineteenth-century Irish nationalist struggles than about the Reconstruction and Redemption South.

The critical response to the novel, on both sides of the Atlantic, was generally hostile, with the exception of some protective southern journalists. The book was condemned for avoiding complex racial and ethnic issues, not least for misrepresenting the complexity of Irish people and politics. American critic Patricia Storace accused Ripley of "whistling Dixie," and bowing to a "literary Nuremberg law" by accepting the contractual clause forbidding the representation of miscegenation, while M. G. Lord deplored the removal of Scarlett from a South of "poll taxes, grandfather clauses or other obstacles to black suffrage" to a "Disney World" Ireland. British writer Kate Saunders described the Irish characters as "hundreds of grinning, barefooted leprechauns who speak like fund-raising pamphlets for Noraid." The *Irish Independent*'s Justine McCarthy believed that, with Tom Cruise's return from Eire to Hollywood, the Irish movie industry should be grateful to Ripley "for creating a gap in the County Meath market for film locations." None made the connection between lines of attack on the book by pointing out that the novel Ripley had written was as polemical as Mitchell's original. Its audacity and strongly antiliberal line lay in its epic and romantic celebration of Celtic white southernness that simply rendered southern African Americans irrelevant and aspired to take cracker history and culture to new mythic heights. Mammy's killing off in chapter 1 was symbolically apt. As African American critic Alvin Poussaint predicted (arguing that the sequel failed to "take corrective action" over *GWTW*'s political agenda), "the white thing will be re-awakened, without much critical outlook." The reawakened "white thing" had its resurgence in a romantic and politically soft-focused worldwide television serialization of the novel. The miniseries featured a host of British stars, including its two main protagonists (Joanne Whalley-Kilmer and Timothy Dalton), designed to give the production both Euro-U.S. commercial appeal and also that "touch of class" conveyed in the 1939 film with Vivien Leigh and Leslie Howard.[21]

21. Patricia Storace, "Look Away, Dixie Land!" *New York Times*, 19 December 1991, 37; M. G. Lord, "*GWTW II*" *Newsday*, 25 September 1991; Kate Saunders, *Sunday*

*   *   *

However, that reawakened white thing was to come under increasingly serious challenge around the Millennium. In the mid-1990s, the Mitchell Estate commissioned a second sequel by the sophisticated, ironic Scottish writer Emma Tennant, with a view to attracting the critical acclaim that had eluded *Scarlett,* but then the Estate sacked Tennant after finding she had failed to honor their thematically restrictive agenda. Tennant went on scathing record about the squeamish and reactionary attempts to censor and control her work.[22] Her contempt for the Estate was echoed by southern novelist Pat Conroy, who in 1998 announced his own sequel, *The Rules of Pride: The Autobiography of Capt Rhett Butler.* His "companion" to the original was intended to kill off Scarlett O'Hara and—in defiance of the Estate's proscription of any whiff of homosexuality or miscegenation—would open with the sentence, "After they made love, Rhett turned to Ashley Wilkes and said, 'Ashley, have I ever told you that my grandmother was black?'" The novel has not yet appeared, but upstaging Conroy's mischievous approach, an important intervention in the *GWTW* saga hit the headlines in 2001. Alice Randall's "parody" novel, *The Wind Done Gone,* was taken to an Atlanta court by the Mitchell Estate for violating copyright laws with "blatant theft" of Mitchell's novel's themes and characters; U.S. District Court Judge Charles A. Pannell Jr. agreed and banned publication. Leading intellectuals and writers led an outcry against the Estate, claiming censorship of free speech. Randall's publishers, Houghton Mifflin, successfully appealed the decision on the grounds that the novel was a "political parody" and was thus protected by the First Amendment, as well as presenting a new perspective on the original story. In June 2001, the novel appeared to considerable critical and public interest, with blurb endorsements from Tony Earley and Jay McInerney that claim it as "the connective tissue that binds the fairytale of *Gone With the Wind* to the gothic nightmare of *Absalom, Absalom!*" and "a brilliant meditation on a modern myth."[23]

Times, 6 October 1991, 6; Justine McCarthy, *Irish Independent,* 26 October 1991, n.d. (Macmillan Publishing, New York, Macmillan cuttings file, October 1991); Alvin Poussaint, quoted in Jacobson, "An Author Tiptoes Through the Times," 61.

22. Emma Tennant, "Gone!" *Telegraph Magazine,* 7 September 1996, 24. For extended discussion of this, see Helen Taylor, *Circling Dixie: Contemporary Southern Culture Through a Transatlantic Lens* (New Brunswick, N.J.: Rutgers University Press, 2001), ch. 2, "*Gone With the Wind* into the Millennium: Sequels, Borrowings, and Revisions."

23. Alice Randall, *The Wind Done Gone* (Boston and New York: Houghton Mifflin, 2001). Subsequent references will be included parenthetically in the text. Also see Paul Gray, "The Birth of a Novel," *Time,* 7 May 2001, 4; Christina Cheakalos et al., "Wind

The narrative is a diary "discovered" in the 1990s in an assisted-living center outside Atlanta, written by Cynara, named after the eponymous Ernest Dowson poem from which the "Gone With the Wind" title derives. She is half-sister to Other (Randall's neatly reversed racial stereotyping of Scarlett), daughter of Planter (Gerald O'Hara) and Mammy, who all inhabit Cotton Farm, Tata (Tara). Cynara's diary records her story for posterity, partly to challenge *Uncle Tom's Cabin* ("I didn't see me in it"), partly to testify to a particular slave history that would otherwise be forgotten (as with Frederick Douglass, who is named, and Toni Morrison's "rememorying," which is woven intertextually throughout). Events progress the story after Rhett has abandoned Scarlett and she has returned to Tara and Mammy; the ur-novel's characters, themes, and phrases are referenced throughout. *The Wind Done Gone* documents the deaths of both Mammy and Other herself—the literary murder planned by Pat Conroy, whose gay scenario is also echoed in Randall's bisexual Ashley. These deaths produce in Cynara a crisis of confidence and direction, resulting in her confused marriage to her long-term lover and Other's widower, a bewildered, broken "R." (Rhett Butler).

Increasingly, Cynara and R. are driven apart by their different responses to memory: when they live together in R.'s Atlanta house, R. tells her, " 'Don't bring your past into this house,' " while she is acutely aware he has brought into it "his history" (27). The novel traces her painful past as a mixed-race slave whose family is riddled with both long-standing miscegenation secrets and secrecy, and whose life is blighted by her attempts to come to terms with them and to move on in an uneasily multicultural nation.The lack of love between Cynara and her real mother is contrasted with the passionate bonding between her and "Lady" (Ellen O'Hara), the latter explained in terms of Lady's own mixed-race heritage, which prevented marriage to a beloved cousin. The companionate and sexually charged love between R. and Cynara is challenged by Other's death and R's subsequent return to Cotton Farm and white southern traditional values; she meanwhile escapes that alien past by moving to Washington, D.C., for an unmarried liaison and baby with a black congressman, before contracting lupus from which she eventually dies.

Part of this escape from a fraught past is reflected in Randall's revisionary view of European values and qualities—the very elements that are so mythified in Mitchell's original and Ripley's sequel. With ironic

Storm," *People,* 7 May 2001, 91–92; John Sutherland, "A Satirical Take on *Gone With the Wind?* You Might as Well Burn the American Flag," *G2 The Guardian,* 7 May 2001, 6.

echoes of the Paris sojourn of Thomas Jefferson and Sally Hemings, Cynara is sent on a "Grand Tour" of European cities, crossing the ocean on the *Baltic,* a ship that carried supplies for the relief of Fort Sumter. Cynara hates her journey, discovering a fear of seawater that recurs in her stay in European cities on rivers. R. plans to take her to London, where they will marry and live as a "passing" white couple. However, Cynara's resistance grows as she considers herself part of "a sailed people" (156) who crossed to America, so that fear of "crossing the water" is the only thing she retains of her mother's and grandmother's, described with echoes of the Middle Passage section of Toni Morrison's *Beloved* as "a heavy lump of an unexplored thing, like a clod of brown-red mud giving off some old mother heat" (156). Cynara's only European yearning is for London, a city known through her reading of the inevitable Walter Scott and Jane Austen (the latter loved only for *Mansfield Park* because "Fanny hated slavers," [157]).

Celticness is never celebrated as in *GWTW* or *Scarlett,* nor is Gerald O'Hara's mystical relationship with Irish land and heritage. Ireland is described only as a country from which Planter fled from the law, wanted for murder and theft. Cynara's Irish heritage is not the red soil of Tara but (as Lady warns her) the reddening face and thickening nose characteristic of the drinking Irish. For Randall, the Atlantic crossing, and transatlantic connections, were bringers not of nostalgia or celebration but rather of terrible racial memories and fears.

Until the end of the twentieth century, *GWTW*'s characters, images, key scenes, and phrases were constantly recycled in popular novels, magazines, TV shows, and colloquial conversation. Publishers, film-makers, and writers quoted and parodied its various elements, straining to titillate new markets. The commercial success of the Ripley sequel and TV version seemed to ensure a robust continuation of the novel's ideological work. And indeed, its power must not be underestimated. *GWTW* was able to hold its own as a world cultural icon throughout two-thirds of the twentieth century. At the 1996 Olympics, international visitors poured out of the Atlanta airport asking to see Tara; a year later, a German-sponsored Margaret Mitchell Museum opened to satisfy tourist demand; memorabilia-collectors and anniversary-watchers are well served by an efficient, lucrative *GWTW* industry; a respected Scottish novelist had a go at the second sequel to the novel; an English journalist complained that the thirty-six-tape "audio book" version of the novel occupied an entire seat of her car; throughout the world, TV comedies, chat shows, and arts programs reference the work constantly. The Celtic theme of the Ripley sequel and the choice of British stars for the mini-series have given a new relevance to the story for British reader-viewers. Its manifold global circulations and reinterpretations have coincided with, and imaginatively played into, a rise in reactionary movements such as the League of the South and the new academic challenge to multiculturalism, "White Studies," together with neo-fascist groups in many European countries. As with southern groups' appropriations of *Braveheart, Gone With the Wind,* the romantic epic that has appealed so widely to international audiences, received in *Scarlett* a new Celtic transatlantic spin that allowed millennial readers to forget that work's negative and oppressive influence on representations and aspirations about race and gender throughout the twentieth century.

Yet Alice Randall, of mixed-race ancestry with a Confederate general ancestor, has reminded the world that there is another story to tell, and that is a story of miscegenation, mixed histories and loyalties that must be addressed before the myth of Tara can be laid to rest. Her bold and witty novel was written to "help more healing to occur," and its affirmative, semi-utopian conclusion—in which Tata is bequeathed (albeit reluctantly) by R. to his black butler and all its black, white, and mixed-race inhabitants are buried together—offers a gesture of national reparation and conciliation. The novel elegantly fits the bill proposed by Maya Angelou when she wrote prophetically,

> You are gone but not forgotten
> Hail, Scarlett. Requiescat in pace.[24]

24. Maya Angelou, "Miss Scarlett, Mr. Rhett, and Other Latter-day Saints," in *Just Give Me a Cool Drink of Water 'Fore I Die: The Poetry of Maya Angelou* (London: Virago, 1988), 28.

The South of the Mind

Diane Roberts

It was supposed to be gone by now, the South, all difference swept away in America's mass-culture tsunami. Malls, McDonaldses, interstate highways, agribusiness, suburbanization, tourism, cable television, Sunbelt migration, and global capitalism were supposed to have inundated the South's otherness by now, rendering the region indistinguishable (except for a few geographical and meteorological quirks) from Michigan or Kansas or the San Fernando Valley. Psychically, the South would be like one of those legendary drowned lands, Ys or Lyonesse, where at certain times, if you listen carefully, you can hear the church bells, the sounds of the old ways, under the water—but not very distinctly and not very often.

The South has always been disappearing, or about to disappear. When the Nashville Agrarians warned in 1930 that the South had "shown signs of wanting to join up behind the common or American industrial ideal" and predicted dire, deracinating consequences, there was already a body of endangerment literature before them. The sense of impending loss, of a whole order of life slipping away, has been expressed by both progressives and conservatives in the South. The South as its people knew it was perpetually on the brink of disintegration, about to reach the Promised Land or else about to slide into apocalyptic chaos.

In 1972, when southern states still clung to Jim Crow, when most southern schools were still segregated, when southern legislatures were defeating the Equal Rights Amendment on the grounds that it would "destroy the Christian home," and southern whites still stood when the band played "Dixie," journalist Marshall Frady was planning the South's funeral: "The South is being etherized, subtly rendered pastless, memoryless and vague of identity. What we are talking about is the passing of a sensibility."[1]

Frady was hardly ahead of the curve: in 1948, William Faulkner waxed bitter over the replacement of the southern wilderness by suburbs with houses "designed in Florida and California set with matching garages in their neat plots of clipped grass and tedious flower beds."[2] In 1936, Margaret Mitchell's *Gone With the Wind* eulogized a bucolic Old South while expressing mixed emotions about an avaricious New South. The be-columned Big House, the grumpy Mammy, the happy field hands, the rakish Gent, and the flirtatious Belle all became part of the nation's— not just the South's—reservoir of nostalgia, valued precisely because it was all lost, or almost lost. The Big House was burned, Mammy dead, the field hands gone north to Chicago or Detroit or Harlem, the Gent ruined when the bottom fell out of the cotton market, and the Belle now short-skirted, short-haired, and addicted to gin and cigarettes.

But even *Gone With the Wind* was just another in a long line of books, plays, and films feeding the national sense that the South was at once "another land, sharply differentiated from the rest of the American nation," as W. J. Cash put it, and being rapidly (and tragically) assimilated into the American melting pot. Around the turn of the twentieth century, writers like Thomas Nelson Page celebrated the *neiges d'antan* of the old feudal order in *Marse Chan and Other Stories* (1887) and *In Ole Virginia* (1912). Joel Chandler Harris eulogized slavery days in his plantation novels and Uncle Remus stories. In reaction to all this backward-looking (but best-selling) moonlight-and-magnolias prose, Mark Twain was inclined to sneer. In *Life on the Mississippi*, when someone remarks on the beauty of the southern moonlight, an archetypal old mammy, perverse keeper of the antebellum flame, replies, "Ah, bless yo' heart, honey, you ought to seen dat moon befo' de WA!"[3]

1. Marshall Frady, *Southerners* (New York: New American Library, 1980), 23.
2. William Faulkner, *Intruder in the Dust* (New York: Random House, 1948), 198.
3. W. J. Cash, *The Mind of the South* (New York: Knopf, 1941), vii; Mark Twain, *Life on the Mississippi* (New York: Harper, 1923), 365. Twain took a very dim view of the

Place is always entangled with history in the South. How we feel about, or write about, Vicksburg or the Blue Ridge or Selma is colored by the long, exhaustively reiterated list of events that happened there. Slavery is the still-crippling catastrophe that haunts black southerners as the Civil War is the still-obsessed-over central moment in the white southern psyche, the catastrophe that wrecked the plantation Eden (as it was represented by the upper classes) and destroyed the slave economy.

Yet even as early as the 1820s, the white South felt under attack from the North. The Missouri Compromise of 1820, in which a line on the map of the nation was drawn—36 degrees 30' of latitude—dividing the country into slave territory and free territory, underscored the South's difference. Subtler lines were drawn, too, between proslavery and abolitionist forces, between the plantation elite and poor whites, between an agrarian economy and an industrializing one, between states' rightists and believers in the supremacy of the federal government. What Richard Gray calls "Southern self-fashioning" hit high gear in the 1830s, driven simultaneously by threats from outside and the conviction that white southerners were the exemplary Americans, ordained by God to uphold highly defined (and quite conservative) race, gender, and class roles.

To some extent, the plantation South was always under attack. In 1831, Nat Turner, a charismatic slave preacher, led a revolt in Virginia. Sixty whites died. In 1832, South Carolina defied the federal government over tariffs, but ultimately lost, and William Lloyd Garrison began publishing *The Liberator*, calling for immediate emancipation of all slaves with no compensation for plantation owners. Southerners such as John C. Calhoun felt they might have to ignite a second American Revolution to assert the sovereignty of the states.[4]

---

white South's look-back pathology, even going so far as to blame the Civil War on Sir Walter Scott. Scott's novels, read as an endorsement of romantic nationalism, were wildly popular among the upper classes in the ante- and postbellum South.

Moreover, one of the oddest ways conservative white southerners had to express the fineness of the world destroyed by the Civil War was to put the nostalgia in the mouths of black characters. Mammy characters, in particular, were pressed into service by Margaret Mitchell, Sara Haardt, Stark Young, Thomas Nelson Page, and Thomas Dixon Jr. to embody the glories of the ancien régime.

4. On the Missouri Compromise, the Nullification Crisis of the 1830s, and the hardening of sectional definitions and race, gender, and class roles in the South, see Charles S. Sydnor, *The Development of Southern Sectionalism* (Baton Rouge: Louisiana State University Press, 1948); Joel Williamson, *New People: Miscegenation and Mulattoes in the United States* (New York: Free Press, 1980); Bertram Wyatt-Brown, *Southern Honor* (New York: Oxford University Press, 1982); Eugene Genovese, *The Political Economy of Slavery* (New York: Pantheon, 1965) and *The World the Slaveholders Made* (New York: Pantheon,

The white South, ever bellicose, defended itself. Calhoun, James Henry Hammond, and other Tenth-Amendment literalists argued an exceptionalist position for the South. Hammond defended his "country" as a land "whose men are proverbially brave, intellectual and hospitable, and whose women are unaffectedly chaste, devoted to domestic life, and happy in it," with all credit due to the South's "peculiar institution of slavery, not merely a necessary evil but a positive good.[5]

But important as states'-rights politicians were, even more profound ideological work was carried out by fiction writers. When *Uncle Tom's Cabin* came out, the proslavery *Southern Literary Messenger* saw it as "evidence" of how "our enemies are employing literature for our overthrow." The anonymous writer calls on "Southern authors" to defend slavery. Scores of novelists, many of them women, heeded the cry, churning out stories in which slaves learn that abolitionists are racist or lascivious or both, that life with Massa and Ole Miss is God-ordained, and that there's no place like (the plantation) home. Mary H. Eastman's *Aunt Phillis' Cabin* (1852), Caroline Lee Hentz's *The Planter's Northern Bride* (1854), Caroline Rush's *The North and the South* (1852), and J. Thornton Randolph's *The Cabin and the Parlor* (1852) are just a few of the counter-fictions produced to praise and "protect" the South in the 1850s.[6]

Twenty years before, in an attempt to become the South's Scott, William Gilmore Simms also tried to justify the ways of his people to the North. He spent the 1830s producing novel after novel about South Carolina during the Revolutionary War, presenting its Great Chain of Being—God, master, mistress, slave, livestock—as an order for all of America, indeed, the world, to envy. Caroline Gilman, a New Englander "converted" to the southern sensibility, wrote of the kindliness and high

---

1969); C. Vann Woodward, *American Counterpoint: Slavery and Racism in the North-South Dialogue* (Boston: Little, Brown, 1971) and *The Burden of Southern History* (Baton Rouge: Louisiana State University Press, 1969); James C. Cobb, *The Most Southern Place on Earth: The Mississippi Delta and the Roots of Regional Identity* (New York: Oxford University Press, 1992); and William Ferris and Charles Reagan Wilson, eds., *The Encyclopedia of Southern Culture* (Chapel Hill: University of North Carolina Press, 1989).

5. See James Henry Hammond, *Letter to an English Abolitionist*, 1845. Quoted in *The Literature of the American South*, ed. William L. Andrews et al. (New York: W. W. Norton, 1998), 96.

6. *Southern Literary Messenger*, 23 October 1856, 242–43; Diane Roberts, *The Myth of Aunt Jemima: Representations of Race and Region* (London and New York: Routledge, 1994), ch. 2.

moral tone of the southern plantation family, broadly, almost biblically, defined as master, mistress, their children, and their slaves—children of another sort.[7]

John Pendleton Kennedy, progenitor of the plantation novel, represented the slave South as Arcadia where high-spirited heroines fell in love with romantic gentlemen, where servants were comical, fathers bluff, mothers gentle, and houses gracious. Kennedy's stories are balm to soothe an unstable South nervous about slave uprisings, angry over federal "interference," obsessed with racial definition.[8] In *Swallow Barn* (1832), the main business is getting the lovely but tomboyish Bel Tracy suitably married, but there is a subplot involving a potentially rebellious slave. Still, this watered-down echo of Nat Turner ends up sacrificing himself for his white folks, reassuring the reader that the slaves love their owners and truly don't want to be free. Real slaveholding whites, outnumbered 10 to 1—sometimes 100 to 1—on their isolated plantations, may have lived in terror of the next Denmark Vesey, Nat Turner, or even Toussaint L'Ouverture, but *romanciers* like Kennedy affirmed at least the theory, if not the practice, of slaveholding in fiction.

Kennedy, Simms, Gilman, Eastman, and other writers taking their stand pre-Modernism tend to look at least one generation back to more effectively defend and celebrate the region. The past is solid, safe, and fixed; the present is conditional, fragile, the site where the old verities are attacked and might be destroyed. The South as an ideal can only exist on the edge of extinction, can only be valued as a sacred and beloved location when it might be extinguished altogether.

The praising and preserving of this South is largely a project of the white establishment. This is not surprising, since the differences that defined the South from its colonial beginnings—slavery, exaggerated gender, race, and class roles, a land-based social and economic order, and a fixation with honor—are conservative by their very nature. The landowning elite (and the poor whites who had only the color of their skin to lend them dignity in this system) were heavily invested in a status quo that derived some of its appeal from a posited state of endangerment. To

---

7. See William Gilmore Simms, *Guy Rivers* (1834), *The Yemassee* (1835), *The Partisan* (1835), etc.; and Caroline Gilman, *The Planter's Northern Bride* (1838).

8. The more the plantation South felt itself to be under threat from "outside" (the federal government) as well as "inside" (slave rebellions and home-grown abolitionists), the more racial boundaries were drawn. Free blacks were denied property and political rights; racial ambiguities were ironed out. See Williamson, *New People*, 12–20.

this day, the South remains more conservative than the nation as a whole, reinforcing its separateness, its specialness, through the time-tested means of identifying, then resisting, threats from the world north of the Mason-Dixon Line.[9]

Of course, the American South isn't the only place to behave in this way: all conservatives want to "conserve" the past, constructed as the font of virtue. British Tories look to imperial history, the monarchy, the military, and an imagined pre-industrial pastoral economy. They used to look to the Church of England, but lately it has become a hotbed of (relative) liberalism. The Roman Catholic Church has fought off attempts to democratize its structure and dogma, recently reasserting its primacy in Christendom by reiterating its origins two thousand years ago in the ministry of the Apostle Peter. White Americans, faced with the feared loss of their social and political hegemony (though a quick glance at big corporations and the U.S. government reveals that white men are, almost without exception, still in charge), have singled out the 1950s, World War II ("the greatest generation"), even the 1880s as times of special virtue.

What all these eras have in common is a top-down power structure, a decorum in which gender and race roles are obviously and concretely assigned. But what the *evocation* of these cultures and times has in common is a willful ahistoricity, a refusal to acknowledge that during these halcyon days, women had few rights and opportunities, and blacks fewer still. The subtext is that these times are celebrated precisely *because* blacks, women, and the poor were powerless. While other nations, and other groups within nations, were skilled at concocting self-aggrandizing, comforting, highly edited pasts to get nostalgic over, the South remains the champion, concocting ways to glamorize the time when most of its people were poor, when almost all blacks were enslaved, and when few people of any race could vote.

The white South is expert at "inventing traditions" to bolster its simultaneous sense of exceptionalism and endangerment. Invented tradi-

9. A number of writers have addressed the South's conservatism and its influence on the nation as a whole. Peter Applebome's *Dixie Rising: How the South Is Shaping American Values, Politics, and Culture* (New York: Times Books, 1996), is a good exploration of Southern dominance of the national political scene. Even better is John Egerton's *The Americanization of Dixie: The Southernization of America* (New York: Harper's Magazine Press, 1974). See also Earl and Merle Black, *The Vital South* (Cambridge: Harvard University Press, 1992); Dan T. Carter, *The Politics of Rage* (New York: Simon and Schuster, 1995) on George Wallace; Cobb, *The Most Southern Place on Earth*; and Dewey W. Grantham, *The South in Modern America: A Region at Odds* (New York: Harper Collins, 1994).

tions are, as Eric Hobsbawm says, "responses to novel situations" with reference to "a suitable historic past." The Confederate battle flag, for example, never flew over any southern capitol building, nor was it used as an official standard signifying the southern "nation" in the Civil War. It was revived in the 1950s as a symbol of resistance to the Supreme Court's 1954 decision mandating desegregation. Georgia incorporated a battle flag into its state flag in 1956; Alabama began to fly it in the early 1960s to spite U.S. Attorney General Robert F. Kennedy when he demanded that the University of Alabama admit black students.[10]

Yet many white southerners are convinced that the banner flapped from the domes of state houses from time immemorial (or at least from 1861), a praiseworthy reference to the Confederate past. The battle flag has become the key symbol of what some southerners claim as the region's "heritage," and a reminder that the South has "always" been different. This accounts for the recent controversies over de-emphasizing or removing Confederate flags from official buildings in South Carolina, Florida, Mississippi, and Georgia. Florida had it easiest: the governor simply had the "Third National" flag of the Confederacy removed from the capitol grounds and placed in a museum. In Georgia, the state legislature approved a new flag that incorporated various flags from the state's past in tiny rectangles labeled "Georgia's History." Groups such as the Sons of Confederate Veterans and the League of the South protested vociferously, but most Georgians, mindful of their image in the global village, went along with the redesign.

In South Carolina, however, the fight over emblems of the past was messier, with boycotts and demonstrations by the National Association for the Advancement of Colored People. Conservative white groups charged (as usual) that "outside agitators" were trying to besmirch the sacred legacy of their ancestors who had "resisted invasion." But most of those "outside agitators" were black South Carolinians, descendants of the slaves whose labor built the big houses and bought the English silver and paid for the Sully portraits and generally made the lingering image of the "gracious" Old South possible.[11]

10. Eric Hobsbawm and Terence Ranger, eds., *The Invention of Tradition* (Cambridge University Press, 1983), 1–2 (this volume contains a variety of excellent essays on how the past is appropriated, manipulated, and edited to serve particular ideologies); E. Culpepper Clark, *The Schoolhouse Door: Segregation's Last Stand at the University of Alabama* (New York: Oxford University Press, 1993).

11. Conservative heritage groups ranging from the comparatively moderate Sons of Confederate Veterans and Daughters of the Confederacy to the Council of Conservative

And in Mississippi, in the spring of 2001, the fault line between competing definitions of the South became even more apparent. A coalition of progressive whites, led by former governor William Winter, business leaders, and black groups spent a great deal of time and money trying to persuade Mississippians to vote for a new flag, one without the St. Andrew cross and stars.[12] It didn't work. Voters rejected the new flag and clung to the Jim Crow banner by a huge margin. White southerners, especially white southern men, cling to the counter-intuitive notion that they are a minority in their own region, constantly under attack from within and without. It didn't matter that some businesses might not relocate to Mississippi because of the flag; it didn't matter that the outside world could continue to see Mississippi as racist and backward. Mississippians chose to embrace the "poor but proud" cliché, affixing "Surrender, hell!" bumper stickers to their cars and running up rebel flags in their front yards. Once again, place, history, and the fear of imminent loss got all knotted up into an act of resistance that in itself defines the South as separate and distinct. Mississippi, at least, will not yet join the Union.

This has been the conservative South's *modus operandi* since before the Civil War: locate a threat and resist it. Governor George Wallace of Alabama was particularly adept at reinventing the South through creating a sense of embattlement. During the 1950s and 1960s, he characterized Alabama as "the last stronghold of the Anglo-Saxon civilization," ranted against the threat to the "Southern way of life" (segregation), and campaigned using posters depicting a little white girl surrounded by black boys and the screaming caption "Blacks Vow to Take Over Alabama." Wallace himself was just following in the tradition of politically astute writers such as Thomas Dixon Jr., who in 1905 lamented the loss in the South of the old "aristocracy of brains, culture and blood," trading the righteous order of slavery for a world where white men are powerless

---

Citizens, the neo-secessionist League of the South, and the various white supremacist groups are still arguing that slavery had nothing to do with the Civil War. They claim that the war was fought over "states' rights" (though the chief "right" the states were interested in was the "right" to own slaves) and cast the war as a patriotic resistance to centralized power. See Diane Roberts, "A League of Their Own," *Southern Exposure* 25 (1997): 18–23; see also Applebome, *Dixie Rising*; and Tony Horwitz, *Confederates in the Attic: Dispatches from the Unfinished Civil War* (New York: Pantheon, 1998).

12. Mississippi incorporated the battle flag emblem into its state banner in 1894, around the time many segregation laws were coming into effect.

and white women constantly menaced by black rapists bent on creating a new master race of mulattoes.[13]

Although the act of fabricating the nexus of heroic history, romanticization of place, and expectation of loss which has constructed the mythic South has been largely a conservative enterprise, it is important to note an alternative tradition with its roots in the South's small but tenacious pockets of progressivism. This tradition also laments the loss of old ways but focuses on romantic notions of the Folk and the Land. The plantation past inspires anger at the suppression of African culture, the abuses of slavery, and the damage done to the land when it was cleared for cotton. W. J. Cash and the North Carolina school of new historians and sociologists of the 1930s and 1940s tried to debunk the Lost Cause version of the Old South while sorrowing over the retreat from old southern virtues and resisting both the incursions of "the Yankee" and its own "too great attachment to racial values and a tendency to justify cruelty and injustice in the name of those values."[14]

Folklorists went to the mountains to collect ballads unchanged since the Battle of the Boyne and tried to document ways of life being eroded by roads and radios. Blues scholars sat on Delta front porches listening to old men pick and improvise, fearful that the ancient, raw sound could disappear without a witness. Zora Neale Hurston recorded the stories of Eatonville and the black communities of Florida, Georgia, and the Caribbean, knowing that they would soon disappear. Native American activists see their South being destroyed over hundreds of years, ever since the arrival of the Spanish with their swords and their smallpox, and fight to preserve pieces of it. Environmentalists, sometimes sounding a little like the Nashville Agrarians, locate virtue in a past time of less population, less technology, and less capitalism. But instead of looking to religion, racial decorum, and a "shared" culture, they seek to protect pieces of a much older Old South against developers, paper mills, and agribusiness.

No matter what the political persuasion, the need to declare the South endangered is itself an act designed to insist on the South's distinctiveness, to shore it up, then to recast it. Poor paranoid Wilbur Cash tried, in 1941, to encompass the "mind" of the South when what he was really after was the South of the mind, the imagined, yet geographically, historically, and culturally locatable place that so enraptures and enrages.

13. Carter, *The Politics of Rage*, ch. 10; Thomas Dixon Jr., *The Clansman* (New York: Doubleday, 1905), 5.

14. Cash, *The Mind of the South*, 440.

As these essays show, that region, that state of being, that category we call "the South" is expanding as much as it was ever in danger of contracting. Southern no longer means "white," as it used to, nor does it imply a simple white/black binary, but now includes Latinos and Asians in its mix. The South retains its place on the margins of America—still poorer, still more violent, still more past-obsessed, race-aware, and gender-traditionalist—while also finding itself at the center.

The protean, paradoxical, changing South was wonderfully illustrated during the postelection imbroglio in Florida.[15] The various lawyers, spin doctors, political consultants, party hangers-on, and journalists who descended on the state in November 2000 could not work out how to tag it. Is Florida in the South? Those billeted in Tallahassee saw that the place is as southern as Georgia: tea is sweet unless otherwise specified, everyone says "y'all," there are big white houses, Spanish moss, and a Confederate memorial in front of the capitol building. Those closer to the bilingual tropics kept flirting with the term "banana republic."

The infusion of Caribbeans and Latinos, not to mention Yankees and Snowbirds, inspired many to knock Florida off the "southern" roster. But the inarguably "southern" North Carolina gets more northern *émigrés* every year. Workers of Mexican and Jamaican extraction are picking fruit in Georgia and Alabama, many of them settling down to raise families in Cordele or Anniston or wherever. As for the Cubans in Miami, no immigrant group came more readily equipped to be called "southern." Like the traditionally defined southerner, the Exiles come from a rich mix of African and European influences, cherish a pathological sense of loss, cling to an old-time religion, and have mythologized history out of all accuracy. Cuba was a plantation society, too.

So it was exquisitely appropriate that in the 2000 presidential election, a Tennessean and a Texan strove for the office held for eight years by an Arkansan in a state that may be said to represent the newest of New Souths. Indeed, as many have pointed out, it is no longer adequate to speak of the South; we must have *Souths,* a plural land now reflecting the multifariousness of its cultures and peoples.

And as for the disappearing South, the South that must be (to paraphrase Faulkner) destroyed in order to have existed at all, well, some Souths will carry on teetering on the brink of the abyss while others arise

15. Many in the old cotton belt of Florida took to referring to the postelection kerfluffle as "the Late Unpleasantness," which is what many of their great-grandmothers called the Civil War.

to take their place. Many old ways have passed—and thank God for that—but we are still debating the Confederate battle flag, creationism and evolution, and public prayer. The state of Alabama voted to remove a provision in its 1901 constitution banning interracial marriages, but not until November of 2000.[16] Yet Alabama lawyers from the Southern Poverty Law Center recently bankrupted a white supremacist organization—in the Pacific Northwest.

Southerners now dream new ways of being southern, drawing new boundary lines between the (however reluctantly) multicultural "us" and the nonsouthern "them." We still speak with a variety of southern accents, we still eat grits (quite unself-consciously), we still get shivers at the sound of Martin Luther King Jr.'s voice. Sure, the South, described by Cash as "a sort of cosmic conspiracy against reality in favor of romance," still colludes in its own production, its own legendizing. But then, it always has. The "newcomers" will invent and invest in their own Souths and so change the region. But the old core of difference—however defined—will continue to flourish. The flames of sheer perversity must be tended; the crop of paradox must be laid. Keeping up mythic property is hard work.

16. The federal Constitution has, for years, protected marriages between blacks and whites in Alabama, superseding the eccentricities of the state constitution. Nonetheless, a September 2000 poll conducted by the University of South Alabama reveals that nearly one-third of Alabamians (mostly white) still oppose miscegenation (AP wire story, *Tuscaloosa News*, 11 September 2000).

CONTRIBUTORS

ERIC GARY ANDERSON is associate professor of English at Oklahoma State University, where he teaches American and American Indian literatures. He is the author of *American Indian Literature and the Southwest: Contexts and Dispositions* and of various articles on topics ranging from Native film and Trickster stories to Linda Hogan's *Mean Spirit*.

WES BERRY teaches fiction writing and twentieth-century literature at Rockford College in northern Illinois. His published work includes short stories, creative nonfiction, and critical essays on Walter Inglis Anderson, Wendell Berry, Cormac McCarthy, and Leslie Marmon Silko. He is completing a book entitled *Landscapes of Healing in Contemporary American Prose*.

MARTYN BONE teaches American literature at the University of Copenhagen. Bone's essay on the postsouthern sense of place in Walker Percy's *The Moviegoer* and Richard Ford's *The Sportswriter* appeared in the "South to a New Place" special issue of *Critical Survey*. He has also published articles on William Faulkner and Barry Hannah in *Mississippi Quarterly* and on Ford's *Independence Day* in *American Studies in Scandinavia*.

DEBORAH COHN is assistant professor of Spanish at Indiana University, Bloomington. She is the author of a book, *History and Memory in the Two Souths: Recent Southern and Spanish American Fiction*, and her articles have appeared in *Comparative Literature Studies*, *The Comparatist*, *Latin American Literary Review*, *Hispanofila*, *Revista Hispanica*

Moderna, and other journals. Her current research interests include comparative literature of the Americas, the promotion of Boom literature in the U.S., and the intellectual infrastructure of Mexico City in the mid-twentieth century.

AMY J. ELIAS is associate professor and director of undergraduate studies in the English Department at the University of Alabama at Birmingham. Her published work includes *Sublime Desire: History and Fiction Since 1960* and articles in *Contemporary Literature, Modern Fiction Studies,* and *Critique.* She is currently working on a study of postmodern ethics and aesthetics.

CHRISTINE GERHARDT teaches American literature and culture in the Department of English and American Studies at the University of Dortmund in Germany. Her book on fictional interpretations of the Reconstruction era in nineteenth- and twentieth-century literature defines the Reconstruction novel as formula literature that has kept alive the memory of a culturally and politically distinct South. She is now working on a book about nature and ecology in nineteenth-century American poetry that explores intersections between place, environmental politics, and poetics.

RICHARD GRAY is professor in the Department of Literature at the University of Essex. He is the author of *The Literature of Memory: Modern Writers of the American South, Writing the South: Ideas of an American Region* (which won the C. Hugh Holman Award from the Society for the Study of Southern Literature), *American Poetry of the Twentieth Century, The Life of William Faulkner: A Critical Biography,* and *Southern Aberrations: Writers of the American South and the Problems of Regionalism.* He has edited two anthologies of American poetry, two editions of the poetry of Edgar Allan Poe, a collection of original essays on American fiction, and a collection of essays on Robert Penn Warren, and has published a number of essays and articles on American literature. He is currently editing *A Companion to the Literature and Culture of the American South* and writing a history of American literature. A regular reviewer for various newspapers and journals, including the *Times Literary Supplement,* he is editor of the *Journal of American Studies* and the first specialist in American literature to be elected a Fellow of the British Academy.

MATTHEW GUINN is managing editor in the Division of Publications and Periodicals at the University of Alabama in Birmingham. He is the author of *After Southern Modernism: Fiction of the Contemporary South* and *Murk*, a novel. He has published articles on southern writers in *Southern Quarterly*, *South Atlantic Review*, and *Resources for American Literary Study*.

CAROLYN M. JONES is associate professor of Religion and African American Studies at the University of Georgia. She is the author of articles on a wide range of writers from Toni Morrison and Harper Lee to D. H. Lawrence. She has just completed a book on Toni Morrison.

SUZANNE W. JONES is associate professor of English at the University of Richmond. She is the editor of a collection of essays, *Writing the Woman Artist*, and two collections of stories, *Growing Up in the South* and *Crossing the Color Line: Readings in Black and White*. Her articles on southern fiction have appeared in a number of journals and collections. She is finishing a book on the representation of race relations in contemporary southern fiction.

MICHAEL KREYLING is professor of English at Vanderbilt University. He is the author of *Eudora Welty's Achievement of Order*, *Author and Agent: Eudora Welty and Diarmuid Russell*, and *Inventing Southern Literature*. He held the Fulbright Chair in American Studies at the University of Naples in 1994.

BARBARA LADD is associate professor of English at Emory University in Atlanta, Georgia. She is the author of a book, *Nationalism and the Color Line in George W. Cable, Mark Twain, and William Faulkner*, and her articles have appeared in *American Literature*, *Mississippi Quarterly*, *Bucknell Review*, and elsewhere.

PAUL LYONS is associate professor of English at the University of Hawai'i at Manoa. He is at work on a manuscript on American Pacific Orientalism, sections of which have appeared in *Arizona Quarterly*, *Boundary 2*, *ESQ: A Journal of the American Renaissance*, and the volume of critical essays *Inside/Out: Literature, Cultural Politics, and Identity in the New Pacific*. The essay in this collection was originally printed in *Studies in American Fiction*.

ROBERT MCRUER is an assistant professor of English at George Washington University. He is the author of *The Queer Renaissance: Contempo-*

rary American Literature and the Reinvention of Lesbian and Gay Identities, and his articles have appeared in *Genders, GLQ: A Journal of Lesbian and Gay Studies,* and the *Children's Literature Association Quarterly.* With Abby Wilkerson, he guest-edited a special issue of *GLQ* on the intersections of queer theory and disability studies, and he is currently completing a book, *De-Composing Bodies: Cultural Signs of Queerness and Disability.*

SHARON MONTEITH is senior lecturer in the School of American and Canadian Studies at the University of Nottingham. In addition to articles and chapters in collections on southern literature and American Studies, her publications on the American South include *Gender and the Civil Rights Movement* (with Peter J. Ling) and *Advancing Sisterhood? Interracial Friendships in Contemporary Southern Fiction.* She is working on a book on cinema and fiction about the Civil Rights movement.

DIANE ROBERTS is the author of *Faulkner and Southern Womanhood* and *The Myth of Aunt Jemima,* as well as many articles and essays on southern culture. She writes about southern politics for the *St. Petersburg Times* as well as the *Times* of London and *The New Republic,* and she is a commentator for National Public Radio and for the BBC. She is currently professor of English at the University of Alabama.

SCOTT ROMINE is associate professor and director of undergraduate studies in the Department of English at the University of North Carolina at Greensboro. He is the author of *The Narrative Forms of Southern Community* and articles about southern literature that have appeared in *Mississippi Quarterly, South Atlantic Review, Southern Literary Review, Southern Quarterly,* and *Style.* He is currently working on a study of contemporary southern narrative.

MAUREEN RYAN is professor of English and dean of the Honors College at the University of Southern Mississippi. Her publications include *Innocence and Estrangement in the Fiction of Jean Stafford,* as well as articles on modern and contemporary American women writers and on American literature of the Vietnam War. She is working on a book tentatively titled *The Other Side of Grief: Women and Gender in the American Literature of the Vietnam War.*

JON SMITH is assistant professor of English at Mississippi State University and managing editor of *Mississippi Quarterly: The Journal of Southern*

Cultures. His work on various twentieth-century U.S. writers has appeared in *American Literary History, Modern Fiction Studies, Contemporary Literature,* and the *Faulkner Journal*. He is co-editor, with Deborah Cohn, of *Look Away! Postcolonial Theory, the U.S. South, and New World Studies,* and is completing a book on the legacy of Progressive conservationism in U.S. literature from the 1890s through the 1950s.

HELEN TAYLOR is professor and chair of English at the University of Exeter. She has published, lectured, and taught widely on southern literature and popular culture. Her publications include *Gender, Race, and Region in the Writings of Grace King, Ruth McEnery Stuart, and Kate Chopin, Scarlett's Women: "Gone With the Wind" and Its Female Fans, Dixie Debates: Perspectives on Southern Cultures* (co-edited with Richard H. King), and *Circling Dixie: Contemporary Southern Culture Through a Transatlantic Lens*.

INDEX

Abbey, Edward, 148, 158; *Desert Solitaire,* 162, 164, 177

Ackerman, Charlie, 209

Affirmative action: opposition to, 54

African American literature: hybridity of, 162–63; and intellectualism, 70; and nature writing, 147–49, 164n.23; regional identity, 265; and rural communities, 151–52; and rural landscapes, 152n.7; and the southern landscape, 150–51, 161; and land ownership, 144–45, 144n.34. *See also* Race relations

African American culture: Great Migration, 121; and homosexuality, 184–95; and the rural South, 121; and migration to city, 15; and return migration, 122, 122n.1, 123

Afrocentrism, 72

Agee, James, 17, 288, 297–302; *Let Us Now Praise Famous Men,* 297

Agrarianism: interracial, 132; contemporary agrarians, 121–46

Agrarians, 29–32; *I'll Take My Stand,* xv, 14, 17, 27, 34, 43, 80, 129, 121, 131, 140, 237, 288, 294, 363, 371; definition of place, 32; and industrialism, 124, 143; and literary-critical canon, 210; neo-Agrarian, 40, 212; real estate development, 125; revision of, 13, 146; similarity to Levi, Carlo, 301–302

Aldridge, John W., 280n.23

Alexander House, 70

Allen, Paula Gunn, 105

Allende, Isabel: *The House of the Spirits,* 333n.21

Allison, Dorothy: *Bastard Out of Carolina,* 106n.14, 206

Amerasian Homecoming Act, 249

American Indians: Claims Commission, 168; discrimination of, 165; and ecocriticism, 176–83; Florida Indian History, 166; and government policy, 168; intraregional conflict, 169; literature of, 171–72, 175, 179; and power, 180; removal of, 165n.2; Removal Act of 1830, 179; in the South, 165; and stereotypes, 176. *See also* Native Americans

American Indian culture, 167, 176–79, 180–83; misconceptions of, 170–71; regional identity of, 169; and sense of community, 173; tribes of, 168. *See also* Native Americans

American Revolution, 340, 365, 366

Anderson, Benedict: *Imagined Communities,* 103n.10; globalization, 276; nationalism, xix; 88–89

Anderson, Eric Gary, 15

Andy Griffith Show, 90

Angelou, Maya, 347, 362; autobiography of, 345

Appalachian literature, 35
Applebome, Peter, 5, 4, 253
Arnold, Matthew, 344
Arrington, Richard, 253
Astronauts (band), 93
Atlanta: and black middle class, 225; and capitalist production, 209; in capitalist world system, 209; and new immigrants, 223, 227–29; identity of, 226; as international city, 208, 219–20, 223–24, 233; and international investments, 220n.22; and land speculation, 214–18, 220; and the literary-critical map, 210; and local poverty, 224, 224n.27; multicultural population, 226–27; national city, 210n.6; representation of residents, 209; sense of place, 210; social geographies, 211; and the socio-spatial chasm, 222–23; uneven development of, 225; Vietnamese immigrants in, 228; Wolfe's depiction of, 221n.23
Atlanta Constitution, 128
Auden, W. H., 60
Augé, Marc, 115, 105n.11
Austen, Jane, 361
Autoethnography, 132–33, 133n.19
Awiakta, Marilou, 171
Ayers, Edward L., 246

Bach, Johann Sebastian, 67
Bakhtin, Mikhail, 75, 194
Bain, Robert, 35
Baldwin, James: 5, 6; and black middle class, 225; contradictions of the South, 5; intimacy and race relations, 61–62
Bambara, Toni Cade: *Those Bones Are Not My Child,* 226
Bancroft, George, 55
Barker, Roger, 127
Barthelme, Frederick, 43
Barthes, Roland, 41, 87
Bartram, William, 80n.9
Basie, Count, 70
Bass, Rick, 80n.9
Baudrillard, Jean, 264, 42, 258
Beam, Joseph, 189n.12
Becquer, Marcos, 186–89

Bell, David, 77
Bell, Madison Smartt: and the Agrarians, 124–33; emotional response to place, 139; representation of contemporary agrarian South, 123; rural experience of, 124n.5; *Soldier's Joy,* 125–32; 144–46
Benjamin, Walter, 116
Bennett, Tony, 264
Bentley, Jerry, 67
Bercovitch, Sacvan, 3
Berendt, John: *Midnight in the Garden of Good and Evil,* 208
Berlin Wall, 94, 318
Berret, Jesse, 94
Berry, Wendell: 121, 123, 146; on nature and healing, 153; on pastoralism, 113; on regionalism, 54–55; on southern identity, 10; on use of land, 152n.7
Berry, Wes, 6, 14
Berube, Michael, 195
Bhabha, Homi K., 64, 89
Biko, Steve, 17
Billie, James, 170n.7
Blake, William, 298
Blount, Roy, 279
Blues music: and identity, 74; and intellectualism, 75; and literature, 70–71, 71n.23; and racial discourse, 64–65; blues metaphor, 9, 12, 62; function of, 65–66; identity and community, 66; idiom of, 63; survival of, 73
Boaz, Franz, 121
Bombal, Maria Luisa, 18; *The Shrouded Woman,* 331
Bomboras (band), 92
Bone, Martyn, 15
Bonetti, Kay, 196
Borges, Jorge Luis, 18, 321
Bourdieu, Pierre, 218n.17
BR-549 (band), 91
Bradley, David: *The Chaneysville Incident,* 122
Bredel, Willi: "Petra Harms," 305, 306–9, 312
Brer Rabbit, 69
Brian Setzer, 92
British influence, 343–44: on southern literature, 345–46; British Tories, 368

Brodhead, Richard, 115n.20

Brooks, Cleanth, 78, 238, 343

Brown v. Board of Education, 139

Brown, Larry: 2, 15; *Joe,* 12–13, 103–17; and sense of place, 2; as southern realist, 206

Brown, Rita Mae, 351

Browning, Robert, 344

Buell, Lawrence, 14, 80, 148, 163

Burke, James Lee, 346

Bush, George W., 82n.12

Butler, Jack, 239

Butler, Judith, 193

Butler, Octavia, 6; *Kindred,* 122

Butler, Robert Olen, 16, 241, 245; "The American Couple," 242–43; biracial literary history, 8; "Ghost Story," 243; *A Good Scent from a Strange Mountain,* 235; "Letters from My Father," 250; "Love," 247; "Relic," 240

Cable, G. W., 109

Caldwell, Erskine: *God's Little Acre,* 19; *Tobacco Road,* 17, 19

Calhoun, John C., 365–66

Calvo, Lino Novás, 321

Campbell, Bebe Moore: *Your Blues Ain't Like Mine,* 122

Cao, Lan, 16, 245, 250, 251; *Monkey Bridge,* 7–8, 237, 241–42, 245

Carlyle, Thomas, 19, 344

Carruthers, William Alexander: *The Cavaliers of Virginia,* 342; *The Knights of the Golden Horseshoe,* 342

Carson, Warren, 64, 60, 72–73

Carter, Hodding, 61

Carter, Jimmy, 4

Cartland, Barbara, 351

Carver, Raymond, 279

Cash, Johnny, 76, 90

Cash, W. J., 35, 98, 364, 371; *The Mind of the South,* 293

Castells, Manuel, 209, 219

Cather, Willa, xiii

Cavour, Count Camillo, 285, 289

Cawelti, John, 25

Celts: and cultural conflict, 354–56; and myth, 19; in the South, 340; immigration of, 354; mythology of, and white supremacy, 341

Censer, Jane Turner, 289

Certeau, Michel de, 221

Chapel Hill Progressives, 294

Chappell, Fred, 34

Chatwin, Bruce, 110

Chaucer, Geoffrey, 70

Cherokee memorials to Congress, 168, 168n.5

Chesnutt, Charles: "The Passing of Grandison," 309–14

Chicken processing, 228, 229n.34

Childress, Mark, 280

Chin, Frank, 99

Chodorow, Nancy, 81

Choi, Susan, 7

Chomsky, Noam, 276

Church of England, 368

Churchill, Winston, 89

Citizens' Council, 139

Civil Rights movement: 17, 35, 54, 94, 105n.12, 111, 139, 349; Freedom Riders, 1; honors to leaders of, 47; memory of, 52n.14; and racial discourse, 72

Civil War: 35, 53–54, 100, 122, 237, 251, 261, 305, 318, 340–44, 354, 365, 369; books about, 110; defense of, 369–70n.11; and *Gone With the Wind,* 348–49; historical reenactments of, 122n.2; historiography of, 53–54; honors to heroes of, 47; and Lost Cause, 12; memory of, 52n.14; reenactments of, 346; southern attitudes toward, xvi; and southern rock music, 12. *See also* Confederacy; Confederate flag

Cleaver, Eldridge, 151, 159

Clifford, James, 286–87, 296–98

Clinton, Bill, 57n.19, 347, 358

Cobb, James C., 81, 86; defending the South, 4; sense of place, 2; on southern identity, 84–85, 264

Cohen, Ed, 188

Cohn, Deborah, 9, 18, 76, 333n.21

Cold War, 52, 92, 93

Comer, Krista, 176–78

Confederacy, 77, 344, 369, 369–70n.11
Confederate flag, 4, 82, 82n.12, 369–70,
370n.12
Conley, Robert, 171
Conroy, Pat: *The Rules of Pride: The Auto-
biography Capt Rhett Butler,* 359–60
Consumer culture, xx, 106, 111, 201
Council of Conservative Citizens, 369–
70n.11
Cousins, Tom, 209
Covington, Vicki, 279
Creole-French tradition, 344
Crèvecoeur, Jean de, 104
Crews, Harry, 279, 124
Cronon, William, 14, 149
Cuban Revolution of 1959, 323, 334
Cultural exchange: and race relations, 67,
69, 69n.21, 74; and white intellectuals,
68; cultural homogenization, 201–2
Cunningham, Malena, 253
Custer, George Armstrong, 273

Dabbs, James McBride, 35
Daimler Benz AG, 350
Dainotto, Roberto Mario, 97–98, 109
Dale, Dick, 91n.24, 93; "Miserlou,"
90n.23
Daniels, Jonathon, 69
Darwin, Charles, 344
DATO Award, 278
Daughters of the Confederacy, 369–70n.11
Davenport, Jim, 82n.12
Davidson, Donald, 30, 33, 35, 202, 210;
literary regionalism, 38; sense of place,
29–32
Davidson, Phebe, 169
Davis, Thadious M., 35, 123, 166, 166n.3
Davis, Townsend: *Weary Feet, Rested
Souls,* 1n.1
Dead Man Walking: stereotypes in, 102n.9
Debo, Angie: *The Road to Disappearance,*
171
Debord, Guy, 217
Defoe, Daniel: *Moll Flanders,* 19
Deforest, John William: *Miss Ravenel's
Conversion from Secession to Loyalty,*
289

Deforges, Régine, 351
Degler, Carl, 3–4
Deloria, Philip, 175–76
Demetrakopoulos, Stephanie A., 152,
156n.13, 163n.22
D'Emilio, John, 189
Dent, Tom: *Southern Journey,* 1, 7
De Roberto, Federico, 291, 292, 293; *I Vic-
ere, 290–91*
Descombes, Vincent, 105n.11
Detweiler, Robert, 66
Dexter, Pete: *Paris Trout,* 6
Di Lampedusa, Giuseppe: *Il Gattopardo
(The Leopard),* 292–93
Díaz, Porfirio, 333
Dickens, Charles, iii; *A Christmas Carol,*
185
Dickey, James, 4
Dickinson, Emily, 164n.23
Dillard, Annie, 148, 158, 162; *Pilgrim at
Tinker Creek,* 156, 164
Dirlik, Arif, 103
Dixon, Melvin, 159
Dixon, Thomas: *The Clansman,* 289, 341,
370
Dodd, Elizabeth, 147
Dollard, John, 31
Donoso, José, 321, 323
Donaldson, Susan, 87n.20
Donovan, Josephine, 103n.10
Douglas, Ellen, 132n.18; *Can't Quit You,
Baby,* 144n.34; and the contemporary
agrarian South, 123; response to Faulk-
ner, 133–34, 143–44, 144n.33; *The
Rock Cried Out,* 13–14, 132–46
Douglas, Marjorie Stoneman, 15
Douglas, Mary, xxii
Douglas, Norman, 17; *South Wind,* 295
Douglass, Frederick, 342, 360; *Narrative of
the Life of Frederick Douglass, an Ameri-
can Slave,* 344
Dowson, Ernest, 360
Du Bois, W. E. B., 60
Duggan, Lisa, 191
Dunbar, Leslie W., 4

Earle, Steve, 90
Early, Tony, 359

Eastman, Mary H.: *Aunt Phillis' Cabin,* 366–67

Echenique, Alfredo Bryce, 335

Eckart, Gabriele: "Feldberg and Back," 18, 314–18

Ecocriticism, 14, 15, 165–83

Edgerton, Clyde, 2, 25

Elias, Amy J., 16

Ellington, Duke, 64, 70

Ellison, Ralph, 70, 75, 121

Emancipation, 54

Emerson, Ralph Waldo, 148, 157

Environmentalism, 111–14, 371

Eplan, Leon, 226

Equal Rights Amendment, 364

Erdrich, Louise: *Love Medicine,* 152

Ethnic diversity, 7–8, 235–52

Euro-American colonization, 167–68

Evans, Walker, 288; *Let Us Now Praise Famous Men,* 297

Evers, Medgar, 6

Faludi, Susan, 87n.20

Fanon, Frantz, 302

Farm Security Administration, 297

Faulkner, William, xv, 2, 9, 14, 17–18, 25, 39, 83, 110, 123–24, 136–37, 143–44, 169, 197, 202, 210, 257, 279, 293, 364, 372; *A Fable,* 198; "A Rose for Emily," 236, 327–30; *Absalom, Absalom!* 81–82, 327, 330–34, 333n.21, 335–38, 359; *As I Lay Dying,* 325–26, 330–31; "The Bear," 13–14, 107, 129–30, 134, 158, 173; biography of, 6n.9; blues idiom, 71n.23; "Delta Autumn," 129n.11, 143; Ellen Douglas's response to, 133–34, 143–44, 144n.33; *Go Down Moses,* 134; "The Hamlet," 134, 290; historical paralysis, 327–28; influence of, 18, 287; literary matrix of southern culture, 107n.15; and Latin American literature, 262, 320–339; *Light in August,* 327; modernist techniques, 329–30, 322–25; *Mosquitos,* 295; narrators in the works of, 325–26; "The Old People," 130; and the representation of community, 326–27; sense of place, 2, 35; *The Sound and the Fury,* 71, 82, 320–22, 325–26, 335–38; southern authenticity, 226; southern white guilt, 121; "Spotted Horses," 2

Featherstone, Mike, 114

Feminism, 36, 105n.12, 111; opposition to, 54

Ferguson, Charlie, 265–67

Fernández, Roberto G., 7

Ferré, Rosario, 18, 321; *Maldito Amor,* 336–37; *Sweet Diamond Dust,* 335–38

Fetishism, 213; and commodification, 83; and the Confederate flag, 82; narrative, 78, 82; and the southern past, 78; southern personal identity, 83–84

Finance capitalists, 214–216

Fisher, Philip, 97–98, 100

Fitzgerald, Frances: *Fire in the Lake,* 237

Flora, Joseph M., 35

Flynn, James, 259

Folks, Jeffrey J., 25

Forbes, Steve, 82n.12

Ford, Richard, 25, 196, 345; *Independence Day,* 197–99, 203–6; sense of place, 2; southern identity, 279; *The Sportswriter,* 197–203; *An Urge for Going,* 207

Foster, Stephen Williams, 101n.7

Foucault, Michel, 187n.6

Fowler, Connie May, 15

Frady, Marshall, 364

Frampton, Kenneth, 100, 103, 115

Frank, Thomas, 92

Franklin, Cindy, 99n.4

Franklin, John Hope, 4–5

Freedman, Estelle B., 189

Freud, Sigmund, 8, 77–78

Fuentes, Carlos, 321, 323, 324, 339; *The Death of Artemio Cruz,* 328, 329–30, 331, 333

Fuss, Diana, 188

Gabbard, Krin, 92

Gaines, Ernest, xv, 34–35; *A Gathering of Old Men,* 129, 145

Gallagher, Winifred, 138n.25

Gardner, Mary, 16, 245; *Boat People,* 241, 242, 246, 247

Garrison, William Lloyd, 365
Gates, Henry Louis, Jr., 15, 185, 186n.4, 194
Gebhard, Caroline, 87n.20
Geertz, Clifford, 264
Gellner, Ernest, xviii
Gender issues, 87n.20; in Faulkner's "The Bear," 173–74; in Hogan's *Power,* 173–74
Gerhardt, Christine, 18
German Democratic Republic, 18, 304–5; literature of, 303–19
Giddens, Anthony, 44n.2
Gilchrist, Ellen: *In the Land of Dreamy Dreams,* 345
Gilman, Caroline, 366–67
Gilman, Owen W., Jr., 250
Gingrich, Newt, 358
Glasgow, Ellen, xiii; *The Man of the People,* 290
Gleason, William, 210
Glissant, Edouard, 67
Globalization, 90n.23, 276; American superculture, 347; in music, 90–91. *See also* Transnationalism
Goldfield, David R., 144n.32
Goldstein, Richard, 92, 94
Gore, Al, 50
Gramsci, Antonio, 109; and the southern problem, 294–97; on southern Italy, 17; on southern problem in politics and poetics, 288
Gray, Richard, 4, 10, 88, 126, 134, 238–39, 347, 365
Great Depression, 350
Gretlund, Jan Nordby, 2, 146
Grewal, Gurleen, 152, 159
Griffith, D. W.: *The Birth of a Nation,* 341
Grigsby, John L., 138n.26
Grimshaw, James A., 25
Grisham, John, 346
Grove, James, 25
Guinn, Matthew, 14–15
Gurganus, Alan: *Oldest Living Confederate Widow Tells All,* 1

Hallam, Russell, 238
Hamilton, Gerald, 70

Hammond, James Henry, 344, 366
Hannah, Barry, 40, 43, 279
Hardy, Thomas, xiii, 25
Harjo, Joy, 171
Harlem Renaissance, 121
Harris, Eddy, 6, 122n.1, 148; *Mississippi Solo,* 147, 150; nature and healing, 149; *South of Haunted Dreams,* 121, 150
Harris, Joel Chandler, 364
Hartmann, Charles: *Jazz Text,* 63, 66
Harvey, David, 209, 214, 221; on globalization, 276; on symbolic capital, 218n.17; on postmodern geographies, 36; on postmodernity, 261
Hau'ofa, Epeli, 110
Hays Rule, 184
Hebdige, Dick, 84, 86–89
Hegel, Georg Wilhelm Friedrich, 67n.20
Helms, Jesse, 84
Hemingway, Ernest, 40, 70; *A Farewell to Arms,* 66
Hempel, Amy, 279
Hemphill, Essex, 189, 189n.12
Hentz, Caroline Lee: *The Planter's Northern Bride,* 366
Heym, Stefan, 53; "Mein Richard," 309, 311–14
Hobsbawm, Eric, 369
Hobson, Fred: on old southern themes, 2; on postmodern criticism, 33–35; on postmodernism, 196; on southern literary influences, 279; on southern role reversal, 253; *Tell About the South,* 123
Hogan, Linda: background of, 169; *Mean Spirit,* 170; *Power,* 15, 165–83; sense of place, 169–70
Holman, C. Hugh, 2, 35, 238
Holman, David Marion, 27
Holmes, Steven A., 82n.12
Holocaust, 78
Homosexuals, 145, 184–95; African American, 184–95; and migration to the city, 185, 185n.2; and religion, 190–91; and sense of community, 186; and sense of place, 185; and teenage suicide, 193–94, 193n.17
Horton, Hamilton C., 144n.32

Horwitz, Tony, 102n.9, 122n.2, 286
Houston, James D., 100
Howorth, Lisa, 85
Hubbell, Jay B., 3
Humphreys, Josephine: *Rich in Love,* 239
Humphries, Jefferson, 38–39, 101
Hurston, Zora Neale: *Their Eyes Were Watching God,* xxiii, 15, 19, 121, 148, 150, 163n.22, 164n.23, 178, 371
Hyatt Regency Hilton Head, 265n.14; 265–67

Ihimaera, Witi, 163n.20
Imbrie, Ann E., 153n.9
intertextuality: cross-cultural 163n.20
Intimacy: and colonialism, 61–62; and multiculturalism, 63; and race relations, 58–75; and the homeplace, 62–63
Italian literature, 289–90; and cultural stereotypes, 293; and the exotic, 299; and genealogy, 291; and religion, 294–95; and socioeconomic class, 292–93
Italy: commodification of, 300–1; politics of, 296–97; urban intellectuals in, 297

Jack Daniel's, "Tennessee Squire Program," 343
Jackson, Andrew, 168; era of, 343
Jackson, Miss., 207
Jacobs, Harriet: *Incidents in the Life of a Slave Girl,* 344
Jacobs, Robert D., 32
Jameson, Fredric, 200, 209, 221; on communal ritual, xxiii; on aesthetic populism, 199; on finance capital, 216, 218; on globalization, 276; on postmodernism, 201, 212, 261, 264
Jarvis, Brian, 221
Jefferson, Thomas, 39, 288, 295–96, 343
Jim Crow laws, 6, 364, 370
John Birch Society, 341
Johnson, Charles: *Middle Passage,* 122
Johnson, James Weldon, 64
Johnson, Lyndon B., 71
Jones, Anne Goodwyn, 36, 87n.20
Jones, Carolyn M., 12
Jones, Madison, 124

Jones, Suzanne W., 6, 13
Jordan, David, 240
Joyce, James, 60, 322; *Ulysses,* 331
Jung, Carl, 32
Justus, James, 238–39, 251–52

Kafka, Franz, 298, 322
Kant, Immanuel, 162
Karlin, Wayne, 16; *Lost Armies,* 240–42, 244; *The Prisoners,* 237, 249–50
Kawaharada, Denis, 110
Keely, Karen A., 289
Kenan, Randall: land ownership, 145; *Let the Dead Bury Their Dead and Other Stories,* 195; "Run, Mourner, Run," 145; *A Visitation of Spirits,* 15, 184–95; *Walking on Water,* 10
Kennedy, John F., 358
Kennedy, John Pendleton: *Swallow Barn,* 289, 367
Kersey, Harry A., 168
Keyes, Frances Parkinson, 346
King, Martin Luther, Jr., 5, 14, 61–62; holiday of, 253; and southern identity, xix
King, Richard H., 230
Kingsolver, Barbara, 182
Kingston, Maxine Hong: *China Men,* 152
Kirby, Jack Temple, 3
Kowalewski, Michael, 11, 47, 51, 100n.5
Kreyling, Michael, 41–42; critical regionalism, 117; on ethnicity, 7; postmodern geographies, 15; postsouthern condition, 39–40; sense of past, 238; southern identity, 88–89, 251; southern Italy, 17; the Agrarians, 29–30
Kristeva, Julia, 86
Ku Klux Klan, 128, 131–32, 139, 142, 215, 247, 253, 341

LaBastille, Anne, 153
Ladd, Barbara, 11–12, 27, 58, 90n.23
Laika and the Cosmonauts (band), 93
Land distribution, 140–41, 143
League of the South, 341, 354, 369, 369–70n.11
Lee, Robert E., 39
Lennon, John, 241

Lenz, Gunter, 18
Leopold, Aldo, 148
Lester, Julius: *And All Our Wounds Forgiven,* 14
Levi, Carlo, 17, 288; *Cristo si è Fermato a Eboli,* 297–302
Lewis, Jerry Lee, 90
Lewis, John: *Walking with the Wind,* 4–5
Lewis, Peirce, 259, 259n.7
Lewis, Sinclair: *Babbitt,* 206; 324
Lincoln, Abraham, 285
Littlefield, Daniel F., 171
Livingston, Jennie: *Paris Is Burning,* 187
Llosa, Mario Vargas, 287, 321, 335; *The Cubs,* 329; *The Real Life of Alejandro Mayta,* 333n.21
Logue, John, 259n.7, 277
Lohmann, Larry, 278
Long, Charles, 73
Lopez, Barry, 14, 54–55, 149,158
Lord, M. G., 358
Loriggio, Francesco, 252
Lost Cause, 77–78
Louisiana Purchase, 53
L'Ouverture, Toussaint, 367
Lowe, John, 239
Luce, Henry, 297, 298
Lutwack, Leonard, 3
Lyons, Paul, 12–13; 15
Lyotard, Jean-François, 36, 41, 261, 264, 276
Lytle, Andrew, 124, 126, 132; "The Hind Tit," 124; *I'll Take My Stand,* 214; *A Wake for the Living,* 196

MacKethan, Lucinda, 36
Mailer, Norman, 232
Malek, Anwar Abdul, xvii–xviii
Malle, Louis: *Alamo Bay,* 244, 247
Mandela, Nelson, 347
Manifest Destiny, 273
Mann, Thomas, 60, 70
Manzoni, Alessandro: *I Promessi Sposi,* 289
Marchessault, Janine, 264
Márquez, Gabriel García, 287, 321, 323; *The Autumn of the Patriarch,* 331, 334;

Chronicle of a Death Foretold, 335; and Faulkner, 262, 320–21; *Leaf Storm,* 326, 328, 331; "Nabo: The Black Man Who Made the Angels Wait," 326; *One Hundred Years of Solitude,* 328, 333n.21, 333–35; Spanish American Writers, 18
Marshall, John, 168, 168n.5
Martin, Russell, 117
Martineau, Harriet, 6
Marxism, 30, 217
Mason, Bobbie Ann, 34, 43, 239, 279
Mason-Dixon Line, 7, 83, 339, 368
Massell, Sam, 210n.6
Massey, Doreen, 35
McCain, John, 82n.12
McCalla, Gary, 259n.7, 277, 280; *Life at Southern Living,* 258n.5
McCarthy, Cormac, 25, 279
McCarthy, Justine: *The Irish Independent,* 358
McClain, Larry, 11
McCullers, Carson, 5
McDonald, Forrest, 354
McGill, Ralph, 17
McInerney, Jay, 279, 359
McKay, Claude: *Banana Bottom,* 49
McMath, Robert C., Jr., 253
McRuer, Robert, 15
McWhiney, Grady: *Cracker Culture,* 341, 354–56
Mencken, H. L.: "The Sahara of the Bozart," 294
Meredith, James, 94
Mexican independence, 333
Mexican Revolution, 333
Michaels, Walter Benn, 77
Michaud, Charles: *A Piece of My Heart,* 198, 205
Middleton, Joyce Irene, 156n.13
Mill, John Stuart, 344
Miller, Rick, 87n.19, 88; 91, 92
Milton, John: *Comus,* 344; *Paradise Lost,* 344
Missouri Compromise of 1820, 365
Mitchell, Margaret, 79–80, 360–61; and relationship to the land, xiv–xv; *Gone With the Wind,* 19, 79, 210n.6, 226, 346,

348n.12; 350–54, 359, 361–62; literary estate of, 351, 359; museum of, 350
Mixed-race identity, 249–50
Mohanty, Satya P., 60
Mondale, Clarence, 304–5
Moore, Harry, 99
Moore, Marijo, 171
Morris, Willie, 9
Morrison, Toni, 6, 12, 60, 74, 157, 226; and southern identity, 279; and southern-ness, 57n.19; *Beloved,* 46, 82, 122, 150, 361; intimacy and place, 62; place and race, 59; *The House That Race Built,* 59n.2; *Song of Solomon,* 14, 122, 147, 152, 154, 156n.13, 158–60
Morton, Brian, 7
Muir, John, 148
Murphy, Patrick, 177
Murray, Albert, 58–75; *The Blue Devils of Nada,* 66, 70; blues metaphor, 9, 12; *The Hero and the Blues,* 74; *The Omni Americans,* 63
Music: sociopolitical events, 93–95; subcul-tures of, 91–93. *See also* Blues music
Mussolini, Benito, 294

NAACP, 369
Naipaul, V. S., 9
Nairn, Tom, xviii
Najerian, Peter: *Voyages,* 152
Nandy, Ashis, 61–62, 73
Narcissism, 76, 80
NASCAR, 87
Nationalism, xviii–xix
Native Americans: as activists, 371; dis-placement of, 54. *See also* American In-dians
Nature: and ego dissolution, 156; and heal-ing 149, 153; parody of, 160
Naylor, Gloria: *Mama Day,* 122, 148
Neo-Confederate influence, 122n.2, 123, 341
Neo-Fugitive movement, 43
New Criticism, 30
New Historians, 45
New South capitalism, 210
Nietzsche, Friedrich, 103

Nixon, Herman C., 142n.31
Nixon, Rob, 17
Noble, Donald R., 279
Nora, Pierre, 46, 96
Nordan, Lewis, 43; *Wolf Whistle,* 280
Norden, C. Christopher, 163n.20
Novel-in-a-day tradition, 331
Nunn, Alexander, 259n.7
Nuremberg Law, 358
NuSouth emblem, 82–83

O'Brien, Michael, xviii, 26, 32, 84, 127
O'Bryan-Knight, Jean, 329
O'Connor, Flannery, 124, 169, 197, 232; "The Artificial Nigger," 214–15; and southern identity, 102
Odum, Harold, 99, 101
Odum, Howard, 29
Oklahoma Convention & Visitors Bureau, 273
Old South, 231, 371; Chesnutt's view of, 311–12; compared to German Demo-cratic Republic, 305; nostalgia for, 364, 364n.3; and racial stereotypes, 266–67
Onetti, Juan Carlos, 321; "The Purloined Bride," 328
Ortiz, Simon, 163
Owens, Louis, 171
Ownby, Ted, 12

Page, Philip, 160
Page, Thomas Nelson, 310; *In Ole Virginia,* 121, 305, 364; *Marse Chan and Other Stories,* 364; *Polly, A Christmas Recollec-tion,* 305–9
Painter, Nell Irvin, 122
Pannell, Charles A., 359
Parins, James W., 171
Pastoral: 147–64 153n.9; faux, 200
Pastoral ideal, 140
Penetrators (band), 92, 93
Percy, Walker, 1, 68, 61, 125, 211, 280n.23; apocalyptic vision of, 124, 131; defending the South, 5; and heritage, 73; hybridity of southern culture, 12; land speculation, 214; sense of place, 2; south-

ern identity, 279; southern vacation travel, 280
Percy, William Alexander, 41; *Lanterns on the Levee,* 1
Perkins, James A., 25
Peter, Apostle, 368
Peyser, Thomas, 90n.23
Piglia, Ricardo, 335
Plaid Cymru, 341
Poe, Clarence, 259n.7
Poe, Edgar Allan, 39, 52, 109
Polhemus, Ted, 89
Polk, Noel, 198
Ponce de Leon, Juan, 270
Portman, John, 201, 209
Postmodernism, 261; and capitalist production, 213–14; and the South, 211; cartographies of, 221; definition of, 44n.2; high and low culture, 201; and simulation, 42n.25, and southern literature, 33
Poussaint, Alvin, 358
Powell, Padgett, 279
Powell, Timothy, 168
Pratt, Mary Louise, 133n.19
Presley, Elvis, 85–87, 346–47
Preston, Howard L., 253
Proust, Marcel, 322
Provincialism, 100
Pryse, Marjorie, 315
Puerto Rico Tourism Company, 264
Pulp Fiction soundtrack, 90n.23, 92

Queer theory, 188

Race relations, 121–46; and intimacy, 17, 58–75; interracial marriages, 73n.16; and land distribution, 132; and mixed-race characters, 129–30, 129n.11, 138; and racial bigotry, 160; racial conflict and land distribution, 129–30; 129, 142n.31; racial discourse, 71–72
Racism, 122, 128, 146, 214–15, 367n.8; Vietnamese and African Americans, 247–49; racial stereotypes, 267–71
Rahv, Phillip, 52
Randall, Alice: *The Wind Done Gone,* 19, 359–61

Randolph, J. Thornton: *The Cabin and the Parlor,* 366
Ransom, John Crowe, 30, 279
Raper, Arthur, 29, 31–32, 41
Raper, Julius Rowan, 32, 78n.3, 211
Rawlings, Marjorie Kinnan, 178
Reader's Digest, 199
Reagan, Ronald, 358
Realism: dirty, 206; "K-Mart," 280n.23; psychological, 131; socialist, 312
Reconstruction, 54, 141, 141n.30, 305, 348, 353, 358
Reconstruction novels, cultural myths in, 288, 293
Reed, John Shelton, xviii, 36–38, 88–89, 101n.7, 102n.9, 209, 221, 221n.23, 253, 257
Regionalism: and the Agrarians, 29–32; and boundaries, 310–13; and colonization, 103n.10; critical regionalism, 117; and culture, 309; comparative approach in classroom, 303n.1; critical, 100–1, 114–17, 115n.20, 118n.23; cross-regional communication, 314–19; definitions of, xiii, 18, 26, 51n.13, 304–6; eco-consciousness, 13; and ethnicity, 96–98, 97n.2; formation of American, 96n.1, 100n.5; geopolitical, 99, 99n.4; and identity, 305, 312, 314, 318–19; literary perspectives on, xv, 11, 38–39, 55, 240; and politics, 313–14, 317; and pride, 309, 311; regional outsiders, 314; and relationship to the land, xiv–xv; resistance to, 146n.36; and sectionalism, 99n.4; as spatial, 27n.4; stereotypes, 101n.7; transatlantic comparison of, 307
Relph, Edward, 80
Renoir, Jean, 6
Rhys, Jean: *Wide Sargasso Sea,* 19
Rice, Anne, 280
Rich, Adrienne, 99n.4
Richardson, Samuel: *Clarissa,* 19
Riggs, Marlon: *Tongues Untied* (film), 186–88
Ripley, Alexandra: *Scarlett,* 19, 351–54, 356–58, 360–61
Roberts, Diane, 259, 341

Roman Catholic Church, 368

Romine, Scott, 11, 78, 78n.3, 58, 169–70

Rose, Gillian, 212n.10

Rubin, Louis D., Jr., 3, 32, 37, 237, 257

Rulfo, Juan, 18, 321; "Macario," 326; *Pedro Paramo*, 328, 331–33

Ruppersburg, Hugh, 25

Rural South: and industrialism, 144n.32; and land distribution, 128n.10; and race relations, 128; and the past, 122–23, 122n.2; moral and ethical connection to, 127; psychological response to, 127; psychology of, 124; real estate development, 125

Russo, Vito, 184

Ruta, Suzanne, 193n.17

Rutheiser, Charles, 209, 225, 227

Ryan, Maureen, 8, 16

Said, Edward, 7, 63, 66

Saldivar, Ramon: *Chicano Narratives,* 117

San Antonio Convention & Visitors Bureau, 270

Sanders, Dori: *Clover,* 145; *Her Own Place,* 148; rural landscapes, 152n.7

Santner, Eric, 78

Sartre, Jean-Paul, 144n.33

Saunders, Kate, 358

Scott Paper Towel Company, 71, 74

Scott, Anne Firor, 36

Scott, Sir Walter, 345, 361, 366; influence of, 342–43; *The Lady of the Lake,* 342; place-defining fictions, 19

Scottish Nationalist Party, 341

Segal, Hannah, 77

Segregation, 54; Supreme Court's 1954 decision, 369; laws on, 370n.12

Seidman, Ann, 17

Selznick, David, 348, 351

Seminole Land Claims Case, 168

Sense of place, 4, 231–232, 245; and African American musical forms, 12; anxiety of, 12; boundaries of, 49–50, 50n.11; and capitalist production, 217; and the commercial landscape, 203; and commodification, 204; connotation of, 23–24; critical perspectives on, 35–36;

deconstuction of, 197; definition of, 44–46, 58; description of landscape, 134; and ethnicity, 50; and finance capital, 218–20; "Generic Indigenous," 199–200; and geography, 46–47; and the international city, 219; loss of, 218–19; and memory, 46, 46n.6; and middle-class zeitgeist, 199; and nature, 80–81, 80n.9, 135–36; North v. South, 138n.26; and postregional landscape, 202; psychology of, 126–27, 138n.25; and race, 59, 59n.2; reconceptualization of, 48–49; and regionalism, 51–52; and social change, 48–49; and southern identity, 59–60; in southern fiction, 32; and southern literary criticism, 25; and southern literature, 239; and the southern plantation, 229–30; theorizing of, 50–51; and Vietnam veterans, 125

Seton-Watson, Hugh, xix

Shakespeare, William: 70; *As You Like It,* 153n.9; *The Winter's Tale,* 153n.9

Siddons, Anne Rivers: *Peachtree Road,* 223–24, 224n.27

Silko, Leslie Marmon, 110, 171, 164n.23; *Ceremony,* 152

Simms, William Gilmore, 366–67

Simpson, Lewis P., 15, 211, 237

Sinatra, Frank, 343

Slavery: defense of, 366–67; master-slave dichotomy, 67n.20; modern references to, 47n.7; shared slavery, 248–49, 309–11, 314, 344–45, 365

Slotkin, Richard, 149

Slovic, Scott, 155; on ecocriticism, 177

Smith, Dave, on southern culture, 40n.22

Smith, Jennifer, 228n.34

Smith, Jon, 4, 12

Smith, Lee, 279; *Oral History,* 114

Smith, Lillian, 32

Snyder, Gary, 113

Socarides, Charles W., 79n.6

Social activism, southern Italy, 300–1

Soja, Edward, 36, 240

Sons of Confederate Veterans, 369, 369–70n.11

South: Agrarian definitions of, 13; Americanization of, 4; biracial literary tradition, 8n.11; British fascination with, 19; and Celtic influences, 19, 340–42; characterizations, 39; and color line, 60; composition of, 372; condition of, 47; contemporary attitudes of, 198; contradictions of, 5–6; and consumer culture, 111; and Cuban Americans, 7; custodians of, 2; distinctions of, 3–4, 16, 174n.14, 6–9, 255; diversity of, xvii, xxiii, 372; definitions of, 28–29, 88–89, 251; demographics of, 11; as exotic, 296–99; globalization of, 18–19; history of, 365; and humanism, 30; idealism of, 367; immigration to, 372; and Korean Americans, 7–8; literary influence of, 196–97; myths of, 342; New South, 16; perceptions of, 139; political parties of, 122; politics of, 296–97; postmodern geographies of, 15; postmodern literature of, 14–15; and the postsouthern literary condition, 39–41; preserving traditions in, 368–69; psychoanalytic paradigms of, 12; remapping of, 28n.6; Secession, 348; sense of past, 238–40; small towns in, 10; stereotyped characters of, 306–7; stereotypes of, 132–33, 137, 203; survival of, 36–38, 36n.16; symbolic landscape of, 11–12; tourists in, 137, 254; urban intellectuals in, 297; and Vietnamese Americans, 235–52; writers from outside of, 6. *See also* Confederacy; Old South; Rural South; Southern culture; Southern identity

Southeast Indian Tribes, 273
Southeast Tourism Society, 277
Southern Conference on Human Welfare, 142n.31
Southern conservatism, 54
Southern culture: authenticity of, 104, 105n.11; commodification of, 16; and consumer culture, xx, 106; decline of, 363; and *Gone With the Wind*, hybridity of, 12; and influence on Britain, 345–47; 347–50; literary matrix of, 107n.15; and the media, 261n.9; modern concepts of, 101; and pop culture, 12, 106n.14; por-

trayed in *Joe*, 105; portrayed in literature generally, 109; and social movements, 111n.18; and southern rock music, 12; stereotypes of, 102, 102n.9; survival of, 40n.22; traditions of, 106–9
Southern Culture on the Skids (band), 12, 87n.19, 84–88
Southern ecosystems, 175
Southern identity, xix–xxi, 19, 36–37, 87–89, 204, 286–87, 367–68, 373; and communal ritual, xxii–xxiii; defending loss of, 370–71; and discrimination, 368; and globalization, 275–76, 278; and intellectuals, 84–85; lack of, 205–6; in literature, 41–43; and masculine signifiers, 87–88, 87n.20, and orientalism, xvii–xviii; and the posthistorical, 287; postmodern simulation of, 257–58; and postmodern media, 264–65; and postsubcultural age, 89; preservation of, 371; and punk, 86; and the past, xv; and trauma, 76, 81–82; and use of language, xxi–xxii
Southern labor movement of 1930s, 142
Southern literature: canon of, 32; and the Civil War, 52n.14; genres of, 105n.12; and postmodern criticism, 33–36; and postmodernism, 198, 280n.23; and sense of place, 32; and social change, 123–24; and southern regional identity, 279–80; and southern vacation travel, 279–80
Southern Living: "advatorials" in, 258n.6; and the American Dream, 259, 259n.8; circulation of, 256–57; and commodification, 16; distribution of, 256n.3; history of, 255; image of South in, 259, 259n.7; positive multicultural advertising in, 273–74; and southern identity, 257; and southern literature, 279–80; travel editorial in, 277–78; and vacation travel, 258n.5; vision of, 257
Southern Partisan, 122
Southern Progress Corporation, 255, 259, 275
Southern Renascence, 26, 196, 202
Southern Skirmish Association, 346
Southern Surf Syndicate, 94

"Southernization of America," 4

Spanish American literature, 320–39; and national history, 332–35; and the patriarchal system, 333n.21; and similarities to literature of American South, 326n.12; tradition of, 324n.10

Spencer, Jon Michael: *Blues and Evil,* 64

Spenser, Sir Edmund: *The Faerie Queene,* 344

Spindler, Amy, 83

Spivak, Gayatri, 89

Stalinist methods, 312, 314

Starobinski, Jean, 115

State-sponsored nationalism, 51

Stegner, Wallace, 101n.7

Steinbeck, John, 70

Steiner, Michael, 304–5

Stengel, Marc K., 42, 146n.36

Stephanson, Neal, 102

Stepto, Robert, 62

Stereotypes, 101n.7, 102, 102n.9, 306–7, 132–33; American Indian, 176; feminine, 308; German, 307; Italian culture, 293; racial, 266–71

Stevens, Thaddeus, 141n.30

Stoicism, 232–33

Stolorow, Robert, 77, 79

Storace, Patricia, 358

Stowe, Harriet Beecher: *Uncle Tom's Cabin,* 366, 369

Stribling, T. S., 32

Sullivan, Walter, 32

Tallmadge, John, 148

Tarantino, Quentin, on *Pulp Fiction* soundtrack, 90n.23

Tate, Allen, 41, 83, 124, 219, 229, 245; *The Fathers,* 291; and southern literary criticism, 26; southern literature, 32, 109

Tate, Linda, 174n.14

Taylor, Helen, 9, 19

Taylor, William R.: *Cavalier and Yankee,* 289

Tennyson, Alfred Lord: *Idylls of the King,* 344

Thoreau, Henry David, 10, 148, 158–59

Tindall, George Brown, 7; *Natives and*

Newcomers: Ethnic Southerners and Southern Ethnics, 252

Tolson, Melvin, 195

Toomer, Jean, 121, 151; *Cane,* 148

Traditional southern novel, 198

Transcultural crossovers, 8–9

Transnational corporations, 275

Transnationalism, 55–56; and local culture, 98n.3. *See also* Globalization

Trollope, Frances, 6

Turner, Frederick Jackson, 104; critical regionalism, 101; on intellectual historians, 55; on nationalism, 99

Turner, Nat, 39, 365, 367

Twain, Mark, 48, 146, 342; *Life on the Mississippi,* 364

Tyler, Anne, 25

Vacation advertising, 261–64, 262n.11; and Native Americans, 273; and Puerto Rico, 264; and racial stereotypes, 266–71; and regional identity, 265, 276–77; and San Antonio, 270–71

Venturi, Robert, on commercial vernacular, 201

Verga, Catanian Giovanni, Mastro-Don Gesualdo, 290; 293, 293

Vertigo, 93

Vesey, Denmark, 367

Viet Cong, 236

Vietnam: similarities to the South, 6–8, 16, 245; veterans of, 111n.18, 125

Vietnam War, 136, 236, 241, 252; American attitudes toward, 250–51

Vietnamese culture: Americans understanding of, 236; and African Americans, 247–49; compared to the South, 237; and identity, 237; and sense of family, 246; and sense of past, 244; and sense of place, 237–39

Vietnamese refugees: American attitudes toward, 250; American dream for, 241–42; discrimination against, 247–48; sense of past, 252; sense of place, 252; in the South, 235, 244; in southern literature, 236

Vivas, Roberto, 267–69

Wagner-Martin, Linda, 174
Walker, Alice, xv, 164n.23; *The Color Purple*, 163n.22; *Living by the Word*, 147; and southern regional identity, 279
Walker, Herschel, 85–86
Wallace, George, 139, 370
Warner, Michael, 194
Warren, Robert Penn, 12, 26, 38, 61, 68, 70, 124, 231
Washington, Booker T., 70
Waterson, Henry, 36
Weber, David J.: *The Spanish Frontier in North America*, 165n.2
Wells, Paul: *The Lost Cause*, 12
Welty, Eudora, xxiii, 25, 51, 75, 169, 197, 210, 232, 239; *The Bride of the Innisfallen*, 198; *Delta Wedding*, 80, 80n.9; "A Memory," 1; "No Place For You, My Love," 18, 314–18; "Place in Fiction," 4, 44, 58; and regionalism, 100; and sense of place, 27; sense of place and nature, 80–81; southern culture and the landscape, 110; use of language, xxi–xxii; "Where Is This Voice Coming From?" 5
West, Nathanael: *The Day of the Locust*, 200
Westling, Louise, 36
Wharton, Edith, xiii
White, Gilbert: *Natural History of Selbourne*, 148
Wilcox, James, 25
Williams, Philip Lee: *Crossing Wildcat Ridge: A Memoir of Nature and Healing*, 149
Williams, Raymond, xiii, 56, 101n.7, 102, 262

Williams, Sherley Anne, 6; *Dessa Rose*, 122
Williams, Tennessee, 137
Williams, Terry Tempest, 148
Williams, William Carlos, xxii
Williamson, Joel, 6n.9
Wilson, Charles Regan, 85–86
Windham, Donald: *The Dog Star*, 210, 210n.6
Winter, William, 370
Winters, Donald, 144n.32
Wolfe, Thomas, 279
Wolfe, Tom: *The Bonfire of the Vanities*, 208; *A Man in Full*, 15, 208–34, 212n.10
Womack, Craig, 171
Woodward, C. Vann, 12, 61, 43, 231, 257
Woodward, Okla., 273
Woolf, Virginia, 322; *Mrs. Dalloway*, 331
Wordsworth, William, 148, 156
World War II, 50n.11, 52, 92, 110, 343
Wray, Link, 90–91
Wright, Richard, 41, 148; *Black Boy*, 32, 345; *Native Son*, 32; rural South, 121; sense of place, 2; *Uncle Tom's Children*, 150
Wyeth, Andrew, 200

Yancey, William Lowndes, xvi, xvii
Yeats, William Butler, 110
Yeltsin, Boris, 347
Yerby, Frank, 346
Yoder, Edwin, 12, 68–69
Young, Robert, 276
Young, Stark: *So Red the Rose*, 49
Young, Stephen Flinn, 13, 211
Younge, Gary, 1, 6

Zamora, Lois Parkinson, 323